Private and Controversial

Celebrating
30 Years of Publishing
in India

Praise for *Private and Controversial*

'This well-curated volume consists of thought-provoking essays by leading authorities, and is a very significant contribution to the field of privacy and health rights.'

—Justice Ajit Prakash Shah, former Chief Justice of Delhi High Court and former Chairperson, Law Commission of India

'The promise of the computer revolution has to be balanced against the peril of surveillance, of state and private actors that achieve new levels of information about the people and use it against them. Too often, in India, we have rushed ahead into the computer revolution without pondering the implications. Smriti Parsheera has built an important book which examines this tension in the field of health. Everyone interested in the future of freedom in India should read this book.'

—Ila Patnaik, Chief Economist, Aditya Birla Group

'To protect people and provide public services in disease outbreaks, emergencies and so also in normal times, the state must have the trust of citizens as some of its actions may encroach upon the fundamental human rights of people. People will trust the state only if such actions are scientifically needed, are proportionate to the threat and there is reciprocity of compensation and other support for those adversely affected. Above all, a speedy due process must be in place to curb misuse of authority. Scholars in this volume critically examine legal and ethical aspects of one such fundamental right, the people's right to privacy which was often violated by the state and the private players during the COVID-19 pandemic in India. It is essential reading to advocate for a stringent data protection law and to ensure that such violations are not repeated.'

—Amar Jesani, Editor, Indian Journal of Medical Ethics

'Smriti Parsheera tells the story of how the pandemic also became a public debate about health and personal data. While COVID-19 may have receded, digitization of our health systems is here to stay. Here, the fourteen essays edited by her help us in understanding this brave new world. They contain a candid, researched account of how our public health response through digital systems works for the affluent but often undermines privacy and equity. *Private and Controversial* is a timely account by experts written with clarity, meant to be read by every Indian. It presents the work of India's best privacy and public health experts in an engaging, popular narrative.'

—Apar Gupta, Executive Director, Internet Freedom Foundation

Private and Controversial

When Public Health and Privacy Meet in India

EDITED BY
Smriti Parsheera

HarperCollins *Publishers* India

First published in India by HarperCollins *Publishers* 2023
4th Floor, Tower A, Building No. 10, DLF Cyber City,
DLF Phase II, Gurugram, Haryana – 122002
www.harpercollins.co.in

2 4 6 8 10 9 7 5 3 1

Copyright © Smriti Parsheera 2023

Anthology © Smriti Parsheera, 2023
Copyright for individual chapters vests with respective authors.

P-ISBN: 978-93-5629-504-9
E-ISBN: 978-93-5629-505-6

The views and opinions expressed in this book are the authors' own and the facts are as reported by them, and the publishers are not in any way liable for the same.

The authors assert the moral right to be identified as the authors of their respective chapters contained in this work.

All rights reserved. No part of this publication may be reproduced, stored in a retrieval system, or transmitted, in any form or by any means, electronic, mechanical, photocopying, recording or otherwise, without the prior permission of the publishers.

This work was supported by a grant received from the Thakur Family Foundation. Thakur Family Foundation has not exercised any editorial control over the contents of the work.

Typeset in 11/13.5 Dante MT Std at
Manipal Technologies Limited, Manipal

Printed and bound at
Thomson Press (India) Ltd

This book is produced from independently certified FSC® paper
to ensure responsible forest management.

For my father, Bir Singh Parsheera
The stars shine brighter in your company

Contents

Foreword   xi
Preface   xv

1. Introduction: When Privacy Meets Public Health   1
   Smriti Parsheera

PART I
The Current State of the World

2. India's Legal Framework on Public Health and Privacy   21
   Smriti Parsheera and Justice (Retd) B.N. Srikrishna

3. COVID-19 Data Infrastructure in India: Politics of Knowing and Governing the Pandemic   41
   Bidisha Chaudhuri and Meera Muthukrishnan

4. COVID-19 Surveillance in India: A Bridge Too Far?   60
   Vrinda Bhandari

PART II
India's Public Health Machinery

5. On Health Data Architecture Design   83
   Prashant Agrawal, Subodh Sharma, Ambuj Sagar, Subhashis Banerjee

6. Privacy Considerations of Community Health Workers   100
   Vijayaprasad Gopichandran

7. Data Protection in Public Healthcare: An Assessment of Three Government Schemes in India   120
   K.P. Krishnan, Rishab Bailey, Gaurav Jain

8. Trust: The Cornerstone of Health Interventions   140
   Olinda Timms

Part III
Locating the 'Public' in Public Health

9. Regulating the Womb: Reproductive Health, Bodily Integrity and Autonomy in Contemporary India   163
   Anindita Majumdar

10. Confidentiality and HIV/AIDS: The Need for Humaneness and Precision in the Law   181
    Vivek Divan and Shivangi Rai

11. Decisional Privacy and Decisional Autonomy: A Rights-Based Paradigm for Mental Healthcare in India   200
    Arjun Kapoor

Part IV
The Governance of Health Data

12. State Legibility of Personal Health Data in India   225
    Faiza Rahman and Ajay Shah

13. Health-Tracking Technologies: Privacy and Public Health   246
    Smitha Krishna Prasad

14. Data Stewardship: Solutions for Sharing of Health Data   266
    Astha Kapoor

15. Artificial Intelligence and Healthcare   287
    Rahul Matthan and Prakhar Pipraiya

Appendix 1   311
Notes   315
Index   389
Acknowledgements   407
About the Authors   409

Foreword

PUBLIC health is the joint responsibility of the public and the body politic that governs. By public is meant the individual constituents of the community. It is only when each of the players play the role effectively that the health of the community is preserved and protected against ravages by disease and death, the two major concerns of any society. The roles of the players often create tensions and conflicts that may appear to be mutually irreconcilable, but tensions are inevitable in a vibrant democratic polity to ensure its viability.

In a democratic set up individuals consensually surrender some parts of their rights, even fundamental rights, in favour of the state so that the state is empowered to act on behalf of all citizens to protect the rights of individuals against erosion by external forces. Epidemics and wars epitomize such situations. In each such situation, the individual's right to freedom and dignified life is threatened both at the micro and macro level and the response can only be collective if it must be effective. This dilemma of the apparent conflict of collective as against individual rights is the subject of critical analyses in the essays in this anthology.

Healthcare and privacy throw up two extremities of the conflict that appear to be internecine. If the state must live up to its responsibility of protecting the health of citizens, it needs to adopt suitable policies and implement them. No public policy can be formulated unless it is based on analysis of large volume of data which alone can generate a reasonable prognosis that could enable the state to formulate and effectuate appropriate responses. The requisite data, however, resides with the individuals and they may be reluctant to transfer them to the state because of trust deficit. The state might take recourse to legal compulsion to acquire such data. This is a catch-22 situation that requires careful balancing of two apparently conflicting rights. The state's action needs to be proportionately nuanced to avoid overreaction and shun unwanted-intrusions into privacy.

This anthology of essays critically examines several dimensions of the dilemma from different perspectives. What data sets represent, how they are collected and preserved with integrity, how they are analysed to draw conclusions that drive policy responses and the legal implications of each of the steps have been examined by the learned authors who have proffered their views and possible methods of making the exercise harmonious. In view of the sensitivity of the data, how the task of collection of the data of principals can be accomplished without offending their privacy rights is a tightrope walk. Varied ramifications of this act have been presented in these essays. The situation is not a trade-off of one against the other, but a zero-sum game where the rights and liabilities of both players balance each other for advancement of the community's interests.

The topics considered by the essays cover a wide range from constitutional and legal issues, tracking and contact tracing, collection and preservation of health data, trust and confidentiality, decisional autonomy, and technical issues like the consequence of emphasis on digitalization and recourse to artificial intelligence to resolve some of the problems encountered.

Kudos to the authors of the papers for throwing light on different aspects of the problem to lead to greater debates and analyses of the complex facets of collection of health data. The editor Ms Smriti Parsheera has done an excellent job that ensures that the pros and cons of the connected issues are put forward with clarity for consideration of the discerning readers.

My best wishes for greater empowerment to the pens of the authors and the editor of the book.

Justice (Retd) B.N. Srikrishna
Mumbai, India
28 February 2022

Preface

'If we had but the gift of second sight to transmute abstract figures into flesh and blood, so that as we walk along the street we could say "That man would be dead of typhoid fever," "That woman would have succumbed to tuberculosis," "That rosy infant would be in its coffin," – then only should we have a faint conception of the meaning of the silent victories of public health.'
– Charles-Edward Amory Winslow, 1923

IT is often said that a well-functioning public health intervention tends to be invisible. Its success lies in the fact that, when available, one does not question the logic or necessity of things like clean air, safe drinking water, sanitation, basic nutrition and building safety. Rather, it is the absence of these necessities that tends to draw attention and gives rise to public health concerns. Privacy follows a similar pattern. We rarely pause to acknowledge the role that it plays in shaping our meaningful existence, through control over our personal spaces, thoughts, relationships and actions. Much like the problems of public health, privacy issues generally come to the fore in response to perceived threat events – a data breach, an amended privacy policy or the announcement of a new data-intensive government programme.

This collection of essays is an attempt to break this cycle of invisibility. It focuses on bringing out the complex interactions between the fields of public health and privacy, in emergencies and normal times, across populations and for specific groups. Its genesis lies in a research grant received from the Thakur Family Foundation in December 2020 for studying the privacy issues in the system supporting public health in India. In the months that followed I reached out individuals with deep knowledge on issues of public health and data governance, and their interaction with the domains of medicine, law, economics, technology, public administration and public policy, and invited them to be a part of this project. In October 2021 we convened in a hybrid format for an author's workshop in New Delhi. The workshop gave us the opportunity to present, discuss and critique the essays in the company of other domain experts. We hope that the reader will find this knowledge and rigour reflected in the pages that follow.

Like everything else around us, this anthology is a product of its times. It comes against the backdrop of one of the most significant public health emergencies of our times. Discussions about the COVID-19 crisis and its impact on human lives, rights, interaction between citizens and the state, and trust in the health system, therefore, form an integral part of the collection. India's evolving policy landscape on privacy and data governance forms another recurring theme across the chapters. When we started this project, the Justice B.N. Srikrishna – led Committee of Experts had submitted its recommendations on data protection to the government and a bill based on the same had been introduced in Parliament. In the months that followed, a joint parliamentary committee offered further recommendations on the bill and the government ultimately decided to withdraw the existing bill with the promise to introduce a new draft. As we went to press, the government had just put out a new draft, titled the Digital Personal Data Protection Bill, 2022, for public comments. The contents of this draft bill are not reflected in these essays that had already been finalized by then. But much of what we discuss here relates to the first principles of privacy and data protection, which remain as relevant to the new draft as they were to the versions before it.

In parallel, India has witnessed a massive push towards the digitalization of health data, notably under the new health data architecture created the Ayushman Bharat Digital Mission. The essays evaluate these policy developments from multiple lenses, like the role of health data in shaping state legibility, India's artificial intelligence story, the rise of health tracking technologies and future of data sharing arrangements.

In addition to a diversity of disciplines, the contributors represent a diversity of viewpoints. As the editor of the volume, I found myself nodding in agreement on most of the ideas presented by the authors but also disagreeing on some counts. Each reader might find themselves in a similar position. And that is precisely the objective. The book's aim is to trigger a more meaningful conversation around what happens when public health and privacy meet in the Indian context, the tensions that it creates, and where the balance should lie. Agreements, disagreements and other heterogeneous viewpoints are all signs that the need for this conversation is acknowledged and that the debate is moving forward.

1
Introduction: When Privacy Meets Public Health

Smriti Parsheera

EVERYDAY interactions between the individual, community and the state are full of interdependencies and tensions. How should the state achieve its vaccination goals while ensuring meaningful consent? What limits can the government impose on an individual's food and drink choices? What should be the bounds of confidentiality governing the conduct of doctors and community health workers? How does the individual's right to control their health information interact with the state's need to know, plan and implement for better public health outcomes? The answer to each of these questions bears significant implications for the autonomy, liberty and dignity of individuals as well as the achievement of public health objectives.

Developments surrounding the management of the COVID-19 crisis help drive home many of these points. In a bid to contain the pandemic, governments resorted to measures such as contact tracing, travel restrictions, mandatory quarantine and door-to-door collection of health data. The legitimacy of the public health objective of tackling a pandemic like COVID is hard to question. But so is the impact of actions taken in the process on the liberty and privacy of individuals. A deeper investigation into the legality and proportionality of each intervention, and how it balances against the citizen's fundamental right to privacy, therefore, becomes imperative.

To be clear, the relationship between privacy and public health is not always one of strife. For instance, maintaining the confidentiality of a person's mental health records or their HIV status is both respectful of their privacy and helps counter the associated stigma. Ensuring privacy under these circumstances serves to build trust in the system, furthering the public health goals of early detection and management.

To take another example, travellers on overnight trains in India would be familiar with morning scenes of rows of people defecating along the sides of railway tracks. For the passenger this may be a source of discomfort or annoyance. Indeed, this is also how the law treats open defecators, who often find themselves charged under provisions on nuisance and trespass of railway property.[1] But at the heart of this illustration lies an enormous public health problem. The World Health Organization (WHO) describes open defecation as a vicious cycle of poverty and disease, which contributes to over 432,000 diarrhoeal deaths annually.[2] In recent years, India has made significant progress on this front, driven by the Swachh Bharat Mission. But the claims of being open defecation free are still far from being met.

At the same time, open defecation is also a matter of privacy, on at least two counts. Its first intersection with privacy is in the context of human dignity. This relates to the dignity of urban slum dwellers who may have no choice but to relieve themselves in the open, in the sight of passing strangers. It also concerns the dignity of rural women who routinely encounter violence, harassment, shame, and menstrual hygiene issues due to the lack of toilet facilities.[3] The second privacy argument is linked to a person's decisional autonomy, another important facet of the right to privacy. Stretching the idea of personal autonomy to its limit, one could claim that they should enjoy the freedom to defecate in any environment of their choice. As per a 2014 study, the revealed preferences of many Indians did in fact convey a view of open defecation as a more 'pleasurable, comfortable or convenient' experience.[4] Yet, a balancing of this choice against the health, hygiene and environmental threats of open defecation makes it easy to argue for social, and even legal, restraints on voluntary defecation choices.

The same public health intervention can, therefore, have multiple effects, some which restrain while others that complement the right to privacy. These effects may also vary across different subgroups, leading to the important question of who is the 'public' in the pursuit of public health? And what happens when the interests of different publics collide among themselves or with the priorities set by the state?

The essays in this volume touch upon a range of such issues that lie at the intersection of privacy and public health. But before introducing the chapters, it seems pertinent to spend some time setting out the context of what lies ahead. I, therefore, begin with a brief introduction to concepts of 'public health' and 'privacy'. Given the richness of these topics, each one deserves, and indeed has, many volumes dedicated to it. The modest goal here is to provide sufficient background to help one appreciate the interconnections between public health and privacy and the relevance of studying these interconnections at this point of time.

What is Public Health?

In his classic definition from 1920, American public health expert, Charles-Edward Amory Winslow, described it as *'the science and the art of preventing disease, prolonging life, and promoting physical health and efficiency through organized community efforts'*.[5] What makes public health a science? The 'scientific core of public health' lies in epidemiology – the systematic study of health risks and patterns in the population and discovery of solutions based on that study.[6] The development of COVID-19 vaccines and that of smallpox, polio, measles and meningitis before that are all examples of epidemiology's scientific successes. However, even the most well-designed scientific interventions may fail unless the community is willing to engage with them through behavioural modifications. Public health is, therefore, also an art whose value is determined both by the skill of the practitioner and the level of engagement by the public.

Drawing upon the wisdom and context of his times, Winslow had identified four key public health interventions: sanitation of the environment, control of community infections, education about personal hygiene; and organization of medical services to aid early diagnosis. Winslow's formulation continues to hold water a century later, especially in terms of the focus on preventive actions and collective efforts. But the priorities of the field have also evolved in some ways.

Many parallels have been drawn between the current COVID pandemic and the 'Spanish flu' or influenza pandemic of 1918, the most disruptive pandemic of the previous century. India happened to be one of the worst-affected countries, with estimates of twelve to eighteen million people having lost their lives to the influenza pandemic.[7] As per historical data, cholera, plague, smallpox and malaria were some of the other major killers of that era.[8] All of these diseases can be traced to unsanitary conditions, contaminated food and water, or transmission through contact with infected persons. This resulted in two major priorities for public health, globally: first, the prioritization of sanitation, clean water, sewage and waste disposal, and personal hygiene; and second, the containment of infectious diseases and subsequently their prevention through vaccinations. Over the years, the global community has managed to achieve significant success on both these fronts.

Despite continuing disparities between the developed and developing world and the COVID setback, an average person now lives much longer than their ancestors did a few decades ago. Compared to a life expectancy of twenty-one years in 1920, a person born in 2020's India is likely to live closer to seventy years.[9] This longevity comes with an increased likelihood of suffering from, and dying of, a different set of causes than the ones described above. Over 70 per cent of global deaths are now attributed to non-communicable diseases like heart and lung problems, cancer and diabetes.[10] The factors responsible for this include dietary and lifestyle choices, such as smoking, lack of physical activity and unhealthy food, as well as environmental, genetic and socio-economic conditions. The intensity of risk factors (as also the related causes of death), however, varies across regions and population groups. As per the Global Burden of Disease study of 2019, child and maternal malnutrition, followed by air pollution and high blood pressure are the three most significant risk factors driving death and disability in India.[11] In contrast, smoking was the leading factor for several other countries, like Australia, Japan, China and the US.

The varying risk factors illustrate how public health outcomes end up being influenced by country contexts and the actions of a range of different stakeholders. At the centre of this maze are the members of the community. Depending on the issue at hand, the size of this community may vary from the residents living on a small street to the entire population of a country. The policy actors responsible for making and implementing public health decisions can be equally diverse. For instance, India has over fifty health-related programmes at the central level itself, divided into the categories of reproductive, maternal and childcare; nutritional programmes; communicable diseases; non-communicable diseases; and programmes for the overall strengthening of the health system.

In their chapter on the evaluation of public health schemes in India, K.P. Krishnan, Rishab Bailey and Gaurav Jain selected three of these programmes – on tuberculosis elimination, safe motherhood and government-financed health insurance – for a more detailed study. As can be expected, they find significant variations in the technical and administrative design, implementation safeguards and personal data interactions under the schemes. Notably, the authors observe that the more recent initiatives seemed to pay closer attention to issues of data protection, probably on account of the greater reliance on digital technologies under programmes like the Pradhan Mantri Jan Aarogya Yojana. This illustrates how seemingly extrinsic factors, like the extent of digitalization in the society and growing privacy awareness, can have a bearing on policy priorities in public health programmes.

In this case, all three schemes happen to be administered by the health ministry. But this may very well not have been the case. Many public health actions fall outside the control of the health department, lying instead in domains like environmental protection, urban management, road safety and child welfare – all of which are handled by different ministries.[12] To take an example, the Smart Cities Mission is an initiative being led by the Ministry of Housing and Urban Affairs in the central government. Under this, 100 cities across the country have been selected to implement model solutions in areas such as solid waste management, water treatment, sustainable environment and crime monitoring. Each smart city is supposed to set up a special purpose vehicle with nominees from the central government, state government and urban local bodies. The footprint of the Smart Cities Mission, therefore, cuts across multiple domains and levels of the government. Many of its interventions relate directly to issues of public health, although it is not labelled as a public health project.

In addition to institutions and high-level decision makers, numerous street-level bureaucrats also play a critical role in the functioning of the public health machinery. Michael Lipsky first used this term in 1980 to describe front-line public workers who interact directly with citizens, while enjoying a substantial level of discretion in their actions.[13] Examples in the COVID context include the constable on the street who gets to decide how strictly to apply the lockdown rules and upon whom. It also includes the receptionist at the government testing facility who can put a person's name on the RT-PCR (real-time reverse transcription polymerase chain reaction) testing list or send them for a rapid test. Each of these individuals is acting within the scope of the directions issued by the state but also reshaping those bounds based on their own incentives, uncertainties, pressures and threats.[14]

The chapter by Vijayaprasad Gopichandran focuses on the role of community health workers, who are arguably the most important cadre of street-level officials in India's public health set-up. Community workers like the Accredited Social Health Activists (ASHAs) and the Anganwadi workers serve as a critical link between the community and the state, discharging the functions of data collection, communication, health education, advocacy and support. While doing so, they often negotiate complex issues of trust, confidentiality and stigma involving the community, and concerns for their own livelihood, safety and privacy. The interviews conducted by Gopichandran with community workers are particularly illuminating in highlighting the socially constructed nature of privacy for young, rural women. Traditional notions of privacy are intrinsically linked to the safety and privacy of one's home. But Gopichandran's conversations with community workers revealed how for a young woman trying to have a conversation about her sexual health, the home can become a particularly confining space. In contrast, the noise and chaos offered by a village fair creates a sense of privacy that is necessary for the conversation with the community health worker.

While the discussion so far has focused on the state, its functionaries and members of the community, it would be remiss to not highlight the role of private actors in this equation. A large part of what is called public health law focuses on reshaping the behaviour of private actors like hospitals, car and drug manufacturers, tobacco companies, employers and polluting industries through the use of incentives and prohibitions. In addition to these large actors from the old economy, who continue to remain relevant, a new breed of technology sector players have also entered the mix. This includes a host of entities involved in the processing of health-related data for purposes such as consumer targeting, development of AI (artificial intelligence) algorithms and the operation of smart devices.

In her chapter on health-tracking technologies, Smitha Krishna Prasad sets out the vast landscape of apps, devices and other artifacts that interact with the personal health information of users. Some of these, like smart watches, period trackers and calorie counters, are explicitly in the domain of health tracking while other smart devices like thermostats and air quality monitors present a more indirect, but no less relevant, link between privacy and public health. Prasad also focuses on the role of corporate employers in pushing the use of health-monitoring technologies. While this is ostensibly meant to serve the goals of employee wellness, it can also create unfair trade-offs in terms of the employees' healthcare and insurance entitlements.

The constitution of the WHO, adopted in 1946, draws a clear link between the concepts of health and well-being. It defines health to mean not just the absence of disease or infirmity but a state of complete physical, mental and social well-being. By extension, public health experts have also started to focus on mental health and psychological well-being as part of their work.¹⁵ For instance, current wisdom tells us that a healthy workplace is not just limited to preventing unhygienic working conditions and safety from occupational hazards. Rather, it captures a broader sense of well-being, which includes mental health and work–life balance. For many, this balance has been upended by the blurred boundaries between home and work in the COVID-19 context. This is accompanied by growing surveillance at the workspace, with employers resorting to intrusive digital surveillance tools, ranging from CCTV monitoring to logging of keystroke activities, and from automatic webcam access to taking screenshots of the employee's computer.¹⁶ This is likely to have long-term effects on public health that are intrinsically linked to the underlying privacy concerns posed by such technologies. This is only a small illustration in a much larger landscape of datafication and digitalization in the health space, a trend that has become all the more evident in the current context.

Vrinda Bhandari's chapter presents a comprehensive mapping of the different types of physical and digital surveillance measures adopted by the state and by certain private actors to deal with the COVID situation. She classifies these based on the underlying functions of symptom tracking, mobility and density mapping, quarantine enforcement, contact tracing, travel passes, and vaccination. Similar to the experience globally, Bhandari notes that India's response to the pandemic has largely been a tech-centric one. But this has been done without a legal framework on data protection or sufficient focus on the utility, reliability, accuracy and security of many of the interventions. India's legal response to the pandemic has hinged on its classification as a disaster. But Bhandari notes that the 'long tail' of the pandemic makes it very different from other types of disasters that are often of a finite and limited duration. The use of extraordinary technological measures to deal with the crises, therefore, comes with the fear of certain types of surveillance being normalized in the long run.

Bidisha Chaudhuri and Meera Muthukrishnan present a fascinating take on understanding the pandemic in terms of the politics of how COVID-related data sets were being constructed, controlled and used. While there appears to be a general consensus on the importance of evidence-based decision making in public health, this is complicated by the fact that the evidence in question often tends to be incomplete and ambiguous.[17] A purported reliance on data was at the core of many important decisions in the COVID context, such as when should lockdowns be imposed and which areas need urgent supplies of oxygen. Chaudhuri and Muthukrishnan undertake a systematic review of the dashboards maintained by state agencies as well as some prominent private ones and find several gaps and inconsistencies in these data practices. This becomes their basis to question the uncritical reliance on databases as a means of getting to 'know' the pandemic.

The 'Public' in Public Health

Public health is often described as the health of the population. But the term 'population' here is not limited to the geographic notion of a population. In the words of Kindig and Stoddart, population health refers to 'the health outcomes of a group of individuals, including the distribution of such outcomes within the group'.[18] As per this definition, a population could indeed be demarcated based on geographical factors, but also based on other factors like gender, ethnicity, clinical conditions, disability status and nature of employment. Accordingly, public health interventions could be focused on preserving or enhancing the health outcomes for any of these specific population groups. This would, for instance, include measures taken by the government to protect front-line health workers, such as through priority in vaccinations, health insurance facilities and amendments to the Epidemic Diseases Act to criminalize attacks against them. Similarly, there are several other occupation-specific laws in the country, like those for beedi and cigar workers, miners and plantation workers, that put in place requirements of cleanliness, ventilation, rest periods and medical examinations for these populations.

This collection contains three essays that explore the relationship between public health and privacy in the context of specific population groups. The first group, covered by Anindita Majumdar in her essay on the regulation of the womb, is that of childbearing women. More specifically, women who find themselves negotiating their reproductive health choices against the incentives of medical practitioners and priorities set by the state. Majumdar selects three sites of inquiry – surrogacy, hysterectomies and caesarean sections – to demonstrate how bodily integrity and autonomy of women play out in these spaces. One of the key points that she drives home is the role that caste, class and religion continue to play in shaping the outcomes faced by the reproductive body. To turn back to the definition of population health, this illustrates how the distribution of outcomes within a group is not uniform and tends to be shaped by numerous economic, clinical, social and political factors.

The chapter by Vivek Divan and Shivangi Rai focuses on the rights of persons living with HIV/AIDS. The authors make a strong case for a rights-based approach to HIV/AIDS, especially in the context of patient confidentiality, as being both respectful of the right to privacy and serving the goals of public health. They highlight how the legal framework in India has evolved in terms of balancing the patient's right to confidentiality with the duty of notification to their partner. While the HIV and AIDS (Prevention and Control) Act of 2017 has put to rest the legal controversy on this issue through a strong confidentiality framework, there remains a gap in the law as it stands and as it is practised. Divan and Rai demonstrate this with an example of the rules applicable to nursing homes in the state of Maharashtra. The rules single out HIV patients in terms of disclosure requirements, by requiring 'details of those found positive and negative' as opposed to only the total numbers for other notified diseases.

Persons with disability constitute yet another important population group from a public health perspective. Arjun Kapoor's essay looks at issues of decisional autonomy and legal capacity faced by persons with mental illness. The state and society often treat this population group as 'incomplete beings', invalidating their ability to make decisions about their own contractual and property matters, family life and medical treatment. Kapoor presents a critique of this approach, rooting his arguments in the legal and moral foundations of decisional autonomy, including its interpretation by constitutional courts in India. While international standards and the legal framework in India offer sufficient safeguards for decisional, bodily and informational privacy in the mental health context, we are yet to create the frameworks necessary to operationalize these rights. Kapoor highlights improvements in community-based measures, better staffing and training of professionals, and understanding the incentives of families and caregivers as some of the necessary steps for realizing the decisional autonomy of persons with mental illness.

Finally, the mainstreaming of the internet and other new technologies also has an impact on how a population or community can be construed. For instance, users of Facebook, content creators on TikTok and fans of the popular video game Minecraft could all be regarded as different population groups. In her chapter on data stewardship, Astha Kapoor dwells upon the meaning of public interest, a term that often comes up in policy documents, in the context of the sharing and use of health data. She focuses on three main developments, the Personal Data Protection Bill, 2019 (PDP Bill), which has now been withdrawn, the Health Data Management Policy put out by the National Health Authority, and the recommendations of the Non-Personal Data Committee. Kapoor notes that amidst this 'rigmarole of regulation and policy' we are still missing a clear set of principles to guide data sharing. Equally lacking is a bottom-up approach that places communities and individuals at the core of decision making about their data.

Privacy, Data and Beyond

The term privacy has already made numerous appearances in this essay. It is a basic human right recognized under the Universal Declaration of Human Rights. In 2017, a nine-judge bench of the Indian Supreme Court affirmed that it also constitutes a fundamental right under the Indian Constitution.[19] In what is popularly referred to as the *Puttaswamy* verdict, the court recognized the interlinkages between a person's privacy and their right to life, liberty, dignity and various other freedoms. This means that an individual can challenge any state action that violates their privacy. The Supreme Court in *Puttaswamy* offered several useful illustrations of the different facets of privacy. Several of these, such as the protection of personal intimacies, ability to make vital personal decisions and the preservation of one's family life, can have a direct bearing on issues of public health. Public health interventions that restrain individual autonomy, cause physical or mental intrusions, or lead to a loss of control over one's health information could therefore be challenged on the grounds of privacy. It is then the court's responsibility to ascertain if the intervention by the state was lawful, legitimate and proportionate in nature, given the specific circumstances of the case.

Government orders linking the opening up of the economy and delivery of services to the COVID vaccination status of the public presents a live example of such a tension. The question is, can the state directly or indirectly coerce citizens to take the vaccine? A number of high courts in India, followed by the Supreme Court, answered this question in the negative.[20] In the first such decision, the Meghalaya High Court was looking into orders issued by the state's district administrations barring shopkeepers, taxi drivers and other vendors from resuming their businesses unless they were vaccinated. The court observed that the mandatory or forceful vaccination orders were neither permitted under the principles of equity and good conscience, nor would they withhold scrutiny against the rights to privacy and livelihood.[21]

Another way to look at this issue is through the lens of the intervention ladder proposed by the Nuffield Council on Bioethics.[22] Similar to the concept of proportionality adopted by courts, the intervention ladder sets out an eight-step model where each step makes a slightly more intrusive inroad into individual freedom and liberty (see Table 1.1). These steps range from the mildest policy response of doing nothing to guiding choices through defaults, incentives and disincentives, and finally to the most intrusive approach of complete elimination of choice. In the above scenario, the High Court of Meghalaya frowned upon interventions that restrict the livelihood of persons who are not vaccinated but applauded information-based measures, such as a public notice informing potential customers about the vaccination status of an establishment's staff. In Table 1, these could be said to fall under the ambit of steps 6 and 2, respectively, which illustrate the difference in the extent of intrusiveness involved.

Table 1.1: The intervention ladder of public health

1.	Do nothing or monitor the situation.	
2.	Provide information.	Campaigns to encourage people to walk more, wash their hands and wear masks.
3.	Enable choice.	Build cycle lanes, distribute free fruit in schools.
4.	Guide choices by changing the default.	A restaurant providing salad instead of chips as a standard side dish.
5.	Guide choices through incentives.	Tax breaks for purchase of bicycles or electric vehicles.
6.	Guide choice through disincentives.	Higher taxes on cigarettes and alcohol.
7.	Restrict choice.	Removing unhealthy ingredients from foods.
8.	Eliminate choice.	Compulsory isolation of patients with infectious diseases.

Source: Nuffield Council on Bioethics, 2007

There are numerous other situations where courts and policymakers have faced the need to weigh the interests of privacy and public health. The next essay in this collection, co-authored by Justice B.N. Srikrishna and me, provides examples from contexts such as confidentiality of a person's HIV status, prohibition on consumption of alcohol and the right to passive euthanasia. We highlight the pivotal role of the *Puttaswamy* verdict in reshaping how future courts might look at some of these issues. At the same time, we also highlight that a case-by-case review of state actions through the *Puttaswamy* lens cannot remain the primary privacy safeguard, especially when it comes to the protection of sensitive health data.

In the last decade or so, a number of countries have moved forward with the adoption of comprehensive data protection laws, the General Data Protection Regulation in Europe being an oft-cited example. These laws typically set out the individual's rights to exercise control over the collection and use of their personal data and the responsibilities of state and non-state actors carrying out such data processing. In India, the draft PDP Bill, prepared based on the recommendations of an expert committee headed by Justice Srikrishna, was under review by a joint parliamentary committee for almost two years. The committee submitted its report to the parliament in December 2021 suggesting several amendments to the draft bill. The government's recent decision to withdraw the draft bill, however, takes us back to the drawing board on this subject.

While the terms privacy and data protection are sometimes used interchangeably, data protection relates to one specific facet of privacy, namely informational privacy. An insightful analysis by Bert-Jaap Koops and others, which was also referred to by the Supreme Court in *Puttaswamy*, identifies nine types of privacy. The first eight categories are bodily, intellectual, spatial, decisional, communicational, associational, proprietary and behavioural privacy. Then there is a ninth category of informational privacy, which finds an overarching presence across all the other categories.[23] To take an example, a woman's decision to get an abortion is an aspect of her bodily and decisional privacy but a record of having undergone an abortion and the related medical history is an informational aspect. Similarly, the use of global positioning system (GPS) tracking to monitor quarantine violations impacts both spatial and informational privacy, just as the confidentiality of the doctor–patient relationship touches on communicational as well as informational privacy.

The delay in the adoption of a comprehensive data protection law, and the rapid progression of state-led and private health data initiatives in the absence of such a law, is a recurring theme across many of the essays. Some of the essays also engage substantially with the design of the Ayushman Bharat Digital Mission (ABDM), previously called the National Digital Health Mission. This is a large national-level project that sets out to build an integrated health data system for the country.

Its principal components include a health ID to be issued to citizens and the creation of an elaborate health data management architecture around that ID. The mission is proceeding with the full firepower of the government that has created a non-statutory agency called the National Health Authority to implement it. The ABDM has already come into play in the union territories, and other state and private actors are now in the process of being taken on board. In many ways, the roll out of this project is similar to the modus operandi that was seen in the case of Aadhaar. Like Aadhaar, the ABDM is proceeding through executive actions, a government–private human resource model, and insistence on the 'voluntary' nature of the project, which could very easily change over time.

Besides the big question of legality, which is linked to the fact that this mission is not backed by a legislative framework, the ABDM's architecture also merits closer scrutiny on several other counts. The chapter by Prashant Agrawal, Subodh Sharma, Ambuj Sagar and Subhashis Banerjee raises some fundamental questions in this regard. The authors draw a line between talking about the potential benefits of health data, which many recent policy documents have done, and a demonstrable theory of public good. They argue that the latter needs to be grounded in the realities of data use cases, feasibility studies, anticipation of technical and administrative failures, and complex privacy design considerations. Similar to a lot of other policy actions in India, these aspects have not been systematically accounted for in the design and roll out of the ABHM.

Faiza Rahman and Ajay Shah continue this critique, focusing on the harms arising from the extensive and systematic collection of health data. They argue that the increased legibility of citizens by the state comes with a varied set of risks, to the individual, the community and the values of democracy at large. These concerns are only exacerbated by the sensitive nature of health data and the vulnerabilities created by the general sweep of the state's surveillance powers in India. The authors highlight that this is a gap that the current draft of the PDP Bill fails to address. Until these first-order problems of state surveillance can be resolved, the authors believe that a maximalist approach towards health data will only do more harm than good.

But this is not a view that is shared across the board. In their chapter on the use of AI in healthcare, Rahul Matthan and Prakhar Pipraiya argue that the approach of the (now withdrawn) PDP Bill was, in fact, too limiting for the development of a vibrant AI ecosystem. They identify the requirements of obtaining the prior consent of the individual, minimal collection of data; and limits on the retention period, as some examples of obligations that can present roadblocks to the availability of data for the training and deployment of AI systems. Drawing on Matthan's earlier body of work, the authors suggest that replacing the consent framework with an accountability-based one might be better suited for exploring the full potential of AI in the health space, while remaining respectful of user privacy.

Summing up

This book explores the numerous linkages between the disciplines of public health and privacy. While examples of these linkages are all around us, the interdisciplinary academic and public interaction on topics like imposition of quarantine restrictions, reproductive choices, patient confidentiality and health surveillance, to name a few, is less vibrant than it ought to be. This is not to suggest that these conversations are completely missing. As highlighted in this chapter, the public health ethicist's approach of balancing the intensity of public health interventions with the acceptable degree of intrusion into individual liberty and the test of proportionality framed by courts already exist as means to account for privacy interests in health interventions. Further, the field of public health ethics also presents a focus on privacy issues, particularly in the context of patient confidentiality. In keeping with this tradition, the chapter by Olinda Timms identifies 'trust' to be an essential, fragile and powerful component of successful health interventions. She emphasizes the ethical and pragmatic considerations that determine the trustworthiness of health providers, institutions, researchers and the system as a whole, and the role of this trust in shaping the effectiveness of individual and population outcomes.

In addition to these philosophical, legal and practical links that are highlighted throughout the book, there are at least three recent developments that create a fertile ground for the deepening of these debates. The first is the ongoing COVID-19 pandemic, and the extensive use of technology as part of the state's response to it. The second is the rapid push for the digitization of health data in the country, which has now been cemented by the creation of the Ayushman Bharat Digital Mission (ABDM). The third is the policy debate around data governance in India, with the proposals for regulation of personal and non-personal data being its two main components. While the connections between public health and privacy are not limited to the digital sphere, datafication and digitization certainly add new layers of complexity even to age-old problems like the power asymmetry between the doctor and the patient, and the citizen and the state.

The four parts of this book aim to capture the entanglements between privacy and public health that cut across the digital and the analogue worlds. The first part called the 'Current State of the World' describes the Indian legal framework on privacy and public health and the ongoing actions by the state to manage and know the COVID-19 pandemic. The second part on 'India's Public Health Machinery' analyses various components of India's public health apparatus, including data governance under existing government schemes and the ABDM that is in the process of being rolled out. This part also covers the discussion on the role of community health workers as mediators of privacy in the health system. The third part focuses on 'Locating the "Public" in Public Health'. It dwells into population-group-specific privacy considerations, in the context of reproductive rights, HIV interventions and mental health followed by a discussion on the importance of trust in framing public health outcomes. Finally, the fourth part titled 'The Governance of Health Data' is framed around India's health data conundrum, characterized by the scarcity and poor quality of data on one hand and possibilities of unrestricted state and private access to sensitive health data on the other.

PART I

The Current State of the World

2
India's Legal Framework on Public Health and Privacy

Smriti Parsheera and Justice (Retd) B.N. Srikrishna

Introduction

IN 1897, John Woodburn, a member of the Council of the Governor General of India, tabled an emergency bill to control the spread of the bubonic plague in the country.[1] He may not have imagined that 123 years later the Epidemic Diseases Act, 1897, would still remain a key part of India's epidemic diseases management tool kit. This law, along with the National Disaster Management Act of 2005, has been at the core of the government's COVID-19 management strategy. The sweeping powers under these laws form the basis for quarantine norms, compulsory masking, prohibition on spitting in public places and most other public health responses seen over the last two years.

Until its amendment in 2020, the Epidemic Diseases Act consisted of only five sections containing the state's power to declare a dangerous epidemic, adopt necessary measures to deal with it, impose criminal sanctions and immunity for the actions of public officials. Born out of a colonial context, the law bore no mention (and still does not) of the rights of the individual in these circumstances. Its intrusive application is illustrated by a memorandum issued by a group from Poona that called out the British government's Plague Committee for excesses, such as the rough handling of people, indignity of public stripping and the forcible opening of houses and businesses.[2] Cut to 2020 and similar forms of physical surveillance were not only going strong but had been bolstered by a new layer of digital technologies. On one hand, we saw migrant workers arriving home in Bareilly, Uttar Pradesh, being subjected to the indignity of being sprayed with disinfectant,[3] and on the other, officials in Karnataka resorted to what Ayona Datta calls 'self(ie)-governance', using the mobile phone as a tool for the surveillance of intimate life.[4] The necessity of a rights-based approach to the governance of public health emergencies has, therefore, been one of the many lessons taught by the COVID pandemic.

The body of public health–related laws, however, extends much beyond the management of rare but devastating pandemics. Its everyday applications include laws that prohibit certain types of harmful conduct (ban on smoking in public places), set standards and norms for others (food safety standards), and seek to empower specific population groups (occupational safety for workers). This chapter traces the evolution of India's legal framework on public health and its intersection with various facets of the right to privacy using select decisions and policy actions to unravel these complex intersections. We also deal with the proposed treatment of health data under the Personal Data Protection Bill, 2019, placing this debate in the broader context of the move towards digitization of India's health data ecosystem.

Constitutional Framework

The topics of health and public health make several appearances in the Indian Constitution and its interpretation by courts.[5] Article 21 of the Constitution, which guarantees the right to life and personal liberty, has been the medium for the delivery of several fundamental rights, including those relating to privacy and public health. In its landmark decision in *Justice K.S. Puttaswamy v. Union of India*, the Supreme Court declared privacy to be a fundamental right, deriving its basis from Article 21 and other interconnected rights and freedoms under Part III of the Constitution.[6] While not explicitly mentioned in the Constitution, the court found privacy to be an intrinsic element of the right to live meaningfully and with dignity. Accordingly, any state interference in an individual's privacy can only take place in accordance with a procedure established by law, which should be fair, just and reasonable.

At the same time, promoting and protecting the health of the population is one of the core functions of the state. This can sometimes lead to the need for balancing of different rights and interests and, as we illustrate throughout this chapter, courts and policymakers have often resolved conflicts between public health and privacy in favour of the former. But the Supreme Court's *Puttaswamy* verdict now makes it clear that any intrusion into an individual's physical, intellectual or informational privacy has to pass the tests laid down by the court.[7] To be constitutionally valid, any such interference must be enacted by a competent legislature and should clearly articulate the legitimate object that is sought to be achieved. In addition, any privacy inroads must not be disproportionate to such legitimate objective. In other words, if the objective can be achieved without infringing a fundamental right, the state must do so. Another key ingredient, as spelt out in Justice Kaul's order in the *Puttaswamy* judgment, is the need for procedural safeguards in the process. The observations made in *Puttaswamy* have already paved the way for legal reforms on key issues like the permissibility of same-sex relationships[8] and guidelines on passive euthanasia.[9]

As in the case of privacy, the Constitution also does not explicitly refer to a fundamental right of health or public health. Courts have, however, found several aspects of public health to fall within the scope of Article 21. This includes rights that are directly related to medical aid[10] and health information[11] as well as broader public health outcomes, such as the right to a healthy environment, hygienic working conditions[12] and fair pricing of vaccinations.[13] The ideals of public health are also reflected in the rights against exploitation laid down under Articles 23 and 24 of the Constitution that prohibit human trafficking, forced labour and employment of children below fourteen years in hazardous environments.

The recognition of public health as a state goal comes up even more explicitly in the Directive Principles of State Policy laid down in Part IV of the Constitution. Unlike the fundamental rights, the directive principles are not enforceable against the state. Yet, the Constitution makes it clear that they are *'nevertheless fundamental in the governance of the country and it shall be the duty of the State to apply these principles in making laws'*.[14] The directive principles nudge the state towards preserving the health and strength of workers, enabling opportunities for healthy development of children, assistance in case of old age, sickness and disablement, maternity relief and provision of early childhood care.[15] But the one provision that stands out in terms of its specific focus on public health is Article 47 of the Constitution. It provides for the state's duty to raise the level of nutrition and the standard of living and to improve public health. The article identifies these goals to be among the primary duties of the state and its existence has informed judicial decisions in varied contexts, such as approved standards for drugs,[16] sale and consumption of alcohol[17] and health-related budgeting.[18]

Besides articulating the importance of public health, Article 47 also encourages the state to endeavour towards the prohibition of intoxicating drinks and drugs that are injurious to health. At the heart of this provision lies the classic and continuing debate on the bounds of state paternalism and permissible limits on interference with individual liberties. The insertion of this prohibition clause became a matter of significant debate among members of the Constituent Assembly. Those in favour of inserting it invoked grounds of morality, lessons in religious scriptures and upliftment of Harijans and Adivasis, who it was claimed would be the greatest beneficiaries of prohibition. On the other hand, critics like B.H. Khardekar of Kolhapur presented both pragmatic and moral arguments against prohibition, arguing that such coercion by the state *'goes against the very grain of personal liberty'*.[19] Interestingly, the men arguing on both sides could only think of examples of other men as the subjects of the prohibition – from the Santhal farmer toiling in paddy fields to Bombay's young men discussing politics over a beer. This gap in participation and claimed representation remains as relevant to modern-day public health policies as it was more than seventy years ago.

Currently, several states like Bihar, Gujarat, Nagaland and Mizoram impose restrictions on the sale and consumption of alcohol. Others like Andhra Pradesh, Haryana, Tamil Nadu and Kerala have had similar restrictions in the past. The position of the courts on this issue has been that the state has every right to regulate and even ban the sale of alcohol, which constitutes a reasonable restriction on the right to carry out any trade or profession under Article 19(g) of the Constitution.[20] However, an interesting question has now come up before the Gujarat High Court in light of the *Puttaswamy* verdict: would a law prohibiting the consumption of alcohol amount to a privacy violation under Article 21?

A set of petitions filed before the high court have challenged the provisions of the Gujarat Prohibition Act, 1949, the constitutionality of which has been previously upheld by the Supreme Court in a 1951 decision.[21] The high court found the latest challenges to be maintainable in light of the changes in the prohibition statute and the *Puttaswamy* developments. As per the court, the statute in question had *'never been tested before in context of personal food preferences weaved within the right to privacy'*.[22] In the examples below, we discuss a few other instances that bring to light the complex trade-offs involved in balancing public health and privacy interests.

Balancing Attempts by Courts and Policymakers

How should the health system deal with the confidentiality expectations of a person who is found to be HIV positive in the course of a blood donation exercise? This issue came up before the Supreme Court in the case of Mr X v. Hospital Z. The court held that when there is a clash between two fundamental rights, such as the patient's privacy rights and their prospective partner's right to a healthy life that could be disrupted if the partner was not made aware of the HIV status, the court's duty is to advance the right that is in line with public morality or public interest. In this case, this translated into a condonation of the unauthorized disclosure of the patient's HIV status by their doctor. The decision has earned its fair share of criticism from a patient rights perspective and now stands replaced by the specific protections for the disclosure of a person's HIV status, including to their partner, under the HIV and AIDS (Prevention and Control) Act of 2017.[23]

There could also be cases in which an individual's privacy interests come into conflict not with the rights of another person but with the policy priorities of the state. A question of this nature came up before the Bombay High Court in the context of the Pre-Conception and Pre-Natal Diagnostic Techniques Act, 1994.[24] This statute is aimed at deterring the use of prenatal diagnostics to determine the gender of an unborn child and prevent female foeticide. In 2011 the collector and district magistrate of Kolhapur passed an order under this law requiring all radiologists and sonologists to install a 'silent observer' in sonography machines that would automatically capture a video of each sonography test. This was challenged by the Radiological & Imaging Association on the ground that the technology made it possible to remotely scan and view the ultrasound images, amounting to an invasion of the patient's privacy.

The use of the silent observer coupled with online reporting requirements was meant to address rampant misreporting of tests by radiology centres. The collector also clarified that the video recording of the tests would continue to remain at the sonography centre and could only be accessed for audit purposes by authorized personnel. Taking into account these design features and the provisions of the statutory framework, the court held that the petitioner's privacy claims did not hold merit. The court, however, reiterated that only authorized medical personnel and other designated officials should be able to access the information recorded by the silent observer.

This case illustrates two important points. First, courts are sometimes prone to readily accepting the state's ability to access the sensitive personal data of citizens for efficiency and monitoring purposes. While they may call for well-intentioned safeguards and due process, the extent to which these safeguards actually exist and are implemented on the ground tends to remain unverified. Second, the case also offers a lesson in the likelihood of interested parties trying to play up the tension between privacy and public health interventions to their own advantage. For instance, it is possible that some constituents of the Radiological Association were motivated not just by the privacy of patients but also their own desire to avoid meaningful oversight over an immoral but lucrative practice.

State-led population control measures tend to present another battleground for personal liberty, reproductive autonomy and the goals of public policy. The Uttar Pradesh State Law Commission was in the news for proposing a controversial bill that contained a range of incentives and disincentives aimed at encouraging couples to not have more than two children.[25] This included wage increments, Healthcare facilities and housing subsidies for public officials who adopt the 'two-child norm by undergoing voluntary sterilization'. Certain other benefits like construction loans, maternity and paternity leave, and rebates on utilities would also be available to members of the general public who meet the above criteria. Other states like Andhra Pradesh, Chhattisgarh, Haryana, Madhya Pradesh, Odisha, Rajasthan and Telangana have already adopted similar prescriptions.[26]

The position of courts, thus far, has been that the imposition of eligibility restrictions on persons with more than two children for contesting panchayat elections does not violate their fundamental rights. Such measures have been held to be valid, taking into account the public interest of population control.[27] But in a memorandum addressed to the president on the UP bill, several women's rights groups, researchers, health and legal rights networks called out the bill for violating the constitutional guarantees of equality and privacy.[28] Quoting an extract from the *Puttaswamy* decision, the memorandum highlighted that '*the preservation of personal intimacies, the sanctity of family life, marriage, procreation, the home and sexual orientation*' are central to the notion of privacy. Similar to the policies on alcohol prohibition, such population control policies fall under the bucket of public health measures that may need to witness a fresh examination in light of the *Puttaswamy* verdict.

Allocation of Legislative Powers

Given that the first element of the *Puttaswamy* tests relates to legality, namely, the existence of a valid law, we now turn to outlining the legal framework on public health in India. Under the constitutional scheme, legislative responsibilities on various subjects are demarcated between the Centre and the states, and sometimes shared between them. The topics of 'public health and sanitation; hospitals and dispensaries' fall under the State List set out in the Seventh Schedule to the Constitution.[29] This means that state governments have the primary responsibility of framing and implementing laws on these subjects. Pursuant to the 73rd and 74th Amendments to the Constitution, local governance institutions, namely panchayats and urban local bodies, also play an important role in discharging public health responsibilities. States can endow panchayats in rural areas and municipalities in urban ones with the authority to implement schemes on a number of matters related to public health.[30] This supports the logic of subsidiarity, as per which decision-making authority is best placed at a level that has the closest appropriate proximity to the outcomes and reflects responsibility for those outcomes.[31] But these two factors may not always overlap. For instance, gathering knowledge about the state of health at the community level is something that logically falls in the domain of the gram panchayats, given their proximity to the community. Yet, the responsibility for what happens to the information, including how it is processed and secured, is not something that can be fully controlled at the grass-roots level.

The list of issues that influence and shape public health is long and cuts across a number of other entries in the Constitution. Several of these, like the prevention and spread of infectious or contagious disease across state boundaries, fall under the joint control of the Centre and the states.[32] Other key items in the Concurrent List include mental health, adulteration of foodstuffs, drugs and poisons, population control and family planning, and labour welfare.[33] Further, the management of a large-scale public health crisis, such as the one posed by COVID-19, also involves managing the movement of people across national and international boundaries. These matters, of movement of passengers through rail, sea, air and national waterways, inter-state quarantine and quarantine at ports fall under the exclusive domain of the Union government.[34]

The Centre also has the power to enter into and implement international treaties and conventions.[35] India is among the 196 countries that have endorsed the International Health Regulations (IHR) adopted by the World Health Assembly in 2005. The IHR deal with the prevention and management of public health events with cross-border implications and bind member states to build capacities and legal and administrative measures to facilitate its implementation. Article 45 of the IHR relates to the treatment of personal data. It requires that any health information collected or received under the IHR is kept confidential and dealt with anonymously, as required by national law. Further, while personal data can be processed for managing a public health risk, this has to be done in a manner that is fair and lawful, not excessive in relation to that purpose, with safeguards to keep the data updated and accurate, and for a reasonable retention period. The IHR also contains other privacy protections that go beyond the protection of personal data. Notably, it requires that any restrictions on travellers or other health measures should be proportionate in nature – they should not be more invasive or intrusive than reasonably available alternatives to address the health risks.[36]

India's other international commitments include the Universal Declaration of Human Rights, the Alma Ata Declaration, the Convention on the Elimination of All Forms of Discrimination against Women, the Convention on the Rights of the Child, and the Convention on Rights of Persons with Disabilities.[37] Domestic legislations like the Rights of Persons with Disabilities Act, 2016, and the HIV and AIDS (Prevention and Control) Act, 2017, are examples of laws that reflect the commitments made under these conventions.

The central government has also made a few attempts to bring about a uniform legislative framework on public health but this has remained a thorny subject, given the allocation of legislative responsibilities between the Union and the states. Attempts at framing a legal framework on public health can be divided into two tracks. The first category consists of proposals for a comprehensive model public health law, covering areas such as the functioning of health authorities, food safety, sanitation, lodging sites, markets, slaughterhouses and burial grounds. The idea here has been to formulate a model law, which could then be accepted and adopted by the states. Suggestions to this effect have been made by various public agencies and task forces constituted by the government. The second track relates more specifically to situations of public health emergencies, an area over which the central government enjoys greater legislative control.

In 2017, the Ministry of Health and Family Welfare put out a draft of the Public Health (Prevention, Control and Management of Epidemics, Bio-terrorism and Disasters) Act, seeking to replace the Epidemic Diseases Act, 1897, with a more modern legislation.[38] While being more elaborate on the scope of the government's powers in dealing with public health emergencies, the bill was criticized for being equally bereft in its regard for civil liberties.[39] Notably this bill, which no longer happens to be on the table, did not even reflect the basic privacy safeguards required under the IHR. This is ironic given that the Union has previously cited compliance with the IHR and other international treaties as a rationale for bringing about a comprehensive public health legislation in the country.[40]

A recent public interest litigation connected with the affordability of COVID treatment in private hospitals brought to light the fact that at that point we had only eight public health enactments in the country.[41] The oldest ones being the public health laws of Tamil Nadu and Andhra Pradesh that date back to 1939. More recently, states like Kerala and UP have adopted new public health laws. Kerala's public health ordinance that was introduced in February 2021 contains five references to privacy, all of which relate only to the physical aspects of privacy. Moreover, even this need for physical privacy seems to be designed mainly from a gendered lens, regarding women as objects of protection of the law. For instance, the law speaks of privacy in sanitary conveniences, protecting the privacy of women from inspecting officials, and special accommodations for the privacy of women who customarily do not appear in public.[42] In maintaining this focus, the ordinance ignores many other essential facets of individual privacy, including the protection of personal information. This happens to be the case despite Kerala's recent encounter with data protection concerns in connection with its use of a US-based firm, Sprinklr, for collection and processing of COVID data.[43]

The Uttar Pradesh Public Health and Epidemic Diseases Control Act, 2020, is another example of a law that was brought about amidst the COVID crisis.[44] The legislation is geared towards empowering the state to undertake interventions like lockdowns, isolation, quarantine, contact tracing and sealing of localities. But we found that it did not even contain the limited references to privacy that were seen in the Kerala law. This is disconcerting given that such laws are being brought about in a context that is shaped both by the requirements of the *Puttaswamy* verdict and the apparent impact of official COVID management strategies on the rights and liberties of individuals.

A Categorization of the Statutory Framework

In addition to the dedicated public health laws discussed above, there is a broader ecosystem of laws that intersects with different aspects of public health, such as food safety standards, restrictions on smoking in public places, and protection of persons with disabilities. Based on their scope and objectives, such laws can broadly be classified into four groups: (i) laws dealing with public health emergencies, (ii) criminal sanctions, prohibitions and standards, (iii) protection of specific groups, and (iv) provision of health services. These categories are not mutually exclusive. Neither is this an exhaustive list. But this classification serves our purpose of illustrating the spectrum of legislative instruments (focusing only on central laws) relating to public health and analysing whether any specific efforts have been made to account for privacy concerns in each context. In addition, there is also a fifth category of laws governing the protection of health data – that has been discussed separately in the next section.

Public Health Emergencies

The Epidemic Diseases Act, 1897, and the Disaster Management Act, 2005, are the two main central legislations dealing with the declaration and management of public health emergencies in India. As noted previously, these laws are fairly open-ended in nature with tremendous scope for discretion in the hands of the state. This is particularly true for the 1897 legislation that allows state governments to take any measures that seem necessary to control the outbreak and spread of any 'dangerous epidemic disease', a term that has not even been defined in the law.[45] The Disaster Management Act, on the other hand, defines a disaster to mean a natural or man-made occurrence that bears widespread implications for human life or the environment, and managing which is beyond the capacity of the local community.[46]

Ghosh and Ray Choudhury note that the legal labelling of the COVID crisis as a disaster (rather than a health crisis) led to the 'normalization of the controlling measures', with a disaster situation being seen as a justification for adopting extraordinary measures with reduced accountability.[47] This observation becomes all the more significant in light of the fact that neither the Epidemic Diseases Act nor the Disaster Management Act addresses the need for balancing privacy interests and other civil liberties with adopted emergency measures.

Criminal Laws, Prohibitions and Standards

The legislations discussed above make it an offence to refuse compliance with the orders issued by an authorized agency.[48] In addition, the Indian Penal Code, 1860, also contains an entire chapter on offences affecting public health, safety, convenience and morals. The range of activities covered under this chapter include negligent or malignant actions likely to spread the infection of a dangerous disease, disobeying quarantine rules, sale of adulterated food, drinks or drugs, contamination of water sources, rash driving and overloading of vehicles, and negligent conduct involving machinery or buildings.[49] Section 144 of the Code of Criminal Procedure is another notable provision. It allows a district magistrate to pass short-term directions to prevent any 'danger to human life, health or safety'. This provision has been widely used during the COVID pandemic for purposes such as lockdowns and restrictions on public gatherings. Courts have, however, made it clear that orders issued under this section should be restricted to emergent situations and cannot be permanent or even semi-permanent in character.[50]

The next subcategory is a fairly broad one, consisting of a variety of laws that do not necessarily have much in common except for the fact that they all deal with the setting of prohibitions and regulatory standards around specific activities. Such laws include rules relating to environmental protection, such as the Environment Protection Act, 1986, rules on air, water and noise pollution, regulation of insecticides and biomedical wastes. Next, they also cover laws prohibiting certain types of conduct that are deemed harmful to individuals or society at large. The prohibition on smoking in public spaces and health warnings on cigarette packets,[51] bar on prenatal diagnostics, prevention of human trafficking are some examples. Finally, there are laws that establish regulatory standards for the production and sale of goods meant for human consumption. This includes laws such as the Food Safety and Standards Act, 2006; the Drugs and Cosmetics Act, 1940; and the Infant Milk Substitutes, Feeding Bottles and Infant Foods Act, 1992.

Most of these laws do not deal specifically with privacy issues, although they may contain some ancillary privacy-linked restrictions on the exercise of state powers. For instance, the law on cigarette regulation limits entry and search of premises by regulatory agencies only during 'reasonable hours'.[52] In another example, the Food Safety Act provides that any confidential information received by the Food Safety and Standards Authority of India should not be disclosed to third parties unless found necessary in order to protect public health.[53] This represents an attempt to balance business information interests against larger goals of public health, with a clear prioritization of the latter.

Protections for Specific Groups

Just as the previous category was about the regulation of specific types of activities and conduct, this one relates to the legal protections that are extended to specific groups, often categorized based on the vulnerability of the population. These special groups could consist of consumers, workers, persons with disabilities, and persons living with

HIV/AIDS. The laws geared towards the protection of these groups reflect a slightly more meaningful engagement with privacy concerns compared with all the other categories discussed above. This may be due to a combination of factors, including the recent vintage of some of these laws and their adoption of a rights-based approach, which often flows from India's international commitments.

For instance, the confidentiality of personal information is given utmost importance under the laws applicable to persons with mental illness and those living with HIV. In each of these cases, the law not only contains a requirement to maintain confidentiality but also spells out the limited grounds on which an exception can be made. The Mental Healthcare Act, 2017, restricts health professionals from sharing any information received in the course of a person's treatment, except on grounds such as preventing threat of harm or to a person's life or in the interests of public safety.[54] The statute also recognizes that every person with mental illness has a right to live with dignity. This includes conditions of a safe and hygienic environment, sanitary facilities and respect for their privacy.[55] Similarly, the new legislation on rights of persons with disabilities that was adopted in 2016 contains explicit references to the dignity and privacy of individuals. Dealing with the important issue of legal capacity, it also restricts anyone from exercising undue influence over a person with disability and compels respect for their autonomy, dignity and privacy.[56]

Provision of Health Services

Our last category of laws deals with the provision of healthcare services and regulation of medical establishments and practitioners. The National Medical Commission Act adopted in 2019 is the result of a long-drawn effort to reform the regulation of the medical profession. It creates a new National Medical Commission (NMC), with an Ethics and Medical Registration Board under it, to replace the erstwhile Medical Council of India. But until the NMC formulates its policies on professional ethics for medical professionals, the Indian Medical Council's regulations on professional conduct, etiquette and ethics continue to remain in effect. These regulations bar medical practitioners from disclosing information that they learn about their patients in a professional capacity, except on three grounds: a court order, serious and identified risk to a specific person or community, and information to public health authorities in case of notifiable diseases.[57] Further, practitioners are required to maintain the health records of patients for a period of three years and are obliged to make these available to the patient upon request.[58] This corresponds with data retention and access requirements that are typically seen under data protection frameworks.

Next, the Clinical Establishments (Registration and Regulation) Act, 2010, lays down the minimum standards of operation of medical facilities and services in states that have adopted the Act. As per the rules framed under this law, every registered clinical establishment is required to maintain electronic health records (EHRs), as notified by the government.[59] While the rules themselves do not deal with the data protection in connection with EHRs, the Ministry of Health and Family Welfare has separately issued a set of recommended EHR standards for healthcare institutions.[60] The current version of the standards, issued in 2016, defines privacy in a fairly narrow sense, as authorization by the patient to view their health records. But the document separately captures various other elements of health data protection through recommendations on confidentiality of the data, the patient's right to access and correct their information, and maintenance of security standards. These are voluntary standards that do not have the teeth of the law but, as we discuss below, certain other legal and administrative measures are currently under way to try and meet this end.

Data Governance in the Health Sector

Health data, which can be defined to mean data related to the state of one's physical or mental health, forms one of the most sensitive categories of personal data. It is categorized as such due to the expectation of confidentiality in such dealings and the extent of harm that the person could face from unaccountable processing of health data. Further, unlike some other types of data that could be changed or replaced – for instance, a credit card number – medical data is 'non-perishable' in nature.[61] The effects of its breach and unauthorized use are therefore permanent and non-reversible. Unfortunately, this realization about the sensitivity of health data is accompanied by the reality of its frequent disregard and abuse.

Research found that the Department of Health and Human Services in the United States had reported over 173 million breach entries involving health data between 2009 to 2017.[62] While this does not reveal the number of unique individuals who were affected, the authors estimate that the breaches could have affected up to one-third of the US population. Closer to home, a report by Oommen C. Kurian brought to light a major data breach involving the complete patient records of a large multi-speciality hospital in Kerala.[63] The data included information such as patients' names and contact details, diagnostic test results, prescriptions and consent forms. Other known incidents include the publication of COVID lab tests of Delhi residents on government websites[64] and reports of over six million records associated with an India-based healthcare being available on the dark web.[65] These incidents highlight the need for an effective data protection framework to regulate the collection and use of personal health data and consequences for its misuse.

At present, the Information Technology Act, 2000, and the rules on reasonable security practices under it constitute India's primary legal framework for the protection of personally identifiable information. Section 43A of the Act entitles a person to claim compensation for any negligence in maintaining reasonable security practices with respect to their sensitive personal data by a body corporate. The rules under it define sensitive data to include information about a person's physical, physiological and mental health conditions, sexual orientation, medical records and history, and biometric information.[66] Going beyond the scope of Section 43A, which is limited to security practices, the rules also set out fairly detailed requirements on other aspects of data protection. This includes requirements of consent from the individual, limitation on purpose of use, retention period, and conditions for disclosures and transfers.[67]

Despite the existence of these rules, the framework under Section 43A has seen limited effectiveness for various reasons. This includes issues of scope – the focus only on sensitive data, exclusion of entities other than body corporates – and limited implementation in actual practice. These limitations build the case for introducing a comprehensive data protection law in the country the foundation for which was laid in 2018 by the Justice B.N. Srikrishna–led Committee of Experts on Data Protection.[68] The committee recognized the need for a robust law governing the protection of personal data, covering both private and state entities, and the establishment of a competent and independent regulator to enforce the law. The recommendations and draft bill prepared by the committee became the basis for the Personal Data Protection Bill, 2019 (PDP Bill, 2019). This Bill received a series of suggested changes in 2021 on account of the recommendations made by a joint parliamentary committee that was constituted on this subject. However, in August 2022, the government announced its decision to withdraw this draft in its entirety with a promise to introduce a new version in the coming months.

The PDP Bill contained a general set of protections for all personal data and certain enhanced standards for the governance of sensitive personal data. This included health data, such as health records and data generated during the provision of health services, as well as genetic and biometric information.[69] One of the additional safeguards applicable to such sensitive data was the requirement of 'explicit consent' from the data principal, which should be context-aware and granular in nature.[70] While consent remains the standard basis for data processing globally, there are certain grounds that can override the need for consent. Relevant conditions in the context of health data under the withdrawn PDP Bill included medical emergencies, health services rendered during an epidemic or other threat to public health, and disaster situations.[71] This indicated a prioritization of health and public health goals over the individual's autonomy and control over their data in these circumstances. A similar prioritization could also be seen in the context of cross-border data flows. The general position under the PDP Bill was that certain types of critical personal data, to be notified by the government, would need to be processed only in India. Yet, such data would be permitted to be transferred abroad for the provision of prompt health or emergency services.[72]

When adopted, a data protection law will create a baseline data protection framework for the country. But it may still need to be supplemented by higher standards of protection applicable to specific sectors. The Data Protection Committee had identified the draft Digital Information Security in Healthcare Act, 2017 (DISHA), drafted by the health ministry as an example of such a proposal.[73] DISHA aimed to set up digital health authorities at the national and state level to implement privacy and security measures for digital health data and create a mechanism for exchange of electronic health data.[74] But as the discussions on the PDP Bill gathered steam, it was decided that DISHA would be subsumed in the PDP Bill, to avoid the duplicity of effort by different ministries.[75] Yet, even as the data protection proposals continue to remain at the discussion stage, and have in fact taken a step backwards after the withdrawal of the PDP Bill, several elements of the health data governance framework have already started taking shape as part of the government's Ayushman Bharat Digital Mission (ABDM).

Initiatives under the ABDM include the creation of a National Health Authority, emphasis on interoperability of health data, and operationalization of health data exchanges. The difference, however, is that while DISHA was meant to be a statutory initiative, the digital health agenda under the ABDM is being pursued based on a cabinet approval and through executive actions. This highlights a quintessential 'cart before the horse' problem of creating digital systems and infrastructures without the legislative frameworks necessary to legitimize and steer such proposals, including on account of the impact on the privacy of citizens.

The conversation around the governance of non-personal data, which either does not relate to an identifiable individual or has been anonymized to remove identifiable markers, is another evolving policy track in India. While the joint parliamentary committee on the PDP Bill had recommended that both personal and non-personal data should be subsumed under one law, another committee headed by

Kris Gopalakrishnan had proposed a separate regulatory framework for the aggregation and sharing of non-personal data. The committee offered several examples of such data, many of which, like pollution data, road safety and traffic conditions, patient data and consumption of utilities, can be traced to different elements of public health. Their report also elaborated upon the mandatory sharing of designated 'high-value' data sets on subjects such as healthcare, urban planning, environmental planning and energy.

The parallel processes on the personal and non-personal data protection create a grey area of regulation with clear overlaps between the two proposals. Alongside this, there is the third track of non-legislative policy measures such as the Data Access and Knowledge Sharing Protocol developed for the Aarogya Setu app and ABDM's Health Data Management Policy. The Aarogya Setu's data protocol was introduced in response to criticisms against the contact tracing app for its non-voluntary use, lack of transparency and absence of safeguards in the processing and collection of personal data. While the protocol helped bring some clarity on these issues, its effectiveness remained marred by the lack of a strong grounding in the law – the protocol could be modified at any point by the empowered group that had notified it.[76] Similarly, ABDM's data management policy is not backed by a law. Yet, the digital health system continues to gain scale even as the statutory conversations on data governance remain stuck at the stage of policy proposals.

Conclusion

Achieving better public health outcomes is one of the core functions of the state. The central and state governments have, therefore, enacted various laws to deal with different aspects of public health, in line with their legislative competencies. Some of these laws relate more explicitly to the subject of public health, such as the state laws covering topics like sanitation, functioning of local health authorities, lodging sites, markets, slaughterhouses and burial grounds. In addition, there are laws like the Epidemic Diseases Act and the Disaster Management Act that deal with powers of both the centre and the states in case of public health emergencies. There are also a number of other laws that intersect with the goals of public health, even though they may not be described as such. This includes laws setting out various prohibitions and standards, such as environmental protection and food safety norms, protections for vulnerable groups like persons with disabilities, provision of health services, and proposals for the governance of health data.

In a few of these cases, the law contains specific references to the concept of privacy, in the form of confidentiality requirements, right to dignity, physical privacy during inspections and respect for individual autonomy. Yet, there are many other laws, most notably those on management of public health emergencies, that are completely silent on the need for proportionality and respect for privacy in the interventions. This runs contrary to the safeguards guaranteed by the Supreme Court's *Puttaswamy* decision, highlighting the urgent need for a new rights-respecting framework for the management of health emergencies.

In the years to come, the *Puttaswamy* verdict is also likely to reshape the boundaries between privacy and public health on many other aspects. The examples discussed in the chapter include the prohibition on consumption of alcohol in some states, regulation of reproductive choices, and the state's ability to access and process the health data of citizens. The last one becomes particularly relevant, given the significant push towards the digitization of health records in the country. Even as the proposal to introduce a personal data protection law remains under consideration, the government is moving rapidly on the roll out of the ABDM, a project that will significantly reshape both the extent and purposes for which health data is processed in India. The project, however, does not rest on the edifice of a legal framework, the first requirement for an intervention to be regarded proportionate under the *Puttaswamy* judgment.

But, as evidenced by the Supreme Court's verdict on Aadhaar, there are limits on how far the optimism of *Puttaswamy* might take us. It is, therefore, imperative that the talks of data protection be urgently translated into statutory law before public and private systems for the processing of citizen's health data end up acquiring an irreversible scale.

3

COVID-19 Data Infrastructure in India: Politics of Knowing and Governing the Pandemic

Bidisha Chaudhuri and Meera Muthukrishnan

Introduction

THE global COVID-19 pandemic has emerged as the single-most impactful event in recent times. This event has impacted every aspect of our lives – social, economic, cultural, political, technological, scientific and medical, in many ways. While the challenges and learnings continue to evolve, a very distinct feature about this pandemic has been the data-driven approach to understand and tackle the nature of the crisis. Most of the governmental and popular responses to the COVID-19 pandemic have been dominated by this data-driven approach. This means that different kinds of data available about the virus and its impact – ranging from positivity rate to mortality rate, from recovered cases to active cases – have not only shaped public health policies and government actions but also largely shaped our understanding of the global health crisis.[1] A variety of policies at different levels of restrictiveness and stringency have been implemented on the basis of such data. Some, like the internal and external travel and business restrictions, complete lockdown or curfew, restrictions to public events and gatherings, result in severe disruption of the social and economic lives and livelihoods of people. The decisions for the implementation as well as relaxation of the policies have been data-driven.

The public discourse on the pandemic has also been data-driven, to a great extent. Increasing proliferation of statistical terms such as 'flattening the curve', 'doubling the rate' into our news and everyday conversations stand witness to the datafied discourse on the pandemic. While data and numbers have largely provided a stable platform for engaging with the crisis amidst uncertainties, they also have been at the centre of much of the debate on policies and actions around the pandemic. Lack of data, lack of trust in data, counter-data practices (where, for example, data becomes a site for debate or when different actors enumerates different sets of data) – all have come to the fore of the public debate around the pandemic.[2] On 27 February 2021, *The Hindu*, a leading national daily newspaper, published a claim by scientists from IIT Kanpur that a second wave is unlikely in India as their model showed that around 60 per cent of the Indians had already been exposed to the virus and the country had reached herd immunity. Their claim was contradictory to the ICMR's (Indian Council of Medical Research) measure of 20 per cent prevalence but was backed by their in-house model's prediction based on the number of symptomatic cases being reported. This news story that was based on a study that used data and mathematical models from a reputed university did not carry any disclaimer about its methodology and any possible caveat in its data or the analysis. In hindsight, we know this prediction was wrong as India suffered a devastating second wave in the following months. What this story, however, reveals is the contested nature of a data-driven discourse on the pandemic, especially when it steers policy decisions and public imagination around the crisis.

Drawing on Mayer-Schoenberger and Cukier (2013)[3], we refer to this data-driven discourse around the pandemic as datafication of the pandemic, that is, transformation of all medical, public health and social practices around the pandemic into quantified data, allowing for ubiquitous tracking and analysis of the pandemic. In this chapter, we unravel to what extent the pandemic in India was datafied and how this datafied discourse shaped our understanding of the pandemic. We see two paradoxical trends around data and the pandemic. The first trend sees a burgeoning number of data projects by state, private and volunteer collectives that report on various dimensions of the pandemic on a regular basis, while the state remains the main source of most of the data. These data projects are seen as an attempt to generate an accurate and objective understanding of the crisis amidst growing uncertainty about the virus and its impact.[4] The second trend sees an increasing mistrust of public data[5] coupled with floods of misinformation and fake news ushering in a 'post-truth pandemic'.[6] So, on one hand, data becomes the most trusted source of enumerating and explaining the crisis. On the other hand, fragility and inconsistencies of the same data open them to sharp criticism and an overall scepticism around them. We position our findings about COVID-19 data infrastructures in India within this broader paradox. The challenge of COVID-19 data veracity and the controversies around it makes it a perfect site to unravel the socially constructed nature of data and politics of data shaping our perception and decision making, which have long been discussed within the field of science and technology studies (STS).[7] Porter argues that reliance on numbers, especially in public life, does not emerge from their inherent rigour but from political, social and cultural contexts with which science interacts with bureaucracy.[8] While this contested and political nature of data has been well established within STS, the current moment of crisis has brought this to the forefront of public debates as manifested through debates around credibility of data sources, claims and counter-claims around data.[9] In this paper, we focus on this contested role of data in shaping the ways of knowing and governing the pandemic and the process through which it becomes apparent.

With this larger research objective in mind, we take a critical data studies lens to explore a series of COVID-19 data sets on and in India and how the data and socio-political response to the crisis co-constitute each other. While asking questions such as, what kind of data gets captured, who are the actors in setting up and maintaining this data infrastructure and who have access to such data infrastructure, we situate our enquiry in India within the global politics of data practices around construction, curation, maintenance and sharing. In analysing the diverse and emerging sets of data, we invoke the concept of infrastructure to highlight, firstly, the evident focus on data availability as a way to deal with the pandemic and secondly, the invisible or 'behind the scenes' practices and actors that make such data available in the first place. In doing so, we rely on an interpretive approach to examine and analyse the selected data sets and to make sense of their social embedding. Through this study, we aim to show the infrastructural motifs of the COVID-19 data and how, as a data infrastructure, it builds our understanding of the world amidst the pandemic and governs our response actions. Our objective is to lay bare the fragile and precarious nature of this data infrastructure that otherwise hides behind strong claims of 'truth'. It is important to underline here that we do not intend to discard the COVID-19 data projected by these sets of data sites, but rather to highlight how these data are socially and politically shaped and how that in turn shapes our knowledge (or lack thereof) of the pandemic.

Datafication of the Pandemic: Relevant Work

Ackoff, in his data-information-knowledge-wisdom (DIKW) hierarchy, provided a pyramidal visualization with the voluminous data being the base and the pointed wisdom churned out continuously by filtration, reduction and transformation at the peak.[10] In this framework, data was considered as an important yet basic tool to the analytical process, which ultimately depended on expertise and experience in a certain domain. However, with technological advancement in digital data storage and archival techniques in the last decade or so, this hierarchy is somewhat challenged.[11] With big and small data becoming accessible either as complete data sets or through specific queries, all kinds of processing – filtering, reducing, correlations, etc. – can be done to suit one's specific requirements and draw out the information required. In this sense, information, knowledge and wisdom can be generated through a set of tools that work on the data as required, where data controls and shapes the new paradigm of knowledge.[12]

This paradigm of accessing, understanding and monitoring human conduct through data has come to be known as datafication.[13] While datafication as a new paradigm of knowing and doing has become normalized, scholars have also engaged with datafication critically.[14] These studies reveal the underlying ideology of datafication. On one hand, they discuss the larger power dynamics that valorize datafication and build trust in institutions that collect, interpret and share data,[15] while on the other, they focus on the materiality and performative agency of the data and data infrastructures as mediating the lived experiences and shaping the possibilities of action.[16]

When it comes to critical understanding of datafication of health, we see a growing influence of Foucault's idea of bio-politics (albeit digitized) that seek to govern the population by means of collecting data about birth, mortality, disease, fertility and so on.[17] However, others have suggested the inadequacy of bio-politics as a conceptual framework to capture the recent trends of datafication that thrive on real-time, predictive analytics permeating into fields of everyday behaviour, choices and preferences of the population.[18] Amidst the growing trend of data-driven medical research and practices and public health infrastructure and attempts to critically engage with such infrastructure, the COVID-19 pandemic has unleashed the fragile and messy nature of such datafied understanding of the status of the health at a level of the population. Some proclaim COVID-19 to be the first data-driven pandemic[19] – it has not only put quantification at the centre of experiencing the pandemic,[20] but also made everyday conversations about the pandemic among the common public being steered by data.

However, amidst this enormous volume of data, which claim not only to represent the crisis but also drive intervention during the crisis, we see a lack of comprehensive data and its inability to influence fitting policy response in times of uncertainty.[21] In fact, in many cases, the policy inputs by various governments have shaped the availability of data.[22] For example, active contact tracing was a prevalent practice in the initial days of the pandemic as the number of cases were low. As the number of infected patients surged, this data was not collected or reported by the state.[23] Sites that used this data to provide visualizations of the spread had to stop doing so in the absence of data. Similarly, since the ICD (International Classification of Disease) code for confirmed and suspected COVID-19 conditions were announced by the WHO in February 2020, the guidelines and additional codes around it kept evolving, leading to different categories of data being collected and documented.

These examples highlight how policies and guidelines shape not only what data gets collected (or not) but also how data often gets categorized and reported. Consequently, there has been much debate about the mismanagement of data and mistrust in data that marked the datafied discourse of the pandemic.[24] Hence, the datafication of the pandemic has highlighted the paradoxical nature of the relationship between the pandemic and its representation in data. While critical data studies have often highlighted the contested nature of data and the insights generated by them,[25] the pandemic and its data-driven discourse has provided an unfortunate yet scholarly opportunity to foreground the paradoxical nature of data and reality through what Shelton[26] calls a 'post-truth pandemic' where emotions and ideologies tend to dominate our understanding of the pandemic rather than the facts.

While COVID-19 data infrastructure lends visibility to the extent of the crisis, it also creates deliberate or unintended unknowing and ignorance about the crisis through decontextualization, obfuscation and misrepresentation of information about the pandemic.[27] In this paper, we focus on these paradoxical functions of the COVID-19 data infrastructures in India by critically engaging with different kinds of dashboards run by public, private and voluntary organizations. Our aim is not to undermine the importance of these data platforms, but to demonstrate what they reveal or do not reveal, and to whom and for what purpose.[28] We argue that a nuanced and critical understanding of the datafication of the pandemic will help us cautiously trade the thin line between over-reliance and dismissal of data.

Methodology

In India, there are three types of actors that have been regularly reporting on the pandemic since early 2020 through data dashboards: the state, private companies and voluntary organizations or collectives. At the state level, data is collected using the existing public health infrastructure. It is then rolled up to the centre which in turn publishes the aggregated all-India-level data. Even though some data is common, there is a lot of variation in the content reported, the method or channel of reporting, and the presentation of the data itself. While some differences can be expected, given that health being a state subject and not handled by a common central agency, the discrepancies in the semantics of the data reported could make comparisons among the states as well as the aggregations of the national-level data difficult and inaccurate. This becomes a prominent source of contention around data in India. To foreground these discrepancies, we surveyed all the available state-led data sites and categorized them based on the content, form and dissemination of the data. Once we surveyed all the state data platforms, we created a master catalogue to capture what was available and what was not, the accessibility and usability of the data and functions presented. We drew on existing work by Vasudevan et al.[29] as they analysed the Indian data platforms during the first wave of the pandemic in India along the dimensions of data availability, accessibility, granularity and privacy, and calculated a COVID data reporting score (CDRS) to rank the state data platforms in order of merit. While we draw on such quantitative studies to underline the degree of variance across state platforms, in our analysis, we treat these variations as a point of departure to further question how these variations in data across states shape our ways of knowing and governing the pandemic in India. While categorizing the states' data platforms, we looked for types of data or information that were available, the kind of actions these platforms supported and the modalities and forms through which data was shared, and what kind of networks of governance were these sites embedded in.

Along with this exhaustive list of state dashboards, we also looked at a few dashboards maintained by private organizations and voluntary groups (see Appendix 1). While these dashboards mostly sourced their COVID-19 data from the state-led dashboards, they were interesting data sites for our study due to the different kinds of information they chose to report. For example, some sites reported non-virus deaths during the lockdown, some others published regular blogs to document their processes and challenges of collecting data, or the impact of the pandemic on other aspects of life, some others ran awareness campaigns with health advisories and fake news detectors. We tracked all these kinds of data sites between November 2020 and June 2021. The distribution of the studied sites is as follows: centre (2), states (28), union territories (8), volunteer groups (4), private sites (1) and printed news media (3).

On the basis of our observations of these sites, we categorized the data platforms as performing different functions, namely, (i) information infrastructure, (ii) as enabling actions and (iii) as representations and counter-representations around issues related to the pandemic. It is important to note here that we do not evaluate any of the dashboards against these functions. Rather, we focus on how these data sites as a whole perform these functions which in turn shape the data-driven discourse of the pandemic.

A Data-driven Narrative of the Pandemic in India: A Critical Perspective

Data as Information Infrastructure

The variety of data available varied from one data platform to another. Overall, the platforms covered the following categories of data:

a) Pandemic status data: Status of cases, including quantitative parameters such as counts of confirmed cases, active cases, recovered cases and deaths (daily new count and the cumulative count), recovery rate and qualitative aspects about whether counts as per demography (age, gender, occupation, origin), co-morbidity and so on.

b) Testing data: Counts about tests sent, tests rejected, positive results, negative tests, testing per million, test positivity rate and type of the test conducted (Rapid antigen/RT-PCR).

c) Clinical management data: Including information about the number of hospital beds available (public and private), the facilities available (intensive care unit [ICU], ventilator support), special COVID-19 centres, their addresses, helplines, etc.

d) Procedural data: Data to let people know about the pandemic itself; the symptoms, testing procedure, self-isolation and care procedure, treatment, recovery and post-recovery information to help the public understand the medical and social aspects of the pandemic more clearly.

e) Information about policy guidelines and protocols: Dos and don'ts about mask wearing, testing, local, national and international travel, opening of schools and other institutions, business restrictions, crowd-gathering restrictions, transport restrictions and so on.
f) Vaccination-related data: Data about the number of vaccinations completed (daily and cumulative), number of first doses, number of second doses, percentage of population partially and completely vaccinated. Data could also be grouped by the type of vaccination itself.

We found that most regions reported data about the total number of confirmed cases since the beginning, the incremental change from the last reporting date (usually the previous day), the active number of cases, total and new deaths, total and new recoveries. This data was available at the district level and aggregated at the state levels, which was further rolled up for the national-level counts. When it came to testing, data about the number of tests performed and positivity rate was mostly available across all the states. Vaccination-related information was found to be better tracked than the cases and testing data, with details of first dose and second dose being available for most of the states. In the area of clinical management, the huge demand in hospitalization during the second wave resulted in almost all the states publishing the number of beds (some also published this with the break-up about the ICU beds, beds with ventilators). Hot spot and containment zone information was available on some of the sites only. Some sites also provided dynamic data and the latest information about the pandemic, for example, changing symptoms, home isolation and treatment routine, testing and hospitalization protocols.

While these data were useful on the whole, there was a great variation across states, not only in terms of which categories of data were covered but also in terms of the granularity, complexity and temporality of such data. For example, only limited number of dashboards reported on the co-morbidities of the deceased patients. Different state dashboards were also updated at different frequencies. A narrow focus on the disease also meant that availability of other data, such as information about consultations for non-COVID cases, psychological support, food and shelter support, online registration for vaccination and testing, e-pass application and so on, which are not directly related to the disease but equally relevant during the pandemic, were hardly made available through these data infrastructures, except for four sites we tracked. This implies that despite enormous volumes of data being generated what we know about the extent and nature of the pandemic in each state is extremely skewed and as a whole provides a fragmented (both spatially and temporally) picture of the pandemic at the national level.

The variation also manifested in the form and mode of dissemination of the data. For example, presence/absence of a dedicated dashboard, availability of search feature, frequently asked questions, local- and English-language support, audio, video and text messages, contact information for helplines, accessibility features for differently abled people shaped who could potentially access these data infrastructures for information about the pandemic. While most of the states had a dedicated dashboard or website, some states chose to publish data only through Twitter or other social media handles. This added an additional layer of inaccessibility irrespective of the availability and quality of data.

The format of data presentation plays an important role in determining how accessible the data is. PDF (portable document format) media bulletins were found to be a common form of presentation. Some states only published picture-based reports on Twitter. Dashboards with tables with filters and break-up features were found in some sites. While these forms of presentation are adequate for humans, for data sharing, and academic research, downloadable data sets are more appropriate. These could be done by providing data in comma-separated values (CSV)[30] files or through well-defined application programming interfaces (APIs) to ensure that the data is readable and usable across various platforms without the need for intermediate transformations. The data columns should be well named and should also be accompanied by metadata describing the data type, description, units and any other information needed for unambiguous usage with other systems. We found only six states supported the CSV download, and API support was not provided by any of the state sources. In order to address this issue, some volunteer-led sites resolved to make state data more accessible for further analysis and processing.

Last but not the least, an important factor in leveraging these data infrastructures was centred around the issue of differential access, that is, who could access what information. Role-based login for the same site is a powerful way to restrict access to data based on privileges and functions. Such role-based logins were found to be supported in thirteen of the state sites, where password-protected access was provided to access secure information to administrators. Some states provided default information without login and additional features based on login using password and CAPTCHA (completely automated public turing test to tell computers and humans apart). Some states had built advanced access control. For example, the Chhattisgarh website (see Figure 3.1) identified a number of roles (like state, home isolation control room, primary, secondary and private facilities) on its website. However, neither the roles defined by these sites nor the categories of information that were assigned to be secure across these sites were uniform or consistent.

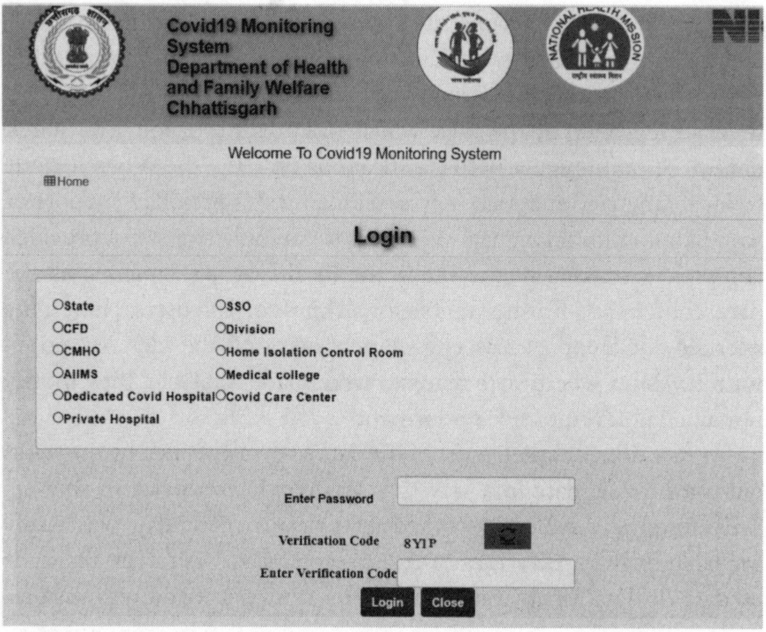

Figure 3.1: Role-based access to site of COVID-19 monitoring in Chhattisgarh

Despite the prevalence of data-driven narrative and a large volume of data projects around the pandemic in India, a close and critical exploration of these data sites reveals two important points. Firstly, the inconsistency of what gets reported and how it gets reported indicates a data overload without a meaningful conversation around why such data is needed, who would need this data and how this data could be useful. Secondly, the fragmented nature of data across states shows how the availability of data is shaped by state policies rather than data leading to policy input. This compels us to think about the extent to which these data sites shaped our actions.

Data as Enabling Actions

Beyond providing information, data platforms also enabled citizen actions such as, self-reporting, test results checking, contact for booking beds, vaccination registration, feedback provision, donations, e-pass applications for local and national movement and so on. However, similar to data availability and accessibility, these actionable features of the data sites were also inconsistent, sometimes across sites and sometimes within the same site over time. While most of the state's data sites provided the guidelines for movement and travel, other actionable features were usually missing from these sites. The social media integration of the sites, which was present for fourteen states, did not respond regularly to clarifications on requests. When it came to local language support, only seventeen states provided support of some kind in local languages. Among them, only five states provided complete rendering of the site in the local language, making all the data, content and features usable for all kinds of end users. Hence, the sites did not support active engagement on or off the sites. Moreover, for a few sites where such features were made available, they mostly remained non-responsive or dormant.

As mentioned earlier, most of the data sites maintained by the states did not provide data in a way that was conducive for open sharing. This closed nature of data worked at two levels: firstly, data was hardly available through CSV files or APIs; secondly, access to certain kinds of data or data forms was regulated by credentials and permissions.

Both these dimensions of closedness meant that despite data being available, most of it was not ready for further processing and analysis. This made most of the data infrastructure inadequate for drawing any data-driven insights and projections around the pandemic. Some of the private and volunteer collectives attempted to fill this gap by aggregating data from multiple sources and making them available in a more accessible manner through open APIs.

Considering that data becomes useful to us in specific contexts for answering different questions about the pandemic, mere availability of data as information infrastructure does not ensure a data-driven discourse on the pandemic, which demands data that is actionable at the same time. In absence of such actionable data infrastructure, most of the data projects, particularly the ones led by the states, appear to be merely reporting mechanism for compliance and do not contribute to any meaningful understanding of the pandemic and future projections.

It is important to note here that we do not intend to undermine the importance of the data reported across these various sites we surveyed. In fact, with the potential to support action, we see them as playing the role of infrastructure. However, in reality, how the data infrastructures facilitated specific actions around the pandemic was not always clear. For example, how data helped making decisions about medical infrastructures in India remains a matter of debate. Moreover, given the issues of data quality, inconsistent reporting and lack of accessibility, drawing any complex and reliable analytical insights from the data became an insipid and inordinate endeavour at once.

Data as Representations and Counter-representations

As a result of many data sites and their diverse range of data reported, without much granularity or complexity, these data sites may appear straightforward and neutral. However, the underlying politics of these sites become apparent when we focus on data that these sites do not report. We found at least one volunteer data site that reported non-virus deaths attributed to suicides due to lockdowns, starvation during migration and so on, and incidence of hate crimes that took place as a result of communalization of the COVID-19 outbreak. This can be easily juxtaposed with the union government's declaration in the parliament in 2020 that no data was maintained on migrant workers who lost their jobs and lives during the early nationwide lockdown in the country.[31] Hence, not capturing certain data meant certain political choices of representation.

We also found some critical data that were missing from most of the data sites which could be framed as misrepresentation or non-representation of the pandemic. These include data on co-morbidities, post-vaccination infection and death, rates of recurring infection, demographic and socio-economic variance in infections and mortality, and contact and cluster tracing. The fact that such critical data were not collected or not made available meant deliberate (or unintended) regulation of the datafied discourse of the pandemic in India.

While the above examples focus on missing data, the pandemic also shows how data can be posed as neutral tool for propaganda. For example, in 2020, media sites were engaged in a 'data debate' over communalization of the pandemic, where one side used a data graphic to show how a certain religious community was responsible for early outbreak of the pandemic in the national capital, whereas the other side pointed out bias in the data representations and alleged deliberate vilification of the religious community.[32] The potential of data to become such a political tool meant that data sites should declare their data sources and methodologies, and be able to explain any discrepancies in the data. Most of the state sites which also acted as the source for non-state sites did not reveal their sources and methodologies for data collection, whereas only four sites provided regular explanations about the data being reported.

As data represented (or misrepresented) the official narratives of the pandemic, with the prevalence of social media, a lot of misinformation has been floated about influencing the decisions of common people who judge the veracity of the information based on their trust of the presenter or the source. Alarmingly, some of this misinformation was circulated on mainstream media, which have conventionally been credible source of information, especially during crisis. The rising challenge of misinformation meant that the state agencies had to actively participate in dispelling fake or wrong news about the pandemic to retain trust on public data and health infrastructures. However, we found only six state-led data sites to engage in detecting fake news and fact-checking. The state of Meghalaya runs a fake news verification service that allows people to submit a query about whether certain news is fake or not. Sikkim provides a service for fake news registration and verification. Some non-state sites we tracked also run fake news detection services along with updated and accurate health advisories.

Hence, the data sites we studied demonstrated how data creates news lines of visibilities and invisibilities, inscribed representational politics and crafted moments of deliberate (or unintended) wisdom and ignorance at the same time. In this sense, sometimes absence of data (for example, the migrant death due to lockdown) opens up new field of political action.

Discussion: Implications of a Data-driven Narrative of the Pandemic

From Datafication to Dataism

Based on our review of the existing data sites, we find that data is treated more as a reporting tool for the purpose of compliance and perception management without any critical engagement with usefulness and effectiveness of data. Hence, from collection to processing, from tracking to reporting, datafication of the pandemic in India was not only fragmented but almost farcical. There was hardly any standardized template or guideline for what categories and forms of data would be collected, how such data would be collected and processed and what kind of reporting mechanism would be deployed. Many volunteers wrote about these discontinuities in the data infrastructure and how that made their job of creating data-based analysis of the pandemic a painstaking endeavour. Moreover, we found that most of data sites we visited did not have any data sharing protocol in place, implying that data-centric collaborations across different states or sites were not practically feasible. The kind of data infrastructure (with necessary human, institutional, procedural and technological resources available within its infrastructural substrates) that is required to build a datafied discourse on the pandemic was by and large missing in India. While this infrastructural inadequacy led to fragmented datafication, ironically, it did not reduce reliance and fervour around data-driven narratives of the pandemic. This, we argue, culminates into the paradoxical trend around data during the COVID crisis in India – data was sought after yet meaningless at once.

Furthermore, as most of the data sites are maintained by state agents (even for the non-state actors the state sites remain the main source), the datafied narrative of the pandemic is controlled by what, how and for whom the state decides to publish. Hence, instead of a data-driven understanding of the pandemic, we see a kind of state-led dataism[33] that promotes certain kind of data as the most objective means to capture the reality amidst uncertainty. On the other side of this state-led data narrative we see two opposite kinds of political actions organized around data and information. The first one attempts to highlight data that are often neglected by the state and thereby underline the politics of visibility and 'truth' claims, and the second one leverages the fragile and messy nature of the data, unfolding during an unprecedented crisis, to promote fake news and unfounded claims about the pandemic by bypassing and often challenging existing data (and scientific knowledge).

In Search of Privacy in a Datafied Pandemic

Concerns about privacy with such data sets may not be evident in plain sight as the data published in the dashboards are mostly collective, aggregated, descriptive statistics, where most personally identifiable information has been removed. However, a more careful look into these data sites reveals otherwise.

While some state dashboards address confidentiality by restricting access to the data itself using role-based logins, most of them do not have a privacy policy to ensure that data collection or sharing adheres to some standard. Dashboards of only five states (Assam, Goa, Karnataka, Mizoram and Nagaland) had a specific page stating the privacy policy, without any mention of data ownership. Even when the privacy policy has been specified in the site, it focused on the privacy of users using the website and did not discuss the guidelines for data downloaded from the dashboard. Some websites explicitly invoked copyright law to declare the legal owners. None of the websites declared the details of whether the data published has been consented to as an individual or a community for publication.

While most of the dashboards display aggregate counts of confirmed cases, active cases, recoveries, deaths, etc. at the district level as well at the state level, there are some cases where personal information about patients are easily discernible despite efforts to anonymize. For example, some states provide detailed information about every death, which, while being useful data from public health perspective, tends to compromise on the deceased's privacy. Data reports from Karnataka and Tamil Nadu reveal the district, state patient number, age, gender, date of admission, date of death, symptoms, co-morbidities, cause of death and place of death for each counted death. Given the patient number, the patient can be located unambiguously with some effort. The Kerala dashboard even gives away the name of the deceased in its dashboard. Thus, the strategy used to anonymize is not rigorous and consistent, keeping possibilities of re-identification of the patient very probable. There are mixed approaches regarding data privacy for deceased people even with established data protection frameworks like the Health Insurance Portability and Accountability Act (HIPPA), 1996, in the US or the General Data Protection Regulation (GDPR), 2016, in Europe.[34] In the Indian context, in the absence of any such robust guidelines, the implications of these fragile data sharing practices for vulnerable populations remain a major cause of concern.

Similar concerns for patient identification arise from initial practices of contact tracing. While due to increasing infections the state stopped publishing these numbers, the potential impact of such data sharing cannot be ignored. Patients who are identified to be the origin of a cluster might face open animosity when identified using such visualizations. The data may also cause wrong conclusions about people who get infected and who transmit the virus based on unscientific generalizations about the other demographic aspects such as caste, religion, profession and so on.

These issues become even more complex when some of the dashboards provide the feature of self-reporting of symptoms and also urge the users to download specific mobile applications to help track the infection and its spread. For instance, the self-reporting feature of Tamil Nadu's dashboard collects personal information (name, age, sex, mobile number, address, symptoms, travel history, contact with other patients, etc.).[35] Even though by accepting these data, the dashboard becomes the custodian of sensitive personal information and comes under the potential purview of personal data protection regulations, it is not clear if the data saved through these sites are stored and maintained along with other non-personal data or they are transferred to the databases guarded by stringent personal data protection practices.

In the absence of a well-defined legal, personal and non-personal data protection framework to enforce, evaluate and seek redress about these complex privacy concerns, it is not possible to predict how the various social and commercial usages of the data published in these dashboards and media bulletins could impact the individual rights of the citizens. A comprehensive regulatory framework for legal protection, data sharing framework for ensuring the right modes of access and authentication for shared users, and an ethical framework to assure controlled scope of usages are all necessary to ensure that these high-value public data sets are not misused intentionally or accidentally.

Conclusion

A critical data approach to the dominant discourse of the datafied pandemic allow us to highlight the opportunities, limitations distractions and concerns brought in by our reliance on data to 'know' the pandemic. It tells us how data renders our knowing, unknowing and deliberate (or unintended) ignorance of certain aspects of the crisis. However, our study also points out that uncritical and almost blind reliance on data brings with it the danger of complete dismissal or denial of data-driven (and scientific) discourse about the pandemic. As Latour in his interview with Kofman[36] points out, the critique of science is premised on the confidence in the authority of science. We argue that a critical deconstruction of the datafied pandemic is necessary to bring back the trust in the authority of scientific knowledge about the public health crisis and create a common world of shared understanding of what the pandemic is and how it should be tackled.

4

COVID-19 Surveillance in India: A Bridge Too Far?

Vrinda Bhandari[*]

Introduction

THROUGHOUT the COVID-19 pandemic, individuals have been asked to accept an ever-increasing number of privacy-violating measures by the government, private employers and resident welfare associations (RWAs). The scope of disease surveillance has expanded, aided in part by the developments in technology and big data. This has significantly impacted our bodily, informational, spatial, decisional, associational and behavioural privacy.

In India, privacy-invading disease surveillance measures – both physical and digital – have taken different forms at the central and state levels. These include contact tracing, quarantine enforcement, affixing posters outside homes of COVID-19 patients, stamping of hands with

---

[*] The author would like to thank Natasha Maheshwari, Ankit Kapoor, Satyender Saharan and Muazzam Nasir for their research assistance at different points of time.

quarantine details, door-to-door data collection by community health workers and mandatory temperature checks by employers. Despite the variety of measures employed, the COVID surveillance debate in India has focused predominantly on the use of contact tracing and the Aarogya Setu app.[1]

The issue of surveillance amidst the COVID-19 pandemic is important for three reasons. First, emergencies help normalize the deployment of surveillance tools. They shift the goal post about the acceptable level of intrusion by the government and private actors into the private lives of citizens.[2] Given the 'long tail' of a pandemic (as opposed to a finite and limited crisis such as a hurricane or tsunami),[3] the extended use of extraordinary technological measures can hasten a shift in privacy norms. This increases an already wide asymmetry of power between the citizen and state/private entities.

Second, even if some of these COVID surveillance measures may not have achieved the desirable level of efficiency, they are now part of the government toolkit and are more likely to be reintroduced (in a modified form) during the next emergency or public health crisis.[4]

Third, the debate in India is further complicated by the fact that both the central and state governments have the power to legislate on preventive aspects of health. Public health is a state subject,[5] while the prevention of the spread of contagious disease across states is on the concurrent list.[6] The result is a patchwork of surveillance measures deployed at the central and the state levels, without clarity on how they interact with each other. Moreover, in the absence of a comprehensive data protection law or a strong conception of data rights, the protection of a citizen's privacy is almost entirely at the mercy of the Indian state.

While studies abroad have analysed the impact of new public and private disease-surveillance measures on the right to privacy, there is a dearth of similar research here. There have been few attempts at comprehensive mapping of the types of surveillance mechanisms adopted during the COVID-19 pandemic in India.[7]

This chapter attempts to present an authoritative account of the physical and digital surveillance measures employed by governments and private corporations across India. It documents the different surveillance mechanisms adopted during the pandemic by mapping them into five public health objectives, namely, (a) symptom tracking, (b) mobility and density mapping, (c) quarantine enforcement and location tracking, (d) contact tracing, and (e) travel passes and vaccination. In articulating these objectives, the chapter adopts the parameters put forth by Boudreaux et al. to evaluate data privacy during pandemics.[8] There is no doubt that the right to privacy is not absolute. It can be validly restricted by the state on grounds of public health, especially in extraordinary times such as the COVID-19 pandemic.[9] However, any such restriction must be backed by a specific law, bear a rational connection to the government's aim, be necessary, and balance competing rights. Next, it evaluates the privacy and proportionality concerns emanating from the use of such surveillance measures. It then considers their suitability and effectiveness, that is, whether the loss of privacy has been accompanied by an appropriate public health benefit. The third and fourth sections will focus on specific interventions, instead of analysing the entire gamut of disease-surveillance measures. Finally, it concludes with recommendations for the way forward.

COVID-19 Surveillance Measures

This section provides an overview of the physical and digital surveillance measures put in place in India during the COVID-19 pandemic and maps them against the five public health objectives mentioned above. While an overlap amongst the different categories is inevitable, this rough categorization provides a useful way to map different forms of disease surveillance.

Data published by the Internet Democracy Project notes the expanse of digital disease surveillance measures employed by state agencies. As of November 2020, at least seventy-two apps were released by public entities across Android and iOS platforms in India, of which three were pan-India apps. These apps covered contact tracing, quarantine monitoring, self-assessment, information dissemination, e-pass integration, etc.[10]

Symptom Tracking

Symptom tracking helps governments understand the geographical distribution of people experiencing COVID-19 symptoms. As a data collection activity, it helps direct users to testing centres, monitors the change in caseloads in a region, and identifies emerging hot spots.[11]

Symptom tracking takes place through self-assessment, third-party assessment (by filling out a questionnaire) or temperature checks. However, these methods suffer from some limitations. Self-assessment or self-reporting relies solely on subjective, user-generated responses, which may not always be accurate, especially because some symptoms may be common with diseases such as influenza, pneumonia or flu. This can result in overestimation of the burden of the disease.[12]

At the same time, many patients with COVID-19 are asymptomatic. In such cases, temperature checks may result in under-reporting and false negatives. The data can get further confounded if gig workers have an incentive to under-report their symptoms to avoid a COVID-positive status.[13] Hospital-based reporting may also contribute to symptom tracking, although during the first few months of the pandemic, access to hospitals was limited.

(i) Self-assessment Tools

The most prominent example of digital symptom tracking is the self-assessment test through the central government's Aarogya Setu app. The app correlates a user's location and proximity to any 'potential COVID hot spots' with self-reported symptoms, and other factors, such as age, gender, recent travel, COVID exposure and pre-existing medical conditions.[14]

Based on the input, the app displays the results in three colours – green (safe or low risk), yellow (moderate risk) and orange (high risk of infection). If an individual tests positive for COVID-19, the testing lab shares this information with the ICMR, and the Aarogya Setu app turns red.[15] Each time a user completes a self-assessment test, the app collects and uploads her location data, results of her self-assessment and unique digital ID (DiD) to the Government of India's server. This data is deleted within thirty to sixty days, depending on the circumstances.[16]

In addition to Aarogya Setu, many private companies such as Reliance Jio and Apollo Hospitals also launched COVID-19 self-diagnostic tools. Users were asked their age, gender, symptoms, duration of fever, highest temperature recorded, etc.[17] However, it is unclear whether this information was anonymized, shared with the government, used for internal purposes or even how long it was stored for.

(ii) Door-to-door Tracking Efforts

State governments have also relied on door-to-door symptom tracking efforts during the pandemic. For instance, in June 2020, the Punjab government launched the Ghar Ghar Nigrani app, for 'house-to-house surveillance'. ASHA workers and community volunteers *had* to use the app to track symptoms, record an individual's co-morbidities, recent medical condition, personal details and occupation, and carry out SARI (severe acute respiratory infection)/ILI (influenza-like illness) surveillance.[18] Interestingly, the health ministry's Model Micro Plan for containing local transmission of COVID-19 did not envisage app-based data collection, and promoted manual human intervention.[19]

A similar effort was also launched by the Greater Chennai Corporation which purchased 13,000 hand-held infrared thermometers to identify symptomatic persons through door-to-door screenings.[20]

(iii) Mandatory Temperature Checks at the Workplace

Private companies also engaged in disease surveillance through symptom tracking by instituting mandatory temperature checks at the workplace. For instance, in April 2020, online food delivery services such as Swiggy, Zomato, Grofers (now rebranded as Blinkit), and companies such as Chaayos and Rebel Foods instituted mandatory temperature checks for their delivery agents and chefs. This was also shared with the customer, via their apps.[21]

Mobility and Density Mapping

To understand the geographical and spatial distribution of infectious disease, public health officials need to track its movement through the country. This involves creating movement and population density maps to identify COVID-19 clusters and hot spots of transmission, to enforce social distancing and to track migration patterns post-lockdown.[22]

(i) Location Tracking and Syndromic Surveillance

In April–May 2020, Aarogya Setu was used to analyse the location history of infected persons and those with self-diagnosed symptoms to forecast over 650 hot spots across the country. Of these, 130 were subsequently declared as hot spots by the government.[23] However, during the devastating second wave in India in April–May 2021, the app had a 'limited function' in identifying emerging hot spots, partly because testing labs were not updating and integrating their results with the mobile numbers linked to Aarogya Setu.[24]

In March 2020, the Karnataka government released a mobile app, Corona Watch, that tracked user location, date and time of movements *before* they tested positive, and recorded their home addresses.[26] This data was accessible to the general public, although in some instances personal details were revealed.[26] The Kerala government combined call data and IP (Internet Protocol) records and security camera footage with manual enquiries to track patients' locations and identify containment zones.[27]

Syndromic mapping undoubtedly has some benefits. Nevertheless, such benefits need to be balanced against concerns of user privacy and must ensure anonymity of infected persons to avoid the risk of stigmatization.

(ii) Drone Surveillance for Density Mapping

During the initial months of the pandemic, Kerala used drones for density mapping and to monitor movement of quarantined persons and movement within containment zones. Those found violating social distancing norms were charged under the law.[28] Drones were deployed by Maharashtra, Tamil Nadu, Gujarat, Uttar Pradesh, Delhi, Karnataka, Punjab, Rajasthan, Assam, Haryana, etc., for similar monitoring purposes.[29]

The use of drone footage, particularly to charge or arrest individuals, is embedded in a criminal justice framework rather than a public healthcare framework, and may have a disproportionate impact on marginalized groups.[30]

Quarantine Enforcement

Since the fourteenth century, when ships arriving from infected ports to Venice were made to sit at anchor for forty days ('*quaranta giorni*'), quarantine enforcement has been used by governments to limit the spread of communicable diseases.[31] During the COVID-19 pandemic, quarantine enforcement took the form of location tracking through app-based surveillance, publication of quarantine lists and lateral surveillance.

(i) App-based Surveillance

During the initial months of the pandemic, various states adopted different app-based modes of surveillance for quarantine enforcement. For instance, in March 2020 the Karnataka government released the Quarantine Watch app, requiring those under quarantine to mandatorily upload geo-tagged 'quarantine selfies' every hour, between 7 a.m. and 10 p.m. A violation of the geo-fence triggered an automatic alert. Defaulters sending 'wrong photos' were shifted to mass quarantine centres.[32]

Surat, similarly, developed an unlisted app, SMS COVID-19 tracker, that required COVID-affected persons to send their GPS location hourly from 9 a.m. to 9 p.m. and '*submit the questionnaire provided in [the] application two times every day with Selfie*'.[33] Defaulters were shifted to public quarantine centres and fined.

Surat's quarantine selfie requirement was replicated in four other cities in Gujarat: Ahmedabad, Gandhinagar, Vadodara and Rajkot.[34]

Equally invasive quarantine and/or contact tracing apps were developed by the states of Maharashtra, Telangana, Himachal Pradesh, Tamil Nadu, Goa, Arunachal Pradesh, Chhattisgarh, Haryana, Madhya Pradesh, Puducherry and West Bengal.[35]

These apps often blur the space between the public and private spheres, with the mobile phone being used to track the live location of quarantined residents or to enforce quarantine. This becomes especially problematic when it involves women sending selfies wearing different attires and against different backgrounds, creating risks of voyeurism, infringing both personal data and bodily integrity.[36] The apps turn the mobile phone into a site for surveillance, and it is unclear whether they even achieved their stated purpose. They introduce a new form of 'self(ie) governance' or 'state at home' governance that transforms facial recognition from the passport photo or Aadhaar card to a 'sentient machine at home'.[37]

Another cause for concern is that most of these apps, such as those developed by Tamil Nadu and West Bengal, have inaccessible and hard-to-find privacy policies, raising concerns about the long-term consequences of such data collection activities.[38]

(ii) Marking Out Those Under Quarantine

The quarantine selfie requirement allowed the state to extend its gaze into the domesticity of our home.[39] This privacy was further invaded when state governments marked out those under quarantine in the initial months of the pandemic. This was done in three different ways.

First, multiple state governments, starting with Karnataka in March 2020, and then in parts of Maharashtra, Rajasthan and Punjab published the personal details of quarantined individuals.[40] These details promptly moved from government websites to mass WhatsApp groups, resulting in serious privacy violations and accompanying social stigma and discrimination.

Second, such publications were often *accompanied* by the stamping of hands of quarantined persons, as in Karnataka and Goa,[41] an example of 'under-the-skin' surveillance.[42]

Third, district administrators in Punjab, Rajasthan and Delhi adopted the practice of affixing posters outside the homes of quarantined or infected individuals, without any authorization under their own lockdown guidelines.⁴³

(iii) Lateral Surveillance

Surveillance, including disease surveillance, traditionally involves asymmetric power relations between the citizen and the state. Here the state can legally authorize the collection and tracking of individual personal data for various purposes. In contrast, lateral surveillance or peer-to-peer surveillance is the *'use of surveillance tools by individuals, rather than by agents of institutions public or private, to keep track of one another'*.⁴⁴ The use of lateral surveillance mechanisms skyrocketed during the pandemic, at the behest of governments and RWAs.⁴⁵

For instance, the Greater Chennai Corporation used FOCUS volunteers – Friends of COVID-19 Citizens Under Surveillance – for quarantine enforcement. Around 5,000 such volunteers or 'quarantine monitors' were reportedly paid in June 2020 to ensure compliance with quarantine requirements.⁴⁶ Kerala adopted a similar strategy, where neighbours of quarantined individuals were encouraged to inform the local police if they left their homes.⁴⁷

At the individual/community level, RWAs emerged as 'mini-sovereigns'⁴⁸ encouraging residents to keep an eye on each other. In Gurugram, the local administration worked with the RWAs, asking them to collect air travel details of their society's residents and share them with the administration.⁴⁹

Contact Tracing

Contact tracing emerged as the primary tool of choice for disease surveillance globally and nationally, particularly during the initial pandemic response. While manual contact tracing has traditionally been employed to trace and inform contacts of infected persons, the COVID-19 pandemic witnessed a surge in popularity of digital contact tracing apps, with equally vigorous debates about privacy concerns.⁵⁰

(i) Aarogya Setu

Contact tracing was embraced by the central government through the development and deployment of the Aarogya Setu app.

There is substantial literature on the privacy and security issues concerning Aarogya Setu. These include concerns of centralization and excessive data collection (through GPS and Bluetooth data), their related security concerns, the absence of clearly defined purpose, the lack of proper data sharing mechanisms, and accountability and oversight measures.[51] Although the Aarogya Setu Data Access and Knowledge Sharing Protocol, 2020 (Protocol), increased some privacy protections for users, it has not been consistently implemented.[52]

In addition to using Aarogya Setu, many state governments developed their own contact tracing apps, which differed in their clarity, transparency and privacy policies.[53] For instance, Punjab's COVA Punjab app was used for geo-fencing, self-screening, reporting mass gatherings and contact tracing (through GPS and call details records).[54]

(ii) Manual Contact Tracing

Apart from digital contact tracing, community health workers were also involved in large-scale manual contact tracing and 'community surveillance'.[55] The health ministry issued a protocol for ASHA workers responsible for contact tracing, covering the enlistment of all contacts of COVID-infected persons – what they should say and do while visiting such contacts and the duration for follow-ups.[56]

Manual contact tracing, accompanied by extensive screening, testing and quarantining, was also one of the strategies employed to control the early spread of COVID-19 in Kerala and in India's largest slum, Dharavi (Mumbai), in June 2020.[57]

Prevention through Travel Passes and Vaccination

Health and immunity passes (e.g., yellow fever passes) have traditionally been used in public health contexts to certify that the bearer of the pass is free from disease and can travel to her destination.[58] Immunization passports were first used in 1796 as proof of having been vaccinated against smallpox.[59] During the COVID-19 pandemic, prevention measures took the form of e-passes and RT-PCR tests prior to travel, and vaccination through registration on the CoWin portal.

(i) E-pass or RT-PCR Test Prior to Travel

During the nationwide lockdown in March–May 2020, nearly all the states and union territories, such as Assam, Bihar, Delhi, Goa, Haryana, Karnataka, Madhya Pradesh, Maharashtra, Puducherry, Uttar Pradesh, started online portals for people to apply for intra-state or interstate travel e-passes.[60] The National Informatics Centre also introduced a centralized portal for e-passes for travel during the lockdown, which integrated the data of at least twenty states and union territories listed on it.[61] The terms of service of Aarogya Setu were modified to introduce an e-pass feature.[62]

However, following the government's guidelines in August 2020 to lift movement restrictions, these mandatory e-passes were discontinued.[63] This was replaced with state-level requirements for mandatory RT-PCR tests prior to entering the state, which was subsequently discontinued.

(ii) Vaccination

Preventive disease surveillance, through the issuance of vaccine passports, has raised various ethical considerations such as inequality in the global vaccine supply (and the ensuing discrimination) and uncertainty about whether vaccines prevent transmission.[64] Therefore, as of April 2021, vaccine passports were not supported by the WHO. There are also security and privacy issues with using a centralized system and ensuring the legitimacy of the vaccination certificate.[65]

Vaccination in India is not mandatory, with the Meghalaya High Court holding that compulsory vaccination is unconstitutional.[66] Vaccination has primarily been carried out through registration on the CoWin app for those over eighteen years of age. The CoWin portal was initially available only in English and was not accessible for persons with visual impairment. It also required digital literacy and access to a smartphone, and did not have any privacy policy. This changed only after significant public pressure and directions from the Delhi High Court.[67]

Privacy Implications

Concerns of Legality and Proportionality

Throughout the pandemic, the central and various state governments collected (through mobility mapping, quarantine selfies, contact tracing) and disclosed (by affixing posters, stamping hands, publishing posters and lists) a vast amount of personal data. While the right to privacy is not absolute, it is well settled after the *Puttaswamy* privacy judgment that all privacy-infringing measures must be backed by law. However, most of the COVID-19 disease surveillance measures discussed in this article were not backed by any specific law or ordinance. In fact, the mandatory imposition of Aarogya Setu was challenged before the Kerala High Court, eventually causing the government to downgrade the obligation to a 'best effort basis'.[68] The directions to affix posters outside homes of quarantined/infected persons was challenged before the Supreme Court for lacking legislative basis. The court observed that states could *only* resort to such action *'when any direction is issued by the competent authority under the Disaster Management Act.'*[79]

Similarly, none of the states or districts published the personal details of quarantined/infected patients, required quarantine selfies or used drones pursuant to any specific statutory authorization.

The government may justify its actions under existing laws, but the Disaster Management Act, 2005, and the Epidemic Diseases Act, 1897, do not provide governments with an express statutory basis for disclosing personal information or deploying such tech-heavy surveillance measures. These laws are open-ended, have no consideration for privacy, have not been tested on the proportionality standard and do not allow the state to coerce individuals to take certain action.[70] Without an anchoring legislation that sets out safeguards, the government can simply use its powers under these two laws to issue *any* executive notification that infringes rights, which cannot have been the intention of Parliament.[71] The Kerala High Court, in fact, stayed a government notification on salary deferrals for lack of statutory basis, necessitating the promulgation of an ordinance.[72]

Even assuming for the sake of argument that there is some statutory basis for the disease surveillance measures; the government still needs to justify that it is necessary *and* proportionate to undertake such measures and there was no less restrictive alternative available.[73] This is particularly important in the absence of any data protection law or statutory requirements of data minimization.

But should courts even engage in rigorous judicial review during an emergency? The role of the courts is not diminished during a pandemic, nor are fundamental rights suspended (unless the government formally declares an emergency under the Constitution). If anything, only courts have the institutional legitimacy and power to protect citizens' rights, especially in times of crisis. The application of the proportionality doctrine does not mean that government's policy decisions will be struck down. It only requires governments to *demonstrate* that they have *some* basis to justify their actions, with courts largely deferring and giving a wide margin of appreciation to government policy choices.[74] Thus, measures taken for symptom tracking, mobility mapping, travel passes, and vaccination are likely to pass the proportionality test.

However, even under a deferential approach, it is hard to see how the statewide publication of quarantine lists with personal details of citizens is proportionate, especially when governments were already stamping hands of individuals and/or affixing posters outside their homes. More importantly, the state was already in possession of the personal data of its quarantined residents and publishing it only led to loss of anonymity and dignity – and vigilantism by RWAs. Such public stigmatization may, in fact, deter individuals from revealing their true symptoms or uploading their test results.[75]

Proportionality would also require that drone-based surveillance and quarantine selfies collect limited information and are narrowly tailored with the images and personal details being immediately deleted and not shared with any other government or private agency.[76] Governments must assess the risk of harm before conducting any surveillance.

Lack of Express or Informed Consent

As demonstrated in the previous section, many COVID-19 surveillance measures have been made mandatory, or de facto mandatory. This means that the privacy of individuals is being infringed without their express or informed consent.

Aarogya Setu was (in)famously made mandatory for a brief period in April 2020, until the government rolled back the mandatory directive in May. Despite the government's changed guidance, which required the app to be downloaded on a 'best effort' basis, many organizations – both public and private – continued to mandate its download.[77] For instance, when it was running special trains for migrant labourers, the Indian Railways required passengers to download the app.[78] Sikkim made it mandatory to install the Aarogya Setu app to be eligible to apply for vehicle e-pass.[79]

Marginalized and vulnerable individuals, including gig workers and ASHA workers, find it disproportionately difficult to dissent to certain COVID surveillance measures. ASHA workers in Punjab protested against the mandatory requirement to download the Ghar Ghar Nigrani app, because of the digital gender divide and resultant lack of smartphones and digital literacy (which introduced another sub-layer of surveillance by their husbands or fathers), technical issues with the app and lack of additional compensation.[80] ASHA workers in Haryana were also forced to download a similar app – MDM 360 Shield.[81]

Privacy concerns are also raised when gig workers are subject to temperature checks, especially if their health data is used to determine pay or insurance.[82]

These concerns get exacerbated in the absence of a national data protection law, and when most workplace surveillance does not comply with the minimal standards of the Information Technology

Act (IT Act).[83] Unlike data protection regulators across the world, the Indian government has not released any updated guidance for data protection under the IT Act to adequately balance public health and safety concerns with individual privacy.

The Personal Data Protection (PDP) Bill, 2019, spoke of permitting the non-consensual processing of personal data to (a) respond to a medical emergency, (b) provide medical treatment or health services during an epidemic, and (c) ensure safety, provide assistance or services during a disaster.[84] Most disease surveillance measures would perhaps get covered within these categories *once* a data protection law is notified. However, questions remain about the proportionality of such measures and the storage and use of the personal data collected. In any event, with the withdrawal of the PDP Bill, 2019, from the floor of Parliament in August 2022, even these limited draft statutory protections have vanished. There was, and continues to be, no specific *statutory* basis authorizing the restriction of the right to privacy.

Lack of Privacy Policies or Protocols for Data Sharing

The concern with symptom tracking and mobility mapping, which are necessary disease surveillance measures to be deployed during a pandemic, arises from the lack of any privacy policies or established data storage, sharing, retention and deletion protocols, which help prevent function creep and maintain confidentiality of data. For example, it does not appear that Punjab's Ghar Ghar Nigrani app has or has published its privacy policy. Upon downloading the app, the author did not find any privacy policy nor could she find the privacy policy online.

The absence of clear delineation regarding the treatment of personal data extends to measures taken for quarantine enforcement and vaccination. For instance, Karnataka and Surat (in Gujarat) introduced mandatory selfie requirements, but their apps did not contain a privacy or data storage/ use/sharing policy. There was no explanation about how the personal data was stored, used, shared and deleted.[85] Karantaka's Quarantine Watch website only linked to the general privacy policy of the Karnataka government, and did not cover the specific data processed by the app. Even the official website to download the Surat Municipal Corporation's app did not provide a link to any privacy policy.

Similarly, despite processing sensitive personal data, the CoWin website and app responsible for booking and tracking the vaccination status of all residents did not have a privacy policy, until the Delhi High Court intervened.[86] In response to an RTI query on the estimate of how long a user's name, gender, date of birth, type of ID proof, photo ID number (i.e., Aadhaar/Passport/PAN/voter ID number) and mobile number would be stored on the CoWin platform, the Ministry of Health and Family Welfare (MoHFW) simply gave a vague answer about how *the data is being managed as per the data extant policy of the Government of India*.[87] The ministry also admitted to using facial recognition authentication technology for a 'touchless' vaccination process, without conducting any privacy impact assessment or accuracy metrics/data.[88]

The MoHFW's protocol on data management focuses on the collection and indexing of information into different groups – number of suspect cases, laboratory confirmed cases, deaths, contacts line listed, contacts tracked, contacts currently under surveillance and number of contacts who have exited the follow-up period of twenty-eight days.[89] Nevertheless, there is no mention of any privacy protocols that ensure storage limitation, use limitation, anonymization or confidentiality.

However, just having a privacy policy is not sufficient. The Aarogya Setu app has a detailed privacy policy and terms of service, but that has not prevented the contact tracing app from metamorphosing from an app to an 'access convenience service', displaying e-passes, and being used for medical research, formulation of treatment plans and vaccine registration.[90]

Involvement of the Private Sector

The private sector disease surveillance measures are subject to even lesser scrutiny. There is little clarity on the protocols for data retention and sharing by organizations such as Apollo, Airtel and Reliance Jio. For instance, the website, https://airtel.apollo247.com, which hosts the self-assessment scan, does not contain any privacy policy or data retention policy. Nor does it explain how it keeps the data 'strictly confidential'.[91]

Chhattisgarh's CG COVID-19 ePass app, which has been downloaded more than a million times, issued interstate/intrastate e-passes to facilitate travel.[92] Its privacy policy clarified that it collected user and log data, which was retained on the *private developer's* servers for 180 days from the date of uploading. Third-party companies were also provided access to users' personal data.[93] However, there were no protections in place to prevent any misuse of personal data by such private third parties.

Similarly, the use of drones for mobility mapping in conjunction with private drone companies and volunteers, as in Gujarat, further increases the risk of breach and underscores the urgency for enacting a data protection law.[94]

Unauthorized Disclosure and Security Breaches

Centralized data collection increases the risk of security breach and/or unauthorized disclosure of information. This is particularly true given the contextual integrity of data,[95] where data collected in one context (e.g., contact tracing) may be legitimate, but when used in another context (e.g., sharing with third parties or law enforcement), becomes illegitimate.

The first prominent case of unauthorized disclosure of personal information came during the *Tablighi Jamaat* event in Delhi in March 2020. The police released a list of names and phone numbers of around 650 people, believed to be present in the vicinity of the Nizamuddin Markaz mosque during the religious congregation. They reportedly obtained this information through tracing the mobile phone data, including GPS locations, of people within the vicinity.[96] Even if the police had legitimately accessed mobile phone data, there can be no legal basis or requirement for publishing the list of persons thought to have attended the congregation. This caused fear, stigma, discrimination and a loss of bodily integrity, apart from being a violation of privacy.

Throughout the pandemic, we have also witnessed reports of security breaches – for example, the breach of Jio's self-reported symptom tracker's database in May 2020, which included a breach of a user's risk status, business type, location details, browser version, etc., until Jio took its systems offline.[97] In Bengaluru, in July 2021, COVID-positive patients were served with targeted ads from hospitals offering beds, insurance companies offering schemes, and pharmacies offering medicines, raising doubts about whether their personal data was leaked.[98] It has also been reported that the health data of the infected patients was being sold on the dark web.[99]

The privacy concerns detailed throughout highlight the urgent need for the enactment of a strong data protection law that enshrines principles of data minimization, data integrity, transparency, accountability, privacy by design and privacy impact assessments.

Suitability and Efficacy

The government may justify the loss of privacy through its disease surveillance measures by relying on their effectiveness in breaking the COVID transmission chain. Unfortunately, their suitability and efficacy are suspect. This is probably best demonstrated by the fact that most of the measures described in this chapter fell by the wayside after the first few months, and during the second wave of the pandemic.

Many researchers pointed to the lack of effectiveness of the Aarogya Setu app and its likelihood of false positives and false negatives, which can result in both overestimation and underestimation of the burden of disease.[100] Technology, today, cannot determine whether someone has been within a six-foot radius of an exposed person, and, therefore, as Susan Landau says, *'it behoves technologists to be honest about what current technology can and can't do – and not to push miracle drugs when they don't exist'* (emphasis added).[101]

For instance, NDTV reported that the central and many state government health officials admitted that Aarogya Setu played 'little or no role' in contact tracing or identifying hot spots; they relied on data collected via manual contact tracing or state-level apps instead.[102] This is in stark contrast to the government's claims, although there is limited transparency around data that can demonstrate the app's alleged success.

Similarly, relying solely on temperature checks of employees may result in under-reporting and over-reporting of the incidence of COVID-19, and can often be inaccurate.[103]

The requirement of quarantine selfies ignores the fact that it can be gamed and that it may be impossible to comply with. On the former, hourly selfies do not prevent an individual from leaving their house and coming back within the hour. It is also possible to falsify the timestamp and GPS of the photo, although very few people would have the technical ability to do that. Depending on the quality of the internet and the mobile device, the GPS coordinates may also be inaccurate.[104] However, in many cases, individuals may wish to comply but are prevented from doing so because either they do not have smartphones or they are unwell (and hence, unable to be awake on an hourly basis), or due to technical glitches preventing them from uploading their photos.[105]

Measures such as affixing quarantine posters or stamping the hands of a quarantined person are likely to be effective in limiting contact between quarantined persons and their neighbours. But they have a significant downside of discrimination and social stigma. Many stories were reported in the first few months of the pandemic about Air India staff (who were part of the international flights to get stranded passengers home) or doctors being harassed or evicted by their RWAs because their houses had a quarantine poster.[106] In Delhi, a woman took a photo of a quarantine sticker on her neighbour's flat and circulated it on the society WhatsApp group as evidence of the person having been infected by COVID.[107]

Way Forward

Sean McDonald aptly notes, 'Pandemic quarantine and social control systems are a rare example of institutional responses that demonstrate the full life cycle of governmental power – from detection and monitoring all the way through to enforcement – with almost no due process.'[108] This allows the government response to an extended public health emergency such as COVID-19, which has no clear 'end date' in sight, to become a prolonged social reality.

India has, by and large, adopted a technology-centric response to the pandemic, relying on various state-level apps to achieve different public health objectives. However, there have been various reports that have questioned the utility, reliability, accuracy and security of such apps. Given the infringement of privacy caused by these surveillance measures, we need to reconsider whether these are the best tools to help check the spread of the pandemic. The focus on rolling out multiple apps comes at the cost of state resources being spent on ramping up testing and rolling out a more effective and privacy-friendly surveillance measure.

Government power, once created, rarely goes away. Aarogya Setu – originally built for contact tracing – is now being used for vaccine registration, even as the original purpose of the app has fallen by the wayside. Therefore, the expansion of surveillance powers must be accompanied with significant oversight and public debate.[109] In the context of the plague, historian Frank Snowden observed:

> Plague regulations also cast a long shadow over political history. They marked a vast extension of state power into spheres of human life that had never been subject to political authority. One reason for the temptation in later periods to resort to plague regulations was precisely that they provided justification for the extension of power, whether invoked against plague or, later, against cholera and other diseases. They justified control over the economy and the movement of people; they authorised surveillance and forcible detention; and they sanctioned the invasion of homes and the extinction of civil liberties. With the unanswerable argument of a public health emergency, this extension of power was welcomed by the church and by powerful political and medical voices.[110]

We must learn from history, and from the present COVID-19 experience, and make sure that the disease surveillance measures adopted during the next public health emergency rely on principles of lawfulness, fairness, transparency, data quality, purpose limitation, data minimization, accuracy, storage limitation, integrity, confidentiality and accountability. After the withdrawal of the Personal Data Protection Bill, 2019, it is even more imperative for the government to enact a new data protection law urgently, providing strong protection for sensitive health data, proactive data breach notification obligations, and requiring governments to conduct privacy impact assessments before deploying surveillance measures. All this will help build trust amongst the citizens and the state.

PART II

India's Public Health Machinery

5

On Health Data Architecture Design

Prashant Agrawal, Subodh Sharma, Ambuj Sagar, Subhashis Banerjee

Introduction

THE National Digital Health Mission (NDHM) – announced by the prime minister on Independence Day 2020 – aims to develop the backbone needed for the integrated digital health infrastructure of India. Developing countries like India, with significant health challenges, perhaps need such an infrastructure the most. This can help not only with diagnostics and management of individual health but also with broader public health monitoring, socio-economic studies, epidemiology, research, prioritizing resource allocation, and policy interventions. Digitization cannot be a substitute for the fundamentals – for example, investment in nutrition and welfare, primary healthcare services and healthcare professionals – but it can potentially make healthcare more organized, efficient and effective.

However, most attempts to build such large-scale, nationwide digital systems for health,[1] and national digital identity systems crucial for supporting such infrastructures,[2] have been mired in controversies. They have often been questioned on privacy and fairness grounds and have been difficult to operationalize. Some have had to be abandoned altogether. In India, too, the recent momentum and concerns around informational privacy guarantees have occurred in the context of the creation of new government databases and digital infrastructures for welfare delivery.[3] The concerns are manifold, and rushing into a design and implementation without adequate due diligence is fraught with risks.

In this chapter we investigate the considerations necessary for building such an infrastructure. We argue that in order to be able to meet the broad social objectives, not only do the crucial privacy and fairness concerns have to be comprehensively addressed, but also the theory of public good based on such an infrastructure needs to be carefully developed, and the operational requirements and risks need to be clearly understood. In particular, an effective proportionality analysis by balancing the utility versus the risks becomes untenable when either the utility or the risks are inadequately or imprecisely modelled. We examine the necessary elements of a conceptual architecture required to enable such a proportionality analysis.

Uncertain Theory of Public Good

That a well-functioning personal health data infrastructure can potentially lead to public good and welfare is undeniable. Individual health records – accessible across healthcare centres and hospitals by treating physicians – can certainly facilitate better management of health episodes. Additionally, reliable history of illnesses, reports and medication may ensure that patients do not have to be treated blind.

As the COVID-19 pandemic has shown, such an infrastructure possibly could also have played a crucial role in public health management. Mandatory recording of test reports and reliable death records would have helped epidemiologists accurately estimate the extent of the disease impact in various locales and geographies as the disease progressed, and plan for eventualities better. This data was sorely missed, and, from several accounts, the deaths were probably under-reported by a significant factor,[4] leading to complacency. Also, real-time availability of test reports with fine-grained, individual-level details like location, occupation, workplace location, environment and commute patterns, etc., could have immediately led to better contact tracing and containment strategies. Moreover, it is obviously helpful to be able to correlate test reports with vaccination records of each individual, and longitudinally track individuals in the population to accurately estimate vaccine efficacy and breakthrough infections. Such data may be crucial both for monitoring variants and future vaccine design. In the absence of a health record infrastructure, we had to make do with tracking small cohorts by independent research groups, and there would always be doubt as to whether such sampled data is representative.

Also, periodic cross-sectional surveys such as the National Family Health Survey (NFHS),[5] Annual Health Survey (AHS),[6] Rapid Survey on Children (RSOC),[7] Comprehensive National Nutrition Survey (CNNS),[8] Surveys of the National Nutrition Monitoring Bureau (NNMB)[9] etc. – though tremendously useful for macro-level understanding of national health indicators – are limited in many ways. For example, definite understanding of the causal factors leading to the alarmingly high rate of stunting and wasting in India[10] has remained elusive. Regression studies using aggregated cross-sectional data can only do so much, and real-time longitudinal tracking of nutrition and health episodes of individual mothers and children through home check-ups, primary care centre visits, pregnancy episodes, childbirth and immunization – for the whole population – may certainly be of immense value. Such high frequency clinical data – in other situations – may also be used for disease forecasting, epidemiology, managing infectious diseases and monitoring public health in general.

However, just highlighting the potentials, as we have done above and as done in the NDHM blueprint,[11] does not develop the full theory of public good using digital health data. That would require clearly identifying the exact data analysis and inference techniques that may be needed and the various outcomes that may be expected, for both diagnostics and public health; analysing the exact requirements for future research and innovation; identifying the correlations with other socio-economic data that may be necessary for research and public health monitoring; and carefully analysing the exact frequency and nature of clinical data that should be recorded at various interfaces, such as at point of care measurements, personal equipment, imaging devices, nutrition records and the observations made by primary healthcare professionals and specialists. It would also require analysis of the feasibility and cost of such recordings, the error models for such data, the error control strategies and assessment of the impact of errors, and missing data on inference and data analysis.

Developing such a theory of public good will inevitably require a multidisciplinary approach – including practitioners and researchers – and should not be left primarily to IT professionals. Otherwise, it may lead to aberrations like CoWin[12] and Aarogya Setu.[13] On one hand, instead of concentrating on the back end, and facilitating the supply chain and the correlation of vaccination records with tests and infection breakthroughs, CoWin focused on centralization of vaccination scheduling, which should ideally have been left to local administrations whose needs and service populations were different and diverse.[14] There is a reason for which health is a state subject in the federal structure of our Constitution. On the other, Aarogya Setu rushed into contact tracing using Bluetooth and GPS without pausing to evaluate what theory, if any, may facilitate computing infection risk estimates from Bluetooth proximity estimates and GPS locations, and what may be the error rates of such estimates.[15] These perhaps exemplify how not to do digitization for health.

Even in the current National Digital Health Mission (NDHM) policy documents[16] there is a serious lack of such analysis, and, as a result, questions regarding the preparedness of the health infrastructure for contributing accurate, standardized and meaningful data remain unanswered.[17]

Operationalization and Use Cases

Even if a theory of public good is well established, it is the translation of the theory into the operational elements that becomes pivotal for the 'utility versus pain' question, and careful design of the use cases – the processes that define the interfaces between the digital and the human elements – is perhaps the most crucial aspect of digitization.

Poorly thought-out use cases that fail to account for the diverse cultural background and social realities can easily lead to unforeseen behavioural adaptations, resulting in unacceptable quality of service delivery. The sheer variety of the actors – ranging from poor rural populace, including children, overworked and understaffed healthcare professionals in primary healthcare centres, midwives and other home care workers, Anganwadi workers in childcare centres, Accredited Social Health Activist (ASHA) workers, patients and health professionals in government and private secondary and tertiary care hospitals, imaging and diagnostic centres, pathology labs, specialists, desk workers, insurance personnel, epidemiologists, researchers, administrators, bureaucrats, policymakers and several others, with widely different levels of digital proficiency – adds to the challenge. Resource crunch, with doubtful internet connectivity in several areas, compounds the problems. Denial of services and exclusions due to authentication failures, internet and server failures or digitization errors, and delays and other increased cost of transactions due to poor scheduling and processing are the typical poor outcomes of digitization use cases that the designers need to explicitly handle. This requires careful modelling of not only the technical and administrative processes themselves but also the risks of technological and administrative failures as part of a threat model, and ensuring that some well-articulated property of non-exclusion is never violated.

Most importantly, proper use case design and analysis will require participation of not only IT professionals but practitioners with ground-level knowledge and users with direct stake in the system. Hence, it is crucial to ensure that they buy in to the proposal, and their participation is eager and voluntary.

The operational requirements also need identifying and understanding the diverse data sources and their complexity. This may involve understanding the constraints of personnel, resources and equipment at various data generation and consumption points, understanding their primary functions and ensuring that they are not hampered in any way. It also requires an understanding of the frequency of data generation, error models, access rights, interoperability, sharing, data analysis, dissemination and other usage requirements, and designing the data organization and application programming interfaces appropriately.

Laying out the use case and operational design blueprints for all to reflect upon is imperative before any implementation is even considered. The NDHM policy documents[18] do not seem to address these considerations adequately.

Privacy and Denial of Rights

In a digitization attempt as complex and sensitive as this, privacy is a crucial concern, and the potential tensions between public good and individual rights are bound to generate disquiet. These concerns must be examined threadbare, as must the suitable ways to navigate them. Any data infrastructure endeavour that fails to effectively address privacy concerns is bound to get mired in controversies and endless litigations. In fact, most attempts at building health data infrastructures worldwide – including in the UK, Sweden, Australia, the USA and several other countries – have led to serious privacy-related controversies and have not yet been completely successful.

In order to develop a suitable operational standard for privacy protection, we must first clearly understand the nature of privacy harms. Often, privacy is conflated with security, that too only against external breaches, and this flawed understanding leads to problematic solutions.

The Privacy Concerns

The most common fear of digitization, especially when enforced by governments, is that of Orwellian mass surveillance and misuse of data. All digitization requires unique digital identities, and the use of a universal health identity across all health-related transactions can create an infrastructure for totalitarian observation of citizen's health data. Also, linking of health identities with general-purpose identities like Aadhaar, as the National Digital Health Blueprint (NDHB) [19] suggests, exacerbates the problem.

The other common fear of digitization is the secrecy aspect of privacy, that is, the fear of exposing one's private world to the public space, which may potentially cause embarrassment or public judgement. The secrecy aspect is obviously important in the healthcare context, and it is primarily the considerations of maintaining secrecy that lead to the emphasis on the prevention of data leaks and identification of specific individuals from statistical database queries.

However, surveillance and secrecy are not the only privacy concerns with digitization. A far more common and subtle manner of erosion of privacy is by way of losing control of information about oneself to insensitive, uncaring and opaque bureaucracies, who may use it for their own interests with little regard to the direct or indirect harms caused to the individual. In the healthcare context, leaking health data to unauthorized entities may result in direct harms through social prejudice and discrimination. Besides, unpredictable use of health information by unpredictable entities may result in indirect harms such as mis-profiling, profiling for commercial interests and predatory targeting, incorrect or unfair scoring using out-of-context data, exposing vulnerabilities to malicious actors, etc. This may lead to fallouts like illegal denial of jobs or jacked up costs of insurance based on individualized health data, direct drug marketing, predatory advertisements targeted to the vulnerable, etc. Solove argues that 'Kafkaesque' is a more appropriate metaphor for describing such a situation and the helplessness of individuals in fixing it.[20]

Big-data analytics and machine-learning algorithms, which are important reasons for building a national digital health infrastructure in the first place, contribute greatly towards Kafkaesque threats to privacy and liberty. It is forcefully argued by O'Neil[21] that big-data analytics systems, by the very fact that they are designed by the privileged and often for profit, magnify inequality and historical biases. Often such systems use poor proxies to make decisions about human life, lack transparency, accountability or flexibility in their decisions, have a tendency to become ubiquitous because of their perceived efficiency gains, and are generally greatly damaging if left unchecked.

Thatcher et al.[22] argue that *'As algorithms select, link, and analyse ever larger sets of data, they seek to transform previously private, unquantified moments of everyday life into sources of profit.'* Similar concerns have also been raised by Zuboff[23] and Eubanks.[24]

Other common Kafkaesque dangers, as also highlighted in the section titled, 'Operationalization and Use Cases', are poorly thought-out use cases, incomplete case analyses and incompetent programming.[25] As common fallouts, one may suddenly find herself being deregistered from services due to no fault of hers, or having to unnecessarily run around to get things corrected when she was not the one responsible for the mistakes in the first place. Being denied hospital treatment, pension or welfare because perhaps a name is misspelt or because fingerprints do not match will be cases in point. Such callous omissions are obvious threats to rights to privacy, liberty and life.[26]

The Orwellian big brother and the Kafkaesque arguments certainly raise crucial concerns, but they do not necessarily imply that privacy protection is impossible with digitization. We first need to carefully model the direct and indirect privacy risks and then evaluate – through the lens of proportionality – how these risks may be balanced against a well-developed theory of the public good. Because of the enormous benefits that digitization and analytics promise in healthcare, we must earnestly look for solutions to mitigate the risks.

Limitations of Standard Approaches for Privacy Protection

The data protection principles for privacy in digital databases have mainly been based on the tenets of informed consent and notice; collection, purpose and storage limitation; participation of individuals; transparency; and regulations, enforcement and accountability.[27] However, the enforcement mechanisms are typically weak. We try to understand why.

Informed Consent

Although there is considerable focus on user consent and notice in much of privacy jurisprudence, consent holds little meaning in case of a nationwide health infrastructure roll-out, presenting a false sense of choice to individuals where actually there is none. Also, it is unreasonable to expect individuals to be able to give *informed* consent because it is unrealistic to assume that they can predict the possibilities and scale of Kafkaesque dangers from an opaque bureaucracy. In general, as pointed out by Solove,[28] and also by Matthan[29] and Srikrishna et al.,[30] notice and consent are generally ineffective because of information overload, limited choice and consent fatigue. This is often reflected in the customary negligent clicking of 'I Agree'. In view of this, NDHM's[31] over-reliance on a consent-based architecture appears to be problematic. There is a strong case for a rights-based approach that shifts a significant part of the responsibility of privacy protection and accountability from the individual to the data controller, irrespective of the level of consent.

Ex Post Accountability vs Ex Ante Protection

Typical methods of ensuring accountability are based on ex post facto auditing and punitive measures in case of breaches or user complaints. However, despite causing grave distress, Kafkaesque privacy harms are very hard to detect. Even when they are detectable, it is hard to show a causal relationship of a tangible harm with a given breach or insider malfeasance at a data controller. For example, it may turn out to be impossible to know for sure whether a person has lost her job because of the officially put out reason or because her personal medical data was accessed without authorization and used to discriminate against her. Thus, privacy violations should be prevented from happening in the first place, that is, privacy protection must be ex ante.

Conflating Privacy with Security

On the technology side, privacy has often been conflated with security and the focus has been on keeping the data secure from *external* threats, more or less ignoring the possibility of insider attacks either due to rogue system administrators or due to conflict of interest of the entire data control organization. This has led to an excessive emphasis on data encryption and other safeguards that are controlled – and are hence potentially susceptible to be overriden – by privileged insiders at the data controller. Moreover, the indirect and subtle nature of Kafkaesque harms mean that often well-intending projects end up having unintended privacy and fairness side effects unless they are carefully controlled. Hence, security, though necessary, is not sufficient for privacy. What we require is ensuring purpose limitation through independent regulatory oversight on the data controller's data-processing activities, careful risk modelling and analysis, and, above all, public participation and transparency.

Anonymization

The other oft-touted solution to protecting privacy while releasing personal data for unrestricted use, as has also been proposed in the NDHB,[32] is *anonymization*. Anonymization is the process of removing personal identifiers from a database by suppressing information, coarsening data or adding noise, with the goal of making it impossible to identify any individual from the released data. However, almost a decade of research in the field of de-anonymization has shown that anonymization is often unreliable. A small number of data points about individuals coming from various sources, none uniquely identifying, can completely identify them when combined together.[33] Reports in the literature have shown that anonymized census data,[34] social-network data,[35] genetic data,[36] location data,[37] credit card data,[38] writing style data,[39] web-browsing data,[40] etc., can be robustly de-anonymized to re-identify individuals.[41] This is backed by theoretical results[42] which show that for high-dimensional data, anonymization is not possible unless the amount of noise introduced is so large that it renders the database useless. Thus, release of even anonymized personal data for unrestricted use must be a strict no-no.

Differential and Inferential Privacy

An absolute notion of informational privacy might be that no information about an individual could be inferred with access to a statistical database that could not be inferred without any such access. In her celebrated result, Dwork[43] not only proved that such absolute *inferential privacy* is impossible to achieve, but also observed that if an adversary has access to arbitrary auxiliary information, an individual's inferential privacy may be violated even when she does not participate in the database, because information about her can be leaked by correlated information of other individuals. This led to the development of the notion of *differential privacy*, which attempts to limit the information gained by an adversary when an individual's data is collected versus when it is not collected, thus limiting the *additional* privacy risk an individual incurs by participating in a database. Note that differential privacy is a considerably weaker notion because even though it guarantees that individuals cannot be identified, de-anonymization and other correlation attacks can still infer a lot of information about them from differentially private databases.[44]

Algorithmic Fairness

Although differential privacy addresses the secrecy aspect of privacy – by preventing re-identification of any individual – the Kafkaesque issues of potential misuse and discrimination due to biased applications of machine learning and big-data analytics remain. The European GDPR has proposed 'right to explanation' as a countermeasure.[45] However, predictive analytics rarely support causal reasoning, and, without expert manual audit of algorithmic and data biases, the algorithmic explanations will most likely turn out to be inane. Moreover, the adverse outcomes of perverse machine-learning applications are Kafkaesque, and the consequent damages are not immediately obvious. So timely explanations may never even be sought or examined.

It is evident from the above discussion that an effective privacy protection architecture must be based on independent regulatory oversight and focus on ex ante prevention of violations by ensuring purpose limitation rather than on fixing ex post accountability. The NDHM's blueprint document[46] does briefly mention a Security and Privacy Operations Centre that appears to be envisaged to play such a regulatory role. However, details regarding not only its legal structure and the precise regulatory obligations, but also how – or on what basis – the regulator may discharge its obligations are completely unclear. Also, there is no well-articulated threat model for privacy protection. As such, the approach appears to be highly non-standard.

We outline below what may be the necessary elements of an effective regulatory architecture.

Elements of a Privacy Architecture

The lack of a standard grammar for articulating the operational requirements for privacy in large public service applications often results in the proponents and the opponents talking past each other in privacy debates, with one side forcefully proclaiming 'privacy by design', and the other side throwing the proverbial 'kitchen sink' of privacy concerns. For example, claims such as 'NDHM has built-in privacy by design because it prevents data aggregation in its federated architecture where the data remains in its original location' or 'storing identity information isolated in separate, hard-to-access, confidential stores mitigates privacy leaks' arise out of imprecise articulation of privacy threat models and do not stand up to scrutiny. It is not at all clear what precise aspects of privacy do these measures mitigate and how, because data aggregation depends more on data access patterns and post-access purpose limitation than on where the data is located; and without an unambiguous specification of their properties it is hard to ascertain what the confidential stores of digital identities actually achieve, especially with possibilities of insider leaks and threats of re-identification with a myriad of correlation techniques. In the absence of adversary threat models, debates on proportionality based on such claims are not particularly useful. Indeed, we have seen in the past that not only did the outcomes in the majority and minority opinions of Aadhåar judgment[47] turn out to be diametrically opposite, but the privacy debates in several other recent applications have also been repetitive in nature without making much headway.

Whereas modelling of utility depends on the context of the application and must vary from case to case, specifying the operational requirements for privacy requires a standard tool. In what follows, we present a conceptual architecture for privacy analysis based on identifying a precise threat model and defining an ideal functionality of use cases.

Privacy Analysis of Use Cases and Ideal Functionality

Any use case of a large public service application will necessarily leak some information at the peripheral interfaces, where it interacts with either humans or other digital systems. There are also other unavoidable risks, such as leakage of control-flow information over a network (for example, which entities have communicated with each other and when), and possible authentication failures and system outages. In an otherwise perfectly secure system, these should be the only risks in an application. Hence the first obligation of the regulator must be to accurately model these inevitable risks and carry out a privacy risk assessment of whether they are acceptable.

This requires first identifying the regulatory boundary of the application, that is, the scope of control of the regulator, analysing the interfaces at the regulatory boundary, and capturing the potential technical and administrative failures as well as malicious actors as parts of an adversary *threat model*. The regulator should then develop a model of the *ideal functionality* of the application that captures the intended ideal-world execution of the application and explicitly models the communications with the adversary under the considered threat model. For example, the regulator must model a health professional to whom a patient's data may be revealed as a potential adversary who may leak or misuse the information, an administrative process as a potential adversary whose errors may cause denial of service, and a researcher with whom certain anonymized statistical data may have to be shared as a potential adversary who may orchestrate a de-anonymization attack using other auxiliary information. It must be the responsibility of the regulator to analyse how or to what extent the use cases may be hardened and evaluate the unavoidable risks.

The ideal functionality thus acts as an abstract specification that sets a standard for real-world implementations. It also identifies and models the unavoidable privacy risks associated with the application.

Making the ideal functionality public allows any analyst to clearly understand the scope of regulatory control, the threats considered, and whether the inherent risks with a proposed use case are acceptable and whether these meet the standards of proportionality. A data protection framework is incomplete till it lays out the operational standards for such an analysis.

The technological obligation for any subsequent real implementation would be to guarantee that the ideal functionality is never violated, or, if unavoidable, to clearly document the gaps if any. In fact, according to computer science security principles, it must be (mathematically) proved that a real implementation is *indistinguishable* from a virtual simulation of the ideal functionality and there are no additional privacy, fairness or exclusion risks except those already modelled in the ideal functionality.

Purpose Limitation through Audited, Tamper-proof Programs

Since unpredictable use of personal data can lead to arbitrary Kafkaesque dangers, one critical component of the ideal functionality must be that all application program are pre-approved by the regulator and run exactly as specified, that is, are *tamper-proof*, even in the presence of malicious privileged insiders. The ideal functionality must also specify that the application program do not leak any information, other than those pre-defined at the interfaces, and that all inter-programme data exchanges and all data storages are secure and the accessed data are used for authorized purposes by authenticating only the approved tamper-proof program.

This would require the regulators to perform rigorous privacy, security and fairness audit of all application program. This is perhaps going to be a predominantly manual review process since, above all, it is hard to encode fairness in an automated algorithm.[48] Once the program are audited and approved, they should be published on a public bulletin board, along with the regulators' digital signatures, to invite public scrutiny and debate. A guarantee must also be provided that indeed it is only the published program that can be executed.

Virtual Identities

All public service applications need a digital identity infrastructure to identify and authenticate individuals. One obvious way to minimize privacy loss across applications is to use different *virtual identities* with different applications, such that the identifiers are impossible to correlate. For example, one may use different identifiers with different care or diagnostic centres for different medical episodes, and they should only be able to correlate or access information that is allowed by the regulator.

Such virtual identities also allow controlled interoperability via anonymous credentials.[49] Anonymous credentials allow one to transform a credential issued against a virtual identity they own to an identical credential against another virtual identity they own, such that the issuing authority does not know the purpose for which the transformed credential is later used, and a service provider obtaining the transformed credential does not know about the individual's information stored with the issuing authority. The unlinkability and untraceability can also be designed so that they may be overridden on case-specific situations, for example, by a regulatory approval, or to permit legitimate analytics by linking of silos.

Virtual identities ensure that ideal functionalities for each application can be predominantly analysed in isolation. It is to be noted, however, that it may still be possible to de-anonymize using other auxiliary information (as discussed earlier), and for this reason, unrestricted release of data should always be viewed as risky and, as much as possible, data should be released outside the regulatory boundary only for human consumption and not for copying or forwarding to other unknown data-processing elements.

A Dynamic Authorization Architecture

Another crucial function of the regulator ought to be to determine and clearly define who can access what data and for what purposes, based on legal sanction or on authorizations, in conformance with approved regulations. Purpose limitation needs to be built into such authorizations, and all-purpose extensions and authorization renewals should be explicitly considered.

This, in turn, would require specification of a dynamic authorization architecture in the ideal functionality. Some of the data access authorizations may be role-based and static; for example, defining what parts of a patient's data a treating physician may be able to access depending on the nature of the complaint. However, granting access to the treating physician in the first place must be a dynamic authorization process, with support for 'grant' or 'revoke' updates. Such authorizations to use personal data should not only be defined for the purposes of operations, investigation and review by human agents, but also for granting programmatic access for data mining to pre-approved tamper-proof programmes.

Implementation Notes

The ideal tamper-proof programmes that we mention above may not be practically realizable and only approximations may be possible. Nevertheless, they are useful theoretical concepts for privacy modelling and defining ideal functionalities. Near tamper-proof programmes may be realized using a variety of emerging technologies such as hardware-based trusted execution environments (TEEs), remote attestation, fully homomorphic encryption, secure multiparty computation, etc. Practicality and the security guarantees offered by the chosen techniques would be important deciding factors to consider. And it will be of utmost importance to document the vulnerabilities and the risks associated with these techniques and factor them into any proportionality analysis.

Virtual identities can be realized mostly using anonymous credential techniques, along with tamper-proof programmes to link them under regulatory supervision wherever required.

The dynamic authorization architecture can be specified as a privacy policy using standard programming language techniques and it can be enforced automatically at run-time using suitable parsers. Standard techniques exist.

To prove that a real implementation is indistinguishable from the ideal functionality, existing proof techniques in computer security can be leveraged.

Finally, it will be necessary to build the required state and regulatory capacity for such analyses. There is really no alternative. Without these capabilities the privacy risk analysis and their mitigation will always be ad hoc and suspect.

Conclusion

Building a health data infrastructure on a national scale is a problem of unprecedented complexity, and it requires the highest standards of due diligence and guarantees. In this chapter, we have tried to highlight some of the considerations that should go into such a design effort, and have suggested an analysis framework through defining an ideal functionality of an application as precisely as possible. It is to be noted that the ideal functionality specification can never be a static, one-time affair, but has to continuously evolve with understanding, analysis and feedback. However, it is an indispensable conceptual tool for analysing the fairness and proportionality of an application.

Also, most importantly, such an endeavour must follow a due process of adequate public consultation and ensure that it is backed by a law. There also has to be the will to build the required regulatory capacity and an effective, rights-based specialized data protection framework for health data infrastructure.

6

Privacy Considerations of Community Health Workers

Vijayaprasad Gopichandran

Introduction

COMMUNITY health workers (CHWs) are trusted members of the community who have an intimate knowledge of the people, their shared values, beliefs and culture. They act as the link between the community and the health system. Their roles include health communication, health education, social support, health advocacy, mobilizing communities towards health action, collecting and reporting health-related information and delivering basic health services such as family welfare and immunization. CHWs often have access to private health information of people including sensitive information about stigmatizing conditions, such as tuberculosis, HIV, infertility and sensitive health-related behaviours like sexual practices. This puts the CHWs in a position of high responsibility as agents of privacy. The legal responsibility to protect health information must also apply to CHWs. They face several unique challenges in protecting private health information of community members.

The Alma Ata Declaration of 1978 aimed at taking healthcare to all. It realized an urgent need to protect the health and well-being of all people in all countries. It made a sound commitment to take the primary healthcare (PHC) approach to achieve the objective of health for all. But the declaration was too broad-based and non-specific.[1] Soon afterwards the global health community adopted the idea of selective primary healthcare in place of a broad primary healthcare, including specific focus areas like child growth monitoring, immunization, oral rehydration treatment, breastfeeding and family welfare. After almost forty years, in the year 2018, the Astana Declaration was proposed. Health for all is still a distant goal and the Astana Declaration made a commitment to strengthen primary healthcare to achieve universal health coverage.[2] In the four decades that have passed between these two major declarations, the important service of primary healthcare has been delivered by community health work in several low- and middle-income countries by front-line CHWs. China was the forerunner of the community health worker movement through their Barefoot Doctors programme. More than one million Barefoot Doctors, who were local farmers trained to identify and treat common minor illnesses, carried forward the goal of taking healthcare to the community.[3] This movement was the inspiration for similar community health worker programmes in many other countries such as India, Indonesia, Tanzania and Venezuela. Following these early innovations in the 1960s and '70s, the Declaration of Alma Ata of 1978 specifically highlighted the role of the CHW, '... primary healthcare relies, at local and referral levels, on health workers, including physicians, nurses, midwives, auxiliaries and community workers, as applicable, as well as traditional practitioners as needed, suitably trained socially and technically to work as a health team and to respond to the expressed health needs of the community'. In most low- and middle-income countries, CHWs are the backbone of the health system.[4]

While much has been researched on the performance, training needs and impact of CHWs, little work exists on ethical issues related to community health work. As CHWs are the first point of contact of people accessing the health system, they are often privy to sensitive health information. This demands a high level of privacy and confidentiality in community health work. There is not much research or writing available on the privacy concerns during community health work, confidentiality requirements, attitudes, practices and training needs of CHWs on these issues. This chapter describes in brief the history and evolution of the CHW programme in India, the concept of privacy in Indian communities, the importance of privacy in community health work, the challenges in operationalizing privacy and confidentiality in community health work, and concludes with a discussion on the role of CHWs as privacy brokers in communities.

Interviews were conducted with CHWs working for the public health system as well as for a non-governmental organization in Tamil Nadu to gain an understanding of the privacy challenges. The findings of these interviews, which are described in this chapter, reveal that CHWs may not have the same power to deny information to the community member as a doctor or a nurse working in a hospital may have. Her ability to negotiate confidentiality of health information may also depend on power dynamics within the community due to gender, class and caste.

Community Health Workers in India

The CHW programme in India has evolved organically over the past seven decades post-Independence. Given the gross inequities in access to healthcare in various parts of India, the Bhore Committee of health planning in 1946 envisaged taking healthcare services to the communities.[5] CHWs would take healthcare to the doorsteps of people. In the early 1960s, there were extension workers who conducted home visits to deliver basic health services such as contraception and immunization of children. The Shrivastava Committee in 1974 recommended a cadre of multipurpose health workers (MPHWs) who would serve as links between the healthcare facilities and communities.[6] A cadre of auxiliary nurse midwives (ANMs) were trained to provide maternal and child health services in rural communities .[7] Traditional birth attendants were also trained in safe delivery services at home and were recruited as CHWs who worked closely with these ANMs and MPHWs. In addition to the ANMs, several voluntary health workers, including schoolteachers, shopkeepers and postmasters, were trained to deliver simple health interventions. The government's community health worker programme was inspired by the Jamkhed project by Arole.[8] Based on this model, the Village Health Guide scheme was formulated and implemented, where, for the first time, the CHWs were paid a modest honorarium.[9] Further, several cadres of workers, including ANMs, male and female MPHWs, Anganwadi workers (AWWs), health supervisors, health visitors and health inspectors, were added to the expanding CHW system in India. In 2006, after the introduction of the National Rural Health Mission, Accredited Social Health Activists (ASHAs) were added to this army of CHWs.[10]

Several unique characteristics of the CHW programme in India have contributed to this organic evolution. The gender of the CHW has been a matter of discussion and debate. There were MPHWs, both male and female gender in the early phases of the CHW system's evolution, with the female health workers focusing more on providing maternal and child health services and the males on outbreak control at the community level. In later years, the Indian health system had an explicit policy to shift towards female CHWs.[11] The need to build greater momentum to achieve the Millennium Development Goals related to maternal and child health was the key factor which drove this shift in policy. Several research studies have also shown that CHWs recruited from among the local communities that they serve lead to better outcomes. This is because such CHWs have a better acceptance by the local communities and they are more efficient in taking the health services to the community.[12] Initially, most CHWs worked on a voluntary basis. However, there is some evidence that performance incentives and honoraria improve the service of the CHWs, and this has influenced the patterns of CHW employment in the public sector subsequently.[13] Given the huge population of India, each CHW is allotted 1,000 households to cover and serve. Moreover, each CHW also integrates the delivery of several services at the community level. For example, the same CHW would also implement the malaria programme, maternal and child health services, immunization, contraception as well as leprosy eradication activities. This has substantially increased the burden of work on the CHWs.

Studies have demonstrated that CHW programmes are very effective in delivering primary care services, promoting equity in health in a cost-effective manner and at the same time promoting the trust of the communities in the health system.[14] However, lack of a good salary structure or incentives, non-standardization of their training and education, lack of career development and upgrade option, lack of a definite work schedule on a day-to-day basis, overburden of the CHWs, and poor supportive supervision have weakened this programme.[15]

Currently, there are three main groups of CHWs who deliver public health services in India, namely, ANMs, AWWs and ASHAs. The ANMs are attached to the health sub-centre, the most peripheral health facility located close to the households and serving a population of roughly 1,000 households. The AWWs are part of the integrated child development services, including nutrition, immunization, child growth monitoring and maternal and child health services. The AWWs work at the village level.[16] The ASHAs constitute the most recent cadre of CHWs who serve as the link between people in the village and the health system. They focus on maternal and child health services, immunization and contraception, and have the key role of promoting institutional deliveries.

The ANMs receive two years of intensive training after their basic schooling. They are employed by the government on a salary. Some of them are regular employees, while most are employed contractually. In contrast, the AWWs and ASHAs undergo less than three months of induction training followed by periodic refresher trainings. Both these cadres of CHWs are voluntary in nature in most states in India and do not draw a regular salary. While AWWs are paid a modest honorarium for their work, the ASHAs receive performance-based incentives. The ANMs are the most educated and trained of these three cadres of CHWs. The ANM trainings are provided by nursing schools which are governed by the Indian Nursing Council.[17] At the end of their training, ANMs are equipped to handle the delivery of basic maternal and child health services including conducting normal deliveries, inserting intrauterine contraceptive devices, performing minor procedures, such as wound dressing, suturing of minor lacerations and administration of basic drugs. The AWWs and the ASHAs receive much shorter training sessions ranging from one to three months.[18] These training sessions include didactic lectures along with practical, field-based, hands-on training. However, evaluations of the delivery of these training programmes of AWWs and ASHAs have revealed that they are grossly insufficient and lack any real skill-building exercises.[19]

The ANMs serve the primary objective of delivering comprehensive primary healthcare services at the community level. They deliver services connected with maternal and child health, family planning, health education of the community, improvement of sanitation, immunization, treatment of common minor ailments and community work during outbreaks. Their newer and expanding roles include medical termination of pregnancy using medicines, recording and reporting of vital events, public health surveillance, and providing supportive supervision and training for the ASHAs and AWWs.

The AWWs primarily run the Anganwadis or the nutrition centres in the village, where they provide supplementary nutrition to children, pregnant and lactating women, and adolescent girls. They are supported by the Anganwadi helper who cooks the meal and serves the children. In addition to running the nutrition centres, these AWWs also support the ANMs in delivery of maternal and child health services, providing health education, conducting immunization activities and distribution of contraceptives in various communities.[20]

The ASHAs create awareness and mobilize communities to utilize health services. They encourage pregnant women to receive antenatal care and undergo delivery in health facilities. They also provide primary care for common ailments like diarrhoea and minor fevers. They carry essential provisions such as condoms, oral contraceptive pills, fever tablets, and iron and folic acid tablets for use. They also liaise with the ANMs in delivering maternal and child health, immunization, sanitation, nutrition and other services.

All these cadres of CHWs encounter sensitive health information of community members. Some of the sensitive, health-related information that these CHWs handle include the following details:

- last menstrual periods, menstrual abnormalities, pregnancy,
- unwanted pregnancies and medical termination of pregnancies,
- contraceptive choices and sexual practices,
- infertility and treatment,
- directly observed treatment for tuberculosis, a stigmatizing illness,
- treatment of other stigmatizing illnesses such as HIV/AIDS, leprosy, mental illness,
- treatment of sexually transmitted infections and reproductive tract infections,
- lifestyle – sedentary life, smoking, alcohol, dietary choices,
- disabilities.

In addition to this sensitive health information, all other health-related information that is required for communities to access appropriate healthcare services from the health system is also shared with these CHWs. Therefore, there are key concerns of privacy and confidentiality of health information handled by them. A brief description of the evolution of the CHW programme in India and the roles and responsibilities of various cadres of CHWs in the country was provided to set the stage for a discussion of the important concern of health data privacy and confidentiality in the context of community health work. The following paragraphs will discuss the issues of privacy and confidentiality in community health work, challenges in upholding them and the training needs to prepare CHWs as privacy brokers.

Concept of Privacy in Indian Communities

In Indian communities with the traditional practice of joint families, privacy is almost a non-existent entity within families. At the village level, there are village courts and panchayats which publicly discuss and debate family issues with onlookers having their opinion on these issues. Privacy is usually associated with matters of stigma or shame. It is common practice for youngsters' mobile devices, especially girls, to be used by everyone in the family and to snoop into their phones. In some communities, it is even accepted as the norm to regulate the behaviour of young girls. Marriage continues to be arranged by the parents and it is often a family decision rather than that of the individuals. In many communities, closing the bedroom door and latching it while sleeping is considered indecent and is not practised. It is very common for a villager to give their ATM card to a total stranger, share their PIN with them and request their assistance in withdrawing cash from the machine. They do not hesitate to share their login passwords in public. In the Indian cultural context, privacy is often confused with secrecy or shame, and it is believed that privacy is a matter of the wealthy who live a luxurious lifestyle.[21]

Despite this loose conceptualization of privacy, matters of health and disease could be strongly private, and communities usually prefer some health-related information to be private. For example, tuberculosis is a stigmatizing illness and community members prefer to protect their privacy if they are diagnosed with the disease. This understanding of the concept of privacy in Indian communities is essential to develop a discussion of privacy in community health work.

CHWs as Agents of Privacy

The role of CHWs as agents of the health system, acting as gatekeepers allowing the health system to access communities, collecting and handling sensitive health information, and keeping channels of communication open between the health system and the community, places them at a key position of responsibility to protect the privacy of the community members.[22] The gatekeeping role is formal and important to the health system. The health system gains access to the community through these CHWs. As CHWs are members of the community they serve in, they also uphold the community's interests in their gatekeeping role. CHWs are effective gatekeepers because they understand the social and cultural milieu of the local community. However, they may sometimes face a conflict of interest because they work for a salary/honorarium/incentive from the health system, for whom they provide access into the community.[23]

CHWs are entrusted with collecting and compiling health-related information from the community. ANMs maintain several registers including lists of eligible couples in the village, women and men who undergo sterilization, women who use intrauterine contraceptive devices, men for whom condoms have been distributed, women who are on oral contraceptive pills, women who have undergone medical termination of pregnancy, women who have delivered, children who have been vaccinated, persons with fever for whom malaria smears have been tested, and presence of other illnesses like jaundice, fever and dengue. Not only do they maintain these registers along with contact details of all these individuals in the community, they also periodically report these to the health system.[24] Though they may be required to report only the numbers for some of these data, for many of them she must perform name-based reporting, especially for notifiable diseases under surveillance such as tuberculosis, leprosy, dengue, malaria, etc. There are several sensitive health information in this list.

Apart from the work of collecting and handling the data of the community members, they also provide healthcare services in the communities. These services include home visits, sometimes repeated visits, and therefore privacy of delivering health services at home is also a major concern.

CHWs also act as channels of communication between the community and the health system. Many times, health system officials and service providers establish communication with the patients through the CHWs. In case the health system wants to conduct a research study on a particular community, not only do the CHWs act as gatekeepers but they also act as links providing communication channels.

The CHWs have sufficient data of the persons in their community to create a complete health profile and, in that regard, they hold the community data repository. They belong to the same community and, in addition to the health profile, they also have a sound understanding of the personal and social profile of the people. These roles make the CHWs brokers of privacy and confidentiality.

Trust in Community Health Workers

CHWs belonging to the same community which they serve may not always augur well for the effective performance of their work. Social dynamics such as caste, class, prior experience and knowledge about the CHW may have adverse impact on her acceptability and respect for her in the community. On the other hand, it may also act in favour of her being highly respected and accepted. Good levels of training and empowerment of the CHW may work towards greater trust and acceptability.[25]

The 5-SPICE model is an important framework that structures discussions about the work of CHWs. It was developed by Partners in Health, Harvard Medical School and Brigham and Women's Hospital, Boston. It has derived extensively from experiences of community health work in resource-poor settings like Haiti, Rwanda, Lesotho, Liberia and Mali. It proposes a theory of community health worker performance.[26] The following help CHWs enhance their performance:

- Supervisory mechanisms within the health system.
- Partnerships, stewardship with dominant power structures within the community.
- Incentives.
- Choice of recruitment – who is able, willing and ready to work? Who is acceptable to the community? How do social and cultural aspects influence this choice?
- Education and training to empower and build capacity.

From this model it can be inferred that the CHW who is poorly selected does not have appropriate partnerships with the power structures of the community, lacks motivation to perform and is inadequately trained and supervised, will not perform adequately and may not earn the trust of the community.

Empirical work with communities about their trust on CHWs has revealed that there is a general sense of mistrust in the CHWs' ability to protect the confidentiality of health information.[27] They have attributed this mistrust to the CHWs belonging to the same community and, hence, there being a chance of letting the information slip to other members, and a lack of training and capacity to protect the confidentiality of their private health information.

Challenges in Operationalizing Privacy and Confidentiality in Community Health Work

Despite the importance of privacy and confidentiality in community health work, CHWs face several challenges in operationalizing privacy and confidentiality. In a recently published case study, a researcher documented her experience of accessing women who are dealing with infertility through ANMs in the village and her ethical dilemma of whether she was compromising the privacy and confidentiality of these women by interviewing them in front of the ANMs.[28] As seen earlier, ANMs act as gatekeepers who help researchers and health system personnel access community members. A few important ethical concerns arise when these ANMs help external parties like this researcher access communities to collect data. In the case described by the researcher, she was studying the social dimensions of infertility. Infertility is a highly stigmatizing condition and information related to infertility and exact cause of infertility are kept confidential. However, the ANM is in a position of trust where she has access to the health condition of the couple with respect to infertility. Is it ethically right for her to allow access to members of the community, using information that she has been entrusted with, under a social and ethical contract of confidentiality? Sometimes such an access happens even without prior permission or notification of the persons involved.

The other ethical issue raised by the researcher is that she was unable to conduct interviews with the couple with infertility without the ANM being present during the interview. She had to use the help of the ANM to locate the house of her research participant. Once she reached there, she could not send away the ANM and request privacy, as it could be seen as being rude.[29] It is difficult to access the community without the support of the ANM. Once the support of the ANM is obtained to access the community, it becomes a challenge to establish privacy and confidentiality of the information collected from the community. This is a major challenge in community health work. Apart from confidentiality of information obtained from the community, privacy in terms of bodily integrity and privacy during examination of the community members by CHWs are also important concerns. Often, when the CHW performs these examinations at the home of the community member, privacy is compromised.

To write this chapter, a few interviews were conducted with CHWs who work both in the public sector as well as in non-governmental organizations in two districts of Tamil Nadu. The interviews were conducted by the author over telephone. The author had prior rapport with one of the CHWs, but the other three were new to him. The author is trained and experienced in conducting qualitative interviews. The author is a male doctor working as a community health physician in the government health system. The interview participants were all women CHWs, one of them working in a rural non-governmental organization and the other three, contacts of the first, working with the public health system. The author contacted the first CHW working for the NGO directly and conducted the interview through telephone. Then he obtained the telephone numbers of the other three CHWs, called them and set up a time for conducting the interviews. He then conducted telephonic interviews with them. All the telephonic interviews were audio recorded on the mobile phone of the author after obtaining permission from the interviewees. They were then transcribed verbatim. The author did preliminary coding to identify the main issues and themes emerging from the interviews. Some of the questions posed to the CHWs during the interviews were:

1. Is there information about patients in the community which needs to be kept secret? Do you come across such information? Can you list a few such examples?
2. How do you protect the secrecy of information collected from patients in the community?
3. What are the sources of leakage of such secret information?
4. When you go and perform your duty in the community, do you get privacy? In other words, do you get the opportunity to talk and interact with people alone?
5. Do people expect this kind of privacy? Can you identify some of the situations where people expect this kind of privacy?
6. What are the difficulties and challenges that you face in maintaining privacy and secrecy of patient's information in the community?

When asked about the challenges in maintaining privacy, one of the CHWs working for a non-governmental organization stated:

> It is almost impossible to maintain privacy during home visits in the community. Some family member is always present. One of the greatest challenges I face is when I have to talk to the daughter-in-law of the house and the mother-in-law refuses to give us any privacy. She is constantly supervising our conversation.

The CHWs interviewed listed some of the common conditions which community members discussed with them after the assurance of confidentiality. These were menstrual problems, sexual problems, reproductive tract infections in men and women, unwanted pregnancy where the couple seek an abortion, and infertility. One CHW working in the private sector mentioned:

> I had a young woman in my village who had recently been married and was pregnant. When I went to visit her at her home, her mother-in-law, sisters-in-law and their children were at home. I could sense that the young woman had some questions she wanted to ask me. But she was shy and hesitant. So I subtly pushed a slip of paper with my phone number written on it into her hands and left. The same evening, she called me, thanked me immensely for understanding, and asked about whether it is all right to have sexual intercourse during early pregnancy.

This CHW had evolved her own strategy to ensure a private safe space for the young woman to discuss her health concerns with her. After the ubiquitous reach of the mobile phone and the privacy that it provides, CHWs have started utilizing its powers to accomplish privacy during their interactions with the community.

One CHW mentioned that the strategy that they use for providing a private safe space for their clients is to meet them in markets, temples, festivals and other such common crowded places. One CHW working for a non-governmental organization said:

> Festivals, markets and such crowded spaces give us adequate privacy. If I talk to a young woman in these circumstances, nobody suspects that we are discussing a health issue. Everyone is busy and there is a lot of noise all around. Amid such crowd, we find safe spaces to discuss menstrual problems, sexual problems and other sensitive issues which the women cannot discuss in their homes.

A CHW working in the public sector said that it is impossible to hide sensitive information and protect confidentiality in the community. She referred to an anecdote where a young girl had become pregnant outside of marriage. The girl's mother secretly called the CHW and informed her and sought her help for obtaining a medical termination of the pregnancy. The CHW had not uttered anything to anyone. But her repeated visits to the girl's house to help her access the health facility roused suspicion among the neighbours. Soon the community figured out that the girl was unwell, and they started pressing the CHW to provide information.

> I tried to protect the confidentiality of that poor young girl. But when community members see me visiting a house more than usual, they automatically know that someone in the house is unwell. They started asking questions and soon the whole village came to know about the girl's pregnancy. This put the whole family to immense shame. I felt bad.

One CHW narrated her experience of being conflicted between her responsibility as a part of the community and as a part of the health system. She said:

> ... the girl's (who had been diagnosed with tuberculosis) parents requested me to not report the disease to the primary health centre. They were worried that if others came to know the diagnosis, it would affect her marriage prospects. But I have clear instructions from the health system to notify any

case of tuberculosis to the primary health centre. I was in a dilemma.

Apart from this conflict of loyalty to both the community and the health system, sometimes CHWs also faced other types of conflicts. One CHW narrated her experience of a strange conflicting situation:

> A person who had lived in Singapore for a long time had returned to his home in the village. There was a rumour going around that he had been diagnosed with some infectious disease and that's why he had returned. Some members of the village started asking me whether he had any disease that could affect them. The person was suffering from tuberculosis, but was on regular treatment. I did not tell the villagers about the diagnosis. But then the village head himself started calling my phone and demanding to know. I did not reveal the information, but I faced a lot of pressure because of this.

Protecting the privacy and confidentiality of patients' information seemed to be challenging at the community level because the CHW could not alienate the local power hierarchies, as she had to come back and continue to discharge her duties in the same community. Other social power structures are also likely to play a role in how much the CHW can protect the private information of individuals. The CHW's gender, caste, class and other social positions may place her at a position of vulnerability, which may not allow her to protect privacy and confidentiality.

COVID-19 has opened up a whole set of ethical issues. Implementation of the Public Health Act and the Disaster Management Act during the COVID-19 times suspended many rights of individuals due to the dire emergency situation. Putting up quarantine stickers on the doors of people who had returned from foreign travel, barricading the streets in containment zones, putting up banners and posters declaring that a house has individuals infected with COVID-19 and such public health measures greatly compromised the privacy of individuals. Many CHWs were actively involved in contact tracing, isolation, quarantine and home-based follow-up of individuals. In Himachal Pradesh, ASHAs were asked to visit individuals who were in home quarantine, click selfie pictures with them on their mobile and share it with the public health authorities. It was not clear what happened to these pictures, who had access to them and what they were used for. In Punjab, the state government released a mobile application into which ASHAs logged in details of persons who had COVID-19 symptoms detected during their routine door-to-door surveillance visits. The central surveillance team then responded to these alerts by picking up the patients for testing and isolation. The community members were upset by this and resorted to violence against the ASHAs. This was another example of how the pandemic led to gross compromise to individual privacy and put the CHWs at risk.

Digital Community Health Work and Specific Issues of Privacy

CHWs are now required to perform much of their work through digital platforms in India. The Maternal and Child Tracking System (MCTS) is a digital surveillance system that collects and handles the pregnancy, childbirth, immunization and contraception details of all women and children in the country.[30] In addition, other national health programmes also have electronic health records such as the Nikshay portal for tuberculosis. ANMs are the primary source of public health surveillance data for the Integrated Disease Surveillance Programme (IDSP) established through World Bank support. This is now subsumed under the Integrated Health Information Platform, which is the primary health management information system in India. Under the Poshan Abhiyan, AWWs use the Information Communication Technology–enabled Real-Time Monitoring (ICT-RTM) to mark attendance in the Anganwadis and distribute supplementary nutrition to children.

CHWs feed in primary data from communities into several of these online portals and electronic health platforms. The privacy of this massive amount of health data can be protected by data encryption and regulating access to the information. Effective encryption is usually applied only at higher levels of data flow, such as central servers where data flows through the networks, and less applied in the peripheral hand-held devices which the CHWs use for collecting and collating the data.[31] These sources are often left vulnerable to data breaches. Very strict encryption can sometimes make the electronic portal difficult to access at the peripheral level through tedious passwords, CAPTCHAs etc. So, the digital health information system at the level of the CHW must strike a balance between ease of access and protection of privacy, which can be a major challenge. The CHW must be provided adequate training on use of mobile devices and computers and on how to protect the privacy of the electronic health records.

Not only the privacy of community members but also the privacy of the CHWs themselves is sometimes compromised due to the proliferation of digital community health work. ASHAs in Gurugram, Haryana, were given mobile phones with a tracking application which tracked their home visits and community work. This greatly compromised the privacy of the CHWs themselves. Often, CHWs share their mobile numbers with all the community members and they get phone calls at odd hours, thus compromising their privacy. Sometimes their mobile numbers are displayed prominently in public places, and this subjects them to online stalking, abuse and harassment.

Empowering Community Health Workers as Agents of Privacy

Though CHWs are sensitive to the privacy and confidentiality needs of people, the above description explained the various challenges they face in operationalizing it in the community. There is a need to provide adequate support to CHWs to enable them to fulfil the ethical responsibility of protecting the privacy of people's health information.

Development of a Clear Code of Ethics for CHWs

One of the important measures is to ensure the drafting of a clear code of ethics for CHWs. The American Association of Community Health Workers has a code of ethics which mentions key principles such as honesty, confidentiality, understanding the scope and ability of work, ensuring quality of work, providing appropriate referrals at the right time, promoting equity, cultural competence, maintaining trust, respect for human rights, anti-discrimination, cooperation with other healthcare providers, and continuing education and advocacy.[32] There is a code of ethics for nurses, which covers most aspects of their duties and responsibilities. However, these ethics codes largely cover hospital- and health-facility-based work and do not extend to community health work. Such a clear code of ethics can help guide the roles and responsibilities of CHWs in India.

Many CHWs have evolved innovative strategies to protect the privacy of their clients. Their innovations and their ground experiences are valuable. These must be documented through extensive case studies. The experiences and voices of CHWs must inform the development of the code of ethics.

Training of CHWs on Ethics and Professionalism

The standard ANM course is a two-year diploma after high school and includes a substantial practical on the field training component. The focus of the syllabus is on community health nursing, primary healthcare, health promotion, midwifery and child health nursing. The whole of second year is dedicated to practical hands-on training in the community. Most of the ethics education happens through observation and is imparted as a hidden curriculum.

The National Health Mission has developed training modules for the capacity building of ASHAs. Book No. 5 of the ASHA training modules covers important issues of self-development and values of ASHA including equality, responsibility, trust, truth and honesty. There are references to Gandhian principles and ethics. This module also covers the issues of human rights, and health as a human right. It discusses respecting individuals in the community and their privacy. The module also covers other important soft skills such as communication and decision making, negotiations and coordination.

The training modules for AWWs include various components that describe their basic jobs including childcare, child health, nutrition, early childhood development and care of pregnant women and lactating mothers. However, they do not have specific components of ethics, values or human rights incorporated in them.

There is a need to standardize the ethics curriculum for CHWs. This ethics curriculum must incorporate aspects of privacy and confidentiality as core principles. In the era of digital health and electronic health records, CHWs are increasingly using digital devices and handling electronic health data. CHWs must also be clearly sensitized to issues of data privacy in this context.

Sensitizing Communities

It is not enough if CHWs are trained on privacy and confidentiality aspects. They must have an enabling environment where they can practise these values. This must be done by sensitizing communities about the right to privacy of each person in the community. The community must also be sensitized about the nature of the CHWs work and the fact that CHWs are brokers of privacy in the community.

Summary and Conclusion

CHWs play a crucial role in the fulfilment of the goal of health for all in India. They handle sensitive private health information of communities and, therefore, carry the huge burden of being responsible for their privacy. There are definite privacy needs for certain sensitive information in Indian communities, to which CHWs are sensitive and try their best to uphold them. However, the nature of community health work is such that there are numerous pressures and challenges that impair the ability of a CHW to effectively protect private health information. Many Indian families, especially in rural areas are joint families and the individual members often lack adequate privacy while interacting with the CHW visiting their homes. CHWs are integral members of communities and are sometimes subject to social pressures and power dynamics in the community to breach confidentiality of health information. The very act of a community member being visited repeatedly by a CHW exposes the detail that the member has a health issue, and this compromises their privacy to an extent. CHWs practise innovative strategies and have evolved local solutions to overcome this challenge to upholding the privacy of the community members. There is a need for a clear code of ethics for CHWs and they must be trained in ethics, especially in upholding privacy of health information. In the era of digital health information, they must specifically be taught about digital data privacy. Empowering CHWs as brokers of privacy is a crucial step in improving the trust in the health system and in improving the quality of healthcare services delivered in communities.

7

Data Protection in Public Healthcare: An Assessment of Three Government Schemes in India

K.P. Krishnan, Rishab Bailey, Gaurav Jain

Introduction

GOVERNMENT programmes play a pivotal role in meeting healthcare needs in India; they cater to millions, particularly the poor and marginalized. Protecting privacy rights while providing public health services can enhance health outcomes, for instance, by reducing dropouts caused by fear of stigma, or indirectly, by enhancing trust between the government and citizens. However, personal data collected during the provision of health services can be useful for a variety of public purposes, not least, improving healthcare schemes and healthcare outcomes. Public health programmes therefore must toe a fine line in balancing these competing interests.

Ensuring that public health programmes account for data protection interests becomes important given that India currently lacks a comprehensive data protection law.[1] While health sector regulation and policies such as the Medical Council of India Code of Regulations, 2002, and the National Health Policy 2017 (NHP), contain certain references to privacy interests, they do not provide a detailed framework for data protection. This is a matter of concern given the quantity and sensitivity of the information collected by health programmes and the consequent risks that beneficiaries may be exposed to.

Accordingly, this chapter examines whether and how three pan-India, flagship, healthcare programmes of the Government of India, consider and account for data protection interests in their design and regulatory structure. The three programmes chosen for study are the National Tuberculosis Elimination Programme (NTEP), the Janani Suraksha Yojana (JSY), and the Pradhan Mantri Jan Aarogya Yojana (PM-JAY).[2] Each of the selected programmes requires the collection and processing of significant quantities of personal data, through means that are increasingly digitized and also increasingly involve private sector involvement.

In this chapter we study the programme literature and applicable laws/policies, and attempt to understand to what extent is data protection a consideration in the design and implementation of these programmes? To do so, we first provide a brief overview of the design and data flows involved in the programmes. We then evaluate the policy and regulatory framework applicable to each of the programmes against ten 'principles' gleaned from an examination of modern data protection laws, as well as best practices in conducting privacy audits and assessments.[3]

The chapter is structured as follows: in this first section, we introduce and provide context for the chapter. In the second section, we describe the data flows under each of the selected programmes and provide a summary of the governance and data protection framework applicable to each. In the third section we examine each programme against ten data protection 'principles', and opine on the overall state of data protection in the government programmes under study. The fourth section concludes.

Understanding the NTEP, JSY and PM-JAY

In this section, we outline the programme design and the regulatory framework applicable to the three programmes under study.

National Tuberculosis Elimination Programme (NTEP)

India has the highest tuberculosis (TB) incidence in the world, with approximately 2.2 million annual cases, which amounts to 24 per cent of global TB incidence.[4] The NTEP, announced in 2020, aims to eliminate TB by mandating the notification of all TB cases and drug sales to the government, enabling surveillance and monitoring of patients, and providing nutritional assistance to beneficiaries.

The governance framework for the NTEP is established by the National Strategic Plan for TB Elimination 2017–25 (NSP, 2017).[5] More recently, the government has published a new draft version of this policy, covering 2020–25 (NSP, 2020).[6] These policy documents are supplemented by various notifications/guidelines, importantly those of May 2012 and March 2018 (that require notification of all TB cases and drug sales to health authorities).[7]

The NSP, 2017, envisages the creation of a multi-tiered governance system which focuses on disease detection and treatment. The mandate of the various governance institutions – the Ministry of Health and Family Welfare, the National TB Elimination Board, and state- and district-level TB centres – does not explicitly extend to issues related to data protection. While the NSP, 2017, is silent on data protection, the NSP 2020, briefly refers to privacy interests in that the policy does mention the need to ensure confidentiality of patient data to prevent stigma. To this end, it also mentions the need to adopt technological measures to limit unauthorized access to beneficiary data. However, the primary focus of both the NSPs is on enhancing data flows. The focus insofar as data protection is concerned is solely on data security.

The centrepiece of NTEP is a platform known as Nikshay, a 'case-based, web-based TB surveillance system'.[8] The platform aims to maintain an end-to-end diagnostic and treatment trail, enable payments, as well as enable surveillance over the entire patient-facing pharmacological ecosystem. All patient data is maintained on the Nikshay platform and access provided to relevant stakeholders based on needs.

Data collection under the NTEP primarily occurs at the time of disease detection, and during treatment. At the diagnosis stage, various personal details including diagnostic reports and prescriptions, demographic information (such as name, ID details, age, gender, mobile number, address, demography details, marital status, occupation, economic status, HIV status, emergency contacts, etc.), financial information (bank account and other details), and health information (basis of diagnosis, patient category, drug resistance information, etc.) are collected.[9] Collection of Aadhaar details is mandatory to access direct benefit transfers (DBT). At the treatment stage, details of tests, prescriptions, treatment and adherence protocols, etc., are added to the record. Even during purchase of drugs, patients are to provide detailed personal data such as the patient prescription, name, address, age, sex, father's name, government-issued ID, mobile number, details of the treating medical practitioner, dates of diagnosis and treatment, details of drugs dispensed, etc.[10]

While typically data collection is done by physical means (say, by healthcare providers reporting to local government officers), these processes are increasingly aided by the use of ICT based tools such as electronic pillboxes, mobile-based pill-in-hand tools, and mobile apps for self-reporting by beneficiaries.

Janani Suraksha Yojana (JSY)

Maternal and neonatal mortality is a significant problem in India, with the country accounting for around 22 per cent of the 10.8 million global child deaths and 25 per cent of the 5,29,000 global maternal deaths.[11] The JSY, launched in April 2005, provides cash incentives to pregnant women and healthcare workers to encourage institutional delivery.

The regulatory and policy framework for the JSY is contained in guidelines issued by the health ministry in 2006 (JSY Guidelines), and guidelines issued under the National Health Mission (NHM)/

National Rural Health Mission (NRHM).[12] The JSY Guidelines mention privacy interests in only one place: they require evaluation of emergency obstetric care service providers insofar as their ability to maintain confidentiality of patient information is concerned. However, there appears to be no details about the process or benchmarks for them.[13]

The regulatory/policy framework for the JSY, therefore, does not account for data protection interests at all. The focus of the policy framework is almost entirely on enabling information flows for healthcare provision and evaluation of programme performance.

The JSY relies on auxiliary nurse midwives (ANMs) and accredited social health activists (ASHAs) to register pregnant women in their localities for the programme. This process involves collection of identity and demographic details (including financial status, religion and caste), mobile number, Aadhaar and bank details, contacts of neighbours and relatives, data on previous illnesses and pregnancies (current and historic) and previous illnesses.[14] The ANM/ASHA enters this in a diary and then uploads the information to the Mother and Child Tracking System (MCTS), a platform maintained by the central government (though various state governments have also developed their own versions of the portal).[15] The MCTS is currently being replaced by the Reproductive and Child Health (RCH) portal, which is referred to as 'an augmented version of MCTS'.[16] The RCH portal is accompanied by an app – ANMOL (Auxiliary Nurse Midwife Online) – which is to be used by ASHAs/ANMs in capturing data and updating patient information.[17] Interestingly, a 2021 study found that ANMs/ASHAs are reluctant to adopt mobile health solutions (including ANMOL and the RCH) due to a perceived lack of usefulness, as well as an absence of technical knowledge.[18]

The JSY policy framework focuses to a large extent on ensuring programme review and to this end places significant reporting/monitoring requirements on healthcare workers and local health officials. Healthcare providers are also required to report health information related to mother and child to local authorities. In order to enable performance monitoring and the use of data for policy/research/statistical purposes, programme data is uploaded to the

Health Management Information System (HMIS) launched by the health ministry in 2008. This data is aggregated and compiled at the district level, and does not appear to enable identification of individual patients.

Pradhan Mantri Jan Aarogya Yojana (PM-JAY)

The high out-of-pocket expenditure required to access health services has been recognized as a significant barrier to healthcare in India, as well as a driver of poverty.[19] The PM-JAY accordingly aims to provide a cashless insurance coverage to over 10 crore poor and vulnerable families.

Unlike the NTEP and JSY, the PM-JAY has been developed on the backbone of digital technologies that constitute an interoperable IT platform consisting of a PM-JAY dashboard, a hospital empanelment system, a beneficiary identification system, a transaction management system, a citizen portal, a citizen mobile app. The system also forms part of the National Health Stack – a pan-India platform that aims to bring together electronic health records registries, insurance platforms and a national health analytics platform, amongst others.[20] The extent of digitization of the scheme is said to have created the world's single largest healthcare data repository.[21]

The primary entity responsible for the governance of PM-JAY is the National Health Authority (NHA), which is established as an adjunct to the MoHFW (the NHA, therefore, does not have statutory authority). At the state level, the PM-JAY envisages the establishment of State Health Agencies (SHAs). The PM-JAY consists of a fairly detailed regulatory/policy framework, of which the most important components are the following:

A. The Cyber Security and Privacy Strategy, 2020:[22] This provides an overarching framework that seeks to ensure the protection of beneficiary healthcare data. It recognizes the importance of identifying risks to data, implementing regulatory frameworks and governance systems, and laying down privacy principles and standards to be followed across the ecosystem.

B. The NHA Data Privacy Policy 2.0:[23] This lays down minimum standards on how entities in the PM-JAY ecosystem, from the NHA and SHA to service providers, are to process personal data of beneficiaries. The policy establishes institutional mechanisms for auditing the PM-JAY ecosystem, and recognizes the obligation of the NHA to ensure compliance with the privacy standards.

C. NHA-Acceptable Usage Policy:[24] This applies to all personnel of the NHA/SHAs and ecosystem partners, and outlines the acceptable uses of the NHA's information systems.

Together with these policies, the NHA issues best practices documents and guidelines on data protection issues. Notably, the NHA Beneficiary Identification Guidelines, 2018, lay down out the processes for verification of beneficiary identities.

As far as data collection and usage are concerned, the key points occur at the time of registration and when accessing healthcare services. Registration occurs on request of an individual to an authorized service point, including if required, at the time of accessing healthcare services. Personal data in the form of specific identification-related documents are collected in the registration process, uploaded to government databases by operators, and put through a verification process (to ensure identification and eligibility). The data collected includes names of family members, mobile number, ration card numbers, family status, etc. Aadhaar details together with other identification documents are used for beneficiary verification.[25] In order to avail of the insurance benefits at the time of accessing health services, beneficiaries must identify themselves to the healthcare centre by providing a scheme-issued e-card and an Aadhaar card (or by undertaking offline verification). Data does not always flow to the insurance provider at this stage, except where pre-authorization for treatment is required. At the time of discharge, the empanelled hospital is to capture discharge details and upload these on the PM-JAY system, based on which payments are made to the healthcare provider by the insurer. Details of the treatment provided and financial information connected to the same are also captured, though these are retained by the healthcare facility. The PM-JAY system maintains links to these records, though the records themselves are not to be shared with any entity, without consent of the beneficiary.

Data Protection under the NTEP, JSY and PM-JAY

In this section we consider how the regulatory framework for the NTEP, JSY, and PM-JAY account for data protection interests. We first analyse the programme literature and regulatory/policy framework from the perspective of ten privacy 'principles'.

Data Protection Analysis

1. *Notice and Consent:* Typically, consent forms the bedrock of data protection regulation the world over. This ensures that individual agency is protected. A key aspect of consent is the need to ensure that the individual is provided sufficient information about the uses to which data will be put. This enables the individual to gauge the possible risks involved and make a reasoned decision about whether to provide the data.

   The NTEP does not specifically recognize the need to secure beneficiary consent at the time of collection of personal data. There is also no requirement for a notice to spell out the possible uses, etc., of the data. Similarly, the JSY framework does not refer to notice/consent at all. That said, informed consent is required under both programmes, for collecting Aadhaar and banking details.[26] However, the purpose of this consent requirement remains unclear, particularly given that the Supreme Court has clarified in the second *Puttaswamy* case,[27] that Aadhaar can be mandated for use in welfare programmes.

   In contrast, processing of personal data under PM-JAY rests on a notice-consent framework. Individuals must be informed about the purpose of the consent in a local language.[28] There are, however, no limitations as to the purposes for which consent can be sought, and no requirements for consent to be granular. Consent must be revocable through a written notice.[29] The PM-JAY envisages a 'consent manager framework' to provide control to beneficiaries.

This raises questions arising from the lack of access to digital technologies and know-how in the targeted population.[30] Some have critiqued the use of such systems, arguing that it will merely legitimize the transfer of control over data to private bodies.[31]

2. *Collection Limitation:* The principle of collection limitation aims to ensure that only that data is collected and retained, which is strictly required for a particular purpose. This limits the ability of service providers to collect information extraneous to the purpose at hand, which could potentially expose individuals to enhanced risks.

Each of the programmes under study requires identification of individuals, collection of demographic data, family records, and maintenance of health records on the beneficiary. In the case of NTEP and JSY the programmes require invasive, long-term monitoring of beneficiary behaviour and habits. NTEP also requires collection of family/neighbour information to enable contact tracing. Thus, a significant amount of personal data in the form of identification, health, financial and demographic data is collected from individuals.

The NTEP and JSY restrict data collection through design of the relevant digital systems and the forms associated with reporting requirements. Neither contains any specific prohibition on unnecessary data collection. The PM-JAY also uses system design and reporting requirements to limit data collection. In addition, programme literature mandates that only data required for identification of beneficiaries and certification of treatment, etc., should be collected and made accessible to relevant stakeholders.[32] This implies that, for instance, health insurers are not normally provided with the beneficiary's medical record.[33]

While each of the programmes does not require Aadhaar to access treatment, in practice it appears that this may indeed be the case.[34] Only the PM-JAY contains a specific mandate to not store physical Aadhaar copies.

The quantity of information collected and the positioning of Aadhaar as a general patient identifier (for instance in the NSP, 2017) is questionable. It should be kept in mind that despite significant efforts to roll out Aadhaar across the population, exclusion-related problems still remain. Linking Aadhaar with medical identities can also enable easier data access across silos, thereby leading to harms arising from aggregation of data or profiling of individuals.[35]

3. *Purpose Limitation:* The principle of purpose limitation implies that data collected for one purpose should not be used for another, unconnected purpose.

All three programmes focus on the need to use personal data for purposes of beneficiary identification, service provision, programme evaluation and research purposes. For instance, a primary focus of the NTEP is on enabling greater information flows for research and policy purposes.[36] However, this is not accompanied by a clear framework on information sharing arrangements or safeguards. The NTEP also does not restrict the use of personal data accessed during the course of service provision for private/commercial purposes (outside that of providing treatment).[37] Even the NSP, 2020, which focuses on innovation and development of platforms/apps with the private sector (such as e-pharmacies), does not address the issue of downstream commercial uses of data. Similarly, the JSY also focuses on use of data for purposes of programme review. It does not prescribe any specific safeguards on the use of data for public purposes, though data on the HMIS is anonymized by aggregation. The NTEP and JSY provide a broad outline of the purpose for which data can be used in relevant notifications and guidelines. However, there are no specific limitations on the uses data can be put to once collected.

In contrast, under the PM-JAY, data can only be used for the purpose it is collected for (as informed to the beneficiary), or for any purpose authorized by law.[38] As a general rule, only that data which is strictly required for any particular purpose is made available to service providers. Crucially, the PM-JAY bars sharing of personal data for commercial purposes.[39] Its data privacy policy also provides that the use of personal data for purposes other than the delivery of insurance services, i.e., for ends such as public health research, fraud management and policy formulation, is to be based on anonymized or de-identified data.[40]

Insofar as private sector data use is concerned, the PM-JAY again stands apart from the older programmes in limiting the uses to which data can be put to. Data is to be shared with service providers only for a specific purpose and in accordance with a contract (containing relevant confidentiality and punitive clauses). Other safeguards implemented include the need for regular review and audit, and due diligence. Biometrics are not to be shared with private sector service providers for any purpose whatsoever. Further, health data (identifiable or anonymized) is not to be accessed or disclosed for any commercial purposes to any person or entity including insurance companies, employees and pharma companies.[41]

4. *Data Quality and Access/Correction:* Ensuring the accuracy of records can be vital in the context of healthcare programmes, as they are the basis on which individuals access rights and entitlements. Errors can risk the health of beneficiaries, and at a macro level, hinder programme outcomes, policy development and research. Providing access and correction rights, therefore, becomes important as a means of promoting autonomy of individuals and also ensure that records are accurate and up to date.

As far as the programmes under study are concerned, the NTEP and JSY were developed based on physical record keeping, a practice which continues to this date. Under the NTEP, typically, diagnostic centres, labs, hospitals, etc., collate relevant records and submit them in physical form to local health officials. This information is then transcribed to digital formats by human operators. This process has been recognized in the National Strategic Plan for TB Elimination, 2020-25, as leading to significant number of errors.[42] Similarly, field studies on HMIS portal implementation have demonstrated implementation problems due to errors and missing data caused by a lack of capacity at the data entry level.[43] Accordingly, both the NTEP and JSY are seeking to move away from physical record collection to digital record keeping.[44]

As far as access and correction rights are concerned, the NTEP permits beneficiaries to access their basic data via the NikshayAarogyaSathi App.[45] Beneficiaries can also utilize the grievance redress mechanism (a call centre) or complain to local health officers to request corrections in their records. The JSY does not specifically provide for access and correction rights, though presumably complaints can be made using the general grievance mechanisms established for the programme.

The PM-JAY provides beneficiaries with the ability to access their own information, learn how it is processed and request corrections.[46] This can be done through digital means (email or calls) or by liaising with the local Aayushman Mitra (an official overseeing the scheme at the local level).

5. *Storage Limitation:* Limiting how long data can be stored or providing individuals the right to seek deletion of their data can reduce the risks of privacy harms by limiting the opportunity for misuse, or by ensuring that decisions are not based on outdated information.

There are no storage limitations provided under NTEP or JSY. Under the Nikshay system, records are frozen on completion of treatment and then archived. There is no provision for erasure or anonymization of records.

PM-JAY does recognize the need to ensure that data is only stored till it is required for a specific purpose or till a data retention limit is reached.[47] However, no such limit has been specified as yet, though the NHA has initiated a consultation process in this regard.[48] Notably, the policy requires third parties dealing with NHA data to keep data inventories, and provide a certificate of erasure at the time of completion of their services (when they must dispose of personal data held by them).[49]

6. *Integrity and Confidentiality:* Ensuring the integrity and confidentiality of data implies that measures are put in place to protect data from unauthorized access or modification. This is clearly vital in the context of healthcare programmes, due to the

nature of data at hand and the significant effects misuse of such data may lead to (harm to health, exclusions, social stigma, etc.).

The NSP, 2017, does not specifically recognize the need to maintain confidentiality of beneficiary data. However, this is acknowledged as a key principle in more recent policy documents including the National Framework for a Gender Responsive Approach to TB in India and the NSP, 2020.[50]

Nikshay training documents indicate that access to the system is based on a credential-based security system.[51] The modular nature of the system means that access is only provided to service providers based on their function and geographical reach, thereby limiting the possibility of privacy harms to patient data. For instance, a health institution at block level can only see data for their own patients.

While the NHM recognizes the need to federate health records and implement certain general privacy safeguards, the JSY itself does not specifically recognize the need to maintain confidentiality of beneficiary data. Indeed, the JSY Guidelines require the compulsory publication of beneficiary names and payment information at the relevant healthcare centre. This is presumably to aid transparency and prevent pilferage of financial incentives by the institutional apparatus. This, therefore, represents an instance where transparency is valued over individual privacy as a systemic choice.

The PM-JAY is developed with a focus on access control and data minimization. The programme provides for data security reviews, data inventories and maintenance of audit trails for all activities.[52] Medical data is to be stored at the healthcare facility, with health records maintained through linkages to primary medical data. Software/hardware used in the ecosystem must be provided by or approved by the NHA. This helps ensure adherence to appropriate standards pertaining to security, openness, etc. Interestingly, operators and implementation support agencies at contact points are required to sign non-disclosure agreements pertaining to the data they collect/upload.[53] This is important as these operators have access to identification data of all individuals on the PM-JAY and connected databases (Rashtriya Swasthya Bima Yojana, family information databases, etc.). There are no geographic or other restrictions placed on whose data they can view (though logs are maintained of all activities carried out by such operators). Regular assessment and audits are also to be conducted on the system by the NHA.

7. *Enforcement and Accountability:* Ensuring that beneficiaries have methods to enforce their rights and hold institutions accountable is essential in protecting privacy. Recognizing possible privacy harms and providing a means to redress as well as award suitable punishments are essential in disincentivizing malpractices involving beneficiary data.

The NTEP under the NSP, 2017, envisages grievance redress mechanisms in the form of call centres as well as committees formed by government officials and community workers.[54] NSP, 2020, clarifies that grievances are to be raised through the NikshaySampark (call centre) system.[55] Data trails are maintained for activities on the Nikshay system, thereby enabling internal audit and accountability.[56] While the JSY Guidelines do envisage creation of a multi-tiered grievance redress mechanism, these do not specifically have the remit to engage with data protection and related issues.[57] These two programmes do not provide for any specific punitive actions in case of grievances related to data protection.

The PM-JAY incorporates a distinct audit and grievance process. It includes a Data Privacy Committee to review compliance on an ongoing basis and also grievance procedures in the form of an NHA data privacy officer (DPO). The NHA contains a Privacy Operations Centre led by a data privacy officer to scrutinize privacy practices and take complaints. All privacy-related complaints must be tracked and closed in a timely manner.[58] The NHA Data Privacy Policy also recognizes that there should be no limitations on the method/channel of raising grievances. However, the primary methods provided to access these mechanisms appear to require some level of (digital) literacy, that is, they require complaints to be sent in writing, via email or using the Central Government Redressal Management System (CGRMS) portal.[59] That said, the grievance policy also recognizes that they may be reported through newspapers or by using a call centre.[60] Enforcement action can range from termination of services to departmental orders.[61] While the DPO may levy penalties on service providers for non-compliance with the Data Privacy Policy, there is no system providing for compensation to beneficiaries.

8. *Openness:* This principle is used to gauge the accessibility of policies and standards for the programmes under study. Openness is important due to the need to ensure transparency and accountability, while also enabling audit and review of the schemes, and, in particular, their technological components. Openness also enables greater participation of stakeholders in programme development processes.

The NSP, 2017, does not recognize the need for openness of the Nikshay system or encourage transparency in data processing protocols. Accordingly, details of the Nikshay system are difficult to come across and require one to scrutinize training modules and other ad hoc documents issued by the government. The NSP, 2020, mentions the need to make more information and data on the 'technology pipeline' available; and also to use open application programming interfaces (APIs). The JSY does not publish sufficient documentation either pertaining to the programme or the digitized systems such as MCTS/RCH/HMIS.[62] On the other hand, information about the NHA's processes and practices relating to handling data are to be reasonably open and accessible.[63] Indeed, ISPIRT (Indian Software Product Industry RoundTable), one of the leading groups behind the development of the health stack, has been carrying out seminars on the design of the stack and safeguards related to data protection in it.[64]

9. *Incident Management:* Ensuring that organizations have in place protocols to deal with data breach and similar incidents is essential

to minimize the risks that may arise due to security breaches or other misuses of data.

Neither the NTEP nor JSY deals with the issue of incident management or provide for data breach notifications to beneficiaries. The PM-JAY framework, however, does envisage a dedicated incident response team at the NHA.[65] While the NHA's Data Privacy Policy requires the formulation of an incident and breach management mechanism, none has been sighted. That said, the policy framework does require the DPO to record, track and close security incidents, while ecosystem partners responsible for a breach must report breaches to beneficiaries (within time limits prescribed by the NHA). The NHA too is required to notify the beneficiary, Indian Computer Emergency Response Team, or CERT-IN, and may also inform the media of data security incidents. There is no publicly available information on whether such reporting has ever occurred.

10. *Prescription of Standards:* This entails ensuring that proper standards are specified can aid in system security, protecting data by implementing protocols for sharing and anonymization/ pseudonymization, etc.

The NTEP and JSY do not reference any particular standards for maintaining system security, etc. The NSP, 2020, prescribes certain security standards for system design, but is silent on the use of anonymization techniques. The PM-JAY prescribes relevant ISO standards for data security.[66] Standards for anonymization/ de-identification and data retention have however not yet been specified despite the policy framework specifying such a need.[67]

Overall Analysis

The JSY and NTEP fail to address data protection issues in their design and regulatory frameworks. The increased digitization of these programmes has not been accompanied by an improvement in data protection frameworks. Both programmes focus on enabling greater information collection and sharing; however, there are no safeguards specified in this respect. These programmes also fail to address issues related to data protection pertaining to healthcare workers. Frontline healthcare workers, usually women, are subject to intrusive surveillance and reporting requirements. Misuse or disclosure of their personal data (such as phone numbers or locations) could expose them to harassment.[68] Indeed, reports indicate that ASHAs in Haryana were on strike in May 2021, protesting against the requirement to install certain apps on their phones that could enable granular surveillance of their activities.[69]

The PM-JAY, in contrast, accounts for data protection interests to a substantial extent. It has a detailed regulatory framework providing for a range of rights and data protection measures, though this is still a work in progress given that certain standards (such as those for anonymization of data) are yet to be published.

While the improvement in regulatory frameworks is to be commended, our analysis also raises some broader concerns.

First, the use of consent as the basis of processing is questionable. Not only one must consider the well-documented problems with 'privacy self-management',[70] but also that denial of consent results in a denial of services (in all the programmes under study). Most beneficiaries will have little choice in accessing alternative modes of healthcare provision. People may also consent to 'unfair' practices during times of duress, say when accessing essential treatment.[71] Reports also point to the misuse of biometric data (which beneficiaries must provide to receive Aadhaar-linked payments), leading to payments fraud.[72] Second, it is unclear to what extent data protection frameworks translate into practice. For instance, while federating records is in theory a good idea, under-resourced healthcare centres may not have the capacity/ability to properly implement secure storage and access systems. Third, concerns have been raised about the extent of digitization in government healthcare programmes. There continues to be suspicion about the motivations of the government in pushing for large-scale digitization, despite the absence of adequate technical capacity, infrastructure or knowhow, particularly in the targeted populations (as well as the meagre financial outlays for health schemes themselves). Some view this as a method to harness data as a resource, say by providing private sector insurance firms with data to enable more profitable pricing or by promoting market growth by enhanced data portability.[73] Fourth, many beneficiaries may not have access to digital infrastructure or know-how to enable protection of their privacy rights. Fifth, the general reliance on Aadhaar as an identity proof (as also proposals to create a universal health ID), raises concerns about exclusions as well as risks arising from data aggregation.[74] Sixth, the use of centralized platforms, databases and identities can be seen as suboptimal system design in that it enables single points of failure. This is particularly important as records on these databases are seen as 'single sources of truth'.[75] Seventh, the ability of the state to access beneficiary data with relative ease (as covered in more detail in Chapter 12, titled State Legibility of Personal Health Data) raises the broader issue of state surveillance over citizens. We have seen, for instance, that data collected by the state is often susceptible to misuse, either for commercial or criminal purposes.[76]

Finally, data protection under the three programmes does not rest on a statutory foundation and is, therefore, subject to administrative/ executive discretion. This implies no statutory recognition of rights or independent oversight mechanisms. Given the government's apparent interest in development of the health stack, for which PM-JAY is seen as a test case, internal oversight and enforcement of privacy norms may lack rigour and transparency. So, it may be advisable to create certainty in this respect, through enforceable laws, that also establish independent oversight.

Despite the above, increasing digitization in the healthcare sector is clearly inevitable to improve efficiency of services, permit scaling and also various other public interest goals such as enabling fraud detention and use of data for making policy and research. However, viewing the issue as a binary between competing goals of public interest and individual liberties is unwise. These interests must be balanced in accordance with the Supreme Court dicta in *Puttaswamy*, by ensuring that interventions with privacy rights are necessary and proportionate, and, importantly, contain safeguards against abuse.

Our analysis indicates that while there is a definite improvement in how privacy rights are recognized in public healthcare programmes over the past few years, there is a scope for improvement. While the general data protection framework in India could be used to mitigate certain privacy harms (or secure compensation in case of data breaches), these are commonly understood as being underdeveloped, with insufficient oversight frameworks or avenues for recourse. Enactment of a specific data protection legislation could therefore enable a clearer recognition of rights and a move from an ad hoc administrative framework to a framework on sound legal footing. It should be kept in mind that while the government has announced implementation of the National Digital Health Blueprint (NDHB), this document, which is intended to guide development of the digital ecosystem insofar as healthcare data is concerned, also does not have legal any standing. However, it does make the regulatory/governance frameworks as applicable to the PM-JAY applicable across the board.[77] This will enhance data protection frameworks applicable to older programmes, though it will not mitigate the general concerns highlighted previously (the absence of independent accountability mechanisms, concerns pertaining to data quality, as well as the centralization of systems, such as through the creation of a national health ID).

Conclusion

This chapter has attempted to provide an overview of the state of data protection in three pan-India flagship public health programmes of the Government of India. We describe the design of the programmes and the nature of data flows in each. We then evaluate the policy and regulatory framework applicable to each against ten privacy 'principles'. We also examine the extent to which data protection is a consideration in the design and implementation of these programmes and the lacunae in the current regulatory frameworks.

Our analysis indicates that data protection rights are barely given any consideration in the regulatory frameworks or design of older programmes such as NTEP and JSY. The programmes were conceptualized in the 'pre-digital' era, and worryingly, the regulatory frameworks have not developed to account for technological progress. Data protection mechanisms are largely based on architectural measures, as opposed to empowering beneficiaries through a recognition of rights. Indeed, to the extent privacy rights are considered, these focus on ensuring data security as opposed to a holistic protection of privacy rights.

The regulatory framework for the PM-JAY is a massive improvement on the low privacy standards in the NTEP and JSY. It includes technical measures as well as legal and institutional frameworks for enforcement of data protection rights.

Despite the increasing recognition of data protection rights, various problems remain, not least arising from the fact that data protection interests are not adequately protected in statute. Even PM-JAY relies on administrative/contractual means to protect beneficiary data. This can create uncertainty, limit the scope of rights and limit accountability. The study illustrates the urgent need for a law that can ensure data protection in a holistic manner. A clear delineation of beneficiary rights, increased routes to enforceability and independent accountability mechanisms would improve programme quality, uptake, and consequently health outcomes. While attempts have been made to put in place horizontal data protection regulations in the health sector, these have not yet borne fruit. The enactment of a data protection law is therefore essential.

8

Trust: The Cornerstone of Health Interventions

Olinda Timms

Introduction

MEDICAL care and health promotion is a universal human need that has a profound and personal impact on individuals. The vulnerability of the sick and the need for care necessitates a trust bond between the patient and the provider. Trust is also essential for effective health outcomes at a population level.[1] Access to health systems and universal healthcare is now regarded as a human right, and the onus is on governments to be trustworthy custodians of this responsibility to prioritize health and social well-being.[2] From an organizational perspective, trust is intrinsically important for effective healthcare and can be described as a collective good or social capital.[3]

An exploration of the dynamics of trust within the healthcare system at each level, involving health providers, researchers and the public health system, therefore, becomes important. It can also inform health planners looking to address privacy concerns while designing successful health interventions and polices. This chapter looks at the underpinnings of trust in the context of informed consent and health data confidentiality, reviewing challenges to trust, as well as strategies that promote trust in health interventions.

Fiduciary Relationship

Trust is a crucial element in the doctor–patient relationship. The human interaction encountered in medical practice, where a patient is dependent on the doctor for expertise and care, is intrinsically asymmetric in an immutable way. Very often, the patient's only option is to trust the doctor's intention, competence and motivation to care. The doctor's power is the advantage of knowledge and his/her expertise is therefore accompanied by the burden to engender trust in the patient through ethical behaviour and compassion. For this reason, the doctor–patient relationship is described as a 'fiduciary' relationship.[4] The power inequality and the dependent, beneficiary status of the patient place a fiduciary duty on the doctor. This understanding of the need to foster trust and place the patient's best interest above all else is at the heart of medical ethics.[5]

Since earliest times, professional ethical guidelines and oaths have described and reinforced values of service and compassion that served to engender trust among patients. Patients are more likely to trust doctors and health institutions, and even accept certain levels of risk, if they believe that their health needs and choices are at the centre of medical decisions.[6]

Education, information and awareness also play a part in equipping the patient with facts and providing reassurance to some extent, but they do not substantially eliminate the need for trust in medical and preventive care situations. The applied nature of medical science, its nuanced approaches and subjectivity, human variability and gaps in medical knowledge, create a terrain that is tough for an untrained person to navigate. Therefore, the patient has little recourse other than to trust the doctor.[7] Reciprocity, which is the tendency to respond positively to a good action, can have a profound role in the trust-building process. This social premise, when applied to healthcare, implies repaying trust with sincere action and beneficial care.[8]

The power imbalance and need for trust apply across health systems, hospitals, research contexts and government health policies. Hospitals are trusted to ensure the safety of patients and quality of care. Governments have a fiduciary responsibility towards citizens to provide the best possible conditions for health and access to medical care. Whereas the doctor–patient relationship involves reposing faith in one individual's ethical behaviour and competence, the situation is aggravated when one has to trust entire systems – hospitals, institutions and government policies. The mechanisms of trust become far more complex and subjective and vary widely, based on earlier experiences, track record and 'trustworthiness' of institutions and governance standards.[9] As opposed to personal risks and benefits, at the level of populations, there are collective risks and benefits and a need to highlight the 'common good'. Common good is defined as 'that which benefits society as a whole, in contrast to the private good of individuals and sections of society'.[10] However, as desirable as the common good may be, it cannot override the rights and health needs of individuals. Here too, reciprocity plays an important role, where receipt of benefits and privileges builds faith in health policy and roll-out of programmes.

Trust and COVID-19

The trust relationship between health providers, health systems and citizens is built on information sharing, inclusion and transparency. In India, this was manifest in interventions and public responses during the COVID-19 pandemic. The sudden lockdown declared at the start of the pandemic, without adequate information, explanation or consideration of possible harms, led to a migration crisis and incalculable suffering in the name of protection against disease.[11] Information from authorities was sketchy and unreliable, access to health was unavailable, and archaic laws like the Epidemic Diseases Act, 1897, and the more recent Disaster Management Act, 2005, were invoked to enforce restrictions on the public.[12] This led to erosion of trust in the government and health systems at a time when trust and compliance were most crucial in order to deal with the pandemic on a national scale. Health workers, who were targeted at their residences, and even chased away while on surveillance duty, most acutely felt the repercussions of distrust.[13]

Fear of quarantine led to denial of symptoms and refusal to test; further spreading the disease. Inadequate oxygen supplies, lack of beds and changing treatment protocols conveyed the gross inadequacies of a broken health system that had simply no answers for the poverty-stricken, marginalized and most vulnerable.[14] Later, when the vaccine became available, there was incomplete information and unequal distribution of limited stocks, once again exposing social injustices. The impact of distrust was felt when people began to refuse vaccinations, thwarting the plan of health authorities of building herd immunity through mass immunizations.[15] The subsequent toll in terms of lives and resources was unacceptably high. The unpreparedness and patchy response of the authorities led to profound insecurity and distrust that may persist indefinitely, and even spill over to other non-health interventions.

Building Trust by Respecting Persons

Respect for the patient is a fundamental guiding principle of medical ethics that contributes to building trust. Not only does this mean treating the physical body and the emotional state of the patient with respect, but also respecting the autonomy of the individual, including health decisions, sensitive personal details, diagnosis, health data and prognosis. Respecting the patient's right to information in order to make decisions about his/her own health and life, and protecting their right to confidentiality, are central in building trust and confidence.[16] It is precisely this confidence and trust that enable the patient to reveal personal details and make truthful disclosures that can assist in accurate diagnosis. It can also result in better compliance with the treatment plan and preventive care. For this reason, informed consent and confidentiality have been highlighted, both in clinical care and health research, as central elements that demonstrate respect for patients and foster trust.

The importance of consent and confidentiality is underscored by the fact that any breach of standard of care related to these aspects, which directly results in patient harm, can be construed as medical negligence and is legally actionable. In this way the law recognizes the obligatory nature of the trust reposed in the doctor–patient relationship, and upholds the right of patients to consent and confidentiality.

Trust and Informed Consent

'Trust is like blood pressure. It's silent, vital to good health, and if abused it can be deadly.'

– Frank Sonnenberg

Communication of information is a critical trust-building component in healthcare. Whether it is clinical care at the individual level, a participant/patient in health research and clinical trials, or at the level of community or population health, adequate information that precedes consent is a prerequisite for successful outcomes. Ethical guidelines across the world highlight informed consent in clinical and research settings.[17] In clinical settings, some aspects of consent are presumed or taken for granted. For example, when a patient pays the registration/consultation fee and enters the doctor's chambers, it is presumed that they agree to receive the care and advice of the doctor. However, if the treatment includes an invasive intervention, like surgery, an additional, signed informed consent is required. Similarly, admission into a hospital and invasive investigations would require specific signed consent. These layers of consent ensure that the patient is aware and willing for the procedures planned, thereby respecting patient autonomy in decision making.

Information for written and signed consent should be communicated by a health professional, preferably the doctor, in the language of the patient and family, and pitched at a comfortable level of understanding. The patient should understand the diagnosis, treatment plan, duration, prognosis, side effects, options of care and cost. In ideal situations, communication flows in both directions as the patient seeks clarifications that may assist the consent process. In the *Samira Kohli* judgment the courts commented on the need for 'real consent' in the Indian context, which is patient-centred and more in line with ground realities of medical care in this country.[18]

In health research and clinical trials, the law mandates a process for informed consent, which may even be audio/video recorded and witnessed. Any abbreviation of this process can lead to litigation and profound loss of trust in vitally needed health research. Even in community settings and epidemiological research, information may be provided to groups, but individual consent is mandated.

Awareness building and information dissemination as part of public health or community health interventions are equally important. These enable engagement, transparency and confidence building in communities and citizen groups. Individual consent may not be possible in population-level interventions, but the success of these programmes is predicated on the awareness, cooperation and trust of citizens. Policymakers have access to population data as well as health resources, based on which they decide the health needs that receive priority. Some policies may apply across the country, like tuberculosis programme, malaria eradication and HIV control, while others may affect targeted populations or communities. Citizens may not have a voice in developing these protocols and may be merely informed, if at all; they may lack the power to influence health policy even within democratic structures. This inequality in public health interventions is a challenge, leaving citizens no choice but to trust the intentions and integrity of policymakers within the health system, and hope their welfare and well-being will be prioritized.

Trust and Confidentiality

'A healthy relationship is built on unwavering trust'
– Beau Mirchoff

The health professional is entrusted with any and all information shared by the patient as part of diagnosis and the course of care. Confidentiality with regard to health information and data is sacrosanct in healthcare relationships and consistently alluded to in medical oaths and ethical guidelines.[19] The right to confidentiality is an extension of the constitutional right to privacy enjoyed by every citizen.[20] Unnecessary or careless disclosure of personal health information can result in serious harm that could be personal, emotional and social in nature. Based on the kind of health or personal information disclosed, it could subject the patient to bias and discrimination; diminish his/her life prospects and curb enjoyment of freedoms. Such harms can even lead to legal action seeking punitive damages against alleged breach of confidentiality by the health worker or institution. Protecting patient confidentiality therefore promotes trust in health professionals and health systems.

For this reason, health documentation and access to health data have always been carefully protected. With computerization and portability of data, this protection has been severely tested and health institutions are wary of linking with other institutions or health networks as hacking, data leaks or crashing of networks could be disastrous. The track record with protection of non-health data has not been inspiring and there are numerous weaknesses in data systems that need to be fixed. In India the Information Technology Act, 2000, has some provisions and the Personal Data Protection Bill, 2019, tried to address these lacunae , but with the withdrawal of the draft bill there is still much ground to be covered.[21]

The Ayushman Bharat Digital Mission launched by the government hopes to build on the 'web' and 'app' data collected during COVID-19 to provide a digital health ID that will hold the health data of each individual.[22] Doctors and authorized parties can access this information with the permission of the user. But there are many unanswered questions with regard to data security, unauthorized access and surveillance, creating tension between personal data protection and overriding interests of national concern and the common good. Further, as health services in this country vary widely, not all physicians would have access to computerization and network connectivity to facilitate safe data storage and transfer.

Protection of Health Data

Protection of sensitive health-related data is an extremely important exercise to build trust in health systems. There are broadly three types of health-related data:

Clinical Data

Clinical data may be stored in medical records, filing systems, hospital data information systems and cloud storage. It includes diagnosis, treatment records, medications, and discharge summaries, as well as data regarding disabilities, infertility, temporary or permanent physical deficiencies, personal habits, mental illness, psychological trauma and drug dependencies. Though not exhaustive, this list underscores the vulnerability of patients to stigma, social harm and discrimination should this sensitive data fall into wrong hands. It would be a total betrayal of trust if such data were inadvertently shared without the express consent of the patient.

Research Data

Research data too requires to be strictly protected, as participants in research have accepted some risk of harm, for the sake of the common good. Betrayal of trust by breaking confidentiality will destroy faith in the research process, ultimately harming society through loss of benefits of medical research. For this reason, guidelines dictate strict confidentiality norms in health research and clinical trials.

Public Health

Public health programmes and interventions also generate copious population data on diet, health habits, mobility patterns, geographical location, endemic disease, health access, family and community life among a plethora of other information. Reciprocity is crucial here, as, it is often the expectations of benefit that motivate persons to surrender personal data. Depending on the handlers of this information and the use to which it is put, there is potential for harm to these communities and families; health data often gets merged with other data and can be misused if not specifically protected. One can imagine this sensitive data potentially being 'weaponized' or communalized, leading to harm, stigma and alienation of communities.

Very Often

Very often information is provided by default to receive public health benefits, as in the case of the Aarogya Setu application that took personal and health details of the beneficiaries in return for free vaccination and testing during COVID-19.[23] The rationale for appropriation of data was epidemic control and surveillance but there was insufficient reassurance regarding data protection and time limits for retention of data. Fear of stigma, quarantine and state action during the pandemic generated a sense of distrust and resentment at having to surrender data, in the absence of transparency and adequate information.

Loss of Trust

'Only those you trust can betray you.'

— Terry Goodkind

A breach of trust, whether at doctor–patient level, in research settings or at a population level, can cause an immeasurable setback and involve costs in terms of harm to the individual and common good. At an individual level, if the patient feels that the health professional or the institution is careless or disrespectful of their health details, they may not comply with treatment protocols and may end the relationship. This could have serious repercussions in situations like HIV-positive cases, disease breakouts, pandemics and mental illnesses. Patients may even seek unproven remedies that may worsen their condition, even as they continue to expose others to harm.

Research and clinical trials are valued for the potential to provide evidence of effective drug therapies and vaccines. Loss of trust in clinical trial design and regulation, participant enrolment, consent process or confidentiality will deter volunteers and breed scepticism regarding evidence generated from such trials. This defeats the entire purpose of clinical research and can be a setback to health benefits for the entire population. The HPV (human papillomavirus) vaccines clinical trial conducted in 1988 is an example of research conduct that diminished trust in the research process in this country.[24]

Epidemiological and community health research also generates health data that can inform public health policy and intervention. Collection of community data for research is governed by guidelines and regulations, particularly with regard to informed consent process and confidentiality.[25] There could be sensitive health or cultural information linked to backward and tribal communities, vulnerable groups and socially marginalized populations. Any breach of confidentiality and trust, no matter how well intentioned, can gravely harm these groups and obstruct efforts to engage with them in the future. In these situations trust is hard-won through persistent engagement, but can very easily be lost.

At community and population level, distrust in health workers and health policies can be catastrophic, as we have seen during COVID-19. Surveillance and testing were obstructed by violence against health workers. In case of vaccines, when there was insufficient supply and the prescribed dose interval kept changing, vulnerable populations refused vaccinations even free of charge, and illness went unreported as patients feared quarantine and isolation. Much of this backlash was due to the absence of trusted channels of communication and information, abrupt and changing information, and the use of force rather than reassurance or appeal.[26] In this life-threatening situation, people turned instead to NGOs working in their communities, and smaller hospitals or doctors that they had come to trust over time.[27]

Other Factors Affecting Trust

The background political climate can also affect public responses at a population level. Those disgruntled in general with governance or discriminatory policies or police action may have less trust in public health interventions, however well intentioned or appropriate.

Another issue is institutional trust, referring mainly to trust in the widely available system of modern medicine and the overarching healthcare delivery system. If government health services are overcrowded, doctors overburdened and the infrastructure outdated or inadequate, patients are often forced to accept substandard care. This failure to provide basic health services coupled with inequities in access and other indignities faced by marginalized groups can erode trust in public health interventions. Patients may be forced to look for alternative healing remedies, some dangerous or uncertified. The brunt of this failure of trust is, of course, borne by poorer sections of society and the most vulnerable, who have limited voice or options.

Structural factors are also integral to promotion of good health. If citizens do not have access to food, housing, employment, education, safety, and affordable healthcare, they are less likely to trust or accept public health interventions prescribed in a heavy-handed manner. Similarly, absence of consistent quality in determinants of health such as clean, unpolluted air, water, food and environment are viewed as a general lack of political commitment to good health and safety. This is the background against which any public health intervention will be judged or trusted.

Trustworthiness of systems plays an important role. Breakdown of democratic structures that allow for diverse voices and opinions in prioritization and rollout of health needs is another cause for concern. Health planning, data collection and public health interventions that are top-down and non-consultative will meet with less cooperation and trust, ending in failure and waste of precious resources. In vast and complex populations such as India's, the principle of subsidiarity may be more efficient, allowing local populations to decide and promote their health priorities, while the authorities provide support and resources as needed.[28]

The expansion of private hospitals and medical colleges and stagnation of governmental health institutions in the last few decades have altered the health sector's landscape.[29] The persistent low health budget (the government spends 1.02 per cent of its gross domestic product on health), among the lowest in the world, has crippled government health infrastructure and expansion plans. The accompanying expansion of high-cost private healthcare has excluded vast populations, and pushed millions into poverty due to health-related debt.[30] Urban and rural poor are left with nothing but electoral promises, destroying trust in health planners and health systems. In a welfare-driven state with a history of socialist measures designed to take medical care to the underserved, this U-turn in policy has left millions with few options and limited access to care.[31]

With ineffective regulation of cost of care and medications, money has soured the trust relationship, making it more transactional. Fees have to be paid or approved upfront and many are turned away at the door. Even those consumers who can afford private care have begun to distrust the motives and priorities of health professionals and management of profit-driven institutions. The conflict of interest is painfully obvious as patients' medical needs can easily be exploited. In corporate hospitals, patient acquisition drives, use of expensive technology, longer hospital stays, batteries of tests and consultations have become commonplace. Feeling trapped and distrustful, patients' families have even resorted to violence against doctors and hospitals.[32] The expansion of for-profit medical colleges, accessible only to those who can afford the high capitation and tuition fees, is of concern as it places pressure on these graduates to recover their cost of education, often through unethical practices. Service, compassionate care and ethics are casualties in this scenario, with the focus shifted to specialization and competition for patients. Most disturbing is the conflict of interest when politicians and regulators themselves have a stake in private medical colleges and corporate hospitals.

News and social media remain an important social voice, but they can also erode trust in health systems and health interventions. The recent trend of going to news channels or print media for alleged negligence or medical error can generate panic and anger against doctors and hospitals even before facts can be verified or explained. The 'trial by media' can be expensive in terms of distrust and fear, triggering defensive behaviour by both patients and doctors. This is detrimental for all concerned, leading to strained relationships and poor medical outcomes. Health professionals feel wronged and bullied, in a bizarre role reversal that is counterproductive. Condemning doctors or hospitals in the media without a fair hearing, just for a brief spike in viewer ratings, in the name of giving citizens a voice, is not beneficial. This is also the case with videos and reports circulated on WhatsApp and social media. With no verification barrier, these forums ravage reputations and disseminate fear instantly, ruining trust in health systems and public health interventions. This was evident during COVID-19 when social media took over, spreading rumours and false data that hampered vaccine roll-out, just when it was most needed. Exposés on corruption and kickbacks in health programmes, medical supplies, infrastructure and drugs have the same effect, ranging citizens and health planners on opposite sides of a trust divide.

Unfortunately a few rotten apples may exist in any system or profession, but the impact here can be devastating in terms of trust destroyed. The power structures at play and vulnerability of health-seekers overtake the narrative, tarring all professionals, hospitals and public health policies with the same brush. However, trust may not always be lost in the entire structure; patients may distrust the system but continue to trust certain doctors, or they may distrust certain doctors, yet retain faith in the hospital or health system as a whole.[33]

Another daunting change in recent decades is the corporatization of healthcare. In many cities, the family doctor and the neighbourhood clinic have all but vanished. These were the trusted faces of care – constant, familiar and recognizable – accompanying the patient over time, embedded within their living environments. Today, for even the slightest ailment, patients are faced with hospital visits, seeing different doctors each time, subject to tests and treatments, in a faceless, business-like set-up. Hospitals have become faceless towers of glass and chrome, with screaming banners peddling wellness and comfort, everything available at a price. Patients are viewed as consumers, some naive and exploitable, others exacting and demanding. Specialists chase down every medical symptom or sign, dragging patients through burdensome treatments, citing early care and eradication.

The splintering of medical care between consultants, laboratories and specialists reduces a patient to a set of deranged tests or scans to be corrected, symptoms to be relieved, and disease and disability to be treated. Sadly, holistic healthcare is abandoned, and patients are left feeling objectified and dissatisfied.

The question is where and how to place one's trust in this new normal? The doctor–patient relationship has transformed into a *doctor–hospital relationship*. The hospital card links the patient to the hospital and provides access to services as required, although the same doctor may not attend at every visit. The patient is then compelled to trust the *system* within the hospital, the *processes* of investigation, the *quality* (competence) of doctors employed – intangibles that impact the care experience. With these changes, in the name of efficiency and viability, a depersonalization of medical care begins to set in. The goals of promoting wellness and preventive health will be at odds with the profit motives of such hospitals, denying patients the benefits of holistic and preventive care. In an interesting twist to the patient–hospital relationship, some patients tend to prefer and trust hospitals with high-tech diagnostics, computerization, quality infrastructure and stylish interiors, equating it to best-in-class services and competent professionals! This change in perception extends to choosing online doctors and telemedicine consultations. Choice can be led by online ratings and reviews, glamorous advertisements and promotions.

Universal health coverage is the WHO's mandate for every country's leadership. Yet, what we see is a move to provide universal health insurance.[34] The Indian government has struggled to extend these benefits to more of the population in the last decade, ignoring hard lessons from other countries. This has led to a *patient–insurance relationship*, with individuals and groups bargaining with their health insurance provider for health benefits, less premium, cashless payments and fancier hospitals, depending on them to come through in an emergency or health crisis. This, in turn, pushes up the cost of care in private hospitals. In this way, patients are forced to trust insurance companies, again a faceless commercial enterprise, driven by actuarial calculations, and ruthless in execution. Inability to understand or negotiate the fine print has left thousands stranded, deprived of care or in debt. Despite this, it appears to be more feasible for the government to promote and insist on some form of health insurance for all, rather than expand low-cost public health services. Even with multiple populist insurance schemes and public and private sector health coverage, there are large swathes of the population left without assured access to quality medical care. Distrust and disenchantment with public health services creep into public insurance schemes, particularly ones that are selective, leaving millions out in the cold.

For the economically distressed and marginalized sections, government health schemes are often the only resort. Getting on to a 'beneficiary list' becomes a feat in itself, with much manoeuvring required to access one's due. Here again, trust is placed in a *patient–government relationship*, one that needs to be nurtured for continued access. Cards based on caste, class, disability, finances, tribe, minority and destitution become instruments of negotiation, condemning families to the indignity and uncertainty of largesse and handouts. In these circumstances, bereft of bargaining or purchasing capacity, the only option is to trust this card and whatever health benefits it brings. Public health programmes are subject to change or may end abruptly without much notice or explanation, based on resources or other priorities; beneficiaries are often left at the mercy of these vagaries within the health system. Coercion of any kind, in development or social security measures, can damage trust in even the best government schemes. Rural communities and the urban poor may receive testing or vaccines focused on one disease, among many that beset such communities. Similarly, sporadic check-ups and health visits without addressing living conditions, social injustices and destitution are meaningless, providing no long-term solutions, leaving beneficiaries jaded and uncooperative.

One is forced to conclude that individual and public trust is a valuable good that must be earned and preserved through consistently respectful and sensitive interventions, ongoing engagement and communication, efficient and robust data systems and commitment to building trustworthy institutions.

Building and Preserving Trust

Clearly, from the preceding discussion, it is far easier to destroy than to build trust. The task of building and preserving trust has to be taken up at every level, with mandated and ongoing investment in terms of resources, training and personnel for awareness building and conflict mitigation.

Training

Health professionals and workers require training in appropriate behaviour towards patients, recognizing the service nature of the profession and need for ethical practices that foster trust. AETCOM (attitude, ethics and communication) modules recently introduced in medical curriculum emphasize empathy, ethics, duties and communication skills.[35] Similar sensitization on ethics, social role and communication must extend as training for all cadres of health workers and health administration. This alignment of objectives and expectations within the health structure can prevent discordant behaviour and promote a better patient experience.[36]

Care Protocols

When doctors are busy in overcrowded hospitals, there should be health workers to step in and guide or assist patients so that they do not feel alienated. Fees should be clearly disclosed and clear process and persons designated to handle legitimate grievances. Disclosure of information and options should be thorough and, where necessary, consent should be taken. Every effort should be made to reassure patients about steps to ensure confidentiality of their health data. Emergency care should never be denied, and patients should not be abandoned when their financial resources run out. Doctors need to advocate for counselling as well as funding for bona fide cases when patient's funds or insurance runs out. Bridges need to be built between modern medicine and other systems of medicine recognized by law in this country, so that, if needed, patients can access other appropriate, less expensive options of care. Despite efforts, it will be a while before we see a respectful integration of all health systems and services, and acceptance of the right to freely access any of these options.

Explanations and rationale should be provided for all tests, scans, referrals and medications, in a language that is understood by the patient, followed by thorough documentation. When things go wrong, there should be a way to openly talk with patients without acrimony or fear. Regular audits of quality of care should be made, as well as 'mortality/morbidity' meetings to learn from errors and avoid them. All this is, in fact, summarized in an ethics aphorism: 'placing the interest of the patient above all other considerations'.

Community Settings

> 'The people when rightly and fully trusted, return the trust'
> – Abraham Lincoln

In rural areas and community settings, health workers need appropriate training to become embedded in and engage with communities, understand the local needs and accurately promote health awareness. The vastness of India's cultural context and languages can be daunting, and acceptance of the health worker is the first challenge. This trust building exercise requires time and support in terms of funds and personnel. Unless there is sufficient outlay of funds for this purpose, at both the state and central level, for training and protection of health workers, these efforts will fall short. Further, health interventions must accompany other social and financial programmes to demonstrate government commitment to social development and holistic change.

Information and conversations about health promotion, disease and research is ongoing and needs to be multidirectional, promoting dialogue and feedback, and allowing dissent. Grass-roots engagement on health needs and preventive health can build a foundation of trust, on which health programmes can successfully be implemented. Health programmes should have scope for adaptation to local needs and culture, respectful of local choices and moving away from the top-down approach. Community advisory boards can help in interpreting policy, translating it in practical terms for the community and relaying feedback. Mindful of the value of subsidiarity, locally derived consensus and acceptance is invaluable in building lasting trust.

In the first decade of the millenium, the term social accountability came into use to describe an aspect of trust building that was relatively underplayed. Empowering communities to participate in self-determination of needs, review of public health interventions and their efficacy, providing feedback and engaging with health policies and health workers is an exercise in democratic processes and human rights. Community of Practitioners on Accountability and Social Action in Health (COPASAH) is an example of an initiative that encourages local communities to seek accountability in health action.[37]

Public Hospitals, Health Services and Health Schemes

> 'The health of people is the foundation upon which all their happiness and all their powers as a state depend.'
>
> – Benjamin Disraeli

Inevitably, the government is the largest health service provider in low- and middle-income countries. They are tasked with the mandate to provide health services and promote health and social development.[38] Article 14 of the UNESCO Universal Declaration on Bioethics and Human Rights also recognizes every person's right to enjoy the highest attainable standard of health. This includes (a) access to quality healthcare and essential medicines; (b) access to adequate nutrition and water, (c) improvement of living conditions and the environment, (d) elimination of the marginalization and the exclusion of persons on any grounds, and (e) reduction of poverty and illiteracy.[39]

In line with the principles of the Alma Ata Declaration of 1978, governments are entrusted to work towards universal health access and coverage, equity, community participation in defining and implementing health agendas and intersectional approaches to health.[40] With a better understanding of what is owed to citizens, public health policy and planning developed as a discipline over the last forty years.

In the early years of the millenium, the Millennium Development Goals and 'health for all' created a push for reforms in the health sector with the roll-out of the National Urban Health Mission and the National Rural Health Mission by the Ministry of Health and Family Welfare.[41] Today, the emphasis is on Sustainable Development Goals, but much has still to be done to include the traditionally marginalized, tribal groups and weaker sections in health protection and promotion schemes.[42] The Human Development Index of 2020 shows India at rank 131 out of 189 countries, having slipped two spots from 2018. In fact, there has been practically no improvement since 2014, when India still ranked 131.[43]

The government must not only aim to provide health services but must also appear to be visibly working towards this goal. This is an important facet of trust building, particularly with dependent populations. Announcement of health benefits and schemes must be backed by financial and resource commitments. Existing health structures, like health centres and hospitals, need to be maintained and upgraded, even expanded, where necessary, to serve growing populations. Inadequate infrastructure, crumbling edifices and absent personnel send the ominous message that people's health needs are not a priority, and the weakest will be at risk when resources are limited. This inequity and injustice is painfully felt in both rural and urban populations. The indignity and loss of trust is aggravated when precious resources are instead spent on image-building exercises, public extravaganzas and vote garnering.

Speaking truth to people in communities, patient groups, activists or a voter is central to building trust and lasting bonds. Information about resources, intention and interventions should be clear and consistent, provided in local languages and open to feedback. Even acknowledgement of uncertainty and confession of lapse can be powerful in public engagement and more likely to foster cooperation. The COVID-19 pandemic provided lessons in the importance of truth and transparency that will hopefully not be forgotten.

To promote trust, governments need to demand larger health budgets at both centre and state levels. This single act can transform the health sector and restore faith in governance. Primary healthcare facilities, health education and preventive health measures, and building resources and capacity are basic requirements. In addition, disease surveillance measures must not be imposed, but supported by communities. Focus on holistic care of communities and monitoring must include mental health, occupational health and environmental risks. A coherent and consistent health policy defined by and for the community is most likely to succeed and be trusted. A long and difficult path, the government can work through its health workers to bring participation in health decisions and health interventions, increasing the chances of success.

As described earlier, determinants of health play a crucial role, and public health interventions in the absence of these would be temporary and wasteful, as the source of disease and ill health is not addressed. Protection of the environment is another important duty that directly impacts public health, and current laws need to be strengthened and enforced to promote clean and wholesome ecological surroundings. Communities can be victims of the climate crisis and ecological damage caused by dams, flooding, deforestation, famine and migration. Inclusion and protection of populations in all planned ecological projects, sensitive to local concerns and engaged with local expertise, can build lasting trust and thriving populations.

Conclusion

'Trust is the highest form of human motivation. It brings out the very best in people.'

– Stephen Covey

Trust is an essential, fragile, yet powerful element running through social structures and human interactions. There is no aspect of healthcare that does not involve trust, whether it is human relationships, health systems or trustworthy institutions. The very nature of healthcare, its sensitivity, complexity and confidentiality requirements, demands trust to be placed in practitioners, hospitals and policymakers. Ethical and compassionate care that is inclusive and collaborative can foster trust in practitioners and health systems. As the largest provider of health in the country, government policymaking and public health interventions must emphasize trust building by including all sections of society in community engagement and sharing of health resources, reducing social and systemic injustices in health and supporting other aspects of social development.

Part III

Locating the 'Public' in Public Health

9

Regulating the Womb: Reproductive Health, Bodily Integrity and Autonomy in Contemporary India

Anindita Majumdar

Introduction

A significant part of the focus on reproduction within reproductive studies is on the uterus/womb. Here, I engage with the theme of the female reproductive body and the violence it faces in contemporary biomedicine. Such an exercise is undertaken by reflecting on the ways in which the uterus and its transformative potential is viewed within biomedicine and legal injunctions. I attempt a discussion on how the uterus is implicated in compromising women's bodily autonomy and privilege through three biomedical interventions: hysterectomies, obstetric violence during birthing, especially caesarean sections, and gestational surrogacy through in vitro fertilization (IVF). I am specifically intrigued by these three as they obfuscate the boundaries of ethical practice around the uterus/womb. The first is the normalization of hysterectomies;[1] second, is the rise in non-essential caesarean sections;[2] and third, the way the womb becomes property that is alienated from the body in commercial gestational surrogacy.[3]

These three sets of practices are especially provocative when seen together and from the vantage point of shifting notions of informed consent regarding bodily autonomy and integrity. Here, informed consent is not part of biomedical practice, instead stemming from socially entrenched ideas (dis)privileging certain wombs over others. 'Unwarranted' hysterectomies are sought by women battling poverty and competitive labour markets, where menstrual cycles and the associated pain can lead to the loss of livelihood.[4] Class and caste differences determine the 'choice' of caesarean sections and the ways in which they are administered in different public health settings.[5] And the disposable/extractable uterus becomes a 'womb' for economically disadvantaged women in order to become gestational surrogates for upper-class and upper-caste women.[6]

The ways in which the womb operates as a uterus and is considered disposable is evident in mass hysterectomies, undertaken often without consent and recourse to bodily autonomy. At the same time, the uterus is identified as a 'womb', the bearer of heirs in the practice of gestational surrogacy, and the legal wrangling over banning commercial surrogacy in favour of 'altruism'. Thus, in a situation where the state actively endorses and supports birth control, each birth becomes part of a larger machination towards control and disciplining the female reproductive self.[7]

Second, the form of care exposes the divide between the patient and her right to bodily integrity and choice within obstetrics and gynaecology. Thus, public–private healthcare in India operates differently, but is nonetheless complicit in usurping bodily autonomy. Whether through the use of assisted reproductive technologies like IVF that render the surrogate and her gestational labour insignificant; or by creating 'experimental' bodies[8] that provide the space for a subjective orientation towards seeking to be medicalized.[9] Under such regimes, women and men are happy to surrender bodily autonomy and privacy for the sake of livelihood,[10] or ideological belonging,[11] or because they are already expendable within state rhetoric, such as illegal migrants, refugees or those who are trafficked.

A significant part of the conversation in contemporary biomedical practice in obstetrics and gynaecology in India has been regarding ethics. Ethically, obstetrics and gynaecology continue to occupy a grey space – a legacy of the state-endorsed, foreign-funded programmes of family planning and population control. Sterilization of Indian women, especially in rural and semi-urban settings has rendered them vulnerable to medical extraction and exploitation in practices such as organ sale and trafficking, also known as being 'bioavailable'.[12] Bioavailability, according to Cohen, emerges from the quality of human bodies as being dispensable to the point that they are available for exploitation and 'extraction' by governments, and biomedical centres like clinics and hospitals – as well as racketeers and illegal organ traders. Thus, Cohen finds that a large number of women who were victims of kidney rackets in southern India had already been subjected to surgical infractions in the public health system through the sterilization procedure. This rendering of reproductive bodies as 'bioavailable' through surgical interventions was not only part of state agenda and promoted in obstetrics–gynaecology practice, but became an aspirational goal amongst the rural and urban poor women seeking to be citizens of a modern nation state.[13]

However, the tone and tenor of the patient–doctor relationship in Indian obstetrics and gynaecology are firmly entrenched in power relations[14] that give medical practitioners the dominant position. Thus, the obstetrician–gynaecologist in India is able to diagnose and make surgical interventions without necessarily seeking consent from the female patient. Consent is a complicated term within medical practice, bordering on ambiguous spaces. However, in the cases discussed with regard to hysterectomies, caesarean sections and commercial surrogacy in India, research suggests that social and economic contexts impact the ways and forms in which consent is sought.[15] Reproductive health in India has a legacy of being extractive especially often through mandated and compulsory practices of family planning. This may not seem to be 'coercive' or lacking in consent – but hide details of varied practices that may overlook minute yet essential processes within diagnosis and medication, which carry subtle shifts towards convincing patients to opt for surgeries that may not necessarily be required. Population rhetoric in India and elsewhere targets women belonging to marginalized communities unable to practise birth control due to multiple factors such as lack of access, intimate partner violence, socio-religious restrictions or chronic conditions. Here, informed consent is not part of biomedical practice, stemming from socially entrenched ideas privileging certain wombs over others.

It is important to note that throughout the forthcoming discussion, I am focusing on institutionalized barriers and systems, such as medicine and law, in how the uterus/womb is constructed through an extensive literature review of systemic changes within obstetrics and gynaecology in India. Unfortunately, I do not engage with lived experiences of women undergoing these forms of reproductive violence and reproductive interventions.

The Dispensable Uterus: The Normalization of Hysterectomies

Hysterectomies are emerging as new forms of invasive technologies that women in rural India are turning to, or being forced to embark upon, in order to avoid being rendered unemployable due to their reproductive exigencies. Agrarian labour, with its seasonal requirements and the precariousness of migrant indentured labour, leads women agrarian workers to make contrarian choices. This is further exacerbated in public health reportage on how 'unwarranted hysterectomies[16] are part' of the emerging new landscape of reproductive violence against women belonging to disenfranchised sections of society. Poverty, unemployment and the demands of an agrarian capitalist market have insidiously entered the lives of women working in these fields.

In the study of hysterectomies, the language of a redundant womb/uterus seems to preoccupy discussions on 'unnecessary' extractive surgeries.[17] Essentially, in the West a majority of hysterectomies have been identified as unnecessary, raising questions regarding bioethical standardization in women's healthcare globally. In India, hysterectomies have been increasingly found to be deeply problematic, raising questions regarding consent and women's bodily autonomy and privacy. Reportedly, in India, studies suggest estimated hysterectomy surgeries are between 1.7 and 9.8 per cent.[18]

According to Desai et al. (2017), '[P]roviders ... viewed hysterectomies as a one-time cure for menstrual problems, cysts, fibroids and other gynaecological ailments for rural, low-income women'.[19] These findings are echoed in Towghi's research amongst women belonging to resource-poor settings such as Balochistan in Pakistan.[20] Such findings implicate practitioners in particular forms of socio-economic appraisals of patients that are often divorced from the actual diagnosis.[21]

Normalization of hysterectomies is an idea that suggests the entrenchment of biomedical diagnosis and routinization in the ways in which the female body is objectified. Both Towghi and Desai et al. (2011) reiterate that normalization of hysterectomies becomes the first line of treatment – surgical intervention – and eventually something that women may seek out in treatment. Thus, rural agricultural workers in India may approach private health practitioners to overcome menstrual pain and fibroids or other debilitating gynaecological issues and agree to hysterectomies to be able to arrive at a more permanent solution to be able to work. This normalization occurs mostly for those who belong to a rural milieu, and is repeatedly performed by medical practitioners in response to what Towghi calls a form of 'social triage for rural women'.[22]

This 'social triage' follows doctors and medical practitioners identifying hysterectomies as the 'best medical decision'[23]– largely influenced by 'women's demographic characteristics such as race, education and socioeconomic [sic] status and insurance status, as well as their physician's gender, training and geographical location'.[24] The academic research into hysterectomies and their recurrence suggests the ways in which, ethically, biomedical interventions occupy questionable spaces. Through the narratives and discussions of doctor–patient interactions in cases of hysterectomies, it is evident that the practice has been subject to ethical scrutiny for long, especially in terms of the ambiguity related to patient consent. A legacy of interventionist sterilization surgeries, the uterus comes to be imagined in hysterectomies as both redundant and dangerous. According to Towghi, such a perception discounts the ways in which women experience their reproductive bodies, reordering them into 'objects' of medical scrutiny and intervention.

Hysterectomies have occupied a chequered terrain in India's medico-political history. As mentioned earlier, the legacy of sterilizations and tubectomies in India's public health practices has a major role to play in how current practices of invasive surgeries that eliminate reproductive potentiality, such as hysterectomies, have come to become dominant forms of reproductive interventions. Rajeswari Sundar Rajan identified the unwarranted mass hysterectomies undertaken on inmates of a state-funded mental health institution in Mumbai in the early 1990s, without their consent, as one of the 'scandals of the state'.[25] The hysterectomies were carried out on women aged between thirteen and thirty-seven years, who were inmates of the facility based on certain medical diagnosis of their mental capabilities, ostensibly to facilitate better care of these women. The caretakers and doctors of the institute maintained that due to their diminished capabilities, 'these young women could not cope with the normal periodically occurring physiological process – menstruation'.[26] Institutionalized medical procedures without consent in spaces such as asylums and prisons continue to be framed as time-saving and 'accepted practice' – but border on the infringement of fundamental human rights.

At the same time, Desai et al. (2011) have also found a damaging nexus between hysterectomies and public insurance amongst women associated with the autonomous women's collective SEWA in Gujarat, as insurance claims come to be largely placed for these surgeries. Rao and Pungaliya highlight the issues that emerged from this encounter in public debates on autonomy and reproductive rights: '(a) The issue of social ethics; (b) the practical problem of physical hygiene and health of the MH [mentally handicapped] in the specific context of menstruation; (c) the issue of social dignity of the MH; (d) consideration for the difficulties and trauma faced by caretakers, with specific focus on parents and/or the families; (e) the right of decision-making on behalf of the MH (the personal vs public issue); (f) sexual abuse and pregnancy related problems ...'[27] These concerns still mark women's engagement with institutionalized public and private healthcare. The exacerbation of the loss of autonomy and choice is clearly evident in the ways in which women who are especially vulnerable, like the inmates of the mental health institution in Mumbai, or incarcerated prisoners, or women belonging to disenfranchised economic and social groups, are subject to extractive surgeries like hysterectomies.

In emerging research and reportage on rural agrarian workers in Maharashtra, rising hysterectomies are a sign of seeking to retain employment in a highly agrarian labour market where a few days off can lead to unemployment and hunger.[28] In Beed district of Maharashtra, many migrant agricultural women labourers working on sugar cane farms lose work if they take time off during menstruation. The labour-intensive, demand-driven sugar cane cutting season requires constant presence, pushing several women labourers to opt for private health practitioners to conduct unnecessary hysterectomies. As Gopinathan suggests, many women in Maharashtra are 'womb-less', especially in rural areas, due to the ways in which unregulated medical intervention has led many women to hysterectomies without proper diagnosis, and often under duress.[29] Chatterjee suggests that close to 4,605 hysterectomies have been conducted in Beed district alone between 2016–19. An unscrupulous private healthcare sector, supported by a lack of laws and equally exploitative sugarcane factory workers, has precipitated the crisis in hysterectomies,[30] which are akin to other forms of gender-based violence.

Obstetric Violence and the Biomedicalization of the Womb

Thus, in thinking through forms of interventionist biomedical imaginings around the uterus, the conceptualization of 'local biologies'[31] is important. By 'biomedicalization' I am specifically asking the following question: How are local biologies implicated in biomedical practice and diagnosis that tend to follow larger social valuations regarding the body? In Lock's work, this is seen through the conflict between Western biomedical definitions of the female reproductive body and the lifeworlds of Japanese women. However, in cultural contexts where biomedicine subsumes – and upholds patriarchal notions of propriety and femininity – the notion of local biologies becomes complicit with a different kind of institutionalized violence.[32] Within Indian obstetric and gynaecological practice, social valuations hamper treatment and diagnosis and the exercise of choice – evident in the practices mentioned.

The state has been part of the reproductive body since Independence through its wide-ranging population control/family planning procedures.[33] Women have sought to refashion themselves as 'modern citizens', and render themselves into 'targets' for mass family planning interventions in the past few decades of engagement with population control in India. However, the increasing biomedical intervention through family planning clinics and compulsory hospital birthing has led to an emerging crisis of high numbers of births through caesarean section. Many women are seeking to opt for caesarean section as a lifestyle choice, and not as an emergency measure. State intervention in highlighting this rising trend in hospital birthing has led to a re-engagement with 'normal birthing', and other forms of practices that encourage natural birthing amongst women.

In a discussion regarding the maternal death register or MDR, Gutschow[34] suggests that Indian healthcare practitioners and the law are deeply complicit in a culture of hiding or euphemizing maternal mortality even in the process of unearthing irregularities in providing care. This continues to be a damning indictment after decades of community and state involvement in ensuring lower levels of maternal mortality. Most importantly, Gutschow finds that as part of the process of seeking to examine how and why a woman dies during childbirth or due to labour-related complications, there is more than negligence involved on the part of public health providers – there is often a form of systemic violence that marks these unfortunate deaths.

Labour room violence, also known as obstetric violence includes, '[p]oor quality of care … disrespectful and abusive care, patient-blaming, purposeful neglect, verbal or physical abuse, disregard for traditional beliefs and the non-use of indigenous languages for patient communication'.[35] Scholars such as Dána-Ain Davis have specifically linked such obstetric violence to a form of 'obstetric racism' that is often seen to occur amongst women of colour in the United States.[36] Thus, Black, Native Indian and Hispanic women are more likely to undergo different forms of obstetric violence in public and private healthcare systems, often irrespective of class or educational background. In India, Gutschow finds this form of violence as endemic amongst women belonging to the scheduled caste and scheduled tribe communities, or those who are economically disadvantaged and unable to access better healthcare.[37]

In this section of the chapter, I examine the ways in which obstetric violence comes to adversely impact the woman's reproductive body through a rise in caesarean sections. I suggest that rising non-essential c-sections in Indian private healthcare services are another form of obstetric violence. The ways in which these rising numbers are explained is through the rhetoric of 'choice' – an oft-repeated trope used to justify increasing biomedicalization and intrusive reproductive technologies.

Births through caesarean section rose from 20 per cent in 2015–16 to 25.4 per cent in 2019–20, and the states that show a steady increase include Telangana, West Bengal, Himachal Pradesh and some states in the north-east.[38] Ghosh and James have been pointing to a steady rise in numbers since NFHS 3 – 10.2 per cent in NFHS 3 (2005–06) from NFHS 2 (1998–99) when it was 7.1 per cent. Some states in India reflect a considerable increase, with Kerala showing the highest number of caesarean section deliveries at 30.1 per cent, followed by Andhra Pradesh at 27.5 per cent and Goa at an alarming 25.5 per cent.[39] In NFHS 4 (2015–16), institutional caesarean deliveries across India had risen to 17.2 per cent, being more than twice as high in urban areas (28.3 per cent) than in rural areas (12.9 per cent).[40]

Ideally, according to the WHO, the permissible number of caesarean sections should range between 5 and 15 per cent of the total population group.[41] The most common form of c-section in India today is the LSCS or lower segment caesarean section, undertaken by 'making a transverse cut in the peritoneum over the lower segment of the uterus'.[42] So, what's wrong with having more c-sections? The reasons for emergency sections range from lack of availability of beds, unavailability or busy schedules of surgeons and doctors, and higher costs involved in conducting c-sections as opposed to normal deliveries, especially in private healthcare facilities.

The impact of unnecessary c-sections is felt on the post-partum health of many women. Those interviewed by Muzaffar and Akram included cases of pus, abdominal pain and fever. But most importantly, the authors note that the surgical intervention had an impact on how women saw themselves and their bodies. The c-section added to the increased surveillance and medicalization of women and their bodies, and also the related undermining of midwives and their knowledge by institutionalized biomedicine.[43]

The linkages with reproductive choice, though provocative, do not necessarily explain the rising cases of c-sections. The suggestion that women, especially those in urban areas, choose c-sections to avoid labour pains, or what is identified through the expression as 'too posh to push',[44] is not as common. Yet, the dynamic of '[w]omen's request for caesarean sections is considered to be an important determinant of birth outcomes, particularly in countries with growing privatization and options for patient choice',[45] cannot be discounted either. That c-sections occur more in the private healthcare industry again brings into focus the failure of public health infrastructure, and the continued medicalization of women's bodies. Private hospitals are able to advertise c-sections as 'women's choice' only amongst those who can afford to make such choices and decisions. Thus, Ghosh and James suggest, 'It is often argued that the power of decision-making in the home and seeking medicalized healthcare are associated with higher maternal education and family incomes.'[46]

But the c-section is also a reminder that the surgeon-doctor holds more power in the patient–doctor dynamic.[47] This power is what has been the source of unwarranted hysterectomies (as discussed earlier), and continues to be the source of obstetric violence across the globe. The institutionalization of the c-section is often orchestrated through a dominant voice and intervention of the surgeon. This may often be undertaken without the tacit or open approval of the birthing woman.

In a detailed study of the kinds of obstetric violence birthing women suffer in north-east India, authors Chattopadhyay et al. identify problematic, biased and insensitive medical training, along with social prejudices, as affecting doctor–patient interactions. They found that episiotomies[48] had become the norm in normal deliveries in many health facilities, especially public ones, where the doctor tended to normalize, or even criticize the articulation of labour pains amongst birthing women. Thus, 'too much screaming', or complaining about birthing practices are not taken kindly by the doctors supervising birthing.[49] There is an overt attempt at disciplining by the doctors and nurses attending the birth, and facilitating it through repeated verbal abuse and humiliation. Many of the doctors actively provide justification for their behaviour by blaming the birthing mother and her background or community practices.[50] Thus, 'the medical construction of what is "risky", in fact, has the impact of normalizing obstetric violence, by not categorizing those very procedures as violent or as iatrogenic practices'.[51] Iatrogenic practices are related to side effects of drugs and other medication, or medical treatment.

And, again, such behaviour may be exacerbated depending on the kind of healthcare being accessed, and the socio-economic background of the birthing woman.[52] Medical practice in India, and globally, continues to mark the woman as an object, and her body as a disciplinary space.[53] But the disciplining is undertaken primarily through markers of social valuation, such as virginity and sexual virtue[54] – which may again be based on socio-economic stereotypes.

Ban or No Ban? The Missing Conversation in Surrogacy Regulation

Since 2005 the Indian state has been deliberating on a suitable law to regulate the practice of commercial surrogacy in India. Despite multiple draft versions, the Assisted Reproductive Technologies (Regulation) Bill remained in the making for too long. However, the proliferation of assisted reproductive technologies (ARTs) such as IVF grew exponentially, especially in relation to the global procreative tourism industry, of which commercial gestational surrogacy is an important part. Concerns regarding the treatment of Indian women belonging to a lower socio-economic group who incubate artificially fertilized embryos belonging to foreign and Indian commissioning couples were a major part of the deliberations on surrogacy regulation. Because commercial surrogacy stands at the cusp of issues that are both intimate and yet have larger social ramifications, any form of regulation leads to endless debates on commodification, technological interventions, family, child rights, kinship and identity. At the same time, commercial surrogacy in India has been mired in accusations of human rights violations and the creation of stateless citizenry. In the absence of any form of legislation, the clamour for stringent legal guidelines kept growing. But who deliberates and directs the public discourse on surrogacy – besides the media and the state?

The Surrogacy (Regulation) Bill, 2016, was unveiled to much public criticism and scrutiny on 24 August 2016. While press releases provoked questions regarding the efficacy of the bill, the medical community went into overdrive appealing against a bill that would effectively end a supposedly Rs 3000-crore industry. The government had suggested a ban on commercial surrogacy and advocated altruistic surrogacy for heterosexual, married, infertile couples who were unable to have a child for five years, having exhausted all aspects of assisted reproductive technologies in their desire to have a biological child. The ban on commercial surrogacy also meant an effective ban on two sets of intended/commissioning parents: those based on citizenship, and those based on sexual, marital status. This meant that foreigners, persons of Indian origin, overseas citizens of India and non-resident Indians would be prohibited from contracting a surrogacy arrangement, along with gay couples, single individuals and live-in couples. They would also be also excluded from participating in an altruistic surrogacy arrangement in India.

What is particularly provocative in this conversation is the way in which surrogacy is being positioned in conversation with larger stories and critiques of childlessness, exploitation and prohibitory mechanisms of the state. Of importance is the way in which the draft surrogacy law came to inhabit a form of legal formulation that signalled the active role of the state in the regulation of the intimate life of its citizenry.

In this part I examine some of the modalities of the surrogacy bill, which has now become a law, from the purview of what it means for larger social questions of exploitation, empowerment, human rights and commoditization of the human body.

Commercial surrogacy has been a part of the draft legislation on assisted reproductive technologies since 2008. There was good reason for its inclusion within this draft law as it provided linkages to how contemporary commercial surrogacy includes the active intervention of ARTs to provide a completely asexual involvement. In-vitro fertilization is in practice both in commercial and altruistic surrogacy arrangements, excluding only traditional surrogacy arrangements where the sexual relationship between the intended father and the surrogate precludes the use of any technological intervention.

The Surrogacy (Regulation) Bill, 2016, created a conversation that excluded the technology and invoked a form of existence primarily marked by commerce. In effect, the concerns raised against the draft ART (Regulation) Bill by Sama and other researchers and academicians went unanswered in the rendering of the arrangement as a transaction of birthing rather than one that involves massive technological intrusions.[55] Many of the concerns raised by the bill were articulated in relation to previous legislation as well, and continue to mark current engagement.

This form of myopia has also marked research on surrogacy wherein the concerns and connection with the IVF technology and its practitioners are usually rather feeble. Thus, in articulating the concerns of the surrogate, her refashioning into an 'automaton' is perhaps fully explored by Sama and Kalindi Vora.[56] Others delve into the exploitation of the surrogate by the nexus of the clinic and agents.[57] This is interesting considering that the technology exists in all recent research on surrogacy as a background to the real machinations of the arrangement.

Thus, elements of the arrangement, such as the surrogacy hostel where surrogates are housed for the period of nine months or the hiring of the surrogate by gay couples, do not provoke the question of the technology involved, which leads to the development of social configurations and arrangements. This is significant, considering the absence of a conversation on ARTs in relation to commercial surrogacy in the bill.

In defining the surrogate and the commissioning couples, the language of medicine and diagnosis was always particularly relevant in draft regulation by the Indian Council of Medical Research (ICMR). The positioning of infertility as a 'disease' meant that the desire to participate in a surrogacy arrangement required medical validation for both the surrogate and the couple. They had to subject themselves to the medical practitioner and the ways in which the medical community constructed the arrangement and its modalities.

The sudden divorce from its technological moorings in the new regulation also means that the practice of surrogacy is now being brought into the realm of completely moral conversation, wherein the amoral technology has to be removed to invoke a ban. The missing technology is now akin to the missing surrogate in the draft ICMR Bill, to give credence to one form of discourse over the other. In a way, the Surrogacy Bill wished to position the surrogacy arrangement as a form of intimate sexual encounter that may only be enacted amongst kin.

The conversation on the ban on surrogacy is primarily consumed with its linkages to commerce. The act of 'hiring' and 'renting' one's body has always led to questions regarding ethics and morality. Here, the sacrosanct position that motherhood occupies within social discourse becomes associated with the idea of commerce, leading to Vivianna Zelizer's conceptualization of 'hostile worlds'.[58] The hostile worlds of intimacy and commerce threaten socially mandated relationships, wherein the power hierarchy of gender, class and race become convoluted and need to be protected.

Take, for instance, the erstwhile, albeit influential, draft ART (Regulation) Bill of 2010, which identified payment as 'compensation' to the surrogate for the services rendered. Thus, it mentioned that the couple hiring the surrogate should bear the expenses incurred in the arrangement, including medicine, hospital visits and insurance. The contours of the compensation identified costs linked to the 'treatment' or the use of the technology and the kind of medical intervention that the doctor provides – but none regarding the labour that the surrogate undertakes. In many ways, the surrogate is subsumed within the technology and seen as an appendage to the miraculous 'cure' rendered by the ARTs. Such a representation has a dual purpose: first, the delineation of surrogacy from its discomfiting commercial linkages, and second, the focus on technological prowess, giving the medical practitioner more power and control over the arrangement and its monetary modalities.

The way in which a 'ban' is envisioned, interestingly, involves the invocation of bodily integrity. In countries such as Germany, France and Sweden, among others where surrogacy is banned in its entirety, the idea of the body has different forms of legal and cultural meanings. In France the human body is indissoluble, making it impossible for it to be broken down and bartered – thereby making both organ donation and surrogacy impermissible by law. In Sweden, the maternal body is 'whole', especially in its gestational role. The woman who carries the child for nine months in her womb is always the mother. Egg donation may be possible but in case of surrogacy, the surrogate is the mother and, therefore, the commercial exchange of a child is a morally problematic concept. In Germany, Spain and the UK (altruistic surrogacy is allowed in the UK), similar concerns regarding the maternal body determine questions of banning the practice.

In India, the Surrogacy Bill of 2016 was particular in this regard: the primary contours of the bill sought to first separate it from the legislative proposals on ART in an important signal to the state's changed stance towards surrogacy. It is important to understand that the ways in which surrogacy came to be understood in the bill necessitated its ban. Thus, the discourse surrounding the bill positioned commercial surrogacy as an exploitative practice that rendered Indian women as subjects of economic exploitation, especially by foreigners. The bill identified the commercial hiring of surrogates as a morally reprehensible act, similar to the laws prevalent in Germany and Scandinavia which position motherhood as absolute. However, there is an important difference here – the identification of the 'womb for rent' becomes the problematic trope for commercial surrogacy. Not only is motherhood threatened, the repository of the family's line and descent is also invaded in the representation of the womb as commercially exchangeable. This is particularly seen in the way in which altruistic surrogacy is endorsed as the only viable form of engaging a surrogate.

While critics such as Mohan Rao suggest that commercial surrogacy is another form of reproductive slavery involving the abuse and exploitation of women belonging to disenfranchised groups by richer women, his support of altruistic surrogacy and ban on commercial surrogacy leads me to think about altruism itself.[59] Altruistic surrogacy, in the way in which it is practised in India, involves kin seeking support from the female members to help fulfil the role of a surrogate. Thus, altruism promises not only the euphemization of commerce, compensation and renting, but hopes that the patriarchal family will control the reproductive potential of its wives by outsourcing their uteruses as a potential fields for gestation to childless family members. The Surrogacy Bill of 2016, in many ways, was proposal regarding the acceptable contours of the Indian family.

As of August 2017, the department-related parliamentary committee on health and family welfare had extensive discussions on the suggested Surrogacy Bill of 2016, recommending important amendments. The Surrogacy (Regulation) Act, 2021, that has now been adopted is a 'breakaway' from the ARTs Bill of 2015, signalling the state's desire to ban commercial surrogacy altogether. At the same time, proposals for the regulation of ARTs have now taken the shape of a legislation called the Assisted Reproductive Technology (Regulation) Act, 2021.

The 102nd Report of the Parliamentary Standing Committee (PSC) was released in August 2017 and involved discussions of all stakeholders, on the Surrogacy Bill of 2016.[60] Civil society participants, government ministries, IVF specialists, gynaecology and obstetrics society, surrogacy lawyers, commissioning couples and surrogates were part of the deliberations. Briefly, the PSC recommended a re-engagement with surrogacy in terms of altruism, commercialization, compensation and access.

The report made an important intervention by questioning the meaning of an 'altruistic' surrogacy arrangement by stating two important issues. One, altruism involves payment for the IVF procedure, medicine and nutrition – however, denying the surrogate her compensation for her reproductive labour is unfair. The PSC was in favour of developing a compensatory surrogacy system that aimed to provide healthcare and compensation to surrogates. Second, the dependence on kin to volunteer for an altruistic surrogacy arrangement was fraught with issues of familial coercion and stigma associated with infertility. The PSC was unsure of whether the infertile couple would be willing to share their infertility with their family, and in a situation of increasing small, nuclear families, whether the kin would be willing to undertake a pregnancy to later relinquish the child.

The suggestion to look at a compensatory mode for surrogacy in India meant, more importantly, that the surrogate would be equitable, she would be provided with insurance, and her post-delivery health would be monitored for up to three months. Such suggestions aimed to move away from a commercialized, industry model of surrogacy in India, recommending a more even-handed arrangement for all concerned, especially the child and the surrogate.

The PSC also noted that access to surrogacy in India, though open to Indian citizens, cannot be discriminatory to unmarried couples (as legally live-in couples are identified as legitimate), single individuals and foreigners. This also meant that the parameters for opting for surrogacy were to be made more stringent, with five years of medically proven infertility after marriage – and the advice to promote adoption before surrogacy as a viable option. This meant that the PSC was also inclined to be critical of surrogacy as an option to earn a living out of poverty, in turn suggesting to the National Commission of Women to encourage vocational training and job creation amongst women belonging to a lower socio-economic category.

Conclusion

In this chapter, the 'womb' is represented through its symbolic value within law, labour and larger conversations on women's health. The focus is on three particular practices in contemporary biomedicine that have led to repeated questions of bodily integrity and autonomy for women in India. Thus, gestational surrogacy, hysterectomies and caesarean sections compromise the ways in which the 'womb' or the uterus has come to mark women and women's reproductive health in the continuing zeal for population control.

I engage in literature review and analysis of contemporary ethnographic and policy documents to reflect upon the ways in which the womb is complicit in medico-social interventions and evaluations of value and worth. The dynamism of the womb as symbolic biocapital is constantly brought to the fore in legislation that is centred on controlling it, and extracting it from the women's bodily choice and autonomy – in the process rendering women themselves into an organ.[61]

The intersection of caste, class and religion continues to mark the engagement between bodily integrity and biomedical and technological interventions into the reproductive body. This is the primary focus. Technological interventions continue to extract the womb from the larger reproductive body and the woman in a process of extraction and invasion. In the process, reproductive autonomy and bodily integrity may be severely compromised. In this chapter, I brought together different strands of research on the value of women's reproductive bodies within contemporary biomedical practice, in order to highlight the 'unnecessariness' of surgical interventions, and the normalization of abuse and violence within obstetric and gynaecological practices in India.

10

Confidentiality and HIV/AIDS: The Need for Humaneness and Precision in the Law

Vivek Divan and Shivangi Rai

Introduction: A Not-So-Hypothetical Situation

IMAGINE a virus that is afflicting humankind, and is known to be transmitted largely through unsafe sexual intercourse. There is great stigma that swirls around this condition. Rigid and uninformed ideas around sex and sexuality pervade the discourse. It is difficult to have honest conversations on these issues whether they be within the family, community or society at large.

Yet the virus must be dealt with, thwarted at the very least. Its unfettered spread has ramifications which are dire – and it has resulted in the annihilation of significant sections of society. Science has not found a cure for the disease; reason and rationality have not been able to penetrate the prejudice that surrounds it.

The policy response is that of panic and repression while the need is to publicly identify those who are afflicted and isolate them so that they cannot infect the uninfected. Directives stipulate that any healthcare worker who encounters a case with this condition must inform the person's family members of the individual's health status. Further, the local health administration must be informed about such a case, including the person's name, address and contact information. Both the concerned healthcare worker and the local administration are expected to identify the sexual partner of the infected person and inform that person too. The local administration is then to take the infected person and place them in isolation.

Now imagine falling sick with this virus or suspecting you may have it due to recent sexual behaviour or symptoms that are manifesting as a result of possible exposure. Would you seek out healthcare knowing that your health status will be revealed potentially to the world (and that you will be isolated)? Or will you try and deal with your condition by self-medicating or seeking spurious solutions? Will you seek authentic health advice from a system that you do not trust in keeping your health status confidential, or will you continue living in denial, and avoid vital behaviour change such as practising safe sex?

Much of the above was the approach through which HIV/AIDS was thought best to be dealt with – a response that identified people by revealing their health status to others so that they could be isolated and their behaviour curbed.[1] In some parts of the world punitive approaches are still viewed as the prescription to curb HIV/AIDS.[2] For example, in the USA 'HIV exposure' laws exist in a vast majority of states, where sexual intercourse using condom by a person living with HIV without disclosing their status is illegal. These laws fail to account for factors that affect actual transmission risk, such as condom use or adherence to antiretroviral therapy. Hundreds of arrests and prosecutions have taken place under these laws, and information points to these laws being enforced mostly against marginalized populations, including people of colour and sex workers. Yet, there is no evidence that these laws reduce HIV transmission or make people more likely to disclose their sero-status or get tested.[3] Of note is the issue of criminalization of the vulnerable. Many persons who are most vulnerable to HIV come from communities that are criminalized by the law – sex workers, men who have sex with men, people who use drugs, transgender people. As pointed out by the Global Commission on HIV and the Law, in Africa and the Caribbean where gay sex is criminalized, HIV among men who have sex with men is far more common than where criminalization is absent and people do not live under the oppressive punitive laws.[4] Where a rights-based approach to HIV/AIDS has been ensured – where a person's rights are assured and respected – it has led to the reaffirmation of rights and contributed to a public health approach that is inclusive and encourages health-seeking behaviour.[5]

One of the more remarkable instances of a successful rights-based approach has occurred in Sonagachi, Kolkata, through the work of the Durbar Mahila Samanway Committee (DMSC) and its self-regulatory boards (SRBs). This seminal HIV prevention initiative was founded on the notion that sex workers themselves are best placed to serve their community's needs through a rights-based approach that empowers and actively involves them in health efforts. It led to the sex work community engaging in solving a host of health and social challenges, including sexual health, violence, trafficking, lack of education and discrimination. Their ability to collectivize and demand rights led to extraordinary health and social benefits. In fifteen years, condom use in the brothel increased from less than 3 to 87 per cent, syphilis rates reduced from 25–30 per cent to less than 1 per cent, and HIV prevalence stabilized at 5 per cent as against rates of over 50 per cent in other Indian metropolises. Moreover, the SRBs regulated entry into sex work, identified abuses and responded when force or presence of underage females in the sex industry was suspected. These efforts saw the proportion of minors in sex work in Sonagachi brothel reduce from 25 per cent to 2 per cent between 1992 and 2011 and the median age of sex workers increasing from twenty-two to twenty-eight years.[6]

The AIDS Paradox

When HIV first started being understood in the early 1980s – as a virus that was most visibly seen spreading in sexually active gay men in the urban West – government reactions were of phobia and apathy. After all, these marginalized communities were of little political value, to be derided or relegated beyond the margins. Once it became clear that HIV and AIDS were as destructive within heterosexual contexts, attention began to increase in seeking ways to control it. Legislators and public health administrators joined the fray in propagating means that were punitive to stem the spread of infection. They believed that coercive approaches – which comprised forced testing, public identification and isolation of the HIV-positive persons – were the only way to restrict the spread of the virus. In India, this became apparent when Goa amended its Public Health Act in 1987.[7] This law required forced testing of anyone suspected of HIV and their immediate isolation.[8] When Dominic D'Souza was incarcerated under this law, he challenged this action as violative of his fundamental rights.[9] While he was eventually released and became a trailblazing champion of the rights of people living with HIV,[10] the Act continues on the books today, a vestige of ill-conceived law-making and a retrograde past.

What changed to make the Goa law dissonant with understandings of how to tackle HIV was the evolution of a critical understanding that coercive approaches were not serving public health imperatives to control its spread. It was Jonathan Mann, the physician, epidemiologist and pioneering head of the WHO's Global Programme on AIDS, who first highlighted a crucial reality: HIV was spreading most in communities of people who were the least empowered in relation to their social status.[11] Women in Africa, women of colour and gay men in North America were the most affected. Mann argued that AIDS was not just a medical condition but a social disease finding fertile ground amidst oppression, gender inequality, economic marginalization and violence. It could only be effectively addressed if the people most affected were buttressed with an assurance of their human rights.[12] Imposing a policy approach that punished them further was not the way in which to draw them towards health-seeking behaviour. Instead, punishment would further fuel the stigma that was extant.[13]

Another leading voice in the HIV movement, Justice Michael Kirby of Australia put it most eloquently. In order to effectively control HIV's spread, it was necessary to respect and protect the rights of those who were most vulnerable to it.¹⁴ This was the AIDS paradox – it was not the intuitive approach of isolation and repression that would prevent the spread of HIV, but the opposite, one of empowerment and the protection of rights of the marginalized. Implicit in this was the conviction that the protection of human rights of those afflicted (people living with HIV) or vulnerable (gay or bisexual men, transgender people, women, sex workers or people who used drugs) was sacrosanct in and of itself. Added to this assurance of human rights was the benefit served to public health imperatives of disease control. While coercive, isolationist strategies push people away from health systems, rights protections and guarantees inculcate health-seeking behaviour and engagement with health services and accurate information. When persons are confident of a system that will not shun them, but respect them and their needs, and support their priorities, they will engage with that system in order to obtain benefits from it. The system will augment its effectiveness in delivering what it is meant to. In the case of health institutions of various kinds – public or private hospitals, clinics, counselling facilities, pathology laboratories, or primary health centres – when they provide empathetic, de-stigmatizing and empowering services embedded in the sharing of accurate health information and health advice, they ensure that people at risk of HIV, those exposed to it or those living with it, access their services, seek their advice and work towards modifying their behaviours so that they and others are protected. Such an approach of empowerment includes the assurance of non-discrimination, respect for bodily integrity and autonomy (through obtaining informed consent before testing along with robust counselling services), and the protection of confidential health information.

Going back to the hypothetical (but very real) situation described above, amongst other things, the assurance of confidentiality of HIV status is critical to a successful public health approach. Knowing that the clinic, physician or healthcare worker is not going to reveal a person's health status instils trust that one can access such health services. At the same time, through non-judgemental and vital counselling services one is encouraged to share one's HIV status to sexual partners in order to protect others. Indeed, there are critical lessons to be gleaned from the adoption of a rights-based approach in the HIV response, which can benefit public health at large, including current challenges such as the COVID-19 pandemic. Fundamental to this is putting to the forefront the needs of the most vulnerable in any public health strategy, and treating these communities as allies and partners who can offer solutions and be strengthened with accurate, relatable, de-stigmatizing, evidence-based and easily available information and services, and the rights to avail these.[15] Equity within and between countries so that all people, irrespective of their financial or geographic locations, are able to access health goods is also essential to a rights-based approach.[16] In the long term, it is critical for health policy to address the social determinants of health, so that the underlying vulnerabilities that cause health setbacks are mitigated. To wholeheartedly engage on this, delivering on a multitude of rights is essential.[17]

Confidentiality and the HIV Response

Confidentiality is rooted in the fundamental rights guarantees in the Indian Constitution. Article 21 protects persons from state action that infringes the right to life and liberty, except as authorized by law. This right to personal liberty has been interpreted to include the right to privacy. The Supreme Court has vigorously articulated the right to privacy as contained in Article 21 in the judgment on *Justice K.S. Puttaswamy v. Union of India*.[18] While doing so, it has noted that the concept of confidentiality is related and derives from the fundamental right of privacy.

Confidentiality of information arises in fiduciary relationships. These are relationships that are inherently imbalanced, where one person is given information by another that would otherwise not be shared, but is revealed to them only because of the particular skill that they possess. Examples of such relationships would be doctors vis-à-vis patients, or lawyers and clients.[19] The notion of confidentiality developed as a legal principle over time, through judicial pronouncements and in various contexts unrelated to HIV.[20] These articulations fine-tuned the understandings of medical confidentiality and informed approaches that were then reflected in HIV-related laws and policies.

Much documentation and research demonstrated that non-consensual disclosure of HIV-positive status resulted in discrimination in the form of denial of work or medical services and social stigmatization.[21] Such disclosure led to extreme and tragic outcomes – from violent death to inhumane isolation, callous neglect and expulsion from schools.[22]

Early in the AIDS epidemic, the issue of confidentiality of HIV status came to be tested in the English courts. In the case of *X v. Y*,[23] information that named two practising doctors as being HIV-positive was provided to a newspaper. Despite the newspaper being restrained by the court from publishing this information, it went ahead and published it without names. To prevent any further revelation, an injunction was sought against publishing of the physicians' names. The court recognized that there were two competing interests – of confidentiality of hospital records and of press freedom. In barring publication of the doctor's names, it held that the former interest outweighed the latter. It noted: 'In the long run, preservation of confidentiality is the only way of securing public health; otherwise doctors will be discredited as a source of education, for future individual patients "will not come forward if doctors are going to squeal on them".'[24]

In doing so it articulated a vital understanding of the value of confidentiality of health information. While such an assurance undoubtedly served the individual interest, confidentiality of HIV status was also seen to serve *public* interest – of fostering and maintaining belief in the health system by society, so that the public is encouraged to access crucial (often life-saving) health-seeking information and services, instead of shying away from them due to concerns that their health status may be publicized. Indeed, public interest is not served if persons know that their HIV-positive status will be revealed if they access the health system, frightening them away from it, pushing epidemics like HIV underground – disappearing them – where effective interventions to control it become even more challenging.

The notions of privacy and confidentiality are well recognized in medical practice. The Hippocratic oath (revised and modernized) states that a physician *'will respect the privacy of my patients, for their problems are not disclosed to me that the world may know'*.[25] The Indian Medical Council (Professional Conduct, Etiquette and Ethics) Regulations, 2002, which govern medical practice in India, state that a doctor shall not disclose confidential information of the patient except if required by law, or when the doctor believes that a 'duty to society requires him to employ knowledge, obtained through confidence as a physician, to protect a healthy person against a communicable disease to which he is about to be exposed. In such instance, the physician should act as he would wish another to act toward one of his own family in like circumstances'.[26] In relation to HIV, the National AIDS Control Programme recognized the protection of confidentiality as crucial to an effective response to the epidemic.[27] As described later, more recently Indian legislation has clearly articulated the assurance of confidentiality of HIV status. Internationally, confidentiality is also recognized in international instruments as central to both the human rights framework[28] and to the HIV/AIDS response.[29]

Disclosure of HIV Status

In a short-lived move that was contrary to rights-based understandings of how HIV should be controlled, the Indian Supreme Court's ruling in *Mr X v. Hospital Z*[30] had significant implications on the confidentiality of one's health status. This case originated in the consumer courts as a breach of service claim by Mr X: the hospital's pathology department where he had tested HIV-positive violated his confidentiality by informing family members and others of his status. Not heard by the consumer courts, the case reached the Supreme Court, which ruled on an issue that was not even before it – it suspended the right of people living with HIV to marry (Mr X was in the process of seeking a betrothal, but had no intention of hiding his HIV status to a prospective spouse). While the court recognized the right to privacy and the duty of physicians to maintain confidentiality of patient information, it held that the Medical Council of India's Code of Medical Ethics created an exception to confidentiality when public interest was at stake and in circumstances where there was a health risk to others. The court held that the disclosure of Mr X's HIV status was justified since the possible spouse's health was protected. While doing so, it did not lay down conditions and protocols by which such disclosure was to be made. It added that a person living with HIV who married and infected a spouse would be liable under Sections 269 and 270 of the Indian Penal Code (IPC), which criminalize those who perform a negligent or malignant act 'likely to spread a disease dangerous to life'. In a 2002 re-examination of this verdict, the Supreme Court noted that Mr X's rights were unaffected by his health status being revealed in the facts of the particular case. However, it set aside its own observations on the right to marriage, privacy/confidentiality and criminal liability.[31]

Although the findings and conclusions of the court regarding Mr X's rights are questionable – he gave no indication that he would not self-disclose his health status to a prospective spouse – there may be reasonable circumstances in which disclosure of HIV status is necessitated, despite confidentiality being paramount. But that is a decision a healthcare worker or a counsellor must make after weighing the balance of two *public* interests as first enunciated in *X v. Y* – on one hand, the public interest to maintain confidentiality, and on the other, the public interest for others to be informed to protect themselves. Importantly, this sensibility demonstrates that rights-based approaches to HIV do not simply pit the false dichotomy of individual rights against societal rights, but support the understanding that protecting individual rights protects and elevates public health and societal rights.

Another influential case in which these nuances came to the fore was *Tarasoff v. Regents of University of California*,[32] albeit unrelated to HIV. Prosenjit Poddar, a university student briefly dated fellow student Tatiana Tarasoff, after which she ended the relationship and started seeing another man. Poddar reacted with anger and distress, and began therapy with a psychologist, Dr Moore. At the final therapy session, he expressed the intention to harm an unidentified female, who was easily identifiable as Tarasoff. The doctor wrote to the campus police regarding Tarasoff's safety and sought assistance in securing the confinement of Poddar in a mental hospital. After an interview, the police assessed Poddar to be rational and released him with the warning to stay away from Tarasoff. The hospital management then retracted Dr Moore's letter and withdrew the request to have him confined. Shortly thereafter, Poddar killed Tarasoff. Her parents sued Dr Moore and the university, arguing that they should have been warned of the threat to their daughter. The question arose whether there was a duty of the doctor to disclose the threat that Poddar posed to Tarasoff despite the confidential nature of the relationship.

In arriving at its ruling, the court weighed the two public interests that needed to be balanced – the patient's right to privacy against the need to warn another of imminent risk. In doing so, it held that once a doctor determines 'or under applicable professional standards reasonably should have determined that a patient poses a serious danger'[33] then there is 'a duty to exercise reasonable care to protect the foreseeable victim'.[34] The disclosure should be made 'discreetly, and in a fashion that would preserve the privacy of his patient to the fullest extent compatible with the prevention of the threatened danger'.[35] Key conditionalities have emerged from this reasoning that have informed disclosure issues in the contexts of both mental health and HIV. They are: first, a determination needs to be made, considered reasonable by a practitioner exercising professional standards; second, the danger posed should be serious; third, the person at risk should be identifiable (and not be based on a general concern of harm being caused to an unspecified person); and fourth, the disclosure should be narrowly made.

India's HIV/AIDS Act

Indeed, the issue of confidentiality of HIV status is closely linked to the issue of partner notification – what are the circumstances in which a needle-sharing or sexual partner can be notified of a patient's HIV status? Since 2017, this has been crystallized in Indian law, influenced by the AIDS paradox, the balancing of public interests to disclose or not to do so, and the *Tarasoff* reasoning. It is stipulated in India's HIV/AIDS (Prevention and Control) Act, 2017 (HIV Act).[36] Section 8 of the law clearly states the rule: No person shall be compelled to disclose their HIV status except for one reason – if required by a court order requiring such information for deciding disputes before it. In addressing disclosure of HIV status by another person to a third party, the law is also very precise. When the HIV status of a person is imparted 'in confidence or in a relationship of a fiduciary nature'[37] disclosure or compelling disclosure of this status to a third party is only permissible after obtaining informed consent in writing or recording such receipt of consent in writing. The law does, however, stipulate certain circumstances of third-party disclosure where informed consent to disclose is not required. These include situations of shared confidentiality between healthcare providers where the disclosure is for the care and treatment of the person living with HIV; if a court order requires such disclosure for adjudicating a case; when made in legal proceedings where such disclosure is necessary; in collecting statistical information not leading to identification of the person living with HIV; for the purposes of monitoring and evaluation undertaken by government AIDS programmes; and in cases of partner notification.

The last ground has been the reason for much discussion and debate over time, and is treated in detail under Section 9 of the Act. It begins by permitting only a physician or counsellor to disclose the HIV-positive status of a person directly under their care to that person's partner. However, before disclosure the healthcare provider must satisfy several conditions, namely, determining that the partner is at significant risk; ensuring that the person has been counselled to inform the partner but will not do so; and then telling the person living with HIV that their partner will be informed. Further, the partner must be informed in person after receiving counselling. The law also explicitly states that it is not the obligation of the healthcare provider to locate the partner, thereby recognizing that the risk must be to an identifiable person as elucidated in *Tarasoff*, and not an unspecific apprehension. An exception is made to partner notification requirements in cases where the person living with HIV is a woman and there is a reasonable apprehension that she, her children or dependents would be subject to violence or abandonment as a result of divulging her HIV status.[38]

While the spectre of criminal liability under Sections 269 and 270 of the IPC looms large for those who transmit life-threatening diseases, the HIV Act focuses on the responsibility of those living with HIV to take a degree of care. This requires that those who are aware of their status, who have been counselled, and, understand the nature of HIV and its transmission, take steps to prevent such transmission by taking reasonable precautions, such as using condoms and clean needles or informing partners of their HIV status in advance. The exception for women in cases of apprehended domestic violence prevails here too.[39]

Grievance Redress

In cases where there are rights violations under the Act, including an impermissible breach of confidentiality, the law provides for a unique method of grievance redress. This was conceived in the backdrop of an overburdened, inaccessible and sluggish judicial system, in which disputes are resolved after an inexorable lapse of time. Rapid resolution of disputes was the need of the hour, especially in the HIV context where lives were precarious at a time when anti-retroviral treatment was far from assured.[40] Under the Act, grievance redress is available institutionally for establishments comprising more than a hundred persons, and for healthcare establishments of more twenty persons.[41] This is ensured by the necessity for such establishments to appoint a complaints officer who is expected to resolve complaints within seven days of receiving them, and within healthcare establishments in emergency situations. If the complaint relates to discrimination, the complaints officer is required to arrive at their decision on the same day they receive them.[42] Moreover, the establishment is required to provide training to the complaints officer on the Act and the gamut of issues implicated in relation to HIV, including information on prevention, care, support and treatment related to HIV, human sexuality, sexual orientation and gender identity, drug use, sex work, stigma and discrimination.[43]

While the procedure to be followed in making and receiving complaints is detailed in the HIV/AIDS (Prevention and Control) Rules, 2018, pertinent to this chapter is the requirement to protect the identity of the complainant, if so requested by the officer.[44] The manner of ensuring suppression of identity is also detailed in the rules, including the provision of pseudonyms and a prohibition from revealing the person's identity in any form of publication. Indeed, the HIV Act stipulates suppression of identity provisions for court proceedings under the law, if requested by a party to the proceedings who is a 'protected person' (a person who is HIV-positive or has lived/ is living with an HIV-positive person – such association being the stigmatizing context that is protected).[45]

While the complaints officer is required to provide remedies at the localized institutional level, the Act also requires pre-court dispute resolution through a state-appointed ombudsperson[46] who is expected to investigate grievances related to discrimination and provision of health services, including issues of informed consent, confidentiality, and a safe working environment (and receive complaints in appeal from the decisions of complaints officers). Provisions for time-bound dispute resolution like the ones mentioned earlier for complaints officers are prescribed for the ombudsperson.[47] The attempt of the HIV Act, therefore, is to offer a speedier, more accessible, and less arcane grievance redress system to complainants. While this law was presented to the government during the the millenium, it was passed and notified only in 2017. Unfortunately, little has been done to ensure its robust implementation.[48]

India's legislative approach to confidentiality in the context of HIV is a finely balanced one. While it is sensitive to the value of ensuring confidentiality as part of a successful rights-based approach, it also allows for exceptions to the rule through clearly laid-out reasoning and protocols that allow for disclosure in defined manners, which protect another person's health and also preserve the overarching imperative for confidentiality in a relationship of trust. It endeavours to serve both individual interests and public health priorities. Little, however, is known of how these protocols have translated into practice. While the Act requires the ombudsperson to report on the number and nature of complaints received, actions taken and orders passed to the state government every six months, together with publishing this information on the office website and forwarding a copy of the report to the central government,[49] it is presently unclear whether state governments have even appointed persons to this office.

Confidentiality of Health Data in the Data Tech Age

The use of digital health technologies is considered an important ingredient in eliminating HIV/AIDS, as a part of the broader public health objective of achieving universal health coverage. In the Political Declaration on HIV and AIDS, to end AIDS by 2030, UN member states committed to enhancing the potential of digital technologies to advance HIV responses consistent with their human rights obligations.[50] Digital interventions are already being used within the global HIV response for a variety of prevention, treatment adherence and surveillance purposes.[51]

With potential benefits that emerging digital technologies present, significant human rights challenges have also been recognized, including possible infringement of the rights to confidentiality, privacy and non-discrimination. UN Resolutions and Political Declarations around Digital Health[52] categorically state that to align with human rights obligations while complementing public health objectives, the harm associated with digital health technologies should be minimized through:

(a) a comprehensive data protection law to regulate collection, processing and sharing of health data;
(b) health system preparedness to ensure digital and technology infrastructure capabilities, human resource training, as well as strengthened data security governance; and
(c) implementation of digital health tools anchored in and guided by existing obligations on the rights to health and privacy, and ethical equity frameworks.

In India, the Supreme Court in *Justice K.S. Puttaswamy v. Union of India*[53] unanimously reiterated that the right to privacy, including privacy of medical data, was a fundamental right. It also laid down guidelines for evaluating constitutionality of any action that encroaches upon privacy: (a) the action must be sanctioned by law, (b) the law must pursue a legitimate aim, (c) the action proposed should bear a rational connection to the aim, (d) it must be the least restrictive option available, and (e) the law must have safeguards from abuse. The court also observed that growth of technology and ubiquitous digitization have created new dangers for invasion of informational privacy by both state and non-state actors, and called for enactment of a comprehensive data protection law.

While the HIV Act prescribes confidentiality requirements in relation to delivery of healthcare, as discussed earlier, it anticipates the era of digital technology by necessitating further assurances of privacy in relation to data protection. All establishments keeping records of a person's HIV-related information are required to adopt data protection measures, which include 'procedures for protecting information from disclosure, procedures for accessing information, provision for security systems to protect the information stored in any form and mechanisms to ensure accountability and liability of persons in the establishment'.[54] However, its provisions on data protection are overarching, and a comprehensive data protection law and health sector specific rules are required to regulate collection, storage, processing and sharing of sensitive health data, including HIV status. This is particularly necessary in the face of increased reliance on information and communication technology (ICT) and burgeoning deployment of digital health tools – electronic health records (EHRs), telemedicine, disease surveillance – to serve public health goals.

In the midst of the first wave of COVID-19, the Indian government launched its National Digital Health Mission (NDHM) and issued a policy document to guide its implementation – the Health Data Management Policy (HDMP). The HDMP seeks to allow a range of entities to collect personal health data of persons and set privacy standards for sensitive health data. However, it fails to fulfil the very first test laid down by *Puttaswamy* – an action which implicates the right to privacy must be based in law. The HDMP is a non-statutory executive instruction; implementation of digital health solely on the basis of the HDMP and in the absence of a law (at the time of writing) makes this architecture constitutionally suspect. Indeed, the absence of a legislative framework suggests that priorities are askew. The cart has been placed before the horse. Before a policy like the HDMP is implemented, it must be preceded by an assurance of fundamental rights expressed in legislation.

The NDHM, among other things, seeks to digitize health records of patients via EHRs, linked to a unique health identity (UHID), which could be created on the basis of government identity cards, preferably Aadhaar.[55] EHRs would include a person's HIV status, being longitudinal electronic versions of patients' demographic details and complete medical history. EHRs would contain all the sensitive health information of patients at a single source, shareable at the click of a button between different healthcare providers as well as multiple private and public entities via numerous interconnected devices and platforms. The increase in access points to sensitive health data that transpires from introducing EHRs is a serious concern to patients and poses new challenges to confidentiality, privacy and security of sensitive health data,[56] and could well violate the allowance for shared confidentiality in the HIV Act.[57] The consequences of data breach can be severe for people living with HIV, ranging from social stigma and embarrassment, discrimination in healthcare settings, employment and educational institutions to violence, abandonment and abuse. The UNAIDS Guidance Document for adoption of UHID cautions against the dangers of having a UHID system compromised or inappropriately used or accessed to track individuals by both state and non-state actors.[58]

Electronic systems must ensure that they have inbuilt technological mechanisms to support the maintenance of confidentiality and privacy of data in order to comply with extant laws on privacy (the *Puttaswamy* ruling) and confidentiality (the HIV Act), as well as the globally recognized principle of 'privacy by design'.[59] However, the HDMP suffers from deficiencies in ensuring confidentiality of sensitive health data.[60] For instance, it does not specifically provide for 'data masking', a technique that contributes to establishing the confidentiality of sensitive medical data. This enables individuals to exercise control over sharing their information with other healthcare providers, if required in the interest of their healthcare, and binds the healthcare provider with the principle of confidentiality, contemplated within the HIV Act. In another example, the HDMP is vague on purpose limitation, considered the cornerstone of privacy and data protection standards. This requires that personal data shall be collected and processed only for specific and lawful purposes, be limited in time and not be processed in any manner incompatible with that purpose. However, the HDMP leaves it to the executive to substantiate the purposes for data collection, processing and sharing at a later date. This lack of clarity on specific purposes for which data can be shared undermines the principles of transparency and accountability and endangers privacy. It also provides too much discretion to the executive to arbitrarily change purposes, without being subject to adequate scrutiny.

The National AIDS Control Programme Data Management Guidelines, 2020,[61] suffer from similar deficiencies as the HDMP. The guidelines lack clarity on which categories of data will be collected and shared, and provide little clarity on purpose limitation, or period of data retention.[62] They also lack clear organizational and technological protocols for ensuring confidentiality of HIV status by concerned entities. And while they state that no personally identifiable data will be shared with third parties for research purposes, the guidelines do not specifically mention the categories of non-personal data which can be shared. Finally, they also fail to recognize that anonymization is no longer considered a foolproof, privacy-preserving measure, as research has shown that in the age of big data and data mining, anonymized data sets can be deanonymized fairly easily.[63]

Although the HDMP states that the use of Aadhaar for creating a UHID is voluntary, experience with COVID-19 vaccination shows otherwise; not only was Aadhaar made de facto mandatory for accessing vaccines, but those who gave their Aadhaar number to access vaccines ended up getting a UHID generated and linked to it unbeknownst to them, and certainly without obtaining their informed consent.[64] This resembles the actions of several state governments that made the submission of one's Aadhaar mandatory for accessing antiretroviral treatment for HIV.[65] The insistence on Aadhaar caused fear of disclosure of HIV status – and for several people disclosure of sexual orientation, or drug use status – which led many people living with the virus to abandon accessing health facilities altogether.[66] When reported in the media, officials said that the use of Aadhaar was encouraged but not mandatory.[67] However, it was clearly being insisted upon at health facilities,[68] much like the experience with COVID-19 vaccination. In the absence of a privacy law, people have very little autonomy over their data and little recourse in case of a breach, as they may not even be notified of its occurrence. The government claims it needs Aadhaar details to track individuals who are lost, to follow up for improving treatment adherence. However, this strategy itself is driving people away from accessing health services as they lack trust in the system.[69]

Conclusion

Legislative and programmatic efforts in HIV point to the value and need for exactitude in the law and in practice in the context of challenging health concerns. Lazy imprecision and thoughtless implementation can be the bane of public health efforts to control the disease. They can carelessly fuel stigma in already difficult, marginalized contexts, encourage distrust of the health system and push people to seek bogus remedies and into dangerous behaviours. Empowering people by obtaining their informed consent after imparting accurate information, protecting them through the assurance of non-discriminatory practices, and guaranteeing their confidentiality so that they are encouraged to modify their conduct while taking responsibility for their actions have all served in ensuring a successful response to HIV.

Yet some concerns persist. One recent example of an action that is contrary to the assurance of confidentiality in the HIV Act is the notification of the Maharashtra Nursing Homes Registration (Amendment) Rules, 2021, by powers granted to the state government under the Maharashtra Nursing Homes Registration Act, 1949. Rule 11-O requires nursing homes to report cases of diseases listed in Schedule-II to the designated authority. Schedule-II currently lists seventeen diseases for reporting, of which Item 10 reads: 'Number of persons tested for HIV, details of those found positive and negative as well as ANC General clients.' While the rules require only reporting of cases of cholera, dengue, infective hepatitis and others, they single out HIV for reporting of additional 'details' without any reasonable basis. Singling out HIV is peculiar, especially in current times when unimpeded access to anti-retroviral treatment has made it a chronic condition. As surprisingly, this effort is at complete odds with the HIV Act, which permits disclosure in very specific contexts as mentioned earlier.

But confidentiality of health status is and should be a concern well beyond the HIV context. In the current digital information age, assuring it has become more complex, and the law mostly lags in keeping up with technology. A policy such as the HDMP and imminent data protection laws that implicate health information should be devised with the kind of precision that is specified in HIV-related laws and protocols. It is the very least that patients are owed in honouring their confidentiality.

11

Decisional Privacy and Decisional Autonomy: A Rights-Based Paradigm for Mental Healthcare in India

Arjun Kapoor

Introduction

HISTORICALLY, societies have failed to recognize persons with mental illness (PwMIs) as complete human beings. Legal jurisdictions across the world deny PwMIs equal recognition before law. Consequently, PwMIs experience structural discrimination and are denied the same legal rights as enjoyed by others in society. This discrimination can be attributed to stigma arising from false and negative stereotypes that PwMIs are irrational and incapable of forming their own decisions or acting upon them. Therefore, in the perception of mainstream society, the existence of a mental illness invalidates an individual's personhood and agency to shape their own life. The prevailing beliefs underlying such stereotypes are that mental illness is an incurable phenomenon, induces irrational behaviour and impairs the individual's decision-making abilities. These beliefs have several implications for how PwMIs are treated in the context of their mental healthcare and other aspects of their lives.

In India, mental healthcare is both a public health and human rights issue. Estimates suggest that anywhere between 70 and 92 per cent of people who have a diagnosable mental health problem do not have access to any form of mental healthcare and treatment.[1] India allocates less than 1 per cent of its total health budget for mental healthcare, despite a severe deficit in mental health services, facilities and trained workforce to meet the increasing demand for services.[2] Social determinants such as poverty, income inequality, unemployment, discrimination, trauma and substance abuse not only exacerbate but are causal factors of mental health problems and high suicide rates. In India, with the advent of the mental health legislation during the colonial era, PwMIs were segregated and institutionalized as they were considered incurable, dangerous and a threat to the social order.[3] Despite legal reforms over the years, PwMIs continue to experience widespread human rights violations and discrimination. For instance, PwMIs continue to be subjected to forced admissions; coercive treatments such as chaining; seclusion; and cruel and inhuman living conditions in mental health establishments. They are also prohibited from making their own decisions regarding different aspects of their lives including their mental healthcare and treatment. Mental health professionals and family members make these decisions on behalf of the PwMIs in their 'best interests', often conflicting with what the individual desires and wishes (this practice is also known as substitute decision making).

This denial of autonomy and agency also extends to legal relationships such as entering into contracts, buying or selling property, opening a bank account, voting, marrying, rearing children or other personal decisions. Often, these disqualifications are justified by mental health professionals or courts on grounds of 'incompetence' or 'unsoundness of mind'.[4] For example, in the Hindu Marriage Act, 1955, and Special Marriage Act, 'mental disorders' are a ground for divorce, annulment and disqualification for marriage. Further, over 150 legislations in India include 'unsound mind' as a criterion for barring individuals from accessing certain rights and entitlements such as voting in elections. However, in India, since mental health professionals, courts and official authorities often falsely equate mental illness with 'unsound mind', PwMIs are barred from enjoying the same legal rights as others do in society.

The practices mentioned above are in violation of international human rights law and fundamental rights enshrined in the Indian Constitution. Article 12 of the United Nations Convention on the Rights of Persons with Disabilities (CRPD) recognizes that all persons with disabilities including those with mental illness (or psychosocial disabilities) have legal capacity on an equal basis with others. Legal capacity is defined in terms of all individuals having equal recognition before law as equal persons. It has two components: (i) all individuals are rights-holders, that is, they have legal rights; and (ii) all individuals have legal agency to exercise rights, make legal decisions or enter legal relationships. Article 12 of the CRPD categorically states that all persons with disabilities should be provided a range of supports to help them exercise their legal capacity by making their own decisions. It calls for replacing substitute decision-making systems with supported decision-making systems to enable such persons to exercise their autonomy and legal capacity. In other words, Article 12 of the CRPD lays down the legal framework for protecting the legal capacity of all PwMIs to make their own decisions regarding all aspects of their lives without interference from others. This has implications for protecting the rights of PwMIs specifically in the context of their mental healthcare and treatment in addition to other aspects of their lives.

This chapter argues that the right to make personal decisions about one's life is a facet of the right to privacy, which is now recognized as a fundamental right under Article 21 of the Constitution. In legal jurisdictions across the world, the doctrine of privacy has expanded to include 'decisional privacy', which is specifically concerned with the freedom of individuals to make personal decisions and choices regarding their own lives.[5] While decisional privacy as a paradigm is evolving within the Indian context, it has direct relevance for protecting the autonomy and personhood of PwMIs, especially for making decisions on mental healthcare and treatment. The recently enforced decisions on Mental Healthcare Act, 2017, (MHCA), embeds decisional privacy and autonomy through a range of provisions which seek to protect the autonomy, dignity and liberty of PwMIs. It does so while balancing the same with other considerations such as access to healthcare, the harm principle and India's socio-economic realities.[6] Decisional privacy can thus inform and shape our understanding of rights-based, legal and public health approaches for strengthening mental healthcare and treatment in India while preserving the individual autonomy and legal capacity of PwMIs. In light of the same, this chapter will identify some of the key conceptual and practical implications of decisional privacy for protecting the rights of PwMIs, especially in the context of their mental healthcare and treatment.

Decisional Privacy, Decisional Autonomy and Questions of Personhood

Decisional Privacy and Decisional Autonomy

'Decisional privacy' has been recognized as one of the core components of privacy by constitutional courts across the world. It has been defined as 'a distinct type of privacy, which protects the autonomy of persons to make decisions about their body or other aspects of their private life'.[7] This concept has also been expanded in the context of health to include 'responsibility for important decisions about treatment, the termination of treatment and the allocation of scarce medical resources'.[8] Simply put, decisional privacy recognizes that individuals must have the liberty to make personal choices to live their lives without any interference from the state or other parties. These decisions are concerned with the intimate or personal aspects of one's life and are not limited to marriage, sexuality, child rearing or healthcare decisions.[9] In order to enjoy decisional privacy, individuals must have autonomy to make decisions. Decisional autonomy refers to the ability of individuals to make their own personal choices or decisions.[10] It comprises two aspects: (i) the freedom to make one's own decisions, and (ii) the ability to make one's decisions and act upon them.[11]

For PwMIs, the freedom to make personal decisions is often contingent on whether they are presumed to have decision-making abilities. In contemporary theories of autonomy and justice rooted in Western liberalism, decisional autonomy is based on whether the individual meets a minimum threshold of 'competence' or 'rationality' determined by their cognitive abilities.[12] In other words, only 'rational' individuals capable of making independent decisions are presumed to exercise decisional autonomy. On the other hand, individuals with intellectual, cognitive or psychosocial disabilities, who do not meet the minimum threshold or may require additional support in making independent decisions, are considered 'incompetent' or cognitively impaired and thus incapable of making their own decisions. As this chapter argues, this is not only a fundamental violation of their basic human rights, but also a denial of their personhood as human beings.

Decisional Autonomy and Decision-Making Capacity: Challenging the Legal Capacity of Persons with Mental Illness

In the context of mental health, decisional autonomy is conventionally determined based on a minimum threshold of decision-making abilities of an individual, also known as decision-making capacity (DMC).[13] There have been primarily three different approaches to assess DMC across various legal jurisdictions.[14] The 'status approach' presumes that all individuals with intellectual, cognitive or psychosocial disabilities are unable to make decisions and lack DMC due to their impairments. In other words, according to this approach, the presence of an impairment is enough to deny DMC to an individual. The 'outcome approach' focuses on assessing DMC based on the outcomes of an individual's decisions. Therefore, if the outcome is likely to be bad, improper or harmful, it is assumed that the individual lacks DMC. The 'status approach' has been widely criticized as discriminatory since it presumes that persons with disabilities are incapable of making decisions solely because they have impairments. The outcomes approach is also considered discriminatory and paternalistic since a certifying authority can impose its own subjective values and beliefs to evaluate whether an individual is making a correct or proper decision.

The third 'functional approach' focuses on assessing the ability of an individual to perform a specific function, such as (i) making mental healthcare and treatment decisions, (ii) entering into legal relationships such as entering into contracts, voting, buying or selling property, marriage, child rearing, and (iii) exercising socio-economic rights such as employment, education, marriage or rearing a family. In the context of healthcare decisions, DMC assessments commonly adopt a functional approach focusing on four broad parameters: (i) understanding, which implies that the individual must be able to 'understand' information or the facts relevant for making a particular decision; (ii) appreciation of the nature, significance and consequences of the decision; (iii) reasoning in terms of ability to reason or weigh options and arrive at a decision; and (iv) communication or expression of one's choice or decision.[15] The functional approach has also been critiqued as discriminatory on the grounds that there is no objective method to determine an individual's decision-making abilities, especially when paternalism and subjectivism in the values and beliefs of certifying authorities 'may distort objective assessments of functional capacity'.[16] However, most DMC assessments fail to consider that while some PwMIs may have impaired decision-making abilities, they are able to make independent decisions if provided adequate and appropriate support. Consequently, the decision-making status of PwMIs is assessed solely on the basis of their cognitive impairments/ abilities, without appreciating the role of support and reasonable accommodation in enabling PwMIs with impaired decision-making abilities to make their own decisions.[17]

As discussed above, Article 12 of the CRPD recognizes that all persons with disabilities have legal capacity irrespective of their impairments and are entitled to a range of supports to exercise the same. Thus, how can PwMIs who require different forms of support to make decisions be supported to enjoy decisional privacy and decisional autonomy over their lives?

Protecting the Decisional Autonomy of Persons with Mental Illness through Supported Decision Making

Bach and Kerzner propose the idea that all individuals have a range of abilities to make decisions and choices in their personal lives.[18] This range of abilities, skills and impairments is a facet of human diversity which must be respected rather than considered as a ground for discrimination or denying personhood to individuals. Thus, decisional autonomy and personhood must be considered inherent in all individuals. It should not be compromised by the presence of impairments, rather it can be enabled through the provision of appropriate supports and accommodation to the individual's needs. Therefore, it is crucial to ask what kind of supports the individual requires to exercise their legal capacity? The determination of this question leads to three different forms of decision-making statuses:

(1) *Independent decision-making* status in which an individual can understand information or foresee consequences of their decisions independently without any support but might require some assistance during the decision-making process. For example, if one has to make a decision about which restaurant to eat dinner at, one might consult a friend or a family member for their recommendations and, based on their advice, make one's own decision eventually.
(2) *Supported decision-making* status in which an individual might have impaired decision-making abilities but can exercise DMC with appropriate supports, and reasonable accommodation through the provision of specific resources or organizational policies. For example, if one has a severe mental illness and is unable to communicate treatment decisions verbally, one's caregiver can provide communication support through visual aids or sign language to interpret one's decision and communicate it to the mental health professional. Here, there would be no requirement to make a decision on behalf of the individual, if they were provided adequate and appropriate support.
(3) *Facilitated decision-making* status in which the individual is unable to make their own decisions despite being provided all forms of support and accommodation. For example, if one has delirium or becomes unconscious, and is unable to make a decision despite any amount of support, a caregiver or mental health professional would be required to take a decision on one's behalf (substitute decision making) after evaluating what one would have preferred or desired if one was conscious or in a condition to make a decision.

Thus, in supported decision making, the support person is bound by the individual's will and preferences, unlike in substitute decision making in which the person can interfere and override the individual's decisions in what is perceived to the latter's 'best interests' but often conflicts with the individual's wishes. However, the Committee on the Rights of Persons with Disabilities mandates that where it is not possible to ascertain the will and preferences of the individual, decisions should be made by another person in accordance with the best interpretation of the former's will and preferences.[19] In other words, decisions should be made after weighing what the individual would have willed, intended or preferred if they were able to exercise their legal capacity, based on the individual's life history, beliefs, values and past decisions.

Supported decision making involves a range of informal and formal supports depending on the individual's specific needs, nature of decisions and relational/social context. For instance, PwMIs may require specific support to help them make decisions regarding their mental healthcare and treatment which may vary depending on the severity of their condition, the nature of treatment decision, presence of known or trusted persons to provide support or the availability of material resources. For example, advance planning through advance directives allows PwMIs to decide how they wish to receive mental healthcare and treatment if in the future they are unable to make their own treatment decisions. Support measures also include 'representational support' such as a trusted person who can interpret and represent the individual's wishes and preferences to others based on personal knowledge of the individual. PwMIs may also require support to build relationships and community-based support networks which they can rely on for their participation and inclusion in society. Other forms of support include communicational support in not only interpreting the individual's actions or intentions but also communicating them to others at the time of making decisions or entering into legal relationships. These include verbal or non-verbal signs, gestures, visual aids, technology-assisted aids or language assistance. Finally, supports for PwMIs also include community-based facilities or services which can facilitate inclusion; legal supports such as powers of attorney, lawyers or legal representation before judicial authorities; caregiving support for managing families or child rearing; or establishment of trusts or financial investment options to ensure financial security.

Nonetheless, the relational nature of this approach renders the individual vulnerable to the possibility of intrusions and interferences in their decisional privacy and autonomy. In the context of mental illness, these situations arise if family members or mental health professionals impose treatment decisions contrary to the individual's wishes. Alternatively, in certain situations PwMIs may be in a facilitated decision-making status, for instance, if the individual is unconscious, in delirium or experiencing catatonic states which make it impossible to discern their will, intention, or preferences.[20] In such situations, across legal jurisdictions, if the individual is at risk of harm to themselves or others, PwMIs may be treated involuntarily, and treatment decisions are made on their behalf till they regain decision-making abilities. As various scholars suggest, this necessitates adequate safeguards such as ensuring that any intrusion or interference in the individual's decisional autonomy, bodily privacy and liberty is authorized by legal procedure, proportionate to the objective, least restrictive and for a limited time period.[21] Further, such instances must be subject to judicial review and, if after legal scrutiny, there are found to be disproportionate, illegal or unjustified, these must be revoked by statutory authorities.

The next two sections of this chapter will contextualize the above discussion in terms of the evolving jurisprudence on decisional privacy and autonomy in the Constitution of India and also the MHCA, 2017, which lays down a rights-based legal framework for protecting the decisional autonomy and bodily privacy of PwMIs through institutional safeguards and supported decision-making approaches.

Decisional Privacy and Decisional Autonomy in the Constitution of India

The Supreme Court of India in its judgments has recognized decisional privacy as integral to the dignity and liberty of all individuals. In *Justice K.S. Puttaswamy v. Union of India*[22] – the Supreme Court's landmark judgment on right to privacy, a nine-judge bench held that privacy is a constitutionally protected right flowing from the right to life and personal liberty under Article 21 of the Indian Constitution. While emphasizing the relationship between decisional privacy and decisional autonomy, the court observed that the ability to make personal choices lies at the inviolable core of the human personality while privacy enables individuals to make these choices. In other words, privacy safeguards individual autonomy and recognizes the ability of the individual to control vital aspects of their life by making personal choices. The Supreme Court in various decisions has also upheld the right to decisional autonomy as an integral aspect of privacy by recognizing and protecting the right to make personal choices in certain contexts.

In *National Legal Services Authority v. Union of India and others*,[23] the court recognized the right of transgender persons to self-identify their gender as integral to one's 'personal autonomy' protected under Article 21 of the Constitution. The court held that personal autonomy implies the negative right of non-interference by others and the 'positive right of individuals to make decisions about their life, to express themselves and to choose which activities to take part in'. In *Navtej Singh Johar and Others v. Union of India*,[24] the court held that Section 377 of the Indian Penal Code, 1890, which criminalized consensual sexual acts between two adults, was unconstitutional on the grounds that sexual orientation is integral to an individual's privacy and decisional autonomy. The court in its reasoning held that the right to privacy was broad enough to encompass decisional autonomy and decisional privacy or the privacy of choice. Consequently, the right to privacy extended to making personal choices without 'unwarranted state interference'. Thus, if Section 377 criminalizes consensual sexual acts between adults, it is unconstitutional since it takes away the decisional autonomy of LGBTQIA+ persons* to make choices consistent with their sexual orientation and live a 'meaningful life as a full person'.

---

* An inclusive term that 'encompasses the entire spectrum of gender fluidity and sexual identities'. (Source: Jennifer Betts, 'What Does LGBTQIA+ Stand For? Full Abbreviation And Other Terms Explained')

The right to decisional autonomy has also been recognized in the context of reproductive rights. In *Sucheta Srivastava v. Chandigarh Administration*,[25] the court overturned the decision of the Punjab and Haryana High Court to terminate the pregnancy of a woman with mental retardation against her consent. In this case, the woman residing in a government shelter had become pregnant after being raped. The high court constituted an expert committee which recommended against abortion since the woman had expressed her desire to give birth to the child. The high court, contrary to the expert opinion, ordered the termination of the pregnancy on grounds that the woman did not have capacity to rear a child. The Supreme Court overturned the high court's decision while referring to Section 3 of the Medical Termination of Pregnancy Act, 1971, which states that the pregnancy of a woman with mental illness or a minor can be terminated only with consent of the guardian in writing, while in all other situations, the pregnancy can be terminated only with the consent of the pregnant woman. The court interpreted this provision to hold that the pregnancy of an adult woman with mental retardation could be terminated only with her consent. The court also recognized that reproductive choices are a component of an individual's personal liberty under Article 21 of the Constitution and further noted that the woman required support from the state to parent the child. It is critical to note that the court's decision was based on Section 3 of the MTP Act, which draws an arbitrary distinction between mental illness and mental retardation by denying women with mental illness the right to consent for abortion. Such a distinction does not rest on any rational or reasonable criteria but rather furthers the false and negative stereotype that PwMIs are incapable of making their own decisions including reproductive choices.

In *Common Cause (A Registered Society) v. Union of India and another*,[26] the Supreme Court recognized the right to passive euthanasia for patients who are terminally ill and have no possibility of recovery. The court held that such patients could exercise their right to withdraw life support by providing informed consent in accordance with the guidelines laid down by the court. The court's reasoning was based on the principle that the right to passive euthanasia flowed directly from the right to life and personal liberty under Article 21 of the Constitution as the right to life also implies the right to die with dignity. Further, the court expanded the scope of 'self-determination and autonomy' of an individual to include their right to decide whether they are willing to submit to medical procedures and treatment, to choose among available alternative treatment or to not opt for any treatment at all in accordance with the individual's aspirations and values. The court's decision was based on the reasoning that an essential attribute of privacy is the 'ability of the individual to refuse medical treatment' while the right to privacy also extends to 'intimate sphere of decisions relating to death ...' The law cannot compel an individual to disclose reasons for refusing medical treatment, nor 'is such a refusal subject to the supervisory control of an outside entity'. Therefore, the court held that continuing treatment against the wishes of a person was not only a violation of the principle of informed consent but also of bodily integrity which was a facet of the right to privacy.

The court also observed that the requirement of informed consent could be met only by those individuals who were 'competent' or who had decision-making abilities, while individuals who were unable to make their own decisions required safeguards to ensure that their wishes were respected without being exploited. Accordingly, the court issued guidelines for authorizing individuals to prepare advance directives (living declarations) to authorize withdrawal of life support if in the future such individuals were unable to make their own decisions due to their condition. The court drew upon jurisprudence on advance directives from across the world, including the provisions of the MHCA, 2017, to hold that 'advance directives as part of a regime of constitutional jurisprudence is an essential attribute of the right to life and personal liberty under Article 21'. It is pertinent that the court did not touch upon the criteria and parameters related to assessment of DMC for terminally ill patients who may have varying decision making abilities with or without other support measures to support decision making. Nonetheless, the court's reasoning expands the scope of decisional autonomy to personal choices such as end-of-life decisions while ensuring safeguards to protect the rights of terminally ill patients who may lose capacity to make decisions regarding withdrawal of life supports but have at a prior time expressed their wishes for the same through advance directives.

Two broad inferences can be drawn from the court's decisions on decisional autonomy which have implications for the rights of PwMIs in India. First, the court's recognition of the right to decisional autonomy is concomitant with the fundamental right to privacy flowing from the right to life and personal liberty under Article 21. At the same time, decisional privacy and decisional autonomy are crucial for making personal decisions regarding one's physical and mental health, such as providing informed consent for treatments, choosing treatments in accordance with one's wishes or refusing any treatment. Thus, decisional privacy and decisional autonomy are crucial for enjoying the right to physical and mental health, which has been recognized by the Supreme Court as an integral component of the right to life under Article 21 in several decisions. At the same time, ensuring access to healthcare and support services for PwMIs is crucial to facilitation of their decisional autonomy. However, the court's judgments have not sufficiently expanded this relationship between decisional privacy, decisional autonomy and the right to health under Article 21 of the Constitution. Second, the court's pronouncements on decisional autonomy have mostly been based on individuals who do not have psychosocial disabilities or are assumed to be 'competent' based on cognitive parameters. Thus, the court's jurisprudence has not expanded on protecting the decisional autonomy of PwMIs who may have impaired decision-making abilities and require supported decision-making resources to make their own decisions regarding different aspects of their lives. This is particularly relevant for the rights of PwMIs who are prohibited from making decisions regarding their mental healthcare and treatment or other personal aspects of their lives, since they are either assessed as lacking DMC or denied support to help them exercise their legal capacity. The recently enforced MHCA, 2017, addresses some of these gaps as it expands the jurisprudence on decisional autonomy in the context of mental healthcare and treatment, beyond the limited scope of the court's decisions which do not specifically address the concerns of PwMIs.

Mental Healthcare Act, 2017: Evolving Jurisprudence on Decisional Autonomy of Persons with Mental Illness

The MHCA enacted in compliance with India's obligations under the CRPD adopts a rights-based approach to mental healthcare and treatment by (i) protecting the rights of PwMIs by placing obligations on mental health professionals and other stakeholders, and (ii) ensuring the right to access mental healthcare and treatment for all persons. The legislation posits a rights-based legal framework for recognizing, protecting and facilitating the decisional autonomy of PwMIs with respect to their mental healthcare and treatment. The MHCA presumes that all PwMIs have the capacity to make their mental healthcare and treatment decisions irrespective of their mental illness. It defines 'capacity' as the ability to make decisions on mental healthcare and treatment in terms of the following three components: (i) understanding information relevant to the decision; (ii) appreciating reasonably foreseeable consequences of a decision; and (iii) communicating the decision by any means including non-verbal signs, gestures, visual aids or any other language.

If a mental health professional has a reason to believe that the individual does not have capacity, they are obligated to conduct a DMC assessment to rebut this presumption. Most significantly, the law also recognizes that PwMIs may have impaired decision-making abilities but can exercise DMC through varying levels of support from their caregivers or mental health professionals. For instance, an individual with severe mental illness may be unable to understand the information required to make their own decision regarding continuing medication. However, with the support of a caregiver who explains the relevant information in a simple language with communication aids, the individual can understand and decide whether they want to continue medication as per their wishes.

Thus, the law creates an obligation on mental health professionals to include supported decision making as an essential criterion while reviewing and deciding the decision-making status of PwMIs. The clinical significance of the presumption of capacity is that no treatment can be provided to an individual without their informed consent while the legal significance is that it facilitates exercise of legal capacity. According to the MHCA, informed consent is always given for a specific intervention or treatment. It can be obtained only after disclosing to the individual adequate information including risks and benefits of, and alternatives to, the treatment in a language and manner understood by the individual. This process must be conducted without any force, undue influence, fraud, threat, mistake or misrepresentation, which compromises the individual's autonomy. The most important implication of informed consent is that the individual can refuse treatment or ask for alternatives which align with their own wishes and preferences. Informed consent is therefore an essential requirement for an individual to exercise their decisional autonomy for mental healthcare and treatment. It protects the individual's decisional privacy and bodily privacy as it enables them to decide whether they expressly permit or refuse outright any intrusion or interference to their bodily and decisional privacy in the context of their treatment and care.

However, the exercise of informed consent or decision making may require varying levels of support to ensure that the individual is able to understand important information such as side effects, risks, benefits and alternatives. The absence of support or relevant information may result in uninformed consent or decisions which are influenced by family members or mental health professionals. It may also result in unwanted intrusions on the person's bodily and mental integrity through coercive treatment.

The MHCA provides for two specific, supported decision-making tools – nominated representatives and advance directives – to enable PwMIs in making their own treatment decisions. The nominated representative (NR) is a trusted and familiar individual appointed by a PwMIs to represent the latter in their mental healthcare and treatment. The NR is required to assist the individual in making their own decisions by providing the necessary support. If the individual is unable to make their own decisions despite receiving support, the NR is authorized to provide informed consent on behalf of the individual (substitute decision making) till the individual regains their decision making abilities. The NR is legally mandated to provide support to the individual while (i) considering the current and past wishes, life history, values, cultural background and best interests of the individual, (ii) giving credence to the views of the person, (iii) applying for admission and discharge, or seeking information regarding the diagnosis, treatment options and alternatives, and (iv) submitting complaints in case of any rights violations.

Advance directive (AD) is a planning document or written declaration where an individual can specify if in the future they have a mental illness and do not have the capacity to make decisions, (i) how they wish to be treated or cared for, (ii) how they do not wish to be treated or cared for and (iii) appoint a nominated representative. Thus, ADs ensure that an individual's will and preferences are respected even if they are unable to make decisions on their own. Mental health professionals are legally obligated to comply with a valid advance directive that has been registered with the Mental Health Review Boards (MHRBs), which are statutory bodies mandated under the law to oversee the MHCA's implementation and redress rights violations.

The MHCA's provisions also protect informational privacy and bodily privacy of PwMIs which, in turn, are crucial for facilitating decisional autonomy. In terms of informational privacy, MHCA protects the right to confidentiality, right to information, right to access medical records, right to receive or refuse visitors or any external communication. PwMIs have a right to non-disclosure of their personal information unless exceptional circumstances require such disclosure to prevent harm to the individual or any other person, facilitate treatment or comply with legal obligations. But the right to information and right to access medical records are crucial for PwMIs to make their own informed decisions regarding their treatment and care in accordance with their preferences.

In terms of bodily privacy, the MHCA provides for certain situations in which the decisional autonomy and liberty of PwMIs may be restricted. It seeks to balance decisional autonomy with other considerations such as ensuring access to healthcare especially for families in low-resource settings who do not have access to resources for non-institutional care or preventing harm to the individual or other persons. For instance, the MHCA authorizes supported admissions in certain situations where the individual does not have the capacity to make decisions, has very high support needs and fulfils any one of the following criteria: (i) recently threatened/attempted or is threatening/attempting to cause bodily harm to self; (ii) has behaved/is behaving violently towards another person or causing them to fear bodily harm to themselves; and (iii) they are at risk to themselves due to an inability to take care of themselves. In such situations, the individual may be admitted and treated without their consent through substitute decision making till such time that they regain their decision-making abilities.

The MHCA places adequate safeguards to ensure that restrictions on decisional autonomy are proportionate and for the least amount of time. All instances of supported admissions including long-stay admissions require periodic review by the MHRBs, which are quasi-judicial authorities and have the power to issue orders. The law also requires a periodic review of the individual's capacity to give informed consent to their decisional autonomy to make treatment decisions. Finally, the MHCA ensures that PwMIs can approach the MHRBs for judicial review and redress of any rights violations at the time of receiving treatment and care from mental health professions, caregivers and family members.

Lastly, PwMIs with impaired decision-making abilities require access to appropriate mental healthcare services and facilities along with supported decision-making tools to exercise decisional autonomy for personal decisions. The right to health recognized under Article 21 of the Constitution places a duty on the state to ensure this right by guaranteeing healthcare services. Section 18 of the MHCA actualizes this constitutional right in the context of mental healthcare by recognizing the right to access mental healthcare and treatment from mental health services run or funded by the state for all persons. Thus, the central and state governments have an obligation to provide minimum mental health services which are affordable, accessible, good quality, culturally acceptable sans discrimination. These services include outpatient and inpatient departments, halfway houses, supported and sheltered accommodations, and community- and home-based rehabilitation services at all levels of the public health system in proportion to the population. Governments are also mandated to provide free mental healthcare to people below the poverty line, reimbursements for accessing private healthcare in the absence of public health services and free medicines on the essential drugs list.

The MHCA also emphasizes a shift from institutionalization to community-based treatment and rehabilitation to reduce restrictive forms of treatment that deny decisional autonomy and legal capacity to PwMIs. The law also recognizes the right to community living which obligates the state to provide supported and sheltered accommodation so that PwMIs can live independently in the community. However, there exists a massive deficit in the availability of community-based treatment, rehabilitation services and support measures, especially in low-resource settings such as rural areas, with most states severely under-resourced to fulfil these obligations. The absence of this vital infrastructure poses a serious challenge to the protection of decisional privacy and autonomy for PwMIs.

Public Health Challenges for Protecting Decisional Privacy of Persons with Mental Illness in India

The public health challenges for protecting decisional privacy of PwMIs can be framed in terms of Isaiah Berlin's distinction between positive and negative liberties.[27] Positive liberty implies that the state is obligated to not only remove unwanted interferences and intrusions to decisional privacy but also take proactive measures to create an environment where individuals can exercise decisional autonomy. In this context, enactment of the MHCA is a watershed moment for public mental health in India since, for the first time, it introduces a rights-based legal framework for protecting decisional autonomy and ensuring the right to access mental healthcare and treatment for all individuals. However, there's much to be desired in its implementation. It has been three years since the MHCA was enforced; however, the Act's basic implementation and governance mechanism comprising the State Mental Health Authorities (SMHAs) and MHRBs are yet to be fully set up and be functional across different states in the country. Many state governments are yet to notify minimum standards for registering and monitoring mental health establishments. Consequently, mental health professionals continue to resist implementing provisions relating to advance directives, admission and discharge procedures, and supported decision making, citing grounds of impracticality and lack of resources.

In the absence of adequate monitoring and oversight by the SMHAs and MHRBs, it is unlikely that PwMIs and civil society can hold mental health establishments and mental health professionals accountable for their obligations under the law. Furthermore, given the wide gap in treatment and care in India, there is an urgent need for community-based mental health facilities and services comprising rehabilitation facilities, supported housing, support services and a trained caregiving workforce which can meet the specific needs of PwMIs.

Positive liberty also implies that the state must enable law and policy reform to ensure that PwMIs can exercise legal capacity and decisional autonomy in other aspects, such as entering into legal relationships, financial security, voting, marriage and family, employment and other civil, political and socio-economic rights. While access to mental healthcare and support is essential for the above, there is also a need for policies and schemes to ensure adequate infrastructure for support services, trained human resources and reasonable accommodation within organizations, such as banks, public service agencies, educational institutions, workplaces, etc., to facilitate decision making and access to public services for PwMIs. For example, due to existing regulations and policies, persons with disabilities face difficulties in opening bank accounts or entering into contractual relationships in the absence of an appointed legal guardian. Mandatory requirements of a legal guardian for exercising one's rights, accessing public services or entering into legal relationships is a denial of the legal capacity and decisional autonomy of PwMIs.

In terms of negative liberties, it is crucial that the state, mental health professionals and law enforcement agencies prohibit unwanted interferences which prevent PwMIs from exercising decisional autonomy. One of the foremost challenges to protecting decisional autonomy of PwMIs in India is the resistance amongst mental health professionals, caregivers and law enforcement officials to accept the view that PwMIs can be autonomous decision makers.[28] As discussed initially, this resistance stems from false and negative stereotypes that persons with severe mental illnesses are irrational or lack decision-making abilities. Mental health professionals are still driven by paternalistic approaches that consider PwMIs as lacking DMC if they make wrong decisions or have values which are incompatible with the world-view of the mental health professionals treating them.[29] This perception flies in the face of contemporary research in behavioural economics and allied disciplines, which have proven that human beings are often driven by irrational motivations while making decisions.[30] Even so, DMC assessments are premised on cognitive parameters which deny legal capacity to many PwMIs who may have impaired decision-making abilities but are able to make decisions with adequate support. Challenging this dominant mode of practice requires a philosophical, ethical and practical revision of our understanding of concepts such as autonomy, decision-making capacity and personhood of those with psychosocial, intellectual and cognitive disabilities. It also necessitates the need for sustained capacity building of mental health professionals, law enforcement officials, caregivers and other duty-bearers in rights-based and CRPD-compliant approaches for respecting the legal capacity of PwMIs.

The role of families, caregivers and support networks is crucial in enabling the decisional autonomy of PwMIs. However, this may be fraught with challenges and dilemmas for family members and caregivers. First, supported decision making requires intimate involvement of a trusted person who has adequate knowledge of the individual to interpret their will and represent them in decision-making processes. However, there's often a thin line between supporting an individual to make their own decision and making decisions on behalf of the individual. If transgressed, this can compromise or interfere with the individual's decisional autonomy. Some strategies to ensure that caregiving and support does not become transgressive include the following: (i) playing the role of an educator by using one's expertise to inform or explain relevant information to the individual in a simple and accessible manner, (ii) assisting the individual in formulating their will, aspirations and preferences with respect to each decision, (iii) reflecting on whether as a caregiver or mental health professional one is imposing one's own values and beliefs on the individual's decisions, (iv) acquainting oneself with the individual's identity, values and life history to authentically represent the individual's wishes, and (v) where the individual is not able to exercise DMC, ensuring that substitute decisions are based on the 'best interpretation' of what the individual would have willed or desired, after taking into account available information regarding the individual's life history, wishes and values.

Second, in the cultural context of India, families play a central role in the treatment and care of PwMIs. However, families are also often a site of violence and trauma marked by authoritative relationships and imposition of moral values that restrain the autonomy of family members.[31] Thus, the family's interests may conflict and prevail over the individual's desires, leading to compromising the latter's decisional autonomy over personal choices. One can witness such dynamics in the experiences of women who challenge patriarchal norms, individuals who identify with alternative genders and sexualities, and individuals who challenge their community's dominant ideals based on caste, religion or other political or social beliefs. Often, in such situations, they require protection from their own families. Here, the MHCA's provisions may provide respite as PwMIs are entitled to appoint, as a nominated representative, any trusted and safe person of their choice even if the latter is not a family member or a relative.

Third, families in low-resource settings are often confronted with financial difficulties or inadequate resources to access less restrictive, community-based services and facilities. This leads to situations where families abandon their loved ones or forcefully admit them in mental health establishments indefinitely. In some instances, forceful admissions are the only resort to ensuring any form of mental healthcare and treatment for the individual, since families do not have access to or cannot afford less restrictive and community-based services.[32] Additionally, families and caregivers are often faced with ethical dilemmas if the individual is engaging in violent behaviour, is at risk of harm to themselves, or is unable to care for themselves. In such situations, due to lack of non-coercive alternatives or community-based support mechanisms, families or caregivers may, even if temporarily, resort to treatment without the consent of the individual. Various international bodies such as the World Psychiatric Association have recommended evidence- and rights-based, non-coercive treatments or alternatives to physical restraints in clinical settings. However, the translation of these approaches in India's context remains a challenge due to inadequate resources and resistance from mental health professionals to transform their perspective and clinical practice.[33]

Conclusion

The right to decisional privacy is fundamental to exercise one's right to life and personal liberty and right to health under Article 21 of the Constitution. For PwMIs, decisional privacy is particularly significant since it facilitates their universal right to legal capacity and decisional autonomy to make decisions about their own lives. However, decisional privacy and decisional autonomy have long been denied to PwMIs in all aspects of their lives including their mental healthcare and treatment. The essence of decisional privacy lies in the right of PwMIs to deny or prohibit any form of interference in their personal decisions including their treatment and care. This implies not just a negative obligation on the state to prevent any interference in private decisions but also a positive obligation to implement laws, policies and programmes to enable conditions and support measures whereby PwMIs can exercise their decisional autonomy. However, this will be actualized only when duty-bearers and society at large first recognize and affirm the inherent personhood and autonomy of all PwMIs as equal human beings before the law.

Part IV

The Governance of Health Data

12

State Legibility of Personal Health Data in India

Faiza Rahman and Ajay Shah

Introduction

PUBLIC and private healthcare providers across the world are implementing different types of digital health systems for record keeping and public health surveillance. The Indian healthcare ecosystem is also on the cusp of adopting a digital health system across the board which centres around digital health records. Many private health sector entities such as pathological labs, digital health trackers, hospitals, insurance providers, etc., have already been digitizing health data of patients. However, most of these systems do not provide for sharing of health records across different healthcare entities.[1] The government is now planning to connect digital health systems operating in silos thus far. Towards this, the central government has announced the launch of the National Digital Health Mission (NDHM), now renamed the Ayushman Bharat Digital Mission (ABDM). The NDHM aims to connect various stakeholders in the health ecosystem such as doctors, hospitals, pharmacies, insurance companies and citizens through an integrated digital health infrastructure.[2] The principal components of this framework will be owned and administered by the government. However, private entities will also be able to integrate with these building blocks and create their own products and services for the market.

The implementation of the digital health systems mentioned above will invariably result in the extensive collection and processing of health data by both government and private entities. The proliferation of such public and private health data systems entails that the government is the generator and processor of health data in some cases, and can access health data through private entities in others. However, the impact this has on the ability of the government to access the vast volume of health data being collected under these digital health systems has received little attention. To capture this phenomenon, we use the term 'state legibility' which refers to the amount of knowledge that a state has with respect to its citizens and their activities.[3] This chapter will seek to understand and discuss the state legibility concerns that stem from the extensive and systematic collection of health data by government and private entities through these digital health systems. It will thereafter set out possible pathways of cautious progress to allay the concerns regarding government surveillance and to minimize the potential harms.

The structure of the chapter is as follows. Section 2 describes the drive for complete digitization of health data, and the concomitant surveillance of individuals through the health data. Section 3 shows the manner in which there has been an increase in health-related surveillance by private and state entities in India. Section 4 envisages the harms to individuals and society that can emerge from the government access to health data. Section 5 details the ways in which state legibility is enhanced in personal health information. Towards this, it discusses the laws that enable the government to access personal data in general and certain types of health data as well. Drawing from these discussions Section 6 elaborates on possible pathways which India can explore to proceed cautiously with digitization of health data. The final section concludes.

The Power and Possibilities of Health Data

In the pre-computer age, doctors and healthcare establishments did not store data about individuals. Each consultation between a doctor and a patient tended to happen in isolation, and was limited by the memory and information management of the patient. Doctors would look at a snapshot of the state of the patient, and were not able to look at the evolution of the condition. Every household valiantly tried to handle pieces of paper containing test results or prescriptions and data objects such as X-ray images.

In an ideal world, all health information pertaining to each individual would be stored in secure and private electronic data systems. This would have enormous benefits:[4]

1. At each consultation, doctors would see the medical history about patients.
2. It would become possible to build statistical models, widely hyped as 'AI systems', which would study this data and help improve decisions by doctors and patients. Systems like this could examine information not just at the level of one individual but also bring together data about family members or neighbours, and thus improve decisions at the level of a community either by way of prevention or by way of cure. In the statistical analysis of data about individuals, a major milestone is the transition from informal/occasional data capture to the systematic process of 'panel data' or 'longitudinal data' where one individual is observed across time.
3. Healthcare providers would be able to monitor doctors, thus modifying their incentives and improving consumer protection.
4. Greater complexity of the healthcare system would become possible, featuring complex contractual arrangements between insurers, healthcare firms, bulk buyers such as employers and individual buyers.
5. Public health functions of the state would be performed better by observing population-level health statistics, which would be

used to better roll out population-scale interventions to prevent sickness.

The Indian healthcare system is at an early stage of development. Health policymakers run the risk of exaggerating the benefits from these data sets; there are fundamental problems which have yet to be addressed. For example, we need to worry about a lack of personnel and equipment, misalignment of incentives between doctors and patients in the private sector driving up healthcare costs, etc.[5] Even if the collection of utopian data sets is successfully initiated, it can yield only small gains in this context. What it most definitely ensures, however, is increased state access to health data of individuals.

The problems of state access to health data about individuals is located in the larger context of the field of state surveillance. The term 'surveillance' is ordinarily understood as a 'close watch kept over someone or something'.[6] A more nuanced way could be to describe it as 'the focused, systematic and routine attention to personal details for purposes of influence, management, protection or direction'.[7]

Both definitions indicate that surveillance can be carried out by anyone. However, till recently, the term invariably led us to imagine activities conducted by powerful government agencies and spies, to collect information on foreign and internal adversaries of the state.[8] The digital revolution that has engulfed all our lives has drawn our attention to 'surveillance capitalism' or the large-scale and systematic collection, processing, analysis and sale of personal data by corporations.[9] Given the state's asymmetric control over coercive organs such as the police and the criminal justice system, the harm that a state can inflict upon an individual often exceeds the harm that can be inflicted by a corporation. At the same time, there is a nexus between information systems built by private firms, which are then legally or illegally accessed by governments. If information about individuals was not captured and stored by private firms, the problems of state surveillance would be much diminished. In this sense, the information captured by firms is an integral part of the analysis of state surveillance.

While both the government and private entities such as companies always engaged in collecting some information on individuals, the rapid development of technology has removed the traditional hurdles that had prevented the systematic amassing, storage and analysis of vast amounts of information.[10] This is further compounded by function creep – the phenomenon where an information system intended for one particular purpose is gradually appropriated for other purposes.[11] The function creep of India's biometric identity project, Aadhaar, for example, has been a major concern for its critics.[12] Function creep, the linking of databases that existed in silos and the improvements in computing power have added up to an unprecedented extent of state legibility. There are now widespread fears about the emergence of a surveillance state where a new phase of democratic institutional design is required to wrestle with this power and ensconce in it commensurate checks and balances.[13] Against this background, we need to envision the consequences of individual health information becoming visible to officials. In this sense, health data is not an isolated problem; it is one part of an overall problem of rising state legibility and the lack of commensurate checks and balances.

In any crisis, state power tends to increase. During the COVID-19 pandemic, governments worldwide deployed new technological tools for contact tracing, monitoring quarantine compliance and vaccine administration. In 2020, governments in at least thirty countries worked together with telecommunications providers and other companies to conduct mass surveillance. More than fifty-four countries launched smartphone apps for contact tracing or quarantine compliance. Facial recognition technology and automated decision making were rolled out with minimal checks.[14] This has directed public attention to the increased collection of health data by governments and corporations alike, and generated discussion around fears of health data surveillance and what this means for democracies.[15]

Interestingly, the term 'surveillance' has specific meaning in the field of public health. 'Public health surveillance' is the systematic collection, storage, usage, and dissemination of health-related information to identify an outbreak and mitigate the spread of disease.[16] There has always been some tension between privacy and public health surveillance. These old difficulties are now manifesting themselves in new ways, for three reasons. First, the improvement in data quality and ease of collection has altered the nature of surveillance in the context of public health. Second, typically, public health surveillance is conducted at community and population level. However, the health surveillance being proposed through digital health systems, such as the one being envisaged under the National Digital Health Mission (NDHM) and contact tracing apps, is more invasive because it collects data at the individual level. Third, the health surveillance through smart wearables or the Aarogya Setu app is not limited to collecting basic health indicators but is also engaging in aggregating and tagging it with other identity data such as demographic data, location data, photograph, etc. The next part of the chapter will discuss these developments that mark a fundamental shift in the manner in which health data is collected and processed in India.

The Emergence of Databases of Personal Health Information in India

Even before the COVID-19 pandemic, public and private healthcare providers across the world were implementing different types of digital health systems both for record keeping and public health surveillance.[17] A number of private healthcare providers in India such as pathological labs, hospitals and clinics already maintain some form of intra-organizational IT system to collect and store medical records of patients.[18] Consumers are also gradually adopting a variety of health-related apps or smart wearables that help users book medical appointments, measure calorie and water intake, physical movements, and sleep quality or keep track of menstruation and ovulation cycle,[19] mental health, etc.[20] As long as this data stays in private or disparate hands, and the linking of diverse databases is hard, the potential for harm is limited. In principle, government officials can indulge in lawful or unlawful information demands addressed to multiple private firms and entities, obtain all this information and link up the records, thus obtaining a comprehensive picture of a certain set of individuals. This is set to change.

An array of developments about health information at the individual level now suggests that this situation is changing. Some of the key developments that will lead to an unprecedented increase in collection, digitization and processing of health data are as follows:[21]

1. Ayushman Bharat Digital Mission (ABDM): In 2018, the union government launched a healthcare insurance scheme, Ayushman Bharat Pradhan Mantri Jan Aarogya Yojna (PM-JAY). This scheme boasts of being supported by an underlying IT infrastructure that is interconnected with the National Health Stack – a 'nationally shared digital infrastructure usable by both Centre and State across public and private sectors'.[22] In 2020, the Ayushman Bharat scheme was expanded by launching the NDHM (now called the ABDM).[23] The NDHM aims to connect various stakeholders in the health ecosystem such as doctors, hospitals, pharmacies, insurance companies, and citizens through an integrated digital health infrastructure.[24] The core elements of NDHM such as Health ID (now the Ayushman Bharat Health Account number or ABHA), Digi-Doctor and Health Facility Registry will be owned, operated and maintained by the government. However, private stakeholders will integrate with these elements and create products for the market.[25] To facilitate this, the government has been developing a 'National Health Stack'.[26] As part of this stack, the government will build master registries of healthcare providers, beneficiaries, insurers, etc. To operationalize this massive public–private system, the government will launch a Unified Health Interface, which will enable users to search, book and access healthcare services such as tele-consultations or laboratory tests.[27] The NDHM will give the central government an unprecedented level of information about and control upon private healthcare transactions.
2. DNA-based tracking: The government's use of DNA technology for the purpose of identification and analysis is also expanding. The DNA Technology (Use and Application) Regulation Bill, 2019, or the DNA Bill in short, was introduced in the Lok Sabha in July, 2019. Given the increase in reliance on DNA evidence in criminal trials, this legislation aims to regulate the use of DNA

technology for establishing the identity of persons in criminal and civil matters (such as parentage disputes, emigration or immigration, and transplantation of human organs). In addition, the DNA Bill establishes a national DNA databank and regional DNA databanks for the storage of DNA profiles retrieved from crime scenes, suspects/undertrials, convicts, missing persons, as well as unknown deceased persons.[28]

3. Aarogya Setu: In April 2020, the central government rolled out the centralized contact-tracing app, Aarogya Setu. This was an unprecedented moment, where real-time location tracking of individuals generated data for the union government. The app was implemented without any specific legislative basis. Even though the use of the app was technically voluntary, it was de facto mandatory for purposes such as air and rail travel during different parts of the pandemic.[29] Government's use of invasive contact-tracing measures during a once-in-a-lifetime pandemic may arguably be justified given the public health necessities, if the use of Aarogya Setu data was strictly limited to the purposes of managing the pandemic.[30] However, this data has since been shared for law enforcement purposes with the Jammu and Kashmir Police.[31] A number of state government and private apps also provide other COVID-related assistance. They have been collecting a range of personal details including Aadhaar number, home and GPS location, demographic data, etc.[32]

4. CoWin: Another digital solution adopted by the government is the CoWin portal, which serves as the main platform for administering COVID vaccines to Indians.[33] State coercion was used to force providers and consumers to not transact without supplying information to this state-run information system, and obeying rules defined by the union government. This policy choice was criticized for being discriminatory towards the digitally challenged sections, inducting a new level of union government control upon individuals everywhere in the country, and intruding on health privacy.[34] CoWin is now being used to connect individuals to the NDHM system as well. This is being achieved by automatically

creating a Unique Health ID for users of the CoWin app who submit their Aadhaar ID to access COVID vaccination.[35]

Further, a number of other government programmes will also lead to the systematic digitization of personal health data. Examples include the National Health Portal's Indradhanush app[36] and state health programmes such as Rajasthan government's Pregnancy, Child Tracking and Health Services Management System.[37]

5. Criminal Procedure Identification Act, 2022: The recently passed Criminal Procedure Identification Act, 2022, authorizes the collection, analysis and storage of biometric data as well as other biological personal data such as iris and retina scans, blood, hair and semen samples, etc., of arrested persons, convicts and habitual offenders. The law permits such data to be stored in a central database by the National Crime Records Bureau for seventy-five years, and shared with various law enforcement agencies. It also allows a magistrate to order measurements of any person to be taken to aid the investigation of an offence under any law. These records will be destroyed for persons who are subsequently acquitted after completion of all appeals, or released without trial, provided a magistrate does not order the retention of such records as well. Further, the resistance of or refusal to provide measurements under this law is a criminal offence.[38]

There is little literature in India which has analysed individual components of state legibility in health. Some researchers have worked on the NDHM,[39] Aarogya Setu and CoWin. In the next section, we envision the harms by looking at the bigger picture of a series of interlinked initiatives involving state actors and private healthcare providers, which come together to deliver a new level of state legibility.

Harms

All forms of surveillance give the observer information about the observed. This augments the observer's power over the observed.[40] The shift in power away from the individual, in favour of corporations and particularly governments, raises concerns for individuals, communities and democratic societies. As is the case with surveillance, in general, government and private-sector surveillance are entangled in the health sector. They often use the same technologies, operate through public/private arrangements[41] and share the benefits.[42] However, given the identified focus of this essay on government access to health data, this part will identify the dangers of government access to large amounts of health data and the creation of health databases.[43] It is difficult to neatly compartmentalize the nature of these dangers, but we analyse them under two broad categories: (a) individual-level and community-level dangers, and (b) dangers to society, democracy and public health.

Dangers Posed to Individuals and Communities

We find that unchecked government access to health data poses the following dangers to individuals and communities:

1. **Loss of dignity and autonomy**: In *K.S. Puttaswamy v. Union of India*, the Supreme Court of India endorsed an 'autonomy-rich understanding' of the right to privacy which seeks to ensure an 'individual's continued capacity to make autonomous choices'. Hence it has been argued that 'a dignified life, being tied to an autonomous life, resists anything which would render the ability to make decisions in the future limited'.[44] Individual consent as the basis for accessing, collecting or processing any personal data including health data is thus indispensable. However, a person does not forgo all her interests in the data upon consenting to its collection or processing.[45] Consequently, even if individuals were to meaningfully consent to isolated or wholesale collection and processing of private health data, it can be argued that the constant subjection of ourselves to the gaze of digital health systems is an attack on individual autonomy and dignity. It interferes with our free will, creates self-consciousness, and makes us susceptible to being controlled. Our inability to withdraw from this constant observation and analysis qualifies as a harm as it infringes individual sovereignty.[46]

2. **Unfair leverage to governments against political opponents**: If a person is observed for a long time, she is at risk of being caught engaging in some form of illegal or immoral activity. This information could then be misused by an authoritarian government or a private individual to either shame or blackmail her. For example, FBI discovered about Martin Luther King Jr's extramarital affairs while surveilling his communications to investigate his ties with communists. The FBI then blackmailed him and leaked the information to discredit him.[47] Government access to health data relating to alcohol intake, medicine use, overall health conditions including health risks, pregnancy, paternity, abortion and contraceptive details can be similarly misused. Authoritarian governments may exploit their access to health data to reap political advantages or cause reputational damage to its opponents. For instance, many apps are collecting deeply personal health details of millions of women such as menstrual and ovulation cycle, frequency of sex, records of unprotected sex, pregnancy plans, recent miscarriages, etc.[48]

In 2019, the pregnancy and period-tracking app Ovia was reportedly sharing user information with employers.[49] It was allowing a company access to aggregate data on employees with high-risk pregnancies or premature deliveries, the key medical queries they had searched and when the new mothers planned to return to work.[50] Such disclosure by a corporation can undoubtedly cause reputational harm, employment discrimination, financial loss or loss of familial or community membership. However, imagine a scenario where an authoritarian government publicly leaks abortion details of a female political opponent or details regarding alcohol consumption of dissidents. Such misuse of access to health data by governments can discredit political adversaries or sway conservative electorates. In the United States, for example, where abortion is a politically polarizing subject, the government has sought to subpoena medical records of women who have accessed abortion services from private clinics.[51] Similarly, sensitive mental health data can be used by authoritarian governments to mischaracterize or discredit the actions of political opponents. Even if governments do not leak health details to the public, government access to interconnected health databases itself can reveal the health conditions of important figures in the opposition. This can be used to improve political strategy and reap electoral advantage. Importantly, the government in power will always have asymmetric access to such information. While we categorize this as a harm mainly impacting individuals, this also has grave implications for democratic societies.

3. **Discrimination and identity-based violence/threats against individuals and communities**: Surveillance is often used to categorize people into distinct groups. Some of these categorizations can be insidious. Public disclosure of personal health data or access of such information by the government may lead to discrimination against individuals or groups by both the state and private individuals.[52] Further, individuals from minority or marginalized communities already face a disproportionately higher risk of discrimination on the basis of prohibited grounds such as sex, caste and religion.[53] The aggregation of health data coupled with public disclosure or government access to such data may increase the risk of discrimination faced by such persons and communities. For instance, COVID-19-related contact tracing in South Korea coupled with publication of infection details led to homophobic abuse being directed at the LGBTQ community.[54] In India, widespread media coverage of COVID-19 outbreak amongst a gathering of Muslims led to reports of discrimination against Muslims across India. This triggered an array of discriminatory behaviour ranging from denial of access to shops to Muslims, refusal to accept services/sale of goods from Muslims,[55] violence[56] and incitement for ethnic cleansing of Muslims from India.[57]

Further, the revelation of extremely personal health-related data to the state can also lead to direct violence by the state. This is not simply academic speculation. The Epidemic Diseases Act, 1897, was used by the imperial authorities in colonial India to demolish the homes of and conduct medical experiments on poorer Indians.[58] Easy and direct state access to health data can only enhance the possibilities of similar state violence at the hands of any authoritarian government.

Dangers Posed to Society, Democracy and Public Health

Digital health databases by themselves, and especially when interconnected with other databases, sweep up every intimate information of ours. This infringes privacy and dignity that form the basis of any rights-based democracy. The existence of such a surveillance apparatus can have a chilling effect on individuals and adversely impact both individual and public health outcomes. We discuss this further below:

Panoptic perils of health databases – impact on society, democracy and public health: The existence of any all-pervasive state surveillance apparatus is itself an infringement into the right to individual liberty as the mere knowledge of being watched inhibits individual expression and openness.[59] The fear of being observed in totality can create a greater chilling effect on individuals known as a panoptic effect. It is based on a thought experiment that revolves around a prison structure called the panopticon. It is designed with the prisoners' cells arranged around a central watchtower where a guard is stationed. While the guard is in a position to observe all prisoners, the prisoners are unable to see the guard.[60] This makes each prisoner conscious of being constantly and completely visible to the guard, even if they are unsure of whether the guard is actually looking at them.[61] Digital informational systems continuously collecting fragments of our personal data operate as all-seeing panopticons. Multiple isolated information systems when interconnected through a common identifier such as the Aadhaar ID or a unique health identifier, as envisaged under NDHM, can reveal an intimate profile of any individual's life including their food habits, medicine use, political affiliations, religion, caste, etc.,[62] thus painting an all-encompassing portrait of the individual to the state.

The chilling effect of such systems can dissuade us from sharing controversial ideas, attending political meetings or associating with a group.[63] However, does this chilling effect translate into anything worrisome specifically in the context of health data being surveilled and individual behaviour towards healthcare? Any health information surveillance architecture will also have panoptic effects on individual behaviour related to healthcare choices. The very existence of a digital health database such as being envisaged by the NDHM changes the fundamental character of any action for an individual. Therefore, the act of visiting doctor X on day D for the purpose of diagnosing disease Z is no longer about just a regular visit to a doctor. It also means that an individual is no longer able to perform this activity without leaving a data trail regarding their most intimate health needs.[64] The panopticon is bound to result in chilling effects in individual behaviour and can manifest in more dangerous forms such as hesitance in accessing healthcare services or reporting communicable diseases. For example, mandatory Aadhaar requirements have caused many persons living with HIV to drop out from government-funded ART treatments due to fear that their health status will be leaked to the wider community.[65]

One empirical study examined the shift in Google search behaviour of users after the Snowden revelations in June 2013 that showed that the US National Security Agency was directly monitoring private email communications on Google, Yahoo and Microsoft. It found that the volume of both personally sensitive and government-sensitive search terms were negatively affected by the revelations. However, the chilling effect was higher with regard to health-related searches as compared to other privacy-sensitive terms on Google, that is, the volume of searches for health-related terms suffered the most both in the US as well as in other countries.[66]

Notably, the government plans to encourage people who do not use government health subsidies to link their Aadhaar ID with the NDHM ecosystem. Aadhaar ID, which is already ceded to distinct government subsidy programmes, will be mandatorily linked wherever government healthcare benefits are being provided.[67] The Aadhaar ID will be used as a bridge across NDHM and other government subsidy programmes, and hence it is critical to undertake studies around the effects of tracking health data on Indian consumers. Given the seriousness of these individual and societal harms, the next section analyses if the law sets out adequate safeguards against government access of health data.

State Legibility in Health Information: Laws and Limitations

Health data is a special case of information about individuals. At present, India has threadbare limitations on government accessing health data of individuals.[68] To understand this more clearly, it is important to first unpack the distinct ways in which government can access personal health data of an individual. This can be done broadly through three means: (i) health programmes and corresponding databases administered by the government itself, such as Aarogya Setu and CoWin data; (ii) indirect access through government-controlled health data processors; and (iii) seeking lawful or unlawful access from private healthcare providers. The government is likely to have almost direct access to health data in the first and second cases. It will have to seek access from private entities in the third case.

The latest developments (NDHM, Aarogya Setu, CoWin) suggest that a significant increase in collection of individual health data may arise, with databases that are often controlled by the state. In an environment where there are threadbare limitations to state access to data, state legibility will increase.[69]

The legal pathway for government access to health data stored with private entities is provided under certain health legislations. For example, the Pre-Conception and Pre-Natal Diagnostic Techniques (Prohibition of Sex Selection) Act, 1994, or the PNDT Act, requires private establishments such as genetic counselling centres and genetic or ultrasound clinics to maintain records including names and addresses of men or women subjected to pre-natal diagnostic procedures, laboratory results, sonographic plates or slides, etc.[70] These records are retained for two years and made available for governmental inspection.[71] The Human Immunodeficiency Virus and Acquired Immune Deficiency Syndrome (Prevention and Control) Act, 2017, or the HIV Act, also permits individual consent for disclosure of HIV-related information to be overridden for when disclosure is made to the officers of the government for the purposes of monitoring, evaluation or supervision.[72]

In terms of the legal protections for health data, collection of health data and access to this data have largely been taking place without checks and balances. For example, the Indian Council of Medical Research requires private labs to collect health-related, demographic and Aadhaar details for every sample being tested for COVID-19.[73] This has no specific legal basis and is drawing its legality from the generic provisions of Epidemic Diseases Act, 1987, and Disaster Management Act, 2005.[74] Similarly, the processing of data by Aarogya Setu and CoWin apps is happening without a specific legal mandate.[75] Now CoWin registration is being used to connect users to NDHM without their consent.[76]

The general legal framework around government access to information stored in computer resources under Section 69 (1) of the Information Technology Act, 2000, can also be used to access health data. It permits the governments to 'intercept, monitor or decrypt' *any* information generated, transmitted, received or stored in any computer resource on grounds including security of the state, public order, sovereignty or integrity of India, defence of India, or for preventing incitement to the commission of any cognizable offence relating to above or for investigation of any offence. The power of authorizing surveillance resides with senior members of the executive and not with a judge. Further, Section 91 of the Code of Criminal Procedure, 1973, allows a court or any officer in charge of a police station to summon 'any document or any other thing' from a person, if it is 'necessary or desirable' for the purposes of any investigation, inquiry, trial or other proceeding under the code. It is usually relied upon by the police to seek information from intermediaries, or to access information not stored in a computer resource.

Peering into the future, the *Puttaswamy* decisions on right to privacy and Aadhaar appear to be the only plausible pathway towards greater privacy protection that could materialize. This is because the government has recently withdrawn the PDP Bill, and a data protection legal regime for India looks unlikely in the near future.[77] However, even the framework outlined under the PDP Bill did not solve the problems described in this chapter. While the PDP Bill categorized health data as sensitive personal data,[78] and imposed basic data protection principles such as collection and purpose limitation, it created wide exceptions for state access to data, including personal health data. For example, the bill allowed the union government to exempt *any* government agency from the application of the entire legislation or any part on grounds such as security of the state and public order.[79] Typically, under this provision law enforcement and intelligence agencies would be exempted, but nothing in the draft stopped the exemption of health agencies when they processed data in the interest of security or public order. It also retained the existing model of review of surveillance requests by the executive without judicial oversight.[80] The state legibility issues outlined in this chapter will therefore not be addressed unless these provisions are completely altered in the new data protection legislation being envisaged by the government.

In light of this development, the only potential pathway to progress is reforms which could flow from the *Puttaswamy* decisions of the Supreme Court. Privacy is a fundamental right under the Constitution of India. The Supreme Court has held that any intrusion into the right to privacy by the state has to satisfy the proportionality standard. Hence, courts will evaluate the legitimacy of any state action impacting individual privacy, including, for example, the creation of digital health systems under the NDHM, on the touchstone of the tests of legality, legitimate aim, suitability, necessity and proportionality.[81]

However, in the years following this ruling, no element of the pre-existing mechanisms for state surveillance has been modified substantially. For example, the PDP Bill was released after the *Puttaswamy* verdicts, but it did not require any government order that exempted an agency from the application of the data protection legislation in entirety or in part, and violated individual right to privacy as a consequence, to be proportionate. This was a clear violation of the verdicts. Similarly, in its decision on the constitutionality of the Aadhaar project, the Supreme Court itself stopped short of mandating prior judicial review of disclosure of biometric/demographic information from the Aadhaar database in the interest of national security.[82] Hence, the policy analysis of health data cannot draw comfort from the *Puttaswamy* verdict and assume that health data of individuals will enjoy protection from state actors.

As a practical matter therefore, the outlook in India is one of unchecked state access to health data about individuals, particularly in cases of databases controlled directly or indirectly by the government.

Pathways for Cautious Progress

Health data is one element of information about individuals. The gains for India from better systems that capture, store and process health data about individuals can be envisioned; however along with these, there are harms in the form of enhanced unaccountable state power. This raises questions about large-scale national systems that will capture data and make it readily accessible to officials of the Indian state, and give the state greater legibility and control over individual healthcare activities. As has been the case in many other fields in India, the state of democratic safeguards within the republic hampers simplistic datafication.

In the field of health policy in India, there are large-scale difficulties in the working of public and private actors. A substantial work programme is pending, through which progress can be made on these fronts. A transformation of the underlying data is neither necessary nor sufficient for solving these deeper problems. In sequence, it would make sense to solve the fundamental problems of health and then come back to large-scale data digitization. We may also hope that there would be improvements in civil liberties in India over this period.

A cautious approach is appealing. Instead of embarking on a maximalist strategy on data capture, and hoping that the health policy and privacy policy work programmes will succeed in parallel, it would be more useful to take one small step at a time, while constantly staying in touch with the costs and benefits, the risk and reward, as understood by researchers in the social sciences and humanities. Such a process, of crossing the river by feeling the stones, is more likely to yield useful results and avoid unpleasant, unintended consequences. Some elements of such thinking may be sketched as follows:

1. **Household panel data**. The maximalist programme is one where data about all or many healthcare transactions is captured by overhauling the informational plumbing of the healthcare system. Such a programme runs into difficulties of privacy (protecting data about individuals from the state) and state control (e.g., central control over vaccination through CoWin). These problems are minimized when longitudinal data is constructed through a random sample of households, and identities are not revealed. Such a dataset holds little possibility of containing data of a person of interest, and it is hence not of interest from the viewpoint of states desiring information about individuals. Many of the objectives of undertaking data analysis that can feed back into a better health system can be achieved using sample-based data sets. Such longitudinal data sets are focused on producing better knowledge, without changing the power structure. Building such data sets is safer when the checks and balances are weak. An example of a broadly similar approach is the COVID-19 Infection Survey, organized by the Office for National Statistics in the United Kingdom, in collaboration with major universities. It is one of the largest coronavirus infections and antibodies surveys in the United Kingdom in which randomly selected households are invited to participate voluntarily by providing their nose and throat swab samples.[83]
2. **Organic evolution of computer systems in private healthcare companies and independent practitioners**. An environment where personal health data is dispersed across a large number of private actors is safer. Under conditions of low state capacity, it would be harder for officials to piece together information about an individual from multiple private firms operating through

multiple technological standards. Some of the efficiency gains from connecting up data across multiple systems would still be obtained when private persons would voluntarily establish mechanisms for interconnection based on business considerations. The enactment of a general data protection statute can help address some of the harms that stem from private aggregation and analysis of health data such as discrimination, loss of employment, subjection to blackmail and extortion, etc. The idea is to avoid the state forcing private persons into using specific standards, or in controlling large quantities of health data.

3. **Caution on data localization requirements.** Another pathway for cautious progress could be rules about data localization. To the extent that data about Indian individuals is stored in countries that have strong privacy protections, with cloud computing contracts given out to firms that do not have a legal person in India, this could create better checks and balances. When this is done, Indian actors and policymakers would freeride on the data protection safeguards that have emerged in other countries. This could be a useful intermediate stage for India, on the path to achieving more robust privacy protections.

4. **Anonymized universal test data collation**. A legal obligation could be imposed on all testing labs in the country to submit anonymized test data to a centralized database. This is, for example, already suggested under NDHM. This database could be controlled by a consortium of universities to restrict the potential for abuse. This data could be used for epidemiological surveillance, such as to obtain daily data on the number of positive dengue fever tests for each city.

These ideas are not exhaustive; they are put forward as illustrations, to find pathways for action in Indian health data, where each step is modest, where each step can be understood deeply in terms of its impact upon society, where the gains appear to be significant but the possibility for harm is low, where the argument does not rest on axiomatic claims that more data always improves the welfare of the people.

Conclusion

Multiple private and public initiatives are presently under way, through which health data about individuals will be collected. Alongside this, there are little checks and balances against lawful and unlawful access to this information by government officials. In this chapter, we have shown specific examples of harms that can flow from this.

In a robust democracy, effective checks and balances are ordinarily in place, through which information systems do not enhance state legibility, and do not concentrate additional power into the hands of government officials and elected politicians. However, in India, where basic privacy protections are not in place or are just developing, electronic systems that hold health data about individuals can enhance state legibility. The simple urge of establishing information systems, is hence a poor guide for action.

Improvements in data can indeed help in improving the health of the people of India. It would make sense to take small steps, constantly weighing the benefits versus the dangers. A research programme is required, where humanities and social science knowledge is brought to bear on envisioning modest initiatives in data, in establishing that benefits to society would actually arise, while the potential harms would be small.

13

Health-Tracking Technologies: Privacy and Public Health

Smitha Krishna Prasad

EARLY in the new millennium, we saw the first of modern preventive health-monitoring technologies, push-button-enabled pendants allowing elderly patients to call for medical assistance, and wireless telemedicine technologies providing home monitoring for the elderly.[1] The premise for the telemedicine technology was simple. It was meant to centre the patient and their need for medical monitoring and assistance, while providing for autonomy over their information. This meant a design that ensured a closed loop of communication, where any data, including medical information, would only pass through the hands, or rather the devices and servers, of the participants, the patient, the doctor and the hospital, and no additional parties. The 'digital representation of the body' that technology enabled was only an enrichment of the pre-existing, intimate relationship between a patient and their doctor, or perhaps family members.[2]

In 2021, the means we have for monitoring and self-tracking health indicators would be unrecognizable in comparison. The sale and use of preventive fitness and health monitoring technologies is largely consumer driven today. While the information gathered using such technology may be useful in understanding patient health, there is typically limited intervention by medical professionals in prescribing or monitoring the use of such technology. Quantification is promoted as a means to understand one's self and body better, and many consider self-tracking essential to 'living a better life'.

The technologies used today range from fitness and activity-tracking wearables (Fitbit and Garmin's watches and trackers, Oura's smart ring, products linked to mobile ecosystems such as the Apple watch and Samsung's Galaxy watches), and home health devices such as weighing scales and mattresses that connect to applications on our phones, to inbuilt features on the smartphones many of us carry with us everywhere (Google Fit, Samsung Health, Apple's fitness app). In addition to tracking mechanisms native to devices, there are several third-party applications available on mobile or even browsers, which track fitness and health-related metrics. This could include auto-tracking of metrics such as GPS location, and some physical activity as well as manual logging of information, or even a combination of the two (activity-tracking applications such as Strava, Move, Zombie Run; workout trackers such as Shred, CureFit and Centr; menstrual-cycle-tracking applications such as Clue, Flo and Maya; diet/calorie-counting applications such as Zero, See How You Eat; applications that log health and fitness information such as MyFitnessPal, HealthifyMe; and mental health services such as Ginger.io). Many apps provide multiple functions, and often include a social aspect encouraging discussion, comparison and even competition among users. Even the everyday use of social media applications contributes to user's understanding and tracking of commonly shared health metrics.[3]

There are also several other health-monitoring technologies within the broader Internet of Things world, or an 'Internet of Medical Things', including connected devices that monitor metrics such as pulse/heart rate, blood pressure and glucose levels, useful for people with specific conditions such as diabetes. Similarly, with the COVID-19 pandemic, devices such as pulse oximeters now connect to mobile/

web applications that help collate readings,[4] as well as wearable devices for this purpose.[5]

Apart from services geared towards monitoring personal health, 'smart, connected lifestyles' now include thermostats that can be connected remotely, air purifiers that record air quality readings and user behaviour patterns, and applications that crowdsource water quality readings.[6]

These technologies collect and process large amounts of data from users, whether actively provided by the user, measured using sensors built into the devices, or tracked based on use. Users can measure some of their tracked data directly, and services offered also include elements of analysis and prediction.

Such information, whether based on self-tracking or the services that the technology provides, is meant to be beneficial to user's health. However, opinions vary on the overall health benefits of preventive health monitoring technologies. Fitness trackers are possibly the most visible/mainstream among the lot, and several studies based on user behaviour and other metrics suggest that while the use of fitness trackers might improve health indicators and promote healthier lifestyles, they are not always beneficial when used or mandated as a part of employee or corporate wellness programmes.[7]

In addition, many of these technologies have competitive/social media elements, which can result in the performance of 'health' and 'fitness', to the tune of metrics that are not always accurate or verified.[8] This disembodiment of tracked and monitored health and other personal data results in data being envisioned as a resource above all else, a performative resource for the individual,[9] and an economic resource for the private sector and often government.[10] The personal, social and cultural effects of the datafication of bodies, where users 'turn bodies and minds into measurable machines and information dispensers',[11] are also of concern, particularly in relation to marginalized groups.[12]

One of the more direct concerns is the impact of these practices on user privacy. Research shows that users have different levels of concern regarding the privacy implications of such technologies,[13] with the 'privacy paradox' (the idea that people value their privacy, but do not reflect such values in their privacy-relinquishing behaviour) being prevalent among users of fitness-tracking devices. Many technologies are also accessible to minors, leading to concerns both about the impact this may have on their privacy, as well as their health if they use services or features that are designed for different age groups and body types.[14]

This chapter will first look at how data protection laws govern the collection and processing of personal data and particularly personal health information. Next, we will look at how privacy and data protection concerns can play out in the context of third parties that support or partner with the technology providers, for instance, as a part of corporate wellness programmes. The third and fourth parts of this chapter will address the use of the data generated by these technologies for research or improving community and public health systems. The last part will present some suggestions on the way forward.

Health Trackers, Personal Health Information and the Law

Most of the devices, applications and services listed above, are positioned as beneficial to the user's health. In some cases, the technology at hand is more in the nature of telemedicine, connecting the user to a medical professional and collecting information that will be beneficial to the medical services provided along the way. Devices that track metrics for the purpose of helping healthcare professionals diagnose, prevent or monitor treatment for diseases or disorders may be considered 'medical devices' and regulated as such under the law.[15] However, while many technologies do not provide any direct medical services, they support and facilitate healthier lifestyles, tracking information that will help users identify the steps they need to take towards better health, and nudging them to take such steps. The common feature is that they collect a variety of personal information from their users, and that the immediate service that is provided is only one of many purposes such information is used for.

Dissecting the different kind of data that a service provider collects and understanding the actual use the data is put to, are complicated when such a wide variety of information is used. This kind of detail is restricted to documents such as a privacy policy or terms and conditions of use, and not often obvious to users from the information provided about the product at the time of marketing or sale.

The nature of user provided information is easier to identify and understand. This could include basic identifying information, name, email, phone number, date of birth; financial information such as credit card or e-banking information for payments; fitness or related information including food and weight logs, information about menstrual cycles, pre-existing health conditions, and health goals relevant to the services they provide.

There is more ambiguity with information that is tracked and measured automatically by the device or application. Some answers are more obvious than others. Fitness-tracking wearables will be expected to collect information about the number of steps a user takes, or the user's heart rate in the middle of an exercise routine. However, devices and applications collect and track several additional categories of data that may not be obvious or known to the user. This could include information about the way users interact with a smartphone or wearable device, the wi-fi access points a device connects to or information that comes from a third party. In addition to information that is simply tracked and captured, they also build profiles based on a user's activity and interaction with the technology. Often, this kind of information is at the crux of our discomfort around the privacy impact of these technologies. At the same time, it could be critical to the service that is provided.

Legal systems vary in how they identify and regulate the collection and processing of different types of personal information. In some cases, all personal information is afforded a certain minimum level of protection, while a defined subset of personal information that constitutes 'health information' is given additional protection either under the same or different sets of regulation. The Indian Personal Data Protection Bill, 2021, or the PDP Bill, which was proposed before the Indian Parliament first in 2019, and has now been withdrawn,[16] the European General Data Protection Regulation, 2016/679 (GDPR), and other laws providing comprehensive data protection regulation follow this approach. Alternatively, specific rules and regulations may be implemented to deal with different types of data, depending on the use case for such data.

Most countries that are discussing data protection regulation today seem to be leaning towards the first option.[17] Countries like the United States of America, take a slightly different approach. The US has sector-specific or use-case-specific regulation such as the Health Insurance Portability and Accountability Act, 1996 (HIPAA), which seeks to protect health information that is received by 'a healthcare provider, health plan, employer, or healthcare clearing house' at the federal level. However, some state governments have a comprehensive law supported by use-case-specific laws in addition to federal law. For instance, the state of California has a Consumer Privacy Act, as well as the California Confidentiality of Medical Information Act.

In India, rules under the Information Technology Act, 2000, currently provide for data protection regulation. These rules aim to protect both personal information, that is, 'any information that relates to a natural person, which, either directly or indirectly, in combination with other information available or likely to be available with a body corporate, is capable of identifying such person'[18] and sensitive personal information which includes personal information consisting of or relating to physical, physiological and mental health condition, medical records and history, biometric information and financial information among other things.[19] These rules are however limited in nature, requiring minimal data protection standards to be followed, by private corporations only.

The PDP Bill (now withdrawn) aimed to regulate the collection and processing of 'personal data', defined to mean 'data about or relating to a natural person who is directly or indirectly identifiable, having regard to any characteristic, trait, attribute or any other feature of the identity of such natural person, whether online or offline, or any combination of such features with any other information'. Personal data also includes any inference drawn from such data for the purpose of profiling.

Processing of such data will only be permitted for a specific, clear and lawful purpose, and subject to the provisions of the law.

Most preventive health-monitoring technologies are likely to collect and process some categories of information that fall within the scope of the wide definitions of 'personal data' provided for under frameworks such as the withdrawn PDP Bill and the GDPR. This can include the basic identifying information provided by the user, such as their name, email, and a myriad of other types of data depending on the technology at hand.

These frameworks also typically recognize health data as 'sensitive personal data', which is afforded additional protections. Under the withdrawn PDP Bill, health data included data that relates to the state of physical or mental health; records regarding the past, present or future state of health; data collected during registration for or provision of health services; and data associating an individual to specific health services. Several data categories relevant to preventive health monitoring technologies, such as user-provided information about pre-existing diseases, symptoms of mental or physical health conditions, or tracked data on user's heart rate and blood pressure, will perhaps fall within the first subset. While other commonly collected information, such as step counts and exercise logs may not directly refer to the state of one's health, the information could still be considered health data, if the technologies are considered to be providing health services. The GDPR, for example, defines 'data concerning health' to mean 'personal data related to the physical or mental health of a natural person, including the provision of healthcare services, which reveal information about his or her health status'.[20] This definition is replicated in the United Kingdom General Data Protection Regulation, and the UK Information Commissioner's Office[21] clearly states that data from medical devices or data from fitness trackers will constitute health data.[22]

While the preventive health-monitoring technologies discussed in this chapter are most likely to collect and/or use personal data and health data, there is a high likelihood that they collect, use or infer other types of sensitive personal data as well, including information about sex life, sexual orientation, biometric data, genetic data, transgender status, intersex status and financial data.[23]

If a data protection law that addresses these issues is passed, we will have more clarity from the law, regulatory action, and independent case law or precedent to help identify how the different types of data commonly collected and processed by preventive health-monitoring technologies are categorized as 'health data' or 'sensitive data'.

However, it is safe to assume that most preventive health monitoring technology will involve the processing of some sensitive personal data. This categorization and its impact could be critical given the nature and use cases for preventive health-monitoring technologies. The journey of self-measurement 'health factors' like weight is not new. However, these actions were usually undertaken at an individual level, in the privacy of a doctor's office or in one's own home, a kind of privacy that was sought after.[24] Today, the kinds of factor that users of preventive health-monitoring technologies use to track 'health' on a daily basis have expanded vastly, and the measurement itself takes place through connected devices always available to the user on their person, at their home, in their offices. However, the data that is measured through these devices is not just available to the user and healthcare professionals. It is available to the parent company that makes the device and/or sells the service, as well as third-party analytics companies.[25] In cases where the user is given the tracking product through their employer, insurance company or even the government, this data will perhaps be shared with these organizations as well.

Studies suggest that while many users care about the impact that such practices have on their privacy, even users of commonly available and well-known products and services have a limited understanding of the personal data that these services collect, and the subsequent use of such data.[26] However, rather than simply acknowledging this contradiction as representative of the privacy paradox,[27] user behaviours that both recognize and seemingly ignore the data protection concerns can possibly be attributed to a combination of a privacy calculus[28](where the benefit of using the technology outweighs the risks to some extent) and cynicism (caused by the recognition that individual-level privacy-protective behaviour is unlikely to be sufficient).[29]

Recognition of the sensitivity of the data collected and processed in the case of preventive health monitoring technologies, as well as the impact of the processing of such data via a regulatory mechanism is therefore critical. For example, the PDP Bill provided for means to determine whether personal data should be considered sensitive personal data, even if not defined as such directly in the law. Some of the key factors that the PDP Bill provided for determining whether personal data should be considered 'sensitive personal data': the risk of significant harm to the individual, the expectation of confidentiality, the risk factor to a 'discernible class' of individuals, and whether ordinary provisions under the law are adequate.[30]

Factors such as 'expectation of confidentiality' may be considered relative, as users' attitude towards measuring their bodies and tracking their activities are continually shifting.[31] But not only do the service providers collect and process user data for profit by means which may not have a direct impact on user's health, they also now often set the standards for 'normalcy' in the context of health.[32] This in turn could have a higher direct impact on user health, and indirect impact on both user's employment, insurance and general financial status, as well as community health and public health measures.

The categorization of personal data as 'sensitive' under privacy laws is significant because of the additional steps required of service providers to reduce the risk of harm to their users. For instance, technologies that process sensitive personal data, or profile users at a large scale will typically trigger the requirement for a data protection impact assessment prior to the use of such technology.[33] Regulation that is specifically applicable to health data, or certain types of sensitive data may also be useful, whether independent of, or in addition to, a comprehensive but basic data protection law. However, as the US experience with HIPAA shows, advances in healthcare technology can outpace privacy and security protections under law, if they are too narrow. In the case of HIPAA, providers that frequently process healthcare information such as health and fitness mobile applications and devices, gyms and fitness clubs are not covered by the law.[34] As a result, additional regulatory mechanisms have become necessary to cater to these digital health services.

Corporate Wellness, Individual Choice, and Third-party Responsibility

One of the distinguishing factors that bring the various products and services discussed in this chapter together is that although they relate to the health and medical fields, they are typically mobile first, and do not require third-party intervention to enable use. This direct-to-consumer approach has meant that many preventive health-monitoring technologies are not regulated, or subject to any soft requirements that they would otherwise need to fulfil to pass muster in the eyes of third parties such as trained healthcare professionals, potentially a key factor in the uptake of such technologies in the market.[35]

Regulatory responses to preventive health-monitoring technologies need to be broad and flexible enough to address the collection and processing of a wide variety of personal and sensitive personal data, with several different aims. However, the identification of the different parties involved in such processing and attribution of roles and responsibilities are not an easy task.

A 2014 study by the US Federal Trade Commission (FTC) revealed that twelve personal health applications and devices transmitted information, including data that could be used to identify users, to seventy-six third parties.[36] In addition, eighteen third parties received device-specific identifiers, and twenty-two received other key health information. One federal trade commissioner also noted that after the audit, they still did not know where that information ultimately went.[37]

Some of the key third-party uses for preventive health-monitoring technology that we do know about are community/corporate wellness programs adopted by employers. Corporate wellness programs are not new, and many large employers especially in the US, have been providing ones that include health insurance and promote better health among their employees for several decades. The addition of health-tracking technologies in the past few years has offered a boost to these programs. Insurers also often work with employers to integrate fitness-tracking information into the plans they offer employees. The providers of many of the popular technologies discussed earlier in this chapter offer their products and services to corporate employers, offering options of buying their products and services for their employees, or incentivizing employees to buy them at discounted rates. In addition, several third-party services offer employers software that collates data across health-monitoring technologies.[38]

There are several incentives for corporate employers to encourage the use of health-monitoring technologies among employees, including the potential reduction in healthcare costs where employers provide health insurance, increased productivity, and tracking of employee safety (in industrial settings).[39] These are often promoted as 'win-win' programs that help employers and employees alike. However, there are significant concerns over privacy, security and discrimination for employees. Although most of these programs start off as voluntary, and are 'encouraged' by employers, they are not often truly voluntary for the employee, given the power imbalance in the relationship between an employer and employee. Information about employee health/well-being (including mental health), or even simply willingness to participate could be used in making (discriminatory) hiring and promotion decisions, and even used against employees in court. Further, the social and competitive aspects of these programs could have a negative impact on the well-being of those employees who do not, and more significantly cannot, use wearables or other technologies in the way employers recommend. For instance, one of the more common features of corporate wellness programs that use fitness trackers is counting steps taken in a day or tracking physical activity, and encouraging friendly competition among employees/teams. One study showed that this could have a negative impact on employees who cannot undertake such physical activity due to illness, injuries or disability.[40]

As discussed in the previous section, preventive health-monitoring technologies invariably collect and process large amounts of personal and sensitive personal information, with limited transparency on the actual use of this data. When the use of such technologies is promoted or required by third parties such as employers, the number of actors that have access to and can process such personal and sensitive personal health information increases, thereby increasing the risks associated with the data processing.

The legality and regulation of such data-processing activities depend on several additional factors, depending on the contractual arrangements between the technology provider, the employer (and/or insurance provider) and the individual user.

The primary questions that typically arise are those of purpose and consent. Corporate wellness programmes can sometimes be linked to health insurance-related incentives, suggesting that some data is shared with an insurance company. In other cases, the use of preventive health-monitoring technologies may be required as a part of performance management or occupational health safety management programmes. In each of these cases, the employer is likely to be considered the controller of data collection and processing activities, with the technology provider acting as a data processor. Any third parties assisting in the administration of the wellness programmes, as well as insurance providers involved, are also likely to be considered data processors providing the employer a service. While there is the possibility of variation depending on the structure of the programme and contractual arrangement between the parties, this reading of such programmes places responsibility for the collection and processing of personal data on the employer.

American scholars suggest that irrespective of the purpose, such collection and processing of data is permitted under US law.[41] On the other hand, the GDPR places an added emphasis on protecting the employee in employer–employee relationships. European scholars argue that employers may not be permitted to run programs promoting or requiring the use of preventive health-monitoring technologies by their employees for the purpose of wellness under the GDPR.[42] In the case of occupational safety programs, employers may meet the requirements for a 'legitimate purpose' for the collection and processing of data, but other requirements under the GDPR will be difficult to comply with, including those for data minimization and accuracy of data. European law also judges the meaningfulness of consent provided by an employee on a harsher metric, given the power imbalance in an employer–employee relationship. This concern is only exacerbated where an employer collects sensitive health information.

The withdrawn PDP Bill in India also recognized some of the concerns prevalent in an employer–employee relationship, and provided for permitted collection and processing of employee data. However, this provision clearly stated that employers could only collect personal data that was not sensitive personal data, where employment was used as a ground for processing data.⁴³ The employer would need consent of the employee for the collection and processing of sensitive personal information.⁴⁴ In such cases, standard requirements specifying that consent would need to be free, clear, informed, specific to the purpose, and given with the option of withdrawal, will be applicable. The employer was also required to ensure that the employee is aware of the (significant) harm that can occur, and provide the employee the option of separately consenting to the different categories of data collection depending on the purpose of collection of such data. While Indian jurisprudence is not as clear as its European counterpart in examining the meaningfulness of consent in such a context, the requirements that are generally applicable in relation to processing of sensitive personal data, combined with those applicable to processing of employee data may regulate, if not restrict, automated collection and processing of data from preventive health-monitoring technologies in corporate wellness programs.

In addition to technology providers, and employers, insurance providers often have an important role in corporate wellness programmes. Insurance companies are required to adhere to minimum requirements to ensure customer data is safe.⁴⁵ However, these requirements are minimal in nature and cannot be considered a substitute for a comprehensive data protection law. Once such a law is in place, insurance providers will perhaps have additional responsibilities in this regard. However, the implications of incentivizing the use of preventive health-monitoring technologies, which among other things do not guarantee accuracy of data,⁴⁶ go beyond data protection alone, and could lead to discriminatory/exclusionary actions that harm users.

The withdrawn PDP Bill famously departed from the standard understanding of stakeholders as 'data controllers' and 'data processors'.⁴⁷ It provided for 'data fiduciaries', who are essentially what frameworks such as the GDPR consider to be 'data controllers'. The drafters of the earlier version of the PDP Bill aspired to incorporate a fiduciary responsibility to protect data.⁴⁸ However, simply using the term 'data fiduciary', in a legal framework that does not otherwise enable or require additional responsibility to be undertaken, may not suffice for this purpose,⁴⁹ as opposed to the health sector where ethical and legal frameworks place certain responsibilities on medical professionals.⁵⁰ In the context of preventive health-monitoring technologies, it would typically befall the service provider, to undertake such a fiduciary duty. When third parties such as employers take on the role traditionally ascribed to data controllers, the distribution of responsibilities becomes murkier.

The fiduciary model may be of value in such cases of heightened responsibility, both by virtue of the sensitivity of the data, as well as the nature of relationship between an employer and employee. However, there is a long way to go once the law comes into effect, to understand how the interests of employees are protected.

Even if the immediate data protection risks are accounted for, the business models discussed above allow employers and insurance companies to use automated data processing by preventive health monitoring technologies to set standards of normality, and good health for employees and communities of workers.⁵¹ This raises questions of algorithmic transparency, ethics and the accountability of different stakeholders. The risks that could arise out of such models are numerous, for instance, if based on inaccurate data, or profiling models, the standards of health that communities of corporate and industrial workers aspire to could in themselves be harmful to mental and physical health. In the absence of adequate anti-discrimination laws, employees could be impacted by hiring, promotion, or even firing decisions taken based on unknown factors deciphered from such (potentially inaccurate) data. In other cases, increasing costs of insurance could have a negative impact not only on an individual employee's ability to access healthcare, but the costs of healthcare for entire communities. Beyond data protection law, there is need for a more holistic approach towards identifying and protecting against the harms that can be caused by large-scale automated profiling activities undertaken in the name of 'health'.

Community Fitness, Digital Governance and Public Health

The other third-party model is government collaboration with companies that offer preventive health-monitoring technologies. For instance, Singapore's Health Promotion Board (HPB) has a history of promoting the use of mobile applications and fitness trackers to encourage healthy lifestyles among citizens and residents.[52] In 2021, it ran multiple programs that involve collaboration with fitness tracker providers Fitbit and Apple. The LiveHealthy SG[53] and LumiHealth[54] programs allow Singaporeans to purchase subsidised subscriptions to health programs provided by the technology providers (and devices in the case of Fitbit). Users are rewarded for completing activities and challenges, which are redeemable in the form of vouchers issued by the HPB. Aggregated, anonymized data is shared with the HPB under both programs. It appears that under LiveHealth SG, a collaboration with Fitbit, the health programs and challenges are administered by Fitbit, and the data collected and processed by Fitbit is shared in aggregate form with the HPB. The LumiHealth program appears to have an additional party involved, Evidation Health, the program operation partner. Evidation Health collects the data and shares randomized data with the HPB, and aggregate program-level data with Apple (users have the option of sharing randomized data with Apple as well). Both the HPB and Apple can in turn share this data with third parties that provide services relating to the program. The aim of the two programs seems to be to promote healthy lifestyles among Singaporeans, and they align with other programs run by the HPB.[55]

In a separate program, Health Insights Singapore, the HPB is conducting a two-year pilot population health study that 'makes use of wearable technology to understand the health behaviours and lifestyles of Singapore residents'.[56] In this case, the HPB issues Fitbit devices to citizens and residents who sign up. The aim of this study is not to promote healthy activity, and users are not expected to change or improve their behaviours in this aspect. However, the HPB collects information regarding their health behaviours and lifestyle patterns, and it appears that later stages of the study will involve understanding user responses to nudges and prompts developed under the program. In this case, the HPB undertakes some responsibility for the personal data it collects and processes under a very simple privacy policy.[57] It is not clear whether the agreement that residents sign when enrolling in the program has any additional terms in this regard. However, Fitbit, as collector of the data, will continue to have access to the data after sharing it with the HPB.

In addition, there is potential for more informal public sector use of preventive health-monitoring technologies, for instance, in the capacity of recommendations and requirements imposed by schools, employers, or even government bodies in relation to the use of wearable devices or mobile applications. In Norway, a municipality was fined after two schools required students to download and use fitness application Strava as a part of their physical education lessons during the COVID-19 pandemic. The Norwegian Data Protection Authority noted that a data protection impact assessment should have been undertaken prior to the use of fitness app Strava, since its use involves processing of particular categories of personal data, including the student's location data. The municipality was fined as no risk assessment had been carried out, and there were no procedures in place to determine which apps could be used for school-related activities.[58]

In India, health policy frameworks that have been central to public health discourse over the past few years have focused on using both digital technologies and data to improve healthcare systems. The key issue has been the digitalization of health records in a standardized manner, to enable access across the country. There are a myriad of privacy and security issues that crop up in this context including questions regarding the potential use of data collected from preventive health-monitoring technologies in identifying and improving public health metrics.

There are limited examples of the Indian government engaging in collaboration with health-tracking technology providers, and any engagement that does exist, appears to be informal in nature. The Khelo India (Play India) program run by the Government of India, has endorsed 'fitness challenges' put out by GOQii, an 'Indian' company that sells fitness trackers.[59] However, the parameters of such an arrangement are not clear.

Other examples include controversial programs such as digital tracking of maternal and child healthcare.[60] Access to maternal healthcare is a challenge for many women in India and such programs may allow for better care for both mother and child. However, privacy concerns remain unaddressed, and with stated aims for some programs including tracking of abortions the potential for discriminatory action is also enhanced.

The immediate area of concern, as the COVID-19 pandemic continues to wreak havoc, is the potential for using data from preventive healthcare technologies to respond to the pandemic. For instance, studies show that wearable devices can potentially flag early signs of COVID,[61] or assist in monitoring patients under quarantine.[62] Other examples suggest that wearable devices already used to promote worker safety in industrial settings could also help ensure social distancing and reduce spread of the infection.[63]

In light of the attempts to engage with digital contact-tracing processes, and many other technologies that aim to monitor quarantine, enable vaccination and otherwise assist in responding to COVID-19, there are legitimate concerns around the use of unproven methods that engage in extensive data collection, without adequate safeguards to protect privacy. Further, while COVID responses were emergent in nature, and are meant to be temporary, the harms that badly planned and executed health surveillance could lead to extend well beyond such scenarios.

Healthcare Technologies and Public Health Research

Many of the preventive health monitoring technologies also use the data that they collect from their users, in aggregate, de-identified form, towards public health or community-based research. For instance, Clue, which runs an application to track menstrual cycles and reproductive health, engages with academic institutions such as Columbia University and Massachusetts Institute of Technology (MIT), to look into questions of public health as they impact people who menstruate.[64] Ginger.io conducts research on mental health, and partners with academic and medical institutions to build on research using data collected from its users.[65] In addition to conducting its own research on health behaviours, Fitbit offers researchers discounts to purchase devices for studies that utilize Fitbit for research.[66] Several of these initiatives can be useful to public health research, particularly in under-researched areas as in the case of menstrual trackers or mental health service providers. However, such research is data-intensive, and adequate care must be taken to protect individual users while promoting public health goals in a balanced manner.

Data protection laws including the GDPR and the now withdrawn PDP Bill that was proposed in India consist of exceptions that permit the use of personal data for research.

The GDPR allows derogations from some provisions where data is used for scientific or historical research. However, it also provides that processing for research must take into account the rights and freedoms of data subjects, and ensure data minimization.[67] The PDP Bill provided that exemptions from compliance with the provisions of the law can be permitted if the processing of personal data is required for research purposes, if: i) compliance with the law disproportionately diverts resources from the research purpose; ii) the research purpose cannot be achieved if the personal data is anonymized, iii) the data has been de-identified;[68] iv) the personal information is not to be used to take any action specific to the individual; and v) the processing is not to cause any risk or significant harm to the individual. The exemption would need to be explicitly provided by way of regulation under the law.

To the extent that this or similar provisions are adopted, it will become important to identify the bounds of such an exception. This may include guidelines on nature of research activities that may be permitted to access personal data and de-identified or anonymized data (differentially applicable to each if required), or the qualification of organizations or persons that may be given exemptions in this regard (factoring metrics such as research for profit versus non-profit, for instance).

To the extent that any public health or research activities envisage the collection or processing of personal and sensitive personal data by the government, the provisions of the law will need to consider whether adequate restrictions are placed on government use of personal data and sensitive personal data under the law. The PDP Bill consisted of some controversial provisions in this respect. Among other things, it provided the government with the power to direct any data fiduciary or data processor to provide the government with any anonymized personal data or non-personal data, to enable better targeting of delivery of services, or formulation of evidence-based policies by the government. The data collected from preventive health-monitoring technologies form only a small part of data that may be required for comprehensive evidence-based policymaking. As a result, it is important to protect the users of such technologies and their data, as well as those citizens/residents of the country who may be impacted by policies made based on data that does not fully account for their needs. As in the case of employer use of preventive health-monitoring technologies for employee well-being, the use of data from such technologies for research, and by government for promotion of public health, demands a holistic approach towards identifying and protecting against the harms.

Apart from concerns that directly concern health or healthcare policy, the PDP Bill was also criticized for the lack of regulation of surveillance activities. The information collected by technologies such as fitness trackers, can be used to track individuals' activities and location in relation to criminal investigations, or even simply government employment.[69] However, considering the risks of inaccuracy of the data collected, among others, it is important to ensure that adequate protections are in place to prevent the misuse of such data.

Going Forward: A Targeted but Holistic Approach

Conversations about health-monitoring technologies and privacy, and health-monitoring technologies and public health, are often on different ends of the spectrum of 'trade-offs', limiting our ability to obtain granular insights on the subject. This is exacerbated by the fact that we do not currently have a legal framework that supports this intersection of policymaking goals, and there is considerable uncertainty on what that framework will look like. However, it seems apparent that with the increasing popularity of self-tracking, these technologies will have a larger footprint in our lives. For many, this technology brings with it a new sense of empowerment. It is, however, argued that using technology service providers with large-scale data analytics capabilities, and profit motives, to engage in such self-tracking empowers the service providers to set the standards we aspire to,[70] impacting our health and healthcare systems in ways that we are yet to discover.

In an idealized version of self-tracking, we would perhaps be able to track our data on specified, limited terms, and practise boundary management at an individual level. In its absence, it is important to consider what is required to protect the individuals and the communities that the health-monitoring technologies serve and draw from. This requires, at the baseline, a comprehensive framework to protect privacy, to enable us to identify the data that is at stake, its potential use, stakeholders we need protection against, and consequential harms.

The use of preventive health-monitoring technologies poses risks of data breach or misuse of data by the technology providers or third parties including, analytics companies, advertisers, employers, insurance providers and governments, as in the examples discussed in this chapter. Where the data is used by stakeholders that have a direct contractual relationship with considerable control over the individual, for instance employers and insurance providers, additional risks of discriminatory actions or increase in healthcare costs become relevant.

When the personal data tracked by such technologies is used by government or in public health research and policymaking, there is a heightened risk at the community level. In this context, we must recognize that most of the examples discussed in this chapter speak to the users' ability to access and use a computer or a smartphone, requiring a minimum threshold of financial and social capital. Even when these technologies are promoted by employers or governments (as in the case of Singapore) there is some semblance of agency on the part of the individual. The use of data generated by technologies with such a limited user base in public health research could lead to inaccurate findings that may be discriminatory to those communities that do not have access to such technologies.

At each of these levels, there is a need for adequate ethical and regulatory guidelines, on both medical research, as well as privacy practices, that take a holistic approach towards addressing these challenges.

14

Data Stewardship: Solutions for Sharing of Health Data

*Astha Kapoor**

Introduction

DURING the Ebola epidemic (2013–15) the World Health Organization (WHO) highlighted the importance of rapid data sharing to investigate and predict the disease and evaluate methods to curb spread. Data on health surveillance, trial data, case reports, etc., was to be shared with public health officials, clinical and aid workers, researchers, governments and non-profits to address the evolving conditions of the epidemic.[1] However, it was realized that there were many gaps in data sharing, even though its value for public health response was clear. These gaps were data protection and confidentiality of individuals, especially concerns around consent, accuracy of data, political and cultural issues such as countries withholding data, reciprocity, poor infrastructure for

---

* The author thanks Soujanya Sridharan and Siddharth Manohar for their inputs.

sharing, and lack of resources.² Therefore, to address some of these concerns, the WHO drafted an agreement on data sharing for public health emergencies.³ Within the world of academic research it was decided that pre-publication dissemination of public health data will be prioritized in case of emergencies, and will be shared with the WHO before publication.⁴

As a result, in January 2020, in an early examination of the unfolding health crisis of the new COVID-19 crisis, the WHO stressed the importance of data sharing. Initial successes such as the release of the full viral genome sequence through public access platform made it possible to diagnose infections much faster than ever before. The mRNA vaccine manufactured by Pfizer and Moderna was a result of data sharing norms established by the Bermuda Principles, to rapidly release DNA sequence data.⁵ However, the process of data generation, sharing and use is more complex in the COVID-19 crisis, largely due to the role of technology (and technology companies) and the abundance and diversity of data. Insights are being generated on the basis of data from phone towers, wearables, smart phones and social media, and harness data not directly related to health but also questions of environment, sanitation, lifestyle, consumption history, etc., to make assessments on the vulnerability to the disease. Fundamentally, in the context of COVID-19, all data is considered health data.⁶ Matters are made more complex by the involvement of technology giants such as Apple and Google in specific instances of digital contact tracing, and also by using the pandemic for wider spherical transgressions.⁷

Even beyond the pandemic, the sharing of data is critical for public health. Individuals are generating data, through wearable devices, e-commerce websites and social media, which is critical for new health research and innovations.⁸ Health data can improve treatment and quality of care, prioritize cost effective responses, enable personalized medication, and allow government in particular to plan resources and workforce among many other impacts.⁹ Governments and funders globally are realizing the value of this and setting up policies, systems, protocols to enable more sharing.¹⁰

In the context of health data there are two major concerns. First, as with the Ebola pandemic, the quality of data – accuracy, granularity and inter-operability and overall usability persist.[11] Health data is also in silos, with one individual's data distributed across different service providers, and similarly, data related to a singular problem also scattered and inaccessible. Second, there are ethical and legal risks of this degree of data processing, and increased vulnerability of individuals and communities to surveillance and tracking. In all of this, the fundamental question of health data as a public good, and the risk its use poses to digital rights, need to be resolved. It is also important to note that given the high levels of sensitivity with regard to health data, sharing must navigate complex questions of data protection, intellectual property rights, etc.

In India, the need for reliable public health data was made clear very early in the pandemic. The country was unable to plan the workforce and resources, and conduct decent surveillance. This resulted in the first and second waves claiming many lives. The difference between jurisdictions that were data-reliant, such as Mumbai's municipal corporation[12] and their response to the second wave was vastly different from Uttar Pradesh where the scale and gravity of the pandemic were poorly understood and managed.

Therefore, globally, but especially in India, policy documents are beginning to address this friction, and highlighting the need to use and to protect health data. Simultaneously, there is also a realization that individuals and communities that share different interests and concerns, and generate health data, should be more active stakeholders in the process of data governance. This is in contrast to them being mere audience to their data use, and instead has the space to deploy health data towards issues that matter to them, and use this data to negotiate better outcomes/services with governments and businesses. This points to a need for a new governance, policy and infrastructural tools to enable greater agential rights for citizens.

This chapter starts with a short overview of the value of data sharing for public health, examining how different sources of data are being deployed to respond to the ongoing health emergency and the benefits and challenges of health data sharing. It will engage with the question of use of data for public health, and the interface with digital rights. Thereafter, the chapter will dive deep into health data sharing in India where, new policy documents and systems such as National Digital Health Mission (NDHM), Health Data Management Policy (HDMP) and the Non-Personal Data Report (NPDR) are trying to regulate the use and reuse of health data. Finally, this chapter will explore new models of responsible data sharing, or data stewardship, which allow individuals and communities to better aggregate and control their data, and make it available for researchers and public health practitioners, as may be needed. The main assertion of the author is that data sharing for public health is critical and needs a combination of top-down regulation and policy frameworks to enable the secure sharing of data, and bottom-up models such as data cooperatives and trusts that are designed to involve people in decisions with regard to what data is collected and how it is used. The creation of this broader ecosystem that both protects and empowers individuals will make the process of data sharing fair and reliable, and in turn impact public health planning and implementation by governments, private sector and non-profits.

Valuing Health Data

There are many questions about the 'value' of public health data, especially now with an increasingly complex data value chain where both machines and humans generate data, and it is processed, analysed and made usable by researchers, technology platforms and governments, who also use different data sets to innovate. Each stakeholder adds value to data, and thus isolating the exact value of health data, and deciding how to distribute and use it are complex decisions. Data is also durable, and non-rivalrous to a certain degree – for instance, the same data set can be used by individuals to receive better patient care, by government to plan assignment of resources for research, and by providers for commercial gain.[13] Despite these multiple layers of value with regard to health data, perhaps due to the complexities of quantification, the primary value is seen as 'economic' – a resource that has property rights attached to it, which need to be protected and/or licensed as such. This reading of data diminishes its public value or value that '*is created, or captured, to the extent that public sector institutions further their democratically established goals, and their impact on improving the lives of citizens*',[14] and makes data less accessible for the purpose of public good.

The COVID-19 pandemic has helped reinforce the idea of data as critical for the generation of public value. In Ed Yong's Pulitzer-winning coverage of the COVID-19 pandemic he says that science, and large-scale scientific collaboration have helped the world deal with virus, and develop solutions for containment and treatment at breakneck speed. He points to many examples that are hinged on data sharing, such as the one presented below:

> Lauren Gardner, an engineering professor at Johns Hopkins University who has studied dengue and Zika, knew that new epidemics are accompanied by a dearth of real-time data. So she and one of her students created an online global dashboard to map and tally all publicly reported COVID-19 cases and deaths. After one night of work, they released it, on January 22. The dashboard has since been accessed daily by governments, public-health agencies, news organizations, and anxious citizens.[15]

However, the idea of public value is vague, and can be interpreted in very many ways by commercial actors to extract more data from individuals and communities. The Nuffield Foundation outlines several public interest uses of data use and reuse in the context of health-efficiency of health services, improving health outcomes by building evidence to predict, respond to and treat disease, and generating economic growth by driving innovation.[16] Private companies use these ideas of public value to ensure strategic infrastructural positions,[17] build market share and become essential to the functioning of public health concerns. For instance, Apple and Google both launched their contact tracing API. This intervention allowed the tech giants to access new spheres of health and medicine, and also provide significant legitimacy among governments and citizens.[18]

A review of qualitative research of public attitudes to data sharing suggests that individuals are more likely to consent to share data in the name of public interest with the private sector[19] and the government,[20] even though concerns exist. This over-sharing can result in 'exploitation' of individuals and series of harms emerging out of loss of privacy such as surveillance, exclusion and distortion.[21] These harms are not just confined to individuals, but also extend to communities that may suffer discrimination. Even where privacy harms are not in question, the essentialization of commercial entities in the name of public interest may diminish and undermine the public sector.

These encroachments on citizen rights in the name of public value are not just initiated by the private sector but also by the government. For instance, in India, the contact tracing app was briefly made mandatory and is still abundantly used despite major criticisms of lack of transparency, excessive collection, processing and sharing of personal data.[22]

It is clear that the idea of data value needs to be expanded to ensure that the public interest that is promised is prioritized in the collection and processing of data. Public interest is often vague and poorly defined but it is critical to pursue and chisel definitions over time. There is a need to build models and policies that enable systematic sharing of data while safeguarding rights. Several jurisdictions are investing in these systems through policies, while more bottom-up movements of data sharing and protection are growing globally. The combination of these efforts, on one hand led by governments and on the other by communities, will ensure that data sharing on the public health is safe and fair. This includes thinking about questions on the purpose of sharing, inter-operability, standards, and learning from international examples. The next section will examine the different policy approaches to data sharing globally, with a focus on India.

Health Data Sharing and Protection: Understanding the Indian Regulatory Landscape

Countries, especially in Europe after the enactment of the GDPR that puts in place a robust data protection architecture, are turning their attention to data sharing. Data sharing is done for many reasons – to address concerns of antitrust and competition by enhancing consumer choice and providing small businesses greater data access to level the playing field. Others view it as a way to ensure efficiencies within sector, bring about sustainability, and bring more data into the domain of research and innovation.[23] At the heart of all the effort is public interest and citizen welfare. Health data and its governance are critical to this conversation and many countries are embarking on, and building specific policies for, encouraging the safe use of health data, recognizing the need for this data to improve health quality and outcomes. These conversations are embedded in ensuring rights-preserving approaches to health data governance, and are implemented with varied effectiveness. Some of the high-level principles that health data governance and use must consider have been highlighted by the OECD.[24] These include enabling the use of health information research to ensure best practices of anonymization, the presence of a data protection framework, public consultation and information on health data use, transparent decision making, and periodic review of governance features to keep up with new technologies and policies. For instance, the UK has launched a new data strategy to improve patient care. This strategy has emerged out of pandemic response, recognizing that 'data saves lives'[25] and enables rapid research and patient care. Therefore, the new strategy will ensure that people are able to view their medical records, keep track of their data and share it with relevant care providers. Other strategic aims of the policy are to increase efficiencies in the National Health Service (NHS) and build AI innovation capacity within the UK.[26]

Patient empowerment and control with regard to health data is not new – HIPAA in the United States aimed to modernize the flow of health information, and safeguard personally identifiable information. It was originally developed to allow portability of health insurance between jobs and encapsulates concerns on privacy giving patients clear rights to request and amend their medical records, and limit access to their health information.

Similarly, Finland has enacted one of the most progressive legislations on the secondary use of health data which facilitates the data-sharing process while safeguarding data rights for individuals. Through an act of legislation, FinData was established in 2019 (Social and Health Data Permit Authority) which is 'a one-stop shop which offers permits, advisory and access to data for research, development and innovations'.[27] Its main aim is to open health data from national registers and patient systems for secondary use such as research, teaching, innovation and public health planning.[28] FinData reviews and grants permissions for data use, and works with all significant government departments, such as, National Institute for Health and Welfare, national e-health records system, Finnish authority for Occupational Health, etc. Individual-level data is made accessible only when de-identified, and in a secure, remote environment for a specific purpose. For statistical data, the requirements are more relaxed – data is transferred to interested parties who are allowed to use it for the purposes specified in the Act on the Secondary Use of Health and Social Data, 2019.[29] However, Finland's journey has been long and has required immense foresight and investment. As early as 2002, Finland had proposed a nationwide interoperable system, and slowly built digital systems for prescriptions and social security, adopted the GDPR guidelines for data protection, and then, after much feedback and experimentation, legislated to create FinData.

Finland's approximately twenty-year journey has many lessons for other countries looking to set up privacy-centric data-sharing systems. The focus of data sharing is public interest but anchored in the idea of individual's rights, where individuals are seen as 'owners' of the data and their rights are protected as under GDPR. FinData, a centralized permit authority, focuses only on reuse of health and social data and ascertains the purpose for data use before granting permission. Interoperability standards as defined by government departments facilitate seamless transfer for data.[30] Finally, FinData in its current form is a result of many previous pilot studies and tests, and has emerged from evidence as opposed to whims of the government. These best practices of community centrism, data protection guidelines, interoperability, technical and human capacity, sectoral decision-bodies, conditions for access and evidence-based legislation[31] are all critical for a health data strategy that aims to unlock the value, and make it usable for public health purposes while safeguarding rights.

It is on these metrics, India's efforts for data sharing and reuse must be evaluated. India has in the last few years proposed several policies and regulations for health data governance, but the landscape is in a state of flux. The government's aims to build a health technology ecosystem are apparent. For instance, the Clinical Establishment Rules (2012) mandate all clinical establishments to maintain electronic health records – this was supposed to build on the rapid digitization of the Indian landscape – and use public infrastructure such as Aadhaar, and also propose registries to build a unified ecosystem that can use technology to improve delivery of healthcare. This vision is made complex by the fact that while India is still missing a data protection framework, it is simultaneously building a complex legal landscape with many overlapping laws and regulations. There are separate regulators proposed for personal and non-personal data, in addition to a health sector authority. India's regulatory limbo is counterproductive, and prevents all stakeholders (government, private sector, academia, non-profits) from acting with reasonable speed and intelligence.

Moreover, the proposals are largely top-down, and the capacity of the community and the lower levels of the government, essential for enacting these regulations on the ground, is not considered. There is also limited space to create evidence before implementation. This means course correction and adaption are almost out of the question. The next section examines three key proposals of the government of India from the lens of health data sharing – personal data protection (PDP), which regards personal information as sensitive; non-personal data (NPD), which is focused on the harnessing of data for public value and which recommends health as primed for implementation of an NPD framework and the national digital health mission (NDHM) which proposes a new National Health Authority (NHA).

Personal Data Protection (PDP Bill) 2019

The Personal Data Protection Bill (2019), which has now been withdrawn, defined health data as 'data related to the state of physical or mental health of the data principal and includes records regarding the past, present or future state of the health of such data principal, data collected in the course of registration for, or provision of health services, data associating the data principal to the provision of specific health services'.[32] This definition encompassed health data across an individual's life cycle, and also every health-related interaction with providers of varied services. Therefore, the PDP Bill had critical implications for the health sector especially as it proposed to extend a broader regime of penalties and liabilities. It is also worth mentioning here, that the draft Digital Information Security in healthcare Act (DISHA), 2018, which was proposed by the Ministry of Health, was fairly progressive, and focused on giving power over data to the individuals. It suggested significant restrictions on the use of health data and placed an individual squarely in control of his data whereas the PDP Bill had a much softer stance on the subject. But the DISHA draft has also been abandoned for now.

The healthcare landscape in India is extremely heterogeneous, and a lot of it is still offline. healthcare providers follow their own protocols and manage their own records and data flows. This lack of process disempowers individual patients, who are unable to understand the processes and the rights and protections offered to them and, therefore, are unable to control the access to and use of their data. The withdrawn PDP Bill aimed to address some of these issues but, most fundamentally, did not afford the individual/patient the clear rights as the chief generators of data, which was critical for enhancing their control and agency. In fact, the PDP Bill also made a case for the government to process health data without consent in cases of emergencies where the definition of emergency was vague. Therefore, the idea of conditional access and purpose limitation was not defined, and could lead to misuse of data.

Further, individual ability to port their data between practitioners and for research, if desired, is seen to be critical both for enhancing user choice and making data more shareable. However, the withdrawn PDP Bill did not adequately discuss interoperability, and did not define standards for sharing, even though ad hoc processes and lack of parity in the health landscape is clear. A clear ontology for health data is essential for any sharing, whether between service providers (hospitals, start-ups) or by patients. Without this, opening the data for research and empowering individuals with the ability to share their data for better care are impossible. Data portability rights were also not entirely defined – the withdrawn bill did not clarify if inferred data or information that was derived without explicit user input by harnessing the digital life of people may not be portable for individuals. Beyond this, service provider liabilities were also not entirely clear, for instance, while larger hospitals may be significant data fiduciaries, the status of general practitioners was not clearly defined. There are also serious questions on the capacity and ability of the health data sector in general, which is overworked and understaffed, to comply with the requirements that were proposed under the PDP Bill. Large-scale investments would have to be made to create the human and technical infrastructure.

The PDP Bill was a necessary step for India – it held the promise of guaranteeing certain data rights for individuals. But it remained insufficient when it came to meaningful protection for individual data, on questions of public interest. The bill made individuals especially vulnerable to the state, which was empowered to extract data in public interest more broadly, and is beginning to set up broader systems like the DNA Databank, to store genetic information.[33] The lack of robust protection also makes it complex to share data with the private sector, researchers and academics for innovation, as individual rights may be compromised, and there may be limited avenues for redress. To enable sharing, without compromising, India will need a stronger framework overseen by the proposed health data authority to nuance the protections laid out for health data, and then over time develop structures that allow for safe reuse of health data for research and innovation. These measures need to be put in place urgently, as the COVID crisis has made the need for data-driven public health planning and implementation apparent.

Non-Personal Data Committee Report (NPD report) 2020

The conversation on the sharing of anonymized data, especially its transfer overseas, has come into focus. In May 2020, the Kerala High Court passed an interim order on the protection of personal data of individuals who have tested positive for COVID-19 in the state.[34] The case came up because the Kerala government had enlisted the support of Sprinklr, a US-based company to help manage its citizen experience.

The state government was collecting and sharing data with Sprinklr for insights that helped plan the response to the pandemic. While the main concern of the petitioner (Balu Gopalakrishnan) was that a foreign entity was being engaged to store and process sensitive personal data of Indians, other arguments such as consent from patients, concerns about commercial exploitation of sensitive data and the interface with the right to privacy were compelling. The state government argued, in its role as the fiduciary of citizen data, that protection of citizen data was guaranteed by the confidentiality clause in the contract, and also claimed to anonymize all data shared with Sprinklr. In its interim order, the court stated that its priorities were to make sure that the state government can continue its work, and that there should be no 'data epidemic'.[35] In essence, the court aimed to balance public health needs with protections. To this end, it ordered that all data be anonymized before providing access to Spriklr. But it did not provide any details on the type and rigour of anonymization. The order also provided for obtaining specific consent for sharing of anonymized data with Sprinklr, returning data to the state government by Sprinklr after the end of the contractual agreement, and finally, banning Sprinklr from using the data for any commercial use.

This case is significant because it highlights the issues and concerns about reuse, even when anonymized, and points to possible ways of addressing some of these questions. The report of the NPD Committee, mandated to think through a framework for governing non-personal data, also aims to do the same and is anchored in the ideals of public interest. It aims to enable a data-sharing framework to enhance the economic, social and public value of data and distribute it to communities and businesses, and also address the harms emerging from the use of this data. Public purpose is defined broadly and encompasses policymaking, and citizen engagement – broadly, socio-economic goals of the country and innovation. The report explicitly excludes businesses' purpose (data sharing between businesses) and sovereign purpose (on security challenges, crime prevention, etc.).

The NPD report is fraught with issues that are layered and complex. It has major implications for how all the data is shared, even though the report highlights health as a space primed for experiments on some of the conceptual frameworks mentioned in the report, such as the identification and mandatory sharing of high-value data sets (HVDs). These are data sets that are of high value for public interest, and can be mandated for sharing. The idea of HVDs does not necessarily account for the implementation realities of the health sector, which is still informal, offline and low on capacity. The building, maintaining and sharing of HVDs by healthcare providers are likely to be time-consuming and expensive, and most stakeholders may be unable to comply with the requirements. This would further harm the cause of data sharing for public health, as data requestors will have to invest in identifying and making HVDs usable. There is also little preparation in the document to set up standards and interoperability. Without these investments the movement of data is encumbered. Finally, the report talks about a new NPD authority which would decide what data is of high value and also develop the functions of the newly proposed data trustees. However, this regulator will serve to add more friction to the process of sharing. Beyond the more fundamental issues of whether NPD should be regulated and how it should be defined (currently by exclusion of data that is not personally identifiable), there are functional issues that will hamper health data sharing instead of achieving the committee's vision of community well-being and public interest through better sharing.

The report is anchored in community rights, which is a novel approach and distinctive from the way the PDP Bill frames rights. It recognizes that the community has rights over data generated by them and must be able to draw both value from this data and be protected from any harms that emerge from data use. However, in the context of health data, especially when considering sharing for public interest, the idea of the community needs to be better defined given that not all individuals/patients may have the same interests when it comes to data reuse. The report does define data trustees to help harness data value, and protect the community, but differences in the vision, intentions and willingness to share within communities such as a group of cancer patients who may want to share their data for specific research and innovation questions, is not effectively addressed. Given the heterogeneity of the health sector, it is possible that small, fissured communities develop, and negotiating data access remains complex, time-consuming and expensive. Other concerns on the NPD report are that individual consent is required only for anonymization, and not for sharing of anonymized data (as ordered by the Kerala High Court). This is not only a concern when it comes to individual interests and protections but is also likely to come into conflict with other health-data-specific regulations such as DISHA.

These features of the report may serve to be counterproductive when it comes to the core purpose of the report – enabling better data sharing in community and public interest given that it does not prioritize the metrics of good data sharing highlighted above. The health sector is underprepared and while public health does need access to quality to improve decision making and planning, it also needs congruent investment in the sector, and thus raise its capacity to enable the implementation of new laws and regulations. The NPD report, though critical in terms of proposing a new way of thinking about data as a community resource, is still far away from implementation.

National Digital Health Mission (NDHM), 2019

The National Digital Health Mission (NDHM) is conceived by the Ministry of Health and Family Welfare (MoHFW). NDHM builds on the National Health Policy, 2017, and aims to create a technology-driven health ecosystem in India. It will establish a Unique Health Identifier (UHID) for all individuals which links to Electronic Health Records (EHRs) that hold complete medical history of people, such that data can be shared seamlessly with healthcare providers. The Government of India has also approved the Health Data Management Policy (HDMP) to guide the creation, processing and sharing of individual EHRs. At the highest level, the NDHM contains four features – Health ID, EHRs, Digi-Doctor and Health Facilities Registry. Over time, it also aims to evolve e-pharmacy and telemedicine services.

In its effort to create a digital infrastructure for health, the government has jettisoned some of the core principles required to make this system accountable and sustainable. First, the idea of putting the data principals, or communities at the heart of any data governance frameworks has been taken lightly by the NDHM and related frameworks. It also does not pay attention to the other requirements of interoperability, conditions for access, and data protection – which need to be institutionalized either through legislation or through practice.

Not just is digitization of health records being done without a complete understanding of its impact on the fundamental right to privacy, but the manner in which UHID is being rolled out, often without the consent of individuals, is a matter of concern. There are also no clear grievance redress systems. Broader capacity concerns on digital and physical infrastructure, interoperability and preparedness on the ground have been deprioritized. As a result, these systems though serving to provide greater security, trust and accountability to new systems of data, lack investment and thought under the new policy. There are also concerns about who can access health data and for what purposes. For example, in the recent vaccination drive, as people use CoWin, digital health IDs are being created without their knowledge and consent.[36] Even on the question of consent, the NDHM does highlight the role of a 'consent manager', an electronic system that interacts with the data principal to obtain consent[37], but the roles of this entity are also without safeguards and restrictions. There are best practices of consent managers globally that serve also as digi-wallets/lockers and provide advisory support to individuals on data sharing and access, and ensure that the rights of the principal are protected (such as Digi.me). However, these practices and roles are not referenced in the NDHM and related documents.

The NDHM does suggest a sandbox to foster integration of current systems and healthcare IT platforms into the framework of building blocks (health ID, DigiDoctor, health registry, telemedicine, etc.) suggested in the NDHM. The sandbox is not set up to test any of the data-principal-centric concerns, like the role of consent managers and how that might interface with the needs of patients. The NDHM guidelines for the sandbox are focused only on a technocratic approach to the health data ecosystem, and not any of the bigger questions on governance.

Data Stewardship: Solutions for Sharing of Health Data   281

Further, another implicit intention of the NDHM is to also ensure smooth financing of healthcare. Therefore, private and commercial entities such as insurance companies are able to access data to process payments, and also for research, analysis and innovation. There are no clear guidelines on the limits to data monetization, and patient data maybe at risk of commodification. These issues are compounded by the fact that there are no clear guidelines for anonymization and de-identification of data – these protocols being left to entities to evolve. This may compromise the privacy and security of health data, which is sensitive by nature. The arbitrariness on data sharing, and the lack of oversight from the National Health Authority (NHA) is likely to add chaos to the landscape. These efforts, though well-meaning, steer the policy away from its intended impact of empowering individuals to better control and harness value from their data.

Implications on Health Data Sharing

The policy landscape in India, and its implications for the health sector, especially from the lens of unlocking data value for public health, makes it clear that this is not just a complex problem but one that the government and regulators are not giving enough thought to. A rigmarole of regulation and policy has been designed to do very many things but a clear framework of principles is missing. The government wants to build a robust data-driven public healthcare system but that requires system investments in top-down legislative action, such as the establishment of data rights, and building a value-driven case for unlocking data value. It also requires regulatory structures that oversee, along with data protection, the enactment of legislations in sectors, and safeguard rights of individuals and communities. Finally, a broader enabling environment needs to be created, without which legislation and regulation will not succeed. The enabling environment must include opportunities for testing technical and governance approaches for the broader health data ecosystem, processes for sharing norms that prescribe suitable standards for the sector, and infrastructure for secure movement of data from individuals to the government and private sector.[38] The enabling environment has to be layered with incentives for stakeholders, including patients, to participate in the ecosystem such that there is buy-in, as opposed to an imposition on the individuals, communities and businesses by the government.

To this end, the government needs to develop a detailed road map[39] that starts with clearly defining rights for the individuals and communities on their data rights, to make these rights unassailable, and give the data principals the rights of portability, and codify the idea of reuse. The government also needs to create strong accountability measures to ensure that individuals/communities are able to track how their data is being accessed and used transparently. While consent managers do provide visibility into who is accessing user data and for what purpose, it does little to minimize data extraction and enhance accountability. Beyond this, there is a need to create evidence through sandboxes and pilots especially on potential ideas that can protect the data principals, like the consent manager in the NDHM and data trustees in the NPD.

India's response to public health questions, innovations and even rapid response to any future health crises can be improved through data sharing, but it remains unable to capitalize on its potential through sluggish and confused policy work that does not consider the well-being of data principals. Further, the top-down efforts from the government need to be supplemented with bottom-up efforts that maybe led by communities or businesses to consolidate the power of data principals, as individuals and at the community level. Bottom-up mechanisms, as discussed in the next section, will ensure accountability from the government and also make current policies more effective.

Bottom-Up Mechanisms for Health Data Governance

A growing body of work demonstrates that for data sharing to be effective, it must consider social and ethical requirements of the data generators, and be able to minimize harm and build trust while achieving scientific progress.[40] Individuals and communities care about both benefits and harms from data sharing, and are beginning to understand the value of their own data. For instance, research carried out in Kenya suggests that stakeholder attitudes were framed by the perceived benefits and concerns for research data sharing, which includes loss of privacy, discrimination and exclusion. If these concerns are addressed through greater awareness, agreements to data sharing, and accountability of governance mechanisms, people are more likely to trust the process of data collection and sharing.[41]

Beyond this, individuals also realize that their personal data is siloed, and it requires significant personal effort and coordination from patients to aggregate, collate and make data usable across providers to draw benefit from their medical journey and history. In the current system, individuals are the only ones who can potentially access their complete medical information. That said, it is also known that personalized medicine also depends on aggregated data. From genome research on one end and smartphone use on the other,[42] this aggregation is complex and expensive. There is a need to create platforms, tools that allow individuals to store, manage and share health-related data such that people can receive more tailored medical response and also make reliable and collated data accessible for research and innovation to third parties, on terms that are agreeable to the data generators, that is, the individuals.

These bottom-up systems or data stewards can take several forms[43] and serve several ends, like giving individuals power over their own data; the ability to store, manage and share data; and aggregating and drawing value from data, both to access healthcare (such as precision medicine) better and also to share it with third parties for purposes that are priorities for the individuals. Finally, if bottom-up systems take on collective forms, that is, cancer patients building bottom-up data governance models, it is also possible to collectivize concerns and aspirations and negotiate with different stakeholders. The design of the data steward is determined by the purpose it aims to fulfil on behalf of its chief stakeholder – individuals and communities.[44]

One of the best tested models of bottom-up data governance in healthcare are data cooperatives. 'A health data cooperative is a collective where health-related data are integrated, stored, used, and shared under the control of the cooperative members.'[45] This structure is not new and exists in different sectors and geographies. Cooperatives have members who pay a membership fee, each member have one vote, and all decisions are decided on democratically. The cooperative is obligated to work in the best interest of its members, and ensure that harms from data use do not come up, and that research, medical interests of members are safeguarded. Data cooperatives are coming up, especially in the European Union, where data portability under the GDPR allows individuals to port their data. In this context, drivers in the Netherlands have been given permission to port their data from platform companies Ola and Uber to a data trust, the form and design of which is still being considered.[46] Another such example is Midata. coop[47] in Switzerland which give people greater control over their medical data. Users can collect different health-related information and encrypt and store it with MiData and share it with researchers working on areas that individuals and the cooperative aim to support. Remuneration from making data accessible is invested back in the cooperative.

In Canada, a health data cooperative was tested to better understand and make visible the health experiences of migrants, while making sure that they remain in charge of their data.[48] It was discovered that cooperatives can fill significant gaps in health research, data and community health more broadly. The cooperative structure was able to give the immigrant community (i) greater control over their data – the cooperative deciding data access, use and governance – and (ii) more data security as cooperatives are able to pull data from different sources and store on their own servers, although this is a cost- and capacity-intensive exercise. Finally, the data cooperative can collect and share longitudinal, aggregated data from individuals and collectives, making it extremely useful to government and policymakers.[49]

Other models of data stewardship, such as personal data stores, perform similar functions but are focused only on the individual and not the collective. Applications such as digi.me encrypt imported data from different social media profiles of an individual, and store it in the individual's personal cloud. The app gives individuals a full view of their online lives, and allows them to draw value from this data in whatever way they want. Other models, such as the health data collaborative,[50] bring together different stakeholders to use data to address health outcomes and deliver on the SDGs. The governance of the data is decided by its institutional members. Finally, there are data trusts[51] that do not exist in the wild at the moment, but aim to use trust law to allow individuals to pool their data rights, and both bargain for better experiences with platforms and make reliable data accessible for research/innovation. Other models, that are more complex to categorize also exist, such as Variant Bio which partners with communities to co-design research that addresses specific needs of the community.[52]

Irrespective of the model, data stewards are critical for redistributing power, and placing it in the hands of the individuals and communities who generate health data. It is focused on ensuring that data value is realized by the generators, and also create mechanisms through which data can be shared effectively to solve for public health questions. It is worth noting that while stewards are in their best form likely to be non-profits, private companies that are committed to data empowerment may also become stewards and discover fair and reliable practices to make stewards sustainable.

Stewards can only be a reality when there are accompanying laws to legitimize their existence and functioning. For instance, the provision of data portability in the EU allows stewards to interpret the GDPR and enact new forms of data rights for individuals and communities. India's proposed data protection bill also allows for portability but its use will have to be understood to exploit it for data stewardship. Further, questions of capacity, and willingness of individuals to participate in these new models of stewardship, remain but can be solved as the landscape matures.

In the context of India, as mentioned above, the NPD report does mention a quasi-steward – the data trustees – to perform the same functions as the stewards, to protect against harm and to guarantee benefits from data. However, data trustees are not supported by accompanying legislations that recognize data rights of individuals, and allow them to entrust a third party with a fiduciary responsibility (trustee) with these rights. The idea of community rights, though mentioned in the NPD is vague, and the PDP bill still awaits parliamentary approval. The design and implementation of the data trustee are vague, so while the intention to create bottom-up structures is well placed, the top-down enablement is slow. This is the same case with consent managers, they are also interpreted as data stewards but their role as a data-blind consent mechanism is insufficient. To be effective, consent managers will have to play a more advisory role to the patients, to make sure data is not being exploited and only shared with individuals and groups that the patient cares to direct their data to.

Conclusion

Data saves lives, the catchphrase of the COVID-19 pandemic, is true in very many ways. On one end it allows for quick and critical collaboration to address ongoing health related questions, and on the other, its protection saves individuals and communities from harm and discrimination. Therefore, it is imperative for all stakeholders – governments, private sector, civil society and communities to come together, innovate and implement methods that allow for simultaneous protection and sharing of health data.

This chapter has discussed that there are two forces that need to act in tandem. First, policy action led by the government that creates legal frameworks to define the contours of data sharing, and give data principals clear rights that need to be safeguarded. Second, bottom-up models that emerge from a community-level realization that data as a good is valuable, and needs to be controlled better by the people who generate it. In the context of India, both these forces are wayward – the policy landscape is in a state of flux and, as a result, innovations from the ground are limited. Civil society organizations and the private sector – the main stakeholders for bottom-up data governance – are unable to navigate the evolving and confusing legal landscape – and, therefore, cannot invest in working with individuals and communities on data governance issues. This is a worrying situation for India, which is still struggling with basic questions of public health – questions that data sharing can solve efficiently. India must streamline its regulatory landscape, create physical and human capacity on data, prioritize standards and interoperability so that in case of the next emergency response, India's public health action can be swift and meaningful.

15

Artificial Intelligence and Healthcare

Rahul Matthan and Prakhar Pipraiya

Introduction

AS the practice of medicine has become increasingly digital, cognitive technologies have made it possible for doctors to use new methods for the diagnosis, monitoring and treatment. In some instances these methods have reduced repetitive tasks, in others support doctors by providing them a basis for their decisions. In some instances, these tools could alter the very practice of medicine.

The use of artificial intelligence in the healthcare space also raises a number of unanticipated challenges – in the form of legal violations, new forms of liability and ethical concerns. In addition, since all medical data is personal and sensitive information subject to the highest standard of protection under data protection law, the privacy impact of artificial intelligence is of significant concern.

Artificial Intelligence

In order to appreciate the privacy impact of artificial intelligence on the healthcare space we need to first understand what artificial intelligence is and how it works.

What is Artificial Intelligence?

The term artificial intelligence was reportedly first used by John McCarthy at a Dartmouth Conference in 1956 to describe 'the science and engineering of making intelligent machines'.[1] It has since been used to describe a range of different techniques but has only come into its own over the past decade when computer scientists could affordably process sufficient quantities of big data to effectively train machine-learning algorithms.

Machine learning simulates human intelligence by iteratively training algorithms to recognize patterns or to perform behaviours using tight feedback loops that improve accuracy. In most cases this involves using specialized algorithms to process vast amounts of training data to iteratively infer connections and patterns in that data. When fully trained, these algorithms are capable of predicting, with a high probability of accuracy, various outcomes without human intervention. In other words, AI systems are prediction engines that take the information you have and use it to generate information you do not.[2]

Today computers can identify human faces[3] and other images[4] with incredible accuracy. They understand what we say to them[5] and can reply with conversational fluency.[6] They can infer contextual meaning from text and can be relied upon to do research previously reserved for humans.[7] Perhaps the most widely cited example of how much machine intelligence has improved is its ability to best humans in games like chess and Go.[8]

AI is often categorized into narrow and general AI. Narrow AI refers machine intelligence that is competent in a narrow field of expertise.[9] This sort of AI performs one task and performs it well. General AI refers to machine intelligence that is more akin to human intelligence where the machine performs a broad range of tasks that require intelligent analysis. While there are numerous examples of narrow AI, we have still to develop general AI.[10]

AI can be further categorized based on how the machine is trained – supervised or unsupervised learning.[11] Supervised learning requires annotated training data sets where the annotations provide the algorithm a supervised framework within which the data is analysed. The algorithm creates models based on its analysis of the data, constantly refitting the models to adhere to the human annotations most closely. In unsupervised learning the algorithm instead finds patterns in the data without the assistance of human annotations.[12] Unsupervised learning algorithms are particularly effective in tightly bounded environments with in-built feedback loops.[13]

Most decision support systems in healthcare use supervised learning.[14] Consequently, this chapter will focus on AI created using supervised learning.

AI in Healthcare

AI is created using a two-step process. The first is the creation of the intelligence required to solve a given problem by getting the algorithms to 'learn' from the historical data they have been provided with. The second is the application of this machine intelligence to new situations to generate insights.

In the first, computationally expensive phase, machine-learning frameworks are trained to process vast amounts of data in relation to identified models of behaviour (such as natural language processing, image recognition and prediction). The algorithm builds models that compress the information latent in the training data sets into a form suitable for making decisions. A prerequisite for this stage is the availability of large sets of annotated data that can be processed to develop the predictive models that will subsequently predict outcomes.[15]

The second, and computationally cheaper, phase involves applying these models to new situations so that insights gleaned through the training stage can be used to predict outcomes. This includes using these models to derive understanding from new information by extracting semantic meaning; identifying words in speech or objects in images; the diagnosis of a disease from its symptoms or the identification of a course of treatment based on clinical diagnosis.

Over the past decade and more, healthcare has become increasingly digital. This has resulted in more data becoming available to train algorithms and identify trends post-training. Now that longitudinal health[16] data records are available, we can gain insights that were not previously possible. In addition, data generated from new sources such as always-on wearable devices or inferred from behaviour tracked by search engines, e-commerce and other digital platforms provide new ways in which to measure health parameters.

The use of AI tools in the healthcare domain has not always resulted in successful outcomes. During the pandemic, a number of AI tools were developed to diagnose infected patients without much success.[17] The use of AI in the medical context also raises questions of ethics, accountability and equity. When a machine learning algorithm is placed in the same situation that was previously handled by human doctors their responses need to not only be accurate and efficient they also need to be ethical.[18] Where machine-learning has contributed to medical negligence it becomes even more difficult than normal to appropriately affix liability. Equally, when the standard shifts from human levels of efficiency to those that incorporate machine intelligence, physicians who eschew the use of these automated helpers can become easy targets to affix blame.[19] At the same time, over-reliance on AI can lead to problems.[20] These concerns are exacerbated in countries like India where social, cultural and economic divides can skew outcomes unfavourably[21] if data pertaining to the sick and the poor are often not considered while designing these algorithms.[22] Finally, given the deeply sensitive nature of personal health, the privacy implications of an excessive reliance on cognitive technologies can be a cause for concern.[23]

Privacy harms could arise at two distinct stages – in relation to the use of personal data to train the artificial intelligence algorithms and in the inferences that these algorithms can derive that could have an impact on personal privacy. Over the next two parts of this chapter, the impact of both these aspects will be discussed.

Data for Healthcare Artificial Intelligence

Healthcare in India has traditionally been analogue. Interactions between the doctor and patient have always been in-person – during which time patients are physically examined, their reports studied and a diagnosis declared (usually as a hand-scribbled file noting accompanied by a prescription). While most ailments are treated by private practitioner/ clinics,[24] in recent times, there has been a shift towards large medical hospitals, especially in urban areas.[25] Most of these hospitals store patient data electronically.[26]

The analogue approach to medical data does not scale in large healthcare facilities. Hospitals have complex administrative operations that call for coordination between different departments. This is why the medical profession has rapidly digitized itself over the past decade or so and has, in the process, created unprecedented volumes of digital medical information.[27] Much of this information resides in the hospitals and other medical facilities within which treatment takes place. However, various other participants in the healthcare ecosystem (diagnostic laboratories, pharmacies, telemedicine service providers, etc.)[28] also have access to medical data.

The increase in digitization has resulted in new technologies that enable the collection and processing of medically relevant data through new means. This includes wearable technologies and the Internet of Things in medical applications. All these sources generate vast volumes of data that can be used as training data sets to build better predictions.

In this chapter we will discuss how medical data sources are used to train AI algorithms with a view to establishing the basis for privacy harm.

Electronic Health Records, Electronic Medical Records and Personal Health Records

The atomic unit of data in a digital health system is the electronic medical record (EMR) – a digital file containing all the information of patient. Most EMRs comprise four types of data:

- Health information,

- Medical history,
- Demographic information, and
- Administrative information.[29]

When amalgamated together, multiple EMRs constitute a single electronic health record (EHR) that provides a record of the medical history of a patient.[30] Most digital health systems in large medical establishments are capable of generating EHRs for patients allowing doctors to pull up the past history of treatment and medically relevant information such as allergies, chronic ailments and medications prescribed. However, given poor standardization across digital health systems used by various medical establishments, EHRs can typically only be generated for interactions that take place within a given facility. This means that where a patient has consulted with doctors practising in different establishments, no single EHR can be generated for all those interactions.

India is attempting to solve this problem by developing a common data exchange standard as part of its National Digital Health Mission to the interchange of data whether or not the same digital systems are being used.[31] This will allow patients to assemble a comprehensive longitudinal record of all interactions with the healthcare ecosystem.[32] The resulting personal health record (PHR) will be the most comprehensive collection of medical data pertaining to a citizen yet created.[33]

Wearables and IoT

The miniaturization of sensor technologies has resulted in the availability of a wide range of wearable devices serving a number of different functions. The most widely recognizable wearable is the smartwatch that, in addition to telling the time is today capable of collecting heart rate, blood oxygen saturation, movement and location information that can be used to generate a range of insights into the wearer's health.[34] There are a range of other devices designed to capture personal parameters over a long period of time including constant glucose monitors,[35] chest strap heart rate monitors[36] and other devices worn on specific parts of the body for long-term monitoring.

Most wearable devices are not classified as medical devices since they lack the level of accuracy that larger medical devices can achieve.[37] However since these devices are worn on the body 24/7 they provide accurate trend lines demonstrating variance over time. The increase in consumer integration of smaller wearable devices into daily life has resulted in a significant rise in the volume of data collected on wearable device users. We have also seen the development of connected devices that collect various other medical parameters (temperature, blood pressure, weight, heart rate, etc.). Since these devices do not have to be worn they are often larger and more accurate. The data they collect is persistent and stored longitudinally providing useful information time series about the patient. Smart thermometers maintain a record of fever,[38] smart weighing scales can track fluctuations in weight and BMI,[39] digital sleep trackers measure sleep patterns[40] and connected BP monitors record and track fluctuations in blood pressure.[41]

Use of EHR Data for Artificial Intelligence

EMRs, EHRs and PHRs provide granular data on a range of medical interactions that can serve as training data sets for machine learning. For instance, in order to build AI solutions for medical imaging, the first step would be to accumulate a large number of radiology scans duly annotated with the diagnosis of a human radiologist.[42] Similarly, to build AI solutions for cancer diagnosis, training data sets comprising reports with the patient's clinical symptoms and the corresponding diagnosis would have to be arranged.[43]

All this data are deeply personal. As such they cannot be used for any purpose other than that for which they were collected. And yet when we realize how valuable this can be in training AI algorithms we rarely stop to consider whether such use would require prior consent. Instead, in most instances we make sure that the data is anonymized, stripping out personally identifiable information to take it out of the purview of data protection law entirely. This process of de-identification is presumed to be sufficient to address the privacy concerns related to their use.

Later on in this chapter we will examine the privacy implications of consent in relation to the forms of health data described above. But before we attempt to address the privacy implications of raw data, let us examine how this data can be used by other cognitive technologies in the context of healthcare services.

Digital Health Applications

For centuries doctors have diagnosed diseases unaided, relying on experience to correctly diagnose the symptoms and prescribe treatment. With advances in cognitive technologies it is now possible to augment (and in some cases replace) human doctors with the data systems that accurately correlate symptoms with recommended treatment.[44] This has resulted in improvements in the quality of medical outcomes by enabling accurate risk modelling, electronic monitoring of patients and the ability to tailor treatment to meet the requirements of the patient using precision medicine.[45]

Digital health applications can be broadly classified into those that use data as an aid to medical decision making and those that apply AI to healthcare. Both categories have been discussed below.

Data-Driven Public Health Interventions

The availability of data lakes (storehouses of data) has made it possible for data technologies to derive inferences that were not previously possible. This includes new ways to identify medical conditions and predict disease outbreaks using signals in data not ordinarily associated with medical outcomes. While these applications use aggregate, anonymized data not associated with identified individuals, the inferences they create could still result in privacy harms.

Syndromic Inferences

The technique of using signs from real-world behaviour to indicate medical outcomes is called syndromic surveillance.[46] It was first developed by DARPA (Defense Advanced Research Projects Agency) in the US in response to the threat of bioterrorism attacks in the aftermath of the 11 September terrorist attacks and has since been used in various different contexts. It is as an additional tool that governments can call upon to identify disease hot spots early to be able to divert resources in order to curb its spread.

Digital technologies have opened up a vast array of new and diverse sources from which medical inferences can be drawn. An algorithm developed by a chain of department stores for the purpose of identifying how best to target new products for buyers to purchase, was able to predict that women in their second trimester of pregnancy favour unscented shampoos and used that knowledge to sell baby products to a young teen.[47] Google Flu Trends a (now defunct) service analysed search requests to predict where flu outbreaks were likely to occur.[48]

In addition to data inferred in this manner, the proliferation of connected devices has made it possible to derive accurate insights from basic home testing equipment like thermometers and blood pressure monitors. Kinsa, a brand of smart thermometers used in over two million homes in the USA, aggregates data across devices, cross-referencing it with positional information to identify flu hot spots.[49] Personal fitness tracking apps are capable of providing insights into health and fitness at population levels across a range of demographic parameters.[50]

Hot spot Detection

Information available at population scale can now be used to identify medically relevant trends. This is useful for healthcare policy interventions as well disease prevention. When visually depicted in the form of heatmaps it provides geographical context to medical information including insights that are actionable both immediately through medical interventions as well as through long-term policy actions.

The Health Heatmap of India aggregates publicly available health data from sources like the National Health and Family Survey, the Annual Health Survey, and the Integrated Disease Surveillance

Programme and presents this information in a searchable, query-able format that is available on an open access platform.[51] By overlaying biodiversity-related data it is possible to include information about environmental factors such as rainfall and vegetation to the visualizations. Heat maps of this sort can help with the early tracking and management of zoonotic diseases[52] and in generating the overall health status at a district level by building a composite index of health indicators.

During the early stages of the COVID-19 pandemic, data collected by the Aarogya Setu app identified disease hot spots. By analysing the location history of the infected and aggregate self-declared symptoms of users collected through the self-assessment feature on the app, the team behind the app was able to forecast over 650 hot spots across the country at a sub post office level. Of those, 130 hot spots predicted by the app were officially declared as such by the Union health ministry three to seventeen days after they were first identified by the Aarogya Setu team.[53] This allowed the government to quickly deploy resources in regions where outbreaks were likely to occur.[54]

Mobility Data

Given that a large percentage of the population owns mobile phones, these devices are increasingly being treated as proxies for human mobility. Mobile phone companies maintain call data records (CDRs) of their customers for regulatory reasons. By triangulating the information contained in CDRs it is possible to derive location information at population scale. During outbreaks of contagious diseases, mobile phone companies have contributed this sort of anonymized positional information to help governments track the movement of people to ascertain where the disease is going to spread next.

This use of CDR was pioneered during the cholera outbreak in Haiti[55] and has since been used in the Ebola outbreak in Sierra Leone[56] and the dengue outbreak in Pakistan.[57] In the context of cholera and Ebola, this sort of granular mobility data has allowed governments to determine the areas most likely to be hit next by the outbreak giving them valuable advance information to halt the spread of the disease.

During the early days of COVID-19, location information was used in different ways to monitor the spread of the disease. Big tech companies like Facebook[58] and Google[59] as well as telecom companies used location data to generate mobility patterns that public health officials then used to assess the impact of mobility restrictions on the spread of the disease.[60]

Artificial Intelligence Applications in Healthcare

The predictive capabilities of AI algorithms can, when applied to various categories of structured and unstructured data, generate medically useful insights. Image recognition algorithms are already demonstrably superior to human radiologists when it comes to interpreting X-rays and other scans. Algorithms that can intelligently parse text can scan through past diagnoses to assist doctors in determining the most suitable course of action for patients. Precision medicine that can today make a diagnosis based on genetic markers and the unique characteristics of the human biome can use AI techniques to create bespoke pharmaceutical remedies. When coupled with always-on wearable devices, these technologies can remotely monitor patients in need of supervision far more effectively than human nurses can.

Image Recognition

Deep learning algorithms can identify feature representations in image data, often without the need for prior definition by human experts. This allows for even the most abstract features in radiology scans to be accurately identified. Today image recognition AI can detect lung cancer by identifying pulmonary nodules, colo-rectal cancer by identifying colonic polyps, breast cancer by identifying micro-calcifications and brain cancer by identifying abnormal tissue growth.[61] In the case of skin cancers, AI algorithms can handle the wide variances in sizes, shades and textures of suspected lesions far better than trained dermatologists could.[62] In all these cases, AI can not only detect but also accurately characterize the tumour as either benign or malignant. Additionally, AI can also be used in the treatment phase to segment tumours so as to optimize the administered dose of radiation.[63]

This is not to say that the use of AI in radiology is not without its challenges. Since most of these tools are narrow AI, they can only perform one task at a time. This means that a given AI will only be able to detect the abnormality it has been trained to detect and if presented with any other abnormality (that a human radiologist would have immediately identified), the AI will not be able to identify it.[64]

There are also question marks around the tendency to generalize AI decisions across the entire population[65] – around whether there is bias inherent in the algorithms since they have been trained on data set notoriously skewed in favour of Caucasian skin types.[66] To address this concern, algorithms need to be trained on image data more fully representative of variations within the population.

Diagnosis, Monitoring and Clinical Decision Support

AI algorithms can also assist doctors with diagnosis. The sum of medical knowledge is far greater than any human being is capable of completely assimilating. AI algorithms can process large volumes of clinical literature, health records, test results and other relevant medical information, and suggest appropriate treatments based on the symptoms of the patient. This was the premise behind Watson Health, IBM's AI offering to the medical community.[67]

AI algorithms have also assisted in other ways. Artificial neural networks have been used as clinical decision support tools in oncology.[68] In cardiology they have improved risk assessment for patients with suspected coronary artery disease.[69] In ophthalmology, they have been used to predict cataract surgery complications and improve the diagnosis of glaucoma and age-related macular degeneration.[70]

This raises the question of whether these technologies should be regulated in some manner. If doctors are relying on AI outputs, would the output of the AI algorithm be equivalent to medical advice? If so, how can anyone other than a licensed medical practitioner provide this advice? This is why these tools are designed to only be used under the supervision of a doctor.

Precision Medicine and Personalized Health

Drug discovery is the process by which chemicals are designed to be effective against identified pharmacological targets.[71] In addition to efficacy, drugs need to operate within safety parameters, display appropriate chemical and biological properties and have sufficient novelty to offer a commercial incentive to continue to invest in research and development.

Traditionally drug discovery is an arduous process. By using AI algorithms it is now possible to design and evaluate molecules *in silico*, reducing the number of potential chemicals to more manageable numbers.[72] There is also interest in repurposing drugs that were developed for one condition and using them to address another.[73] AI has a role to play in poly pharmacology – the design of a single drug molecule to simultaneously interact with multiple targets.[74] By deploying deep learning it is possible to use information from receptors, ligands, and their known interactions from many experiments and multiple targets to improve the per-target performance of suitable drug candidates screened from a library of virtual compounds.

Advances in precision medicine have given us insights into the genetic architecture of diseases and an understanding of the underlying mechanisms of disease pathogenesis in the human body. It has become clear that each patient is unique and needs a bespoke therapeutic journey. Drug development has begun to shift away from merely alleviating symptoms to directly arresting the progression of the disease. AI techniques allow us to learn specific features of biomedical data that will guide the design of new drug molecules and tailor therapeutic agents to work effectively on a given patient.[75]

Artificial Intelligence and Assisted Living

AI is increasingly being used in the care of the elderly. AI-based remote monitoring solutions can detect changes in the activity and behaviour of elderly patients detecting in advance the onset of serious medical conditions. This includes devices that continuously monitor key parameters such as atrial fibrillation and blood sugar.[76] Wearable devices use onboard accelerometers and gyroscopes to detect falls and sound an alarm where the wearer has had a 'hard fall'.[77] While most devices operate on the basis of consent there are legitimate concerns around the governance models they currently operate under.[78]

Voice-based assistants are used to encourage medication adherence in the elderly who struggle with memory.[79] Others are being used to provide companionship through tailored conversations while at the same time extracting necessary data about treatment.[80] Still others engage the elderly to keep their minds alert and connect them with family.

These developments raise questions of autonomy, preferences and overall impact of artificial intelligence on the elderly and infirm. Some complain that these technologies are preferable to care by the children of elderly.[81] Similarly questions arise as to who can share what data and with whom. While the patient might like control over the data, the interests and preferences of family will also have to be appropriately balanced – particularly where it affects the safety of the patient.

Artificial Intelligence and Privacy

India does not yet have a full-fledged privacy law. It is, however, in the process of enacting one that is likely to be conceptually aligned with privacy principles recognized around the world. At the time of writing, the most recent draft of the bill has been withdrawn from Parliament. Consequently, we have referenced language from the 2019 draft. This includes the use of consent as the principal legal ground for processing personal data; the requirement to provide notice prior to the collection of personal data; the obligation to adhere to principles of purpose and use limitation; and the enforcement of data minimization and retention restrictions.

The privacy implications of artificial intelligence operate at two levels. First, at the stage when the artificial intelligence models are being created and then, in the application of these models to derive insights.

Raw Data and Privacy

Training data used to build machine-learning models is accumulated from raw medical data contained in EMRs, EHRs and PHRs. They are supplemented by data collected from wearables and IoT devices. Medical information contained in EMRs, EHRs and PHRs are typically sensitive personal data subject to a higher threshold of compliance and consequently there are privacy implications that need to be addressed.[82]

To assess these privacy implications we need to understand how data protection law will apply to these processes. The discussions that follow contain references to the text of the PDP Bill, 2019, with emphasis added by the authors, that now stands withdrawn.

Consent

The notion of informed consent is well understood in the medical context as the approval that patients provide for the interventions they are about to receive. This is very different from the consent required in the data protection context. According to Section 11(1) of the 2019 PDP Bill (since withdrawn), consent is the fundamental legal basis for processing personal data:

> *(1) The personal data shall not be processed, except on the consent given by the data principal at the commencement of its processing.*

Section 5 of the PDP Bill stipulated that data processing must be fair and reasonable and only for the purpose for which consent was obtained or for anything incidental to or connected with such purpose. Consent must be *free, informed, specific, clear and capable of being withdrawn.*

When patients are admitted into hospitals they consent to having their EMR data used in relation to their treatment. It is unlikely that this consent can be assumed to extend to its use in training machine-learning algorithms. That being the case, this is neither the 'purpose consented to' nor one 'incidental to or connected with such purpose'.

Even if consent was validly obtained for such use, there are questions about whether it was freely given. Under Section 11(2), *free consent* required that it be free from coercion, undue influence, fraud, misrepresentation or mistake. Patients in hospitals are often only capable of processing the decisions that pertain to the medical conditions that brought them there. They are often distraught and coping with various other pressures. Obtaining consent under these circumstances for data to be used to train machine-learning models is unlikely to meet the standard for consent freely given.

What all this suggests is that if EMRs are used as training data, consent must be separately obtained. It is inordinately difficult to obtain consent for data that has already been collected. Patients who might have willingly consented at collection tend to be reluctant to consent after the fact, for a fresh purpose – particularly since they derive no benefit from doing so. For these reasons, rather than seeking consent, EMRs used as training data sets are usually anonymized.

Information collected from wearable and IoT devices are usually compliant with privacy obligations since the consent based upon which they have been collected tends to be phrased broadly to cover the use of AI to derive insights. Even so, the processing of such data would need to meet the other restrictions that were set out in the PDP Bill in relation to purpose and use limitation as well as data minimization and retention limitations.

Purpose and Use Limitation

The PDP Bill additionally imposed restrictions on the purpose for which data can be processed. Section 4 stated that:

> *No personal data shall be processed by any person, except for any specific, clear and lawful purpose.*

Raw data from EMRs and EHRs used to train machine learning algorithms are usually aggregated after the fact, that is, after the primary purpose of collecting the information or conducting a test has been met. Since training machine-learning algorithms is essentially a different purpose from that for which the data was collected, the use limitations under the PDP Bill would have prevented use for these purposes.

Purpose limitation restrictions also limit the purposes to which raw data collected from wearable devices can be put. Since purpose needs to be specific and clear, expansive terms covering a wide range of activities are proscribed. Data collected by these devices must therefore be for purposes clearly and specifically stated.

Data Minimization and Retention Restrictions

Additional restrictions under the PDP Bill limited the amount of data that could, legitimately, be collected. Section 6 of the PDP Bill stated that:

> The personal data shall be collected only to the extent that is necessary for the purposes of processing of such personal data.

This restraint is contrary to how AI is designed to work. Machine learning algorithms excel at deriving insights from large volumes of data. The more data they process the better their predictive capabilities become. While there are techniques such as transfer learning and few-shot learning which perform well even with small amount of data,[83] all these techniques are currently at such a nascent stage of development that their effectiveness is questionable.[84]

Data minimization limits the amount of data that can be collected, restricting the pool of data available to train machine-learning models. While the PDP Bill was addressing the risks of over-collection it would hamstring the growth of AI by restricting the volume of data collected. With data collection proceeding apace in the absence of a privacy regulation there already exist large data sets that would, once the PDP Bill comes into force, stand in violation of the data minimization principle.

Section 9 of the PDP Bill prohibited the retention of personal data for longer than absolutely necessary to satisfy the purpose for which it was processed. In the context of medical data collected to treat a patient, arguably that time, particularly with regard to evanescent markers of the progression of the disease, will expire once the patient has been treated. If this is implemented none of this personal data will be available for use to train machine-learning algorithms. Since the quality of machine learning directly corresponds to the volume of data available for training, restrictions on the size of the training data sets will have a corresponding impact on the quality of the resulting model.

That said, it should be possible to overcome these obstacles by deploying anonymization techniques to ensure that training data sets are de-identified and therefore kept outside the purview of the PDP Bill or similar frameworks focused on identifiable personal data.

Anonymization

The PDP Bill did not apply to anonymized personal data. Section 2(B) of the PDP Bill stated that the provisions of the law:

> *(B) shall not apply to the processing of anonymised data, other than the anonymised data referred to in section 91.*

This approach is aligned with that taken by other countries, where it is only personal data that is regulated under privacy law. This offers a path by which the restrictions imposed by the law can be avoided through the anonymization of data. It therefore becomes important to assess what amounted to anonymized data under the PDP Bill. Section 3(3) defined anonymized data as that which has undergone the process of anonymization. Anonymization was defined in Section 3(2) of the PDP Bill:

> *(2) "anonymisation" in relation to personal data, means such irreversible process of transforming or converting personal data to a form in which a data principal cannot be identified, which meets the standards of irreversibility specified by the Authority;*

The standard for anonymization set out in this definition, is almost impossibly high. No transformation of personal data can ever be completely irreversible. Experience has shown us that with the addition of multiple data sets and the operation of big data analytics even previously anonymized data can be re-identified.[85] That being the case, any exemption available under the PDP Bill would be evanescent. The definition did reference standards of irreversibility prescribed by the Data Protection Authority implying that data anonymized to these standards would be deemed to be anonymized data.

This understanding will be crucial to the development of the AI ecosystem given that it will be impossible, as discussed above, to comply with the obligations set out under the PDP Bill and still have training data sets of the volume and quality that would be required to ensure that the artificial intelligence ecosystem flourishes.

India recently convened a committee of experts[86] to examine whether non-personal data ought to be regulated and if so how. In its interim report,[87] the committee has recommended the establishment of regulatory frameworks that support the creation of high-value data sets (HVDs) comprising non-personal data beneficial to the community at large, which the committee recommends should be shared as a public good.[88] The committee recommends that data collectors who intended to anonymize the personal data they collect, should, at the time of its collection, provide the data principal notice of the proposed anonymization and offer the data principal the choice to opt out of it.

The current NDHM guidelines require that all health information processors (HIPs) make aggregated data available.[89] However, as described above, aggregation and anonymization are often an inadequate safeguard as it is possible to re-identify persons in anonymized data sets. In addition, in order to be useful, interventions in response to clinical and population health require non-anonymized, high-resolution data. Various privacy-enhancing mechanisms modify data to improve privacy but at the cost of the effective utilization of the data.[90]

There are privacy-enhancing techniques that preserve privacy, while still ensuring the effectiveness of non-anonymized data. This includes redaction, pseudonymization, randomization, offsetting, generalization, etc.[91] These methods can be used solely or collectively, depending on the objective sought.[92] At the same time, advances in machine learning that enable efficiency, parallelism, and reductions in communication costs allow for greater value extraction from anonymized data in trusted execution environments. By deploying a combination of these techniques it should be possible to improve the privacy of personal data while still extracting useful value out of the data.

Federated learning sets up decentralized/distributed systems designed to distribute copies of the machine learning algorithm to multiple sites where the data is stored, the training carried out, and results returned to a central repository where the primary algorithm is updated. Differential privacy introduces 'statistical noise' into the data set, depending on what is being queried and by whom. The 'noise' masks the contribution of each individual data point without significantly impacting the accuracy of the analysis thereby maintaining privacy without sacrificing the quality of the output.[93] In all such instances the use of these technologies represents a trade-off between the privacy it secures and the efficacy of the AI model.

The Privacy Implications of the Use of Healthcare Applications

Many of the healthcare applications described in the previous part have privacy implications that extend beyond the process of their creation, to their use and deployment in the field. This often relates to whether the anonymization they rely on actually achieves the privacy objectives of de-identification.

Locational Privacy

Healthcare applications that generate heat maps to provide geographical context to a disease risk having individual patients identified on account of their geographic location. This could be the result of inadequate de-identification of location data in the data set, or faults in its collection. For instance, if geographical anonymity was intended to be preserved by identifying the location so broadly as to ensure that the location cannot be correlated to the individual, any such attempt could be set at naught if data from only very few individuals were collected within that location. To address this, the syndromic information collected by Aarogya Setu was fitted to grids that ranged from 200 metres to three kilometres in size so that, at all times, the details of at least fifty people were mixed in each grid cell. By sizing the geographical area on the basis of the number of individuals as opposed to a fixed physical area, the re-identification concern was mitigated.

Identifiable Images

Any healthcare application that uses image recognition for its outputs operates on the assumption that the training data is de-identified. However, where clearly discernible features are apparent on the image, despite the fact that all other personal identifiers of the patient have been expunged from the record, the presence of the identifiable mark will re-identify the individual. The process of de-identification is often complicated by the nature of the image. A radiograph of a leg is harder to associate with an individual as compared to a scan of their head.[94] Similarly, where the nature of the image is such that the contours of the face are either visible, or can be reconstructed from the image, no amount of pseudonymization of the patient information will be sufficient to de-identify it. Users of image recognition technologies have a greater obligation to ensure that the data sets they use should be processed more rigorously since they are more naturally prone to identification.

Unintended Privacy Consequences

It is possible that artificial intelligence algorithms deployed in a given context do have privacy implications in an entirely different and unrelated context. As useful as precision medicine techniques are in delivering bespoke medical treatments tailored to meet the requirements of individual patients, the accumulation of granular information about the patient carries heightened privacy risks that may not be capable of being mitigation using anonymization techniques.

While assisted living technologies can take care of elderly and infirm patients, the level of persistent surveillance that this entails has privacy implications that have not yet been properly evaluated. The use of voice-based assistants to either provide companionship to the elderly or to coerce them to take their medication implies that these devices are always listening to the persons they are watching over, potentially collecting data from them that are unrelated to the service performed. Since these voice-based services are responsible for the safety of their wards, the privacy constraints on these services are often reduced. For instance, AI designed to care for the infirm may not be capable of being turned off in order to ensure that they are always watching over their wards.

In a study of high-resolution activity data, including spatial memory, dexterity and speed, voice and walking activity using iPhone's ResearchKit feature, it was possible to use AI to analyse baseline variability of Parkinson disease.[95] However a subsequent study[96] pointed out that it was possible to capture high-fidelity information that is capable of uniquely identifying the individuals from whom the data was collected, suggesting that the AI was capturing individualized 'digital fingerprints' of the subject.

The privacy implications of AI are both seen and unseen. In many cases the outcomes discussed above were discovered after many years of having run the programme. This makes it extraordinarily difficult to accurately predict the privacy implications in advance of deployment of these algorithms and consequently to develop a privacy framework for artificial intelligence.

Conclusion

There can be no dispute of the fact that data-driven technologies, when deployed in the medical space, can yield tremendous benefits. However, current privacy law imposes restrictions on the use of medical data that could significantly curtail these benefits. While India does not yet have a privacy law, the draft bill is cast in the mould of data protection laws around the world, requiring consent for the use of data and imposing restrictions such as purpose limitation, data minimization and retention restrictions that significantly restrict the manner and extent to which medical data can be used.

Countries that have more flexible privacy regulations (the US and China) have arguably made greater strides in artificial intelligence than those that do not (countries in Europe). India is blessed with the benefit of hindsight. It has the option to adopt frameworks that facilitate the use of AI while still ensuring the privacy of patients. This will call for the dilution, to some extent, of the strictness with which principles of purpose limitation, use limitation, data minimization and retention restrictions are applied in India. A paper presented by one of authors, describes an alternative accountability framework[97] that replaces the over-reliance on consent with an accountability obligation that requires data fiduciaries to be more responsible for the consequences of their actions. This could address the information asymmetry inherent in data businesses today allowing data principals the recourse they need when the consent they provided results in their data being used in ways that harms them.

Even if this accountability framework cannot be applied in India, we will do well to encourage the use of privacy-enhancing technologies such as differential privacy and confidential clean rooms that facilitate the use of cognitive technologies while at the same time preserve individual privacy.[98] The practice of privacy by design should be encouraged so that engineers bake privacy into their products, securing personal privacy from the ground up.

Finally, it is important to recognize that the use of these technologies present very specific trade-offs. The benefits that cognitive technologies provide must be balanced against the harms they can cause. Practitioners need to be educated about these consequences and trained to appropriately moderate their expectations of what technology can do. While it is impossible to be prescriptive about where this balance should lie, regulators should encourage data fiduciaries to conduct impact assessments to evaluate the harms that could result from the deployment of AI. They need to do this at the time these technologies are rolled out as well as during their operation so as to detect harms on the margin. It is only through continuous supervision and active intervention that AI systems will reach their full potential.

Appendix 1
Data sites reviewed between November 2020 and June 2021

Data Sites	Type	Primary Link
Ministry of Health and Family Welfare, Government of India	Central	https://data.gov.in/major-indicator/covid-19-india-data-source-mohfw* https://www.mygov.in/covid-19 https://pib.gov.in/PressReleasePage.aspx?PRID=1726593
ICMR, India	Central	https://www.icmr.gov.in/
Andaman and Nicobar	UT	https://dhs.andaman.gov.in/
Andhra Pradesh	State	http://covid19.ap.gov.in/* http://hmfw.ap.gov.in/covid_dashboard.aspx*

Data Sites	Type	Primary Link
Arunachal Pradesh	State	https://twitter.com/DirHealth_ArPr
Assam	State	https://covid19.assam.gov.in/*
Bihar	State	https://twitter.com/BiharHealthDept
Chandigarh	UT	http://chdcovid19.in/*
Chhattisgarh	State	http://www.cghealth.nic.in/cghealth17/
Dadra and Nagar Haveli, Daman and Diu	UT	https://dnh.gov.in/category/press-release/
Delhi	UT	https://delhifightscorona.in/
Goa	State	https://www.goa.gov.in/covid-19/
Gujarat	State	https://gujcovid19.gujarat.gov.in/*
Haryana	State	https://gisgmda.maps.arcgis.com/apps/dashboards/5cade394ece3496a9e0c4f168f9536a2
Himachal Pradesh	State	http://www.nrhmhp.gov.in/
Jammu and Kashmir	UT	https://twitter.com/diprjk
Jharkhand	State	http://amritvahini.in/DashBoardNHM.aspx
Karnataka	State	https://covid19.karnataka.gov.in/covid-dashboard/dashboard.html*
Kerala	State	https://dashboard.kerala.gov.in
Ladakh	UT	https://covid.ladakh.gov.in/

Data Sites	Type	Primary Link
Lakshadweep	UT	https://cdn.s3waas.gov.in/s358238e9ae2dd305d79c2ebc8c1883422/uploads/2021/01/2021012428.pdf
Maharashtra	State	https://www.covid19maharashtragov.in/mh-covid/dashboard*
Manipur	State	http://nrhmmanipur.org/?p=5350
Meghalaya	State	http://meghalayaonline.gov.in/covid/login.htm
Mizoram	State	https://mcovid19.mizoram.gov.in/
Madhya Pradesh	State	http://sarthak.nhmmp.gov.in/covid/
Nagaland	State	https://covid19.nagaland.gov.in/
Odisha	State	https://statedashboard.odisha.gov.in/
Puducherry	UT	https://covid19dashboard.py.gov.in/
Punjab	State	https://nhm.punjab.gov.in/media-bulletin_June21.htm
Rajasthan	State	http://www.rajswasthya.nic.in/*
Sikkim	State	https://covid19sikkim.org/*
Tamil Nadu	State	https://stopcorona.tn.gov.in/*
		https://stopcorona.tn.gov.in/daily-bulletin/*
		https://stopcorona.tn.gov.in/dashboard-3/*
Telengana	State	https://covid19.telangana.gov.in/*

Data Sites	Type	Primary Link
Tripura	State	https://covid19.tripura.gov.in/
Uttar Pradesh	State	https://rahatup.in/Dashboard/Dashboard*
Uttarakhand	State	https://covid19.uk.gov.in/
West Bengal	State	https://www.wbhealth.gov.in/
Covid19India	Volunteer Collectives	https://www.covid19india.org/
Covid19Kerala	Volunteer Collectives	https://covid19kerala.info/
CovidIndia.org	Volunteer Collectives	https://www.covidindia.org/*
Thejesh GN	Volunteer Collectives	https://thejeshgn.com/projects/covid19-india/
AptLogica	Private	https://indiacovid-19.in/*
Hindustan Times	NewsPaper	https://epaper.hindustantimes.com/Home/ArticleView
The Indian Express	NewsPaper	https://indianexpress.com/
The Hindu	NewsPaper	https://epaper.thehindu.com/

* These links are no longer available or active. However, the references have been retained in the table to indicate the sources that the authors had looked at for their analysis.

Notes

1: Introduction

1. Pranshu Mishra, 'Caught Defecating Near Railway Tracks, Slum Dwellers in UP Say They Have no Other Option', News 18, 13 December 2018, https://www.news18.com/news/india/caught-defecating-near-railway-tracks-slum-dwellers-in-up-say-they-have-no-other-option-1603157.html
2. 'Sanitation Fact Sheet', World Health Organization, 14 June 2019, https://www.who.int/news-room/fact-sheets/detail/sanitation
3. Mahrukh Saleem, Teresa Burdett and Vanessa Heaslip, 'Health and Social Impacts of Open Defecation on Women: A Systematic Review', *BMC Public Health*, Vol. 19, No. 158, 2019, https://bmcpublichealth.biomedcentral.com/articles/10.1186/s12889-019-6423-z
4. Aashish Gupta et al., 'Revealed Preference for Open Defecation: Evidence from a New Survey in Rural North India', *Economic & Political Weekly*, Vol. 49 No. 38 2014, https://www.epw.in/journal/2014/38/special-articles/revealed-preference-open-defecation.html
5. C-E. A. Winslow, 'The Untilled Fields of Public Health Science', *Science*, Vol. 51, No. 1306 1920, pp. 23–33, doi:10.1126/science.51.1306.23

6 Muin J. Khoury, Wylie Burke and Elizabeth Thomson, 'Genetics and Public Health: A Framework for the Integration of Human Genetics into Public Health Practice', Centers for Disease Control and Prevention, 1999, https://www.cdc.gov/genomics/resources/books/21stcent/chap01.htm
7 Sifra Lentin, 'The 1918 Flu: India's Worst Pandemic', Gateway House, 17 September 2020, https://www.gatewayhouse.in/1918-flu-india/; TV Sekher, 'Influenza Pandemic of 1918: Lessons in Tackling a Public Health Catastrophe', *Economic & Political Weekly*, Vol. 56, No. 21,Vol. 56, No. 21, 2021, https://www.epw.in/journal/2021/21/perspectives/influenza-pandemic-1918.html
8 Chinmay Tumbe, 'Pandemics and Historical Mortality in India', IIMA W. P. No. 2020-12-03, December 2020, https://web.iima.ac.in/assets/snippets/workingpaperpdf/17719931472020-12-03.pdf
9 Aaron O'Neill, 'Life expectancy in India 1800-2020', Statista, 8 April 2020, https://www.statista.com/statistics/1041383/life-expectancy-india-all-time/
10 'Noncommunicable Disease Fact Sheet', World Health Organization, 13 April 2021, https://www.who.int/news-room/fact-sheets/detail/noncommunicable-diseases
11 'Global Burden of Disease Country Profiles – India', Institute for Health Metrics and Evaluation, University of Washington, 2021, http://www.healthdata.org/india
12 Vijay Kelkar and Ajay Shah, *In Service of the Republic: The Art and Science of Economic Policy*, Gurugram: Penguin Random House, 2019, p. 484.
13 Michael Lipsky, *Street-Level Bureaucracy: Dilemmas of the Individual in Public Services*, 30th ed., New York: Russell Sage Foundation, 2010.
14 Smriti Parsheera, 'Street-level Officials in India's COVID-19 Response', LEAP Blog, 6 April 2020, https://blog.theleapjournal.org/2020/04/street-level-officials-in-indias-covid.html
15 Vikram Patel, Alan J. Flisher, Sarah Hetrick and Patrick McGorry, 'Mental Health of Young People: A Global Public Health Challenge', *Lancet*, 369, 2007, pp. 1302–13, doi:10.1016/s0140-6736(07)60368-7; Claudia Trudel-Fitzgerald et. al., 'Psychological Well-being as Part of the Public Health Debate? Insight into Dimensions, Interventions, and Policy', *BMC Public Health* Vol. 19; No. 1712, 2019, https://doi.org/10.1186/s12889-019-8029-x
16 Sandy Milne, 'Bosses Turn to Tattleware to Keep Tabs on Employees Working From Home', *The Guardian*, 5 September 2021, https://www.

theguardian.com/us-news/2021/sep/05/covid-coronavirus-work-home-office-surveillance
17 Nuffield Council on Bioethics, 'Public health: Ethical Issues', 2007, https://www.nuffieldbioethics.org/publications/public-health/guide-to-the-report
18 David Kindig and Greg Stoddart, 'What Is Population Health?', *American Journal of Public Health*. March 2003, Vol. 93, No. 2003, p. 380–383, doi: 10.2105/ajph.93.3.380
19 *Justice K.S. Puttaswamy v. Union of India*, AIR 2017 SC 4161
20 *Jacob Puliyel v. Union of India*, Writ Petition (Civil) No. 607 of 2021, order dated 2 May, 2022, Supreme Court of India; Shreya Shrivastava, 'COVID-19 and Mandatory Vaccination: An Analysis of the Current Status and Legal Challenges', Vidhi Centre for Law and Policy, 19 August 2021, https://vidhilegalpolicy.in/blog/covid-19-and-mandatory-vaccination/
21 *Registrar General v. State of Meghalaya*, PIL No.6/2021, order dated 23 June 2021, High Court of Meghalaya
22 Nuffield Council on Bioethics, 'Public Health: Ethical Issues'.
23 Bert-Jaap Koops, Bryce Clayton Newell, Tjerk Timan, Ivan Škorvánek, Tomislav Chokrevski and Maša Galič, 'A Typology of Privacy', *University of Pennsylvania International Law Review*, Vol. 38, No. 2, 2017, p. 483, https://scholarship.law.upenn.edu/jil/vol38/iss2/4

2: India's Legal Framework on Public Health and Privacy

1 Abstract of the Proceedings of the Council of the Governor General of India', Vol XXXVI, Jan-Dec 1897, https://eparlib.nic.in/bitstream/123456789/783589/1/ilcd_28-january-1897.pdf
2 Cited by Kiran Kumbhar, 'Epidemic Diseases Act, India's 123-Year-Old Law to Help Fight the Pandemic', *The Wire*, 22 March 2020, https://science.thewire.in/health/epidemic-diseases-act-india-pandemic/
3 Omar Rashid, 'Coronavirus: In Bareilly, Migrants Returning Home Sprayed With 'Disinfectant''', *The Hindu*, 30 March 2020, https://www.thehindu.com/news/national/other-states/coronavirus-in-bareilly-migrants-forced-to-take-bath-in-the-open-with-sanitiser/article31204430.ece
4 Ayona Datta, 'Self(ie)-governance: Technologies of Intimate Surveillance in India Under COVID-19', *Dialogues in Human Geography*, 10 no. 2 (2020), https://doi.org/10.1177/2043820620929797

5   K. Raghavendra Rao and. P.R. Panchamukhi, 'Health and the Indian Constitution', *CMDR Monograph Series No. 7*, Centre for Multi-disciplinary Development Research, http://cmdr.ac.in/editor_v51/assets/Mono-7.pdf
6   *Justice (Retd) K.S. Puttaswamy v. Union of India*, (2017) 10 SCC 1.
7   Vrinda Bhandari et al. 'An Analysis of Puttaswamy: The Supreme Court's Privacy Verdict', *The LEAP Blog*, 20 September 2017, https://blog.theleapjournal.org/2017/09/an-analysis-of-puttaswamy-supreme.html
8   *Navtej Singh Johar v. Union of India*, AIR 2018 SC 4321.
9   *Common Cause (A Registered Society) v. Union of India*, (2018) 5 SCC 1.
10 *Consumer Education and Research Centre v. Union of India*, AIR 1995 SC 922.
11 *Mr X v. Hospital Z*, AIR 1999 SC 495.
12 *Bandhua Mukti Morcha v. Union of India*, AIR 1984 SC 812
13 *In Re Distribution of essential supplies and services during pandemic*, Suo Motu Writ Petition (Civil) No.3 of 2021.
14 Article 37, Constitution of India.
15 Articles 39 to 45, Constitution of India.
16 *Vincent Panikurlangara v. Union of India*, 1987 AIR SC 990.
17 *Khoday Distilleries Ltd. v. State of Karnataka*, 1995 (1) SCC 574, *Kanaka Durga Wines v. Government of Andhra Pradesh*, 1995 (3) ALT 228.
18 *State of Punjab v. Ram Lubhaya Bagga*, (1998) 4 SCC 117.
19 Constituent Assembly of India Debates (Proceedings), Volume VII, 24 November 1948, http://164.100.47.194/loksabha/writereaddata/cadebatefiles/C24111948.html
20 *Khoday Distillerie v. State of Karnataka*, 1995 SCC (1) 574.
21 *State of Bombay v. F.N.Balsara*, AIR 1951 SC 318.
22 *Peter Jagdish Nazareth v. State of Gujarat*, Special Civil Application No. 799 of 2019 before the High Court of Gujarat, order dated 23 August, 2021, https://indiankanoon.org/doc/137437893/?type=print
23 Sections 8 and 9, The Human Immunodeficiency Virus and Acquired Immune Deficiency Syndrome (Prevention and Control) Act, 2017.
24 *Radiological & Imaging Association v. Union of India*, AIR 2011 BOM 171.
25 Population (Control, Stabilisation and Welfare) Bill, 2021.
26 Mohan Rao and Aprajita Sarcar, 'Two-child Norm: Curtailing Welfare, Weaponising Demography', *Economic & Political Weekly*, Vol. 56, No. 35 (2021), https://www.epw.in/journal/2021/35/commentary/two-child-norm.html

27 *Javed* v. *State of Haryana*, AIR 2003 SC 3057, *B.K Parthasarthi* v. *Government of Andhra Pradesh*, AIR 2000 AP 156, *Elkapalli Latchaiah* v. *Government of Andhra Pradesh*, (2001) 5 ALT 410.
28 NewsClick, 'UP Population Bill Violates Basic Rights of Women, Says Memorandum Submitted to President', 20 July 2021, https://www.newsclick.in/UP-Population-Bill-Violates-Basic-Rights-Women-Memorandum-Submitted-President
29 Entry 6, List II, Seventh Schedule, Constitution of India.
30 Articles 243G and 243W read with the Eleventh and Twelfth Schedules of the Constitution.
31 P.J. Wolf. 'Authority: Delegation', in International Encyclopedia of the Social & Behavioral Sciences, eds. N. J. Smelser and P. B. Baltes (Pergamon: 2001).
32 Entry 29, List III, Seventh Schedule, Constitution of India.
33 Entries 16, 18, 19, 20A, 24, List III, Seventh Schedule, Constitution of India.
34 Entries 28, 29, 30 and 81, List I, Seventh Schedule, Constitution of India.
35 Entry 14, List I, Seventh Schedule and Article 253, Constitution of India.
36 Articles 17, 23, 31, and 43, International Health Regulations
37 Amit Yadav et al. 'Public Health Law in India: A Framework for its Application as a Tool for Social Change', *The National Medical Journal of India*, Vol. 22, No. 4 (2009).
38 Public Health (Prevention, Control and Management of Epidemics, Bio-terrorism and Disasters) Act, 2017, Ministry of Health & Family Welfare, Government of India, https://main.mohfw.gov.in/sites/default/files/Inviting%20Comments%20on%20Draft%20Public%20Health%20Bill%2C%202017.pdf
39 Menaka Rao, 'A New Bill on Public Health Emergencies Allows For Dubious Restrictions of Citizens' Liberties', *The Scroll*, 31 March, 2017, https://scroll.in/pulse/833283/a-new-bill-on-public-health-emergencies-allows-for-dubious-restrictions-of-citizens-liberties
40 Draft National Health Bill, 2009, Ministry of Health and Family Welfare, Government of India, https://nhsrcindia.org/sites/default/files/2021-06/7.The%20National%20Health%20Bill%202009.pdf
41 Supreme Court's order dated 31 August, 2020 in *Sachin Jain* v. *Union Of India*, Writ Petition (Civil) No. 863 of 2020 and Writ Petition (Civil) No. 489 of 2020, https://indiankanoon.org/doc/104401487/
42 Sections 19, 23, 29 and 40(2), Kerala Public Health Ordinance, 2021

43 Jeemon Jacob, 'Kerala Backs Out of Sprinklr Deal, Cancels Controversial Pact Over Privacy Issues, *India Today*, 21 May 2020, https://www.indiatoday.in/india/story/kerala-sprinklr-deal-covid-19-pinarayi-vijayan-high-court-1680484-2020-05-21
44 The Uttar Pradesh Public Health And Epidemic Diseases Control Act, 2020, https://www.indiacode.nic.in/bitstream/123456789/16571/1/act_epidemic_2020.pdf
45 Section 2, Epidemic Diseases Act, 1897.
46 Section 2(d), National Disaster Management Act, 2005.
47 Ambar Kumar Ghosh and Anasua Basu Ray Chaudhury, 'Pandemic as a "Disaster": Assessing Indian State Response', *The Diplomatist*, 5 September 2020, https://diplomatist.com/2020/09/04/pandemic-as-a-disaster-assessing-indian-state-response/
48 See Section 3, Epidemic Diseases Act, 1897, Section 51, Disaster Management Act, 2005, and Section 188, Indian Penal Code, 1860.
49 Sections 268 to 291, Indian Penal Code, 1860.
50 *Jagdishwaran v. Police Commissioner, Calcutta*, AIR 1984 SC 51.
51 The Cigarettes and Other Tobacco Products (Prohibition of Advertisement and Regulation of Trade and Commerce, Production, Supply and Distribution) Act, 2003.
52 Section 12, The Cigarettes and Other Tobacco Products Act, 2003.
53 Section 16(6), Food Safety and Standards Act, 2006.
54 Action 23, Mental healthcare Act, 2017.
55 Section 20, Mental healthcare Act, 2017.
56 Section 13(5), Rights of Persons with Disabilities Act, 2016.
57 Regulation 7.14, Indian Medical Council (Professional conduct, Etiquette and Ethics) Regulations, 2002.
58 Regulation 1.3, Indian Medical Council (Professional conduct, Etiquette and Ethics) Regulations, 2002.
59 Rule 9 (iv), Clinical Establishments (Central Government) Rules, 2012
60 Notification of Electronic Health Record (EHR) Standards - 2016 for India, Ministry of Health and Family Welfare, Government of India, 30 Dec, 2016, https://www.nhp.gov.in/NHPfiles/EHR-Standards-2016-MoHFW.pdf
61 Waldemar W. Koczkodaj et al., 'Electronic Health Record Breaches as Social Indicators', *Social Indicators Research*, 3 February 2018, doi:10.1007/s11205-018-1837-z
62 Koczkodaj et al., 'Electronic Health Record Breaches'.

63 Oommen C. Kurian, 'Data, Privacy, Pandemic: India Just Had the Biggest Medical Records Breach Ever', *Observer Research Foundation*, 12 January 2021, https://www.orfonline.org/expert-speak/data-privacy-pandemic-india-just-had-the-biggest-medical-records-breach-ever/
64 Ax Sharma, 'Indian Government Sites Leaking Patient COVID-19 Test Results', *Bleeping Computer*, 5 January 2021, https://www.bleepingcomputer.com/news/security/indian-government-sites-leaking-patient-covid-19-test-results/
65 'Hackers Attack Indian Healthcare Website, Steal 68 Lakh Records: Report', *The Wire*, 23 August 2019, https://thewire.in/health/hackers-attack-indian-healthcare-website-steal-68-lakh-records-report
66 Rule 3, Information Technology (Reasonable Security Practices and Procedures and Sensitive Personal Data or Information) Rules, 2011.
67 Information Technology (Reasonable security practices and procedures and sensitive personal data or information) Rules, 2011, https://www.meity.gov.in/writereaddata/files/GSR313E_10511%281%29_0.pdf.
68 B.N. Srikrishna et al., 'A Free and Fair Digital Economy: Protecting Privacy, Empowering Indians', Report of the Committee of Experts constituted by the Ministry of Electronics and Information Technology, 2018, https://meity.gov.in/writereaddata/files/Data_Protection_Committee_Report.pdf
69 Section 2(21) and 2(36), PDP Bill, 2019.
70 Section 11(3), PDP Bill, 2019.
71 Section 12, PDP Bill 2019.
72 Section 33 and 34, PDP Bill 2019.
73 B.N. Srikrishna et al., 'A Free and Fair Digital Economy', p. 98.
74 Milind Antani, Darren Punnen and Anay Shukla, 'DISHA: The First Step Towards Securing Patient Health Data in India', Nishith Desai Associates, May 2018, http://www.nishithdesai.com/fileadmin/user_upload/pdfs/NDA%20In%20The%20Media/News%20Articles/180725_A_DISHA-The-First-Step-towards-Securing-Patient-Health-Data-in-India.pdf
75 Ministry of Health and Family Welfare, Data Transfer of Digital Health Records, 16 July, 2019, https://pib.gov.in/Pressreleaseshare.aspx?PRID=1578929
76 Smriti Parsheera et al., 'Analysis of India's Aarogya Setu App', in *Monitoring, Citizenship and Health: COVID-19 Global Insights*, eds. Lucena C. and Almeda L. (AREPB: 2020).

3: COVID-19 Data Infrastructure in India: Politics of Knowing and Governing the Pandemic

1. Stefania Milan, 'Techno-Solutionism and the Standard Human in the Making of the COVID-19 Pandemic', *Big Data & Society*, 7 no. 2 (2020), doi:10.1177/2053951720966781.
2. V. Aula, 'The Public Debate Around COVID-19 Demonstrates Our Ongoing and Misplaced Trust in Numbers', 2020, https://blogs.lse.ac.uk/impactofsocialsciences/2020/05/15/the-public-debate-around-covid-19-demonstrates-our-ongoing-and-misplaced-trust-in-numbers/
3. Viktor Mayer-Schoenberger and Kenneth Cukier, *Big Data. A Revolution That Will Transform How We Live, Work, and Think* (London: John Murray Publishers, 2013).
4. Milan, 'Techno-solutionism and the Standard Human'.
5. Aula, The Public Debate Around COVID-19'.
6. Shelton, 'A Post-truth Pandemic?'.
7. Geoffrey C. Bowker and Susan Leigh Star, *Sorting Things Out: Classification and its Consequences*, The MIT Press, 1999; Margo Anderson, Martha Lampland and Susan Leigh Star (eds.), *Standards and Their Stories: How Quantifying, Classifying and Formalizing Practices Shape Everyday Life*, Ithaca, Cornell University Press, 2009, *Journal of Interdisciplinary History*, Vol. 41, 2010, pp. 124–125, doi:10.1162/jinh.2010.41.1.124; Lisa Gitelman and V. Jackson, 'Introduction', in *'Raw Data' is an Oxymoron*, ed. Lisa Gitelman, Cambridge: MIT Press, 2013, pp. 1–14.
8. Theodore M. Porter, *Trust in Numbers: The Pursuit of Objectivity in Science and Public Life*, Princeton: Princeton University Press, 1995.
9. Aula, 'The Public Debate Around COVID-19'.
10. R. Ackoff, 'From Data to Wisdom', Journal of Applied Systems Analysis, 16 (1989, pp. 3–9.
11. J. Rowley, 'The Wisdom Hierarchy: Representations of the DIKW Hierarchy' *Journal of Information Science*, 33, Vol. No. 2, 2007, pp. 163–180.
12. Viktor Mayer-Schoenberger and Kenneth Cukier, *Big Data. A Revolution That Will Transform How We Live, Work, and Think* (London: John Murray Publishers, 2013).
13. Mayer-Schoenberger and Cukier, *Big Data*.
14. R. Raley, 'Dataveillance and Countervailance' in Lisa Gitelman (ed.), *'Raw Data' is an Oxymoron*, Cambridge: MIT Press, 2013, pp. 121–146; J Van Dijck, 'Datafication, Dataism and Dataveillance: Big Data Between Scientific Paradigm and Ideology', *Surveillance & Society*, Vol. 12, No. 2,

2014, pp. 197–208; K. Crawford, M.L. Grayand K. Miltner, 'Big Data. Critiquing Big Data: Politics, Ethics, Epistemology', *International Journal of Communication*, 8 (2014): 10.
15   Van Dijck, 'Datafication, Dataism and Dataveillance'.
16   R. Kitchin and T.P. Lauriault, 'Towards Critical Data Studies: Charting and Unpacking Data Assemblages and Their Work', *The Programmable City Working Paper*, 2014; B. Williamson, 'Algorithmic Skin: Health-tracking Technologies, Personal Analytics and the Biopedagogies of Digitized Health and Physical Education', *Sport, Education and Society*, Vol. 20, No. 1, 2015, pp. 133–151; M. Ruckenstein and N.D. Schüll, 'The Datafication of Health', *Annual Review of Anthropology*, 46 (2017): 261-278.
17   E. Ruppert, 'Population Objects: Interpassive Subjects', *Sociology*, Vol. 45, No. 2, 2011, pp. 218-233.
18   Ruckenstein and Schüll, 'The Datafication of Health'.
19   T. Shelton, 'A Post-truth Pandemic?' *Big Data & Society*, Vol. 7, No. 2, 2020, doi:10.1177/2053951720965612.
20   Stefania Milan and Emiliano Treré, 'The Rise of the Data Poor: The COVID-19 Pandemic Seen From the Margins', *Social Media + Society*, Vol. 6, No. 3, 2020, doi:10.1177/2056305120948233.
21   Taylor, 'The Price of Certainty'.
22   Taylor, 'The Price of Certainty'.
23   "But as the cases grew, we dropped the feature. For two reasons - one, the states stopped publishing the contact tracing info, two, the data points to visualize were so many that the browsers crashed." In 'Nodes and links. Links and nodes', 9 July 2020, https://blog.covid19india.org/2020/07/09/nodesandlinkslinksandnodes/
24   Shelton, 'A Post-Truth Pandemic?'
25   Kitchin and Lauriault, 'Towards Critical Data Studies; Gitelman and Jackson, from the 'Introduction' in *'Raw Data' is an Oxymoron*.
26   Shelton, 'A Post-truth Pandemic?'.
27   M. Hoyer, K. Stafford and A. Morrison, 'Racial Toll of Virus Grows Even Starker as More Data Emerges', 18 April 2020, https://apnews.com/8a3430dd37e7c44290c7621f5af96d6b
28   Hoyer et al., 'Racial Toll of Virus Grows'.
29   V. Vasudevan et al., 'Disparity in the Quality of COVID-19 Data Reporting Across India', *Public and Global Health*, 2020.
30   A CSV file, or a comma-separated values file, is a way of storing information in a tabular format in a plain text file. It's a way to exchange

structured information, similar to a spreadsheet, between programs that wouldn't normally be able to talk to each other.' Available on https://www.freshbooks.com/hub/other/what-is-a-csv-file

31 D. Nath, 'Govt. Has No Data of Migrant Workers' Death, Loss of Job', *The Hindu*, https://www.thehindu.com/news/national/govt-has-no-data-of-migrant-workers-death-loss-of-job/article32600637.ece

32 S. Daniyal, 'Explained: How Sampling Bias Drove Sensationalist Reporting around Tablighi Coronavirus Cases', *The Scroll*, 2020, https://scroll.in/article/958392/explained-sampling-bias-drove-sensationalist-reporting-around-tablighi-coronavirus-cases; S. Chandhiramowuli and B. Chaudhuri, 'Perspective, Politics of Data in & as News: A Data Justice' AMCIS 2021 Proceedings (2021):13.

33 Van Dijck, 'Datafication, Dataism and Dataveillance'.

34 Bird and Bird, 'Personal Data of Deceased Persons', 2019, https://www.twobirds.com/en/in-focus/general-data-protection-regulation/gdpr-tracker/deceased-persons.ax

35 Health and Family Welfare Department, Government of Tamil Nadu, 'Self Reporting', https://stopcorona.tn.gov.in/self_reporting.php

36 A. Kofman, 'Bruno Latour, the Post-Truth Philosopher, Mounts a Defense of Science', *The New York Times*, https://www.nytimes.com/2018/10/25/magazine/bruno-latour-post-truth-philosopher-science.html

4: COVID-19 Surveillance in India: A Bridge Too Far?

1 Vrinda Bhandari and Faiza Rahman, 'Constitutionalism During a Crisis: The Case of Aarogya Setu' in Uma Kapila (ed.), *Coronavirus Pandemic: Lessons and Policy Response*, Academic Foundation, 2020; Siddharth Sonkar, 'Guest Report: Bridging Concerns with Recommending Aarogya Setu,' *Centre for Internet and Society*, 20 June 2020, https://cis-india.org/aarogya%20setu%20privacy; Siddhart Deb, 'Public Policy Imperatives for Contact Tracing in India' (Working Paper No. 5/2020, IFF), https://drive.google.com/file/d/1UK5rElhcdP5T3Y-8fYP6cCgQKKpQBeOX/view

2 Yuval Noah Harari, 'The World After coronavirus,' *Financial Times*, 20 March 2020, https://www.ft.com/content/19d90308-6858-11ea-a3c9-1fe6fedcca75

3 Lindsay Wiley and Steve Vladeck, 'COVID-19 Reinforces the Argument for "Regular" Judicial Review - Not Suspension of Civil Liberties - In Times of Crisis,' *Harvard Law Review Blog*, 9 April 2020, https://blog.

harvardlawreview.org/covid-19-reinforces-the-argument-for-regular-judicial-review-not-suspension-of-civil-liberties-in-times-of-crisis/
4   Tiffany Li, 'Privacy in Pandemic: Law, Technology, and Public Health in the COVID-19 Crisis,' *Loyola University Chicago Law Journal*, Vol. 52, 2020, p. 767, https://scholarship.law.bu.edu/faculty_scholarship/973/
5   Item 6, List II, Schedule VII, Constitution of India, 1950.
6   Item 29, List III, Schedule VII, Constitution of India 1950.
7   A notable exception is the report by Chithira Vijayakumar and Tanisha Ranjit, *Virus Detected: A Profile of India's Emergent Ecosystem of Networked Technologies to Tackle COVID-19*, (Internet Democracy, May 2020), https://cdn.internetdemocracy.in/idp/assets/downloads/reports/covid-app-project-india-country-report/Vijayakumar-and-Ranjit-IDP-Virus-Detected_2021-06-03-103842.pdf
8   Benjamin Boudreaux et al., *Data Privacy During Pandemics: A Scorecard Approach for Evaluating the Privacy Implications of COVID-19 Mobile Phone Surveillance Programs* (RAND Corporation, 2020), https://www.rand.org/content/dam/rand/pubs/research_reports/RRA300/RRA365-1/RAND_RRA365-1.pdf
9   K.S. Puttaswamy v. Union of India, (2017) 10 SCC 1 [312].
10 Vijayakumar and Ranjit, *Virus Detected*.
11 Boudreaux, *Data Privacy During Pandemics*, p. 8.
12 Tim Mackey et al, 'Machine Learning to Detect Self-Reporting of Symptoms, Testing Access, and Recovery Associates with COVID-19 on Twitter: Retrospective Big Data Infoveillance Study,' *JMIR Public Health Surveillance* 6 no. 2 (2020), https://www.ncbi.nlm.nih.gov/pmc/articles/PMC7282475/
13 Vijayakumar and Ranjit, *Virus Detected*, p. 39-40.
14 Question Nos. 7 and 16, https://www.aarogyasetu.gov.in/faq/
15 Question No. 9, https://www.aarogyasetu.gov.in/faq/
16 Clause 3, Aarogya Setu Privacy Policy, https://www.aarogyasetu.gov.in/privacy-policy/
17 Vishal Mathur, 'Reliance MyJio App Adds a Coronavirus Self-Diagnostic Tool That is Available For Everyone,' News18, 9 April 2020, https://www.news18.com/news/tech/reliance-myjio-app-adds-a-coronavirus-self-diagnostic-tool-that-is-available-for-everyone-2548619.html; Aastha Ahuja, 'Are You Infected With COVID-19? Check With Apollo Hospitals' Online Coronavirus Risk Scan,' NDTV, 15 April 2020, https://swachhindia.ndtv.com/are-you-infected-with-covid-19-check-with-apollo-hospitals-online-coronavirus-risk-scan-42797/

18 Radhika Radhakrishnan, 'I took Allah's name and stepped out: Bodies, Data and Embodied Experiences of Surveillance and Control during COVID-19 in India,' Data Governance Network Working Paper No. 12, 2020, p. 19, https://internetdemocracy.in/reports/i-took-allahs-name-and-stepped-out-bodies-data-and-embodied-experiences-of-surveillance-and-control-during-covid-19-in-india/
19 'Micro Plan for Containing Local Transmission of Coronavirus Disease', Ministry of Health and Family Welfare, https://www.mohfw.gov.in/pdf/ModelMicroplanforcontainmentoflocaltransmissionofCOVID19.pdf
20 'The Chennai: Together We Stand,' Greater Chennai Corporation, -https://chennaicorporation.gov.in/news_letter/Newsletter%20First%20Issue.pdf
21 Shweta Mohandas and Deepika Srinivasa, 'The Boss Will See You Now – The Growth of Workplace Surveillance in India, is Data Protection Legislation the Answer,' *Centre for Internet and Society*, 31 December 2020, https://cis-india.org/internet-governance/blog/the-boss-will-see-you-now-the-growth-of-workplace-surveillance-in-india-is-data-protection-legislation-the-answer
22 Olivier Telle et al, 'The Spread of Dengue in an Endemic Urban Miliue – The Case of Delhi, India,' *Plos One* 11 no. 3 (2016), https://journals.plos.org/plosone/article?id=10.1371/journal.pone.0146539; Partha Mukhopadhyay and Shamindra Nath Roy, 'Mapping the Lockdown Effects in India: How Geographers can Contribute to Tackle COVID-19 diffusion', *The Conversation*, 22 April 2020, https://theconversation.com/mapping-the-lockdown-effects-in-india-how-geographers-can-contribute-to-tackle-covid-19-diffusion-136323
23 Rahul Matthan, 'Aarogya Setu and the Value of Syndromic Surveillance', *LiveMint*, 13 May 2020, https://www.livemint.com/opinion/columns/aarogya-setu-and-the-value-of-syndromic-surveillance-11589304017285.html
24 Deeksha Bhardwaj, 'Aarogya Setu Fades into Background as India Deals with Second COVID-19 Wave', *Hindustan Times*, 7 May 2020, https://www.hindustantimes.com/india-news/aarogya-setu-fades-into-background-as-india-deals-with-second-covid-19-wave-101620365578382.html
25 Rohini Swamy, 'This is How Karnataka Govt Will Keep Track of Nearly 15,000 People under Home Quarantine', *The Print*, 26 March 2020, https://theprint.in/india/governance/this-is-how-karnataka-govt-will-keep-track-of-nearly-15000-people-under-home-quarantine/388870/

26 Alithea Stephanie Mounika and Sanyukta Dharmadhikari, 'Karnataka's App for Contact Tracing Reveals Home Addresses of COVID-19 Patients,' *The News Minute*, 27 March 2020, https://www.thenewsminute.com/article/karnataka-s-app-contact-tracing-reveals-home-addresses-covid-19-patients-121241
27 Arun Kang Joseph, 'Interview: How Kerala Contained Its Coronavirus Epidemic', *The Wire*, 4 July 2020, <https://thewire.in/government/interview-vijay-sakhare-kerala-triple-lock-strategy-coronavirus-epidemic
28 Press Trust of India, 'Drones Help Cops Nab Over 40 Violating Social Distancing Rule', *Business Standard*, 4 April 2020, https://www.business-standard.com/article/pti-stories/drones-help-cops-nab-over-40-violating-social-distancing-rule-120040400567_1.html
29 Siddharth Sonkar and Divij Joshi, 'COVID-19 Related Government Digital Surveillance and Tech Measures in India,' *Mozilla Pulse*, 15 April 2020, https://www.mozillapulse.org/entry/1647
30 Radhakrishnan, 'Allah's name', pp. 22–23.
31 Boudreaux et al., *Data Privacy During Pandemics*.
32 Anil Urs, 'Karnataka Develops App to Track Home Quarantine Persons,' *Business Line*, 31 March 2020, https://www.thehindubusinessline.com/info-tech/karnataka-develops-app-to-track-home-quarantined-persons/article31214354.ece
33 'COVID-19 Quarantine Reporting App', http://office.suratmunicipal.org/SMCCOVID19/Guest; Rohini Lakshane, 'Tracking Quarantine, Tracing Cases, Sharing Info: Can These Govt-issued Apps Help Fight COVID-19', *Citizen Matters*, 6 April 2020, https://citizenmatters.in/tracking-quarantine-tracing-cases-sharing-info-can-these-govt-issued-apps-help-fight-covid-19-17151
34 'SMC's Home Quarantine App Replicated in Four Guj Cities,' *Times of India*, 28 March 2020, https://timesofindia.indiatimes.com/city/surat/smcs-home-quarantine-app-replicated-in-four-guj-cities/articleshow/74853134.cms.
35 'Analysis of the Indian COVID-19 Apps', *Software Freedom Law Centre*, 20 April 2020, https://sflc.in/our-analysis-indian-covid19-apps
36 Radhakrishnan, 'Allah's name', pp. 15-16.
37 Ayona Datta, 'Self(ie)-governance: Technologies of Intimate Surveillance in India Under COVID-19', *Dialogues in Human Geography* 10 no. 2 (2020): 234, 236.

38 Mira Swaminathan and Shubhika Saluja, 'Watching Corona or Neighbours? – Introducing Lateral Surveillance during COVID-19,' *Centre for Internet and Society*, 21 May 2020, https://cis-india.org/internet-governance/blog/essay-watching-corona-or-neighbours-introducing-2018lateral-surveillance2019-during-covid201919

39 Datta, 'Self(ie)-governance', p. 236.

40 Pooja Jaiswal, 'Privacy of COVID-19 Suspects violated; names, addresses made public,' *The Week*, March 22, 2020, https://www.theweek.in/news/india/2020/03/22/privacy-of-covid-19-suspects-violated-names-addresses-made-public.html; 'Karnataka makes addresses of quarantines residents public, raises privacy concerns,' *The News Minute*, March 25, 2020, https://www.thenewsminute.com/article/karnataka-makes-addresses-quarantined-residents-public-raises-privacy-concerns-121096

41 'Airports in India Begin Stamping Home Quarantine Info on Wrist of All incoming International Passengers,' *News18*, March 20, 2020, https://www.news18.com/news/auto/airports-in-india-begin-stamping-home-quarantine-info-on-wrist-of-all-incoming-international-passengers-2542365.html

42 Yuval Noah Harari, 'Surveillance is getting under our skin – and that should alarm us,' *Al Jazeera*, May 31, 2020, https://www.aljazeera.com/opinions/2020/5/31/surveillance-is-getting-under-our-skin-and-that-should-alarm-us

43 Jaiswal, 'Privacy'.

44 Mark Andrejevic, 'The Work of Watching One Another: Later Surveillance, Risk, and Governance', *Surveillance & Society* 2, no. 4 (2005): 479, 488.

45 Swaminathan and Saluja, 'Lateral Surveillance'.

46 Aloysius Xavier Lopez, '5,000 Focus Volunteers To Be Deployed,' *The Hindu*, 13 June 2020, https://www.thehindu.com/news/cities/chennai/focus-volunteers-to-help-quarantined-persons/article31823473.ece

47 Joseph, 'Kerala'.

48 Sonalakshi Naidu, 'RWA Uncles, Please Calm Down About Aarogya Setu,' *Internet Freedom Foundation*, 1 June 2020, https://internetfreedom.in/aarogya-setu-rwas/

49 Vishaka Chaman, 'Gurugram: RWAs Told To Get Travel Data, Move Triggers Concerns,' *The Times of India*, 7 April 2020, https://timesofindia.indiatimes.com/city/gurgaon/rwas-told-to-get-travel-data-move-triggers-concerns/articleshow/81939372.cms

50 Li, 'Privacy in Pandemic'.

51 Sonkar, 'Bridging Concerns'; Pranav Bhaskar Tiwari et al, 'Privacy Framework for the Aarogya Setu App,' (Working Paper, The Dialogue, 2020), https://thedialogue.co/wp-content/uploads/2020/05/Privacy-Framework-for-the-Aarogya-Set-App.pdf; Binayak Dasgupta, 'Protection or Threat? Experts say Aarogya Setu poses National Security Risk,' *Hindustan Times*, 23 May 2020, https://www.hindustantimes.com/india-news/aarogya-setu-protection-or-threat/story-QmpSP3H60ohkLV3l5ywhBI.html; Vrinda Bhandari, 'Digital Rights and the Covid-19 Pandemic: A Case Study of Aarogya Setu and Why We Should Care,' in *Covid 19: A View from the Margins*, ed. Yogesh Jain et al (2021, forthcoming).

52 Saurav Das, 'Govt. Ignores Its Own Vital Safeguards on Aarogya Setu,' *The Quint*, 30 October 2020, https://www.thequint.com/news/india/exclusive-govt-fails-to-implement-its-own-data-protection-safeguards-under-aarogya-setu-protocol

53 For a list of state apps on contact tracing, see Sonkar and Joshi, 'Mozilla Pulse'.

54 Vijayakumar and Ranjit, *Virus Detected*, pp. 18–19.

55 'COVID-19 Book of Five: Response and Containment Measures for ANM, ASHA, AWW', Ministry of Health and Family Welfare, https://www.mohfw.gov.in/pdf/3Pocketbookof5_Covid19_27March.pdf

56 MoHFW, 'Micro Plan'.

57 Mahaveer Goleccha, 'COVID-19 Containment in Asia's Largest Slum Dharavi-Mumbai, India: Lessons for Policymakers Globally,' *Journal of Urban Health* 97 (2020): 796, https://doi.org/10.1007/s11524-020-00474-2; Niha Masih, 'Aggressive Testing, Contact Tracing, Cooked Meals: How the Indian State of Kerala Flattened its Coronavirus Curve', *The Washington Post*, 14 April 2020, https://www.washingtonpost.com/world/aggressive-testing-contact-tracing-cooked-meals-how-the-indian-state-of-kerala-flattened-its-coronavirus-curve/2020/04/10/3352e470-783e-11ea-a311-adb1344719a9_story.html

58 Boudreaux et al, *Data Privacy During Pandemics*, p. 24.

59 Mira Patel, 'From Smallpox to COVID-19: The History of Vaccine Passports and How it Impacts International Relations,' *The Indian Express*, 4 June 2021, https://indianexpress.com/article/research/from-smallpox-to-covid-19-the-history-of-vaccine-passports-and-how-it-impacts-international-relations-7274871/

60 'Here's How You Can Get an e-pass Across India During the Lockdown', *ET Online*, 30 May 2020, https://economictimes.indiatimes.com/news/

politics-and-nation/how-you-can-get-an-e-pass-across-india-during-the-lockdown/articleshow/75708982.cms

61 Vijayakumar and Ranjit, *Virus Detected*, p. 21.
62 Aparna Banerjea, 'Aarogya Setu App Can Be Used as e-pass to Facilitate Travel Amid Lockdown: Modi', *Livemint*, 11 April 2020, https://www.livemint.com/technology/tech-news/aarogya-setu-app-can-be-used-as-e-pass-to-facilitate-travel-amid-lockdown-modi-11586605016598.html
63 Ministry of Home Affairs, Guidelines for Phased Re-opening (Unlock 4), Order No. 40-3/2020-DM-I(A), 29 August 2020, https://www.mha.gov.in/sites/default/files/MHAOrder_Unlock4_29082020.pdf
64 'WHO Does Not Back Vaccination Passports For Now – Spokeswoman', *Reuters*, 6 April 2021, https://www.reuters.com/article/us-health-coronavirus-who-vaccines-idUSKBN2BT158
65 Patel, 'Vaccine Passports'.
66 *Registrar General, High Court of Meghalaya v. State of Meghalaya*, MANU/MG/0061/2021 (Meg HC).
67 'Delhi High Court Issues Directions on Suggestions to Improve the CoWIN Platform', *Internet Freedom Foundation*, 7 June 2021, https://internetfreedom.in/delhi-high-court-issues-directions-on-suggestions-to-improve-the-cowin-platform/
68 'Aarogya Setu : MHA Dilutes Mandatory Imposition; Says Employers On "Best Effort Basis" Should Ensure Use Of App By Employees With Compatible Mobile Phones', *Livelaw*, 17 May 2020, https://www.livelaw.in/top-stories/aarogya-setu-mha-dilutes-mandatory-imposition-156921
69 *Kush Kalra v. UOI*, (2021) 2 SCC 481[13].
70 Bhandari and Rahman, 'Aarogya Setu'; Suhrith Parthasarathy, 'Coronavirus and the Constitution – IV: Privacy in a Public Health Crisis,' *Indian Constitutional Law and Philosophy Blog*, 29 March 2020, https://indconlawphil.wordpress.com/2020/03/29/coronavirus-and-the-constitution-iv-privacy-in-a-public-health-crisis/
71 Gautam Bhatia, 'Coronavirus and the Constitution – XXI: The Mandatory Imposition of the Aarogya Setu App,' *Indian Constitutional Law and Philosophy Blog*, 2 May 2020, https://indconlawphil.wordpress.com/2020/05/02/coronavirus-and-the-constitution-xxi-the-mandatory-imposition-of-the-aarogya-setu-app/
72 *KVMS v State of Kerala*, WP(C) TMP No. 182/20, order dated 28 April 2020.
73 *K.S. Puttaswamy v UOI*, (2017) 10 SCC 1.
74 Wiley and Vladeck, 'Judicial Review'.

75 Basawa Prasad, 'Coronavirus and the Constitution – VII: Balancing Privacy and Public Health in Karnataka', *Indian Constitutional Law and Philosophy Blog*, 3 April 2020, https://indconlawphil.wordpress.com/2020/04/03/coronavirus-and-the-constitution-vii-balancing-privacy-and-public-health-in-karnataka-guest-post/

76 Rahul Matthan, 'The Privacy Implications of Using Data and Technologies in a Pandemic', *Journal of Indian Institute of Science*, Vol. 100, No. 4, 2020, pp 611–12.

77 'Aarogya Setu Tracker', Internet Democracy Project, https://docs.google.com/spreadsheets/d/19pF6A2GXvbAjSefj_LHT9VC2Ct7h52S0iZsdsAwd5EM/edit#gid=0

78 'Coronavirus: Aarogya Setu App Mandatory for Passengers Travelling on Special Trains, Says Railways', *Scroll.in*, 12 May 2020, https://scroll.in/latest/961719/coronavirus-aarogya-setu-app-mandatory-for-passengers-travelling-on-special-trains-says-railways

79 'Application Form for Issuance of Vehicle e-Pass', https://bit.ly/3DYYgPn

80 Radhakrishnan, 'Allah's name', p. 19-20.

81 Sagrika Kissu, 'ASHA Workers in Haryana Reject Govt. Tracking App over Surveillance Fears', *NewsClick*, 16 June 2021, https://www.newsclick.in/ASHA-workers-haryana-reject-govt-tracking-app-surveillance-fears

82 Meredith Van Natta et al, 'The Rise and Regulation of Thermal Facial Recognition Technology During COVID-19 Pandemic,' *Journal of Law and Biosciences*, Vol. 7, No. 1, 2020, pp. 1, 5–8.

83 Mohandas and Srinivasa, 'Workplace Surveillance'.

84 Clause 12(d)-(f), Personal Data Protection Bill, 2019.

85 Government of Karnataka, 'Privacy Policy', https://www.landrecords.karnataka.gov.in/privacypolicy/; 'Quarantine Watch App', https://www.karnataka.gov.in/common-1/en

86 *Manisha Chauhan v Government of NCT of Delhi*, WP(C) No. 5256/21, Order of the Delhi High Court passed on 2 June 2021.

87 Internet Freedom Foundation (@internetfreedom), 'We filed RTIs on behalf of @no2uid asking the Ministry of Health and Family Welfare questions about how your personal data will be protected while you're using CO-WIN, the COVID-19 vaccination registration platform', Tweet, 18 March 2021, https://twitter.com/internetfreedom/status/1372480031830667272

88 'Facial Recognition Used to Verify Vaccine Beneficiaries', *The Hindu*, 5 July 2021.

89 MoHFW, 'Micro Plan'.
90 See Para 1 of Aarogya Setu, 'Terms of Service', https://web.swaraksha.gov.in/ncv19/tnc/. See also Aarogya Setu, 'Privacy Policy', https://www.aarogyasetu.gov.in/privacy-policy/
91 'Coronavirus Risk Scan', Apollo, https://airtel.apollo247.com
92 'CG Covid-19 ePass App', https://play.google.com/store/apps/details?id=com.allsoft.corona
93 'CG Covid-19 ePass Privacy Policy', https://allsoft.co/cgepass/privacy/
94 Sushovan Sircar and Arun Dev, 'With Humans Under Lockdown, How Drones Are Helping Fight COVID-19', *The Quint*, 10 April 2020, https://www.thequint.com/news/india/covid-19-states-use-drone-volunteers-to-surveil-sanitise-streets#read-more
95 Julie Cohen, 'What Privacy is For', *Harvard Law Review* 126 (2013): 1904.
96 Anindita Sanyal, 'Police Using Cellphone Data to Trace People Linked to Delhi Mosque Event', *NDTV*, 5 April 2020, https://www.ndtv.com/delhi-news/delhi-police-using-cellphone-data-to-trace-people-linked-to-islamic-sect-meet-2206388
97 Zack Whittaker, 'Security Lapse at India's Jio Exposed Coronavirus Symptom Checker Results,' *TechCrunch*, 3 May 2020, https://techcrunch.com/2020/05/02/jio-coronavirus-security-lapse/
98 Akhil Kadidal, 'Data Leak? Bengaluru COVID-19 Patients Flooded with Ads,' *Deccan Herald*, 2 July 2021, https://www.deccanherald.com/national/data-leak-bengaluru-covid-19-patients-flooded-with-ads-1003842.html
99 Devina Sengupta and Saloni Shukla, 'COVID-19 Patients Health Data Being Sold on Dark Web', *Economic Times*, 13 May 2021, https://economictimes.indiatimes.com/industry/healthcare/biotech/healthcare/privacy-fears-around-patients-health-data-breach-amid-covid-surge/articleshow/82600389.cms?from=mdr
100 Sonkar, 'Bridging Concerns'.
101 Susan Landau, 'Location Surveillance to Counter COVID-19: Efficacy Is What Matters', Lawfare Blog, 25 March 2020, https://www.lawfareblog.com/location-surveillance-counter-covid-19-efficacy-what-matters
102 'Aarogya Setu vs Covid: Hype vs Reality', NDTV, 14 January 2021, https://www.ndtv.com/video/shows/reality-check/aarogya-setu-vs-covid-hype-vs-reality-572314
103 Natasha Singer, 'Employers Rush to Adopt Virus Screening. The Tools May Not Help Much', *The New York Times*, 11 May 2020, https://www.

nytimes.com/2020/05/11/technology/coronavirus-worker-testing-privacy.html
104 Lakshane, 'Tracking Quarantine'.
105 Arpita Raj, 'COVID-19: K'taka Govt Asks for Selfies but The App Doesn't Work', *The Quint*, 31 March 2020, https://www.thequint.com/news/india/covid-19-312-low-risk-primary-contacts-to-be-isolated-in-bengaluru
106 Pankaj Upadhyay, 'Facing Discrimination for Flying During COVID-19 Outbreak, Says Air India Staff', *India Today*, 22 March 2020, https://www.indiatoday.in/india/story/air-india-staff-says-facing-discrimination-flying-during-covid19-outbreak-1658518-2020-03-22; Aditya Kalra and Devjyot Ghoshal, 'Indian Doctors Evicted Over Coronavirus Transmission Fears: Medical Body', Reuters, 25 March 2020, https://www.reuters.com/article/us-health-coronavirus-india-doctors-idUSKBN21C12G
107 Prerna Katiyar and Venkat Ananth, 'Leaks, Whatsapp Rumours Add to Quarantine Blues', *The Economic Times*, 28 March 2020, https://economictimes.indiatimes.com/news/politics-and-nation/leaks-whatsapp-rumours-add-to-quarantine-blues/articleshow/74854472.cms?from=mdr
108 Sean McDonald, 'The Digital Response to the Outbreak of COVID-19', CIGI, 30 March 2020, https://www.cigionline.org/articles/digital-response-outbreak-covid-19/
109 Ibid.
110 See Soutik Biswas's tweet (@soutikBBC) dated 29 March 2020 highlighting historian Frank Snowden's opinion of pandemic regulations at https://twitter.com/soutikBBC/status/1243996423772725248?s=20

5: On Health Data Architecture Design

1 James Temperton, 'NHS Care. Data Scheme Closed After Years of Controversy', *Wired*, 6 July 2016, https://www.wired.co.uk/article/caredata-nhs-england-closed; Robert N. Charette, 'Australians Say No Thanks to Electronic Health Records', 27 July 2018, https://spectrum.ieee.org/riskfactor/computing/it/australians-choosing-to-optout-of-controversial-myhealth-record-system; Tammy Lovell, 'Swedish Healthcare Advice Line Stored 2.7 Million Patient Phone Calls on Unprotected Web Server', 20 February 2019, https://www.healthcareitnews.com/news/emea/swedish-healthcareadvice-line-

stored-27-million-patient-phone-calls-unprotected-web; Siddarth Shrikanth and Benjamin Parkin, 'India Plan to Merge ID with Health Records Raises Privacy Worries', *Financial Times*, 17 July 2019, https://www.ft.com/content/4fbb2334-a864-11e9-984c-fac8325aaa04

2 The London School of Economics and Political Science, 'The Identity Project: An Assessment of the UK Identity Cards Bill and Its Implications', June 2005, http://www.lse.ac.uk/management/research/identityproject/identityreport.pdf, GOV.UK Press Release, 'National Identity Register Destroyed as Government Consigns ID Card Scheme to History', 10 February 2011, https://www.gov.uk/government/news/national-identity-register-destroyed-as-government-consigns-id-card-scheme-to-history; Reetika Khera, *Dissent on Aadhaar: Big Data Meets Big Brother*, Orient BlackSwan, 2019.

3 Unique Identification Authority of India, 'Aadhaar', 2020, https://uidai.gov.in; Government of India, 'Direct Benefit Transfer, Government of India', https://dbtbharat.gov.in; Khera, *Dissent on Aadhaar*; Subhashis Banerjee and Subodh Sharma, 'Privacy Concerns with Aadhaar', *Communications of the ACM*, Vol. 62; No. 11, October 2019: p. 80, https://doi.org/10.1145/3353770

4 Paran Balakrishnan, 'Study Estimates 1.21 Million Indians Have Died From COVID-19', *Telegraph*, 31 May 2021, https://www.telegraphindia.com/india/study-estimates-1-21-million-indians-have-died-from-covid-19/cid/1817293; Murad Banaji, 'Estimating Covid-19 Fatalities in India', *The India Forum*, 10 May 2021, https://www.theindiaforum.in/article/estimating-covid-19fatalities-india

5 International Institute for Population Sciences, 'National Family Health Survey, India', http://rchiips.org/nfhs/

6 Office of the Registrar General and Census Commissioner, India, 'Annual Health Survey', https://censusindia.gov.in/vitalstatistics/AHSBulletins/ahs.html

7 Ministry of Women and Child Development, 'Rapid Survey On Children', https://wcd.nic.in/acts/rapidsurvey-children-rsoc-2013-14

8 Ministry of Health and Family Welfare, Government of India, 'Comprehensive National Nutrition Survey', http://www.nhm.gov.in/index1.php?lang=1&level=2&sublinkid=1332&lid=713

9 National Institute of Nutrition, ICMR, 'National Nutrition Monitoring Bureau', https://www.nin.res.in/researchdivision/publichealth.html

10 India State-Level Disease Burden Initiative CGF Collaborators, 'Mapping of Variations in Child Stunting, Wasting and Underweight

Within the States of India: The Global Burden of Disease Study 2000-2017', *EClinicalMedicine*, Vol. 20, No. 100317, May 2020, https://doi.org/10.1016/j.eclinm.2020.100317; Ashwini Deshpande and Rajesh Ramachandran, 'Picture This: How Caste Increases Stunting in Dalit Kids', 29 July 2021, https://ceda.ashoka.edu.in/picture-this-how-caste-increases-stunting-in-dalitkids/

11 Ministry of Health and Family Welfare, Government of India, 'National Digital Health Blueprint',2019, https://ndhm.gov.in/home/ndhb

12 Ministry of Health and Family Welfare, Government of India, 'Cowin', 2020, https://https://www.cowin.gov.in

13 National Informatics Centre, Ministry of Electronics and Information Technology, Government of India, 'AarogyaSetu Mobile App', 2020, https://www.mygov.in/aarogya-setu-app/

14 Apar Gupta and Anushka Jain, 'India's Technocratic Approach to Vaccination Is Excluding the Digitally-deprived', *Indian Express*, 15 May 2021, https://indianexpress.com/article/opinion/columns/indias-technocratic-approach-to-vaccination-is-excluding-thedigitally-deprived-7315442/

15 Subhashis Banerjee, Bhaskaran Raman and Subodh Sharma, 'How Reliable and Effective Are the Mobile Apps Being Used to Fight COVID-19?', *The Wire*, 16 April 2020, https://thewire.in/tech/covid-19-mobile-apps-india; Subhashis Banerjee, Bhaskaran Raman and Subodh Sharma, 'On the Proportionality of Aarogya Setu', 8 July 2020, https://www.livemint.com/opinion/online-views/covid-19-tracking-app-on-the-proportionality-of-aarogya-setu-11594183812518.html

16 Ministry of Health and Family Welfare, Government of India, 'National Digital Health Blueprint'; Ministry of Health and Family Welfare, Government of India, 'National Digital Health Mission – Health Data Management Policy', 2020, https://ndhm.gov.in/healthmanagementpolicy

17 Shefali Malhotra, Rohin Garg and Shivangi Rai, 'Analysis of the NDHM Health Data Management Policy', 2021, https://drive.google.com/file/d/1sEBg-syzsbe159x4PGkAHzcZilct0cQq/view

18 Ministry of Health and Family Welfare, 'National Digital Health Blueprint', 'Health Data Management Policy'.

19 Ministry of Health and Family Welfare, 'National Digital Health Blueprint'.

20 Daniel J. Solove, *The Digital Person: Technology And Privacy In The Information Age*, New York, New York University Press, 2004.

21 Cathy O'Neil, *Weapons of Math Destruction: How Big Data Increases Inequality and Threatens Democracy*, New York, Crown Publishing Group, 2016
22 Jim Thatcher, David O'Sullivan and Dillon Mahmoudi, 'Data Colonialism through Accumulation by Dispossession: New Metaphors for Daily Data', *Environment and Planning D: Society and Space*, Vol. 34, No. 6, 2016, pp. 990–1006, https://doi.org/10.1177/0263775816633195
23 Shoshana Zuboff, *The Age of Surveillance Capitalism: The Fight for a Human Future at the New Frontier of Power*, 1st (Profile Books, 2018)
24 Virginia Eubanks, *Automating Inequality: How High-Tech Tools Profile, Police, and Punish the Poor*, New York, St. Martin's Press Inc., 2018
25 Khera (ed.), *Dissent on Aadhaar: Big Data Meets Big Brother*.
26 Subhashis Banerjee, 'A Welfare Test for Aadhaar', *The Indian Express*, 4 November 2017, http://indianexpress.com/article/opinion/columns/a-welfare-testfor-aadhaar-upa-nda-aadhaar-card-4921582/
27 The Planning Commission, Government of India, 'Report of the Group of Experts on Privacy Chaired by Justice A.P. Shah', December 2011, http://planningcommission.nic.in/reports/genrep/repprivacy.pdf; B. N. Srikrishna et al., 'White Paper of the Committee of Experts on a Data Protection Framework for India', 2017, http://meity.gov.in/writereaddata/files/whitepaperondataprotectioninindia171127finalv2.pdf
28 Solove, *The Digital Person: Technology And Privacy In The Information Age*.
29 Rahul Matthan, 'Beyond Consent: A New Paradigm for Data Protection' *Takshashila Discussion Document*, 2017-03-July, 2017 http://takshashila.org.in/wp-content/uploads/2017/07/TDD-Beyond-Consent-Data-Protection-RM-2017-03.pdf
30 Srikrishna et al., 'White Paper of the Committee of Experts'.
31 Ministry of Health and Family Welfare, 'National Digital Health Blueprint'; 'Health Data Management Policy'.
32 Ministry of Health and Family Welfare, 'National Digital Health Blueprint'.
33 Arvind Narayanan and Vitaly Shmatikov, 'Robust De-anonymization of Large Sparse Data sets', in *Proceedings of the 2008 IEEE Symposium on Security and Privacy*, SP '08 Washington DC: IEEE Computer Society, 2008, 111–25, https://doi.org/10.1109/SP.2008.33
34 Luc Rocher, Julien M Hendrickx and Yves-Alexandre de Montjoye, 'Estimating the Success of Re-identifications in Incomplete Data sets Using Generative Models', *Nature Communications* Vol. 105, No. 1, July 2019, p. 3069; Jonathan Ullman, 'Statistical Inference Is Not a Privacy

Violation', 3 June 2021, https://differentialprivacy.org/inference-is-not-a-privacy-violation/

35 Arvind Narayanan and Vitaly Shmatikov, 'De-anonymizing Social Networks', in *Proceedings of the 30th IEEE Symposium on Security and Privacy*, SP '09 Washington DC: IEEE Computer Society, 2009), pp. 173-87, https://doi.org/10.1109/SP.2009.22; Arvind Narayanan, Elaine Shi and Benjamin I. P. Rubinstein, 'Link Prediction by De-anonymization: How We Won the Kaggle Social Network Challenge', arXiv, 2011, https://arxiv.org/pdf/1102.4374.pdf

36 Melissa Gymrek et al., 'Identifying Personal Genomes by Surname Inference', *Science*, Vol. 339, No. 6117, 2013, pp. 321–24, https://doi.org/10.1126/science.1229566; Yaniv Erlich et al., 'Identity Inference of Genomic Data Using Long-range Familial Searches', *Science*, Vol. 362, No. 6415, 2018, pp. 690-94.

37 Yves-Alexandre de Montjoye et al., 'Unique in the Crowd: The Privacy Bounds of Human Mobility', *Scientific Reports*, Nature Publishing Group, Vol. 3, 2013.

38 'Unique in the Shopping Mall: On the Reidentifiability of Credit Card Metadata', *Science*, Vol. 347, No. 6221, 2015 pp. 536-39, https://doi.org/10.1126/science.1256297

39 A. Narayanan et al., 'On the Feasibility of Internet-Scale Author Identification', in *Proceedings of the IEEE Symposium on Security and Privacy* May 2012, pp. 300-14, https://doi.org/10.1109/SP.2012.46

40 Jessica Su et al., 'De-anonymizing Web Browsing Data with Social Networks', in *Proceedings of the 26th International Conference on World Wide Web*, WWW 2017, Perth, Australia: International World Wide Web Conferences Steering Committee, 2017, pp. 1261-69, https://doi.org/10.1145/3038912.3052714

41 Arvind Narayanan and Vitaly Shmatikov, 'Robust De-anonymization of Large Sparse Data sets: A Decade Later', 2019, http://randomwalker.info/publications/de-anonymization-retrospective.pdf

42 Anupam Datta, Divya Sharma and Arunesh Sinha, 'Provable De-anonymization of Large Data sets with Sparse Dimensions', in Pierpaolo Degano and Joshua D. Guttman (eds.), *Principles of Security and Trust*, Berlin Heidelberg: Springer Berlin Heidelberg, 2012, pp. 229-48; Charu C. Aggarwal, 'On k-anonymity and the Curse of Dimensionality', in *Proceedings of the 31st International Conference on Very Large Data Bases*, VLDB '05, Trondheim, Norway: VLDB Endowment, 2005, pp. 901-09, http://dl.acm.org/citation.cfm?id=1083592.1083696

43 Cynthia Dwork, 'Differential Privacy', in *Proceedings of the 33rd International Conference on Automata, Languages and Programming - Part II, ICALP'06* Venice, Italy: Springer-Verlag, 2006, pp. 1-12, https://doi.org/10.1007/117870061
44 Ullman, Statistical Inference Is Not a Privacy Violation.
45 The European Parliament and the Council of European Union, Regulation (EU), No. 2016/679, https://eur-lex.europa.eu/legal-content/EN/TXT/?uri=celex%3A32016R0679, 2016
46 Ministry of Health and Family Welfare, 'National Digital Health Blueprint'.
47 *K S Puttaswamy and Another v. Union of India*, Writ Petition (Civil) No. 494 of 2012, Supreme Court judgment dated 26 September, 2018.
48 Jon M. Kleinberg, Sendhil Mullainathan and Manish Raghavan, 'Inherent Trade-Offs in the Fair Determination of Risk Scores', arXiv/1609.05807 (2016), http://arxiv.org/abs/1609.05807
49 David Chaum, 'Security Without Identification: Transaction Systems to Make Big Brother Obsolete', *Commun. ACM* Vol. 28; No. 10; October 1985: pp. 1030-44, https://doi.org/10.1145/4372.4373; J. Camenisch and A. Lysyanskaya, 'Signature Schemes and Anonymous Credentials from Bilinear Maps', in Matt Franklin (ed.), *Advances in Cryptology – CRYPTO 2004*, Berlin Heidelberg: Springer Berlin Heidelberg, 2004 pp. 56–72.

6: Privacy Considerations of Community Health Workers

1 See p. 326, n. 15 'Alma-Ata : Rebirth and Revision 4 30 Years after Alma-Ata: Has Primary Healthcare Worked in Countries?', *Lancet*, Vol. 372 2008: pp. 950–61.
2 Sophie Park and Ruth Abrams, 'Alma-Ata 40th Birthday Celebrations and the Astana Declaration on Primary Healthcare 2018', *British Journal of General Practice* Vol. 69, No. 628, 2019, pp. 220–21.
3 A J. Smith, 'Barefoot Doctors and the Medical Pyramid', *British Medical Journal* Vol. 2, No. 5916, 1974, p. 429.
4 Henry Perry, 'A Brief History of Community Health Worker Programs', *Developing and Strengthening Community Health Worker Programs at Scale: A Reference Guide and Case Studies for Program Managers and Policymakers*, Washington, DC: USAID, MCHIP, 2013.
5 Sonu Goel, 'From Bhore Committee to National Rural Health Mission: A Critical Review', *The Internet Journal of Health*, Vol. 7, No. 1, 2008.
6 Ravi Duggal, 'Health Planning in India', *India Health: A Reference Document*, CEHAT, 2002, pp. 43–56.

7   M. Waheed and M. B. Paliwal, 'Effectiveness of Auxiliary Nurse Midwife in Delivering MCH Service', *POPCEN* Newsletter. Population Centre, Lucknow, India, Vol. 4, No. 6, 1978, pp. 10–11.
8   Mabelle Arole and Rajanikant Arole, *Jamkhed: A Comprehensive Rural Health Project*, Macmillan Press Ltd, 1994.
9   A Crandall et al., 'Village Health Workers Improve Child Health: The Jamkhed, India Experience'. *International Journal of Global Health and Health Disparities*, Vol. 5, No. 1, 2007, pp. 41–54.
10 Kerry Scott, Asha S. George and Rajani R. Ved, 'Taking Stock of 10 Years of Published Research on the ASHA Programme: Examining India's National Community Health Worker Programme from a Health Systems Perspective', *Health Research Policy and Systems*, Vol. 17, No. 1, 2019, pp. 1–17.
11 Banuru Muralidhara Prasad and Vangal Muraleedharan, 'Community Health Workers: A Review of Concepts, Practice and Policy Concerns', A working paper as part of ongoing research of international Consortium for Research on Equitable Health Systems (CREHS), 2007.
12 Deborah E. Bender and Kathryn Pitkin, 'Bridging the Gap: The Village Health Worker as the Cornerstone of the Primary Healthcare Model', *Social Science & Medicine*, Vol. 24, No. 6, 1987, pp. 515–28.
13 Hermen Ormel Maryse Kok, Sumit Kane, Rukhsana Ahmed, Kingsley Chikaphupha, Sabina Faiz Rashid, Daniel Gemechu, Lilian Otiso, Mohsin Sidat, Sally Theobald, Miriam Taegtmeyer and Korrie de Koning, 'Salaried and Voluntary Community Health Workers: Exploring How Incentives and Expectation Gaps Influence Motivation', *Human Resources for Health*, Vol. 17, No. 1, 2019, pp. 1–12.
14 Sara Javanparast Alice Windle, Toby Freeman and Fran Baum, 'Community Health Worker Programs to Improve Healthcare Access and Equity: Are They Only Relevant to Low and Middle-Income Countries?', *International Journal of Health Policy and Management*, Vol. 7, No. 10, 2018, p. 943.
15 Peter A. Berman, Davidson R. Gwatkin and Susan E. Burger, 'Community-Based Health Workers: Head Start or False Start towards Health for All?', *Social Science & Medicine*, Vol. 25, No. 5,1987, pp. 443–59.
16 Prakarsh Singh and William A. Masters, 'Impact of Caregiver Incentives on Child Health: Evidence from an Experiment with Anganwadi Workers in India', *Journal of Health Economics*, Vol. 55, 2017, pp. 219-31.
17 Shilpa Karvande, Vidula Purohit, Somasundari Somla Gopalakrishnan, B. Subha Sri, Matthews Mathai and Nerges Mistry, 'Building Capacities

of Auxiliary Nurse Midwives (ANMs) through a Complementary Mix of Directed and Self-Directed Skill-Based Learning – A Case Study in Pune District, Western India', *Human Resources for Health*, Vol. 18, No. 1, 2020, pp. 1–10.
18. PK Garg, Anu Bhardwaj, Abhishek Singh and S. K. Ahluwalia, 'An Evaluation of ASHA Worker's Awareness and Practice of Their Responsibilities in Rural Haryana', *National Journal of Community Medicine*, Vol. 4, No. 1, 2013, pp. 76–80.
19. Shimmila Bhowmick and Keyur Sorathia, 'Findings of the User Study Conducted to Understand the Training of Rural ASHAs in India', in *Proceedings of the Tenth International Conference on Information and Communication Technologies and Development*, 2019, pp. 1–5.
20. Gaurav Desai, Niraj Pandit and Diwakar Sharma, 'Changing Role of Anganwadi Workers: A Study Conducted in Vadodara District', *Healthline*, Vol. 3, No. 1, 2012, pp. 41–44.
21. Osmana Manzar and Udita Chaturvedi, 'Understanding the Lack of Privacy in the Indian Cultural Context,' Digital Empowerment Foundation, New Delhi, 2017.
22. Tracey Shield, 'Community Engagement: Improving Health and Wellbeing and Reducing Health Inequalities', NICE Guidelines, 2016.
23. Wenzhen Li, Yong Gan, Xiaoxin Dong, Yanfeng Zhou, Shiyi Cao, Naomiem Kkandawire, Yingjie Cong, Huilian Sun and Zuxun Lu, 'Gatekeeping and the Utilization of Community Health Services in Shenzhen, China: A Cross-Sectional Study', *Medicine*, Vol. 96, No. 38, 2017.
24. Calvin Sindato, Leonard E. G. Mboera, Eric Beda, Mpoki Mwabukusi and Esron D. Karimuribo 'Community Health Workers and Disease Surveillance in Tanzania: Promoting the Use of Mobile Technologies in Detecting and Reporting Health Events', *Health Security*, Vol. 19, No. 1, 2021, pp. 116–29.
25. Michelle Dynes, Rob Stephenson, Craig Hadley and Lynn M. Sibley, 'Factors Shaping Interactions among Community Health Workers in Rural Ethiopia: Rethinking Workplace Trust and Teamwork', *Journal of Midwifery & Women's Health*, Vol. 59, No. 1, January 2014, pp. S32–43.
26. Daniel Palazuelos, Kyla Ellis, Dana DaEun Im, Matthew Peckarsky, Dan Schwarz, Didi Bertrand Farmer, Ranu Dhillon, Ari Johnson, Claudia Orihuela, Jill Hackett, Junior Bazile, Leslie Berman, Madeleine Ballard, Raj Panjabi, Ralph Ternier, Sam Slavin, Scott Lee, Steve Selinsky and Carole Diane Mitnick, '5-SPICE: The Application of an Original

Framework for Community Health Worker Program Design, Quality Improvement and Research Agenda Setting', *Global Health Action*, Vol. 6, No. 1, April 2013, doi: 10.3402/gha.v6i0.19658.

27 Merridy Grant, Aurene Wilford, Lyn Haskins, Sifiso Phakathi, Ntokozo Mntambo and Christiane M. Horwood, 'Trust of Community Health Workers Influences the Acceptance of Community-Based Maternal and Child Health Services', *African Journal of Primary Healthcare and Family Medicine*, Vol. 9, No. 1, 2020, pp. 1–8.

28 Sunu C. Thomas, 'Maintaining Confidentiality While Gaining Access to the Community', *Indian Journal of Medical Ethics*, Vol. 5, No. 1, 2020, pp. 10–11.

29 Vijayaprasad Gopichandran, 'Community Gatekeepers and the Conundrum of Confidentiality and Coercion'. *Indian Journal of Medical Ethics*, Vol. 1, 2020, pp. 11–13.

30 Anam Feroz, Rawshan Jabeen and Sarah Saleem, 'Using Mobile Phones to Improve Community Health Workers Performance in Low-and-Middle-Income Countries', *BMC Public Health*, Vol. 20, No. 1, 2020, pp. 1–6; Karin Källander, James K. Tibenderana, Onome J. Akpogheneta, Daniel L. Strachan, Zelee Hill, Augustinus H.A. ten Asbroek, Lesong Conteh, Betty R. Kirkwood and Sylvia R. Meek, 'Mobile Health (MHealth) Approaches and Lessons for Increased Performance and Retention of Community Health Workers in Low and Middle-Income Countries: A Review', *Journal of Medical Internet Research*, Vol. 15, No. 1, 2013, p. e17; Kerry Scott, D. Glandon, and B. Adhikari, 'India's Auxiliary Nurse-Midwife, Anganwadi Worker, and Accredited Social Health Activist Programs', in Henry B. Perry (ed.), *Health for the People: National Community Health Worker Programs from Afghanistan to Zimbabwe*, 2020, p. 113; Joyojeet Pal, Anjuli Dasika, Ahmad Hasan, Jackie Wolf, Nick Reid, Vaishnav Kameswaran, Purva Yardi, Allyson Mackay, Abram Wagner, Bhramar Mukherjee, Sucheta Joshi, Sujay Santra and Priyamvada Pandey, 'Changing Data Practices for Community Health Workers: Introducing Digital Data Collection in West Bengal, India,' in *Proceedings of the Ninth International Conference on Information and Communication Technologies and Development* 2017, pp. 1–12.

31 Adeel Anjum, Saif ur Rehman Malik, Kim-Kwang Raymond Choo, Abid Khan, Asma Haroon, Sangeen Khan, Samee U. Khan, Naveed Ahmad and Basit Raza, 'An Efficient Privacy Mechanism for Electronic Health Records', *Computers & Security*, Vol. 72, 2018, pp. 196–211; Pulkit Mehndiratta, Shelly Sachdeva and Sudhanshu Kulshrestha, 'A Model

of Privacy and Security for Electronic Health Records,' in *International Workshop on Databases in Networked Information Systems*, Springer 2014, pp. 202-13.

32 John R. Stone and Groesbeck P. Parham, 'An Ethical Framework for Community Health Workers and Related Institutions', *Family & Community Health*, Vol. 3, No. 4, 2007, pp. 351–63.

7: Data Protection in Public Healthcare: An Assessment of Three Government Schemes in India

1 The framework under the Information Technology Act, 2000, is inapplicable to state entities and is in any event, commonly recognized as being inadequate.

2 The size and scope of the programmes implies that they contact the lives of millions of citizens, often the most marginalized. For instance, PM-JAY is targeted at over 10 crore poor and vulnerable families, and as of August 2020, has been used for over 1.09 crore hospital admissions. Similarly, there are over 40 lakh patients registered on the Nikshay system, which is a critical component of NTEP. As of 2015 – 16, more than a crore of women availed themselves of benefits under the JSY scheme. 'About Pradhan Mantri Jan Aarogya Yojana', National Health Authority, https://pmjay.gov.in/about/pmjay; 'Revised National Tuberculosis Control Programme', Directorate General of Health Services, 6 September 2019, https://dghs.gov.in/content/1358_3_RevisedNationalTuberculosisControlProgramme.aspx; Anumeha Yadav and Menaka Rao, 'The Government Wants Pregnant Women to Enroll in Aadhar to Get Their Social Scheme Benefits', *Scroll.in*, 8 March 2017, https://scroll.in/pulse/831175/the-government-wants-pregnant-women-to-enroll-in-aadhaar-to-get-their-social-scheme-benefits

3 The principles mentioned form the bedrock of modern data protection regulations the world over including the European GDPR and the draft Personal Data Protection Bill, 2019. These also derive from an examination of guidance on how privacy impact assessments and audits are to be conducted, as issued by the Information Commissioner's Office (ICO), UK, the Health Information and Quality Authority of Ireland, and the Office of the Australian Information Commissioner. The framework is also supported by literature on the subject of privacy audits as well as various privacy impact assessments conducted

on healthcare programmes globally. See for instance, 'A Guide to Data Protection Audits', ICO, UK, https://ico.org.uk/media/for-organisations/documents/2787/guide-to-data-protection-audits.pdf; 'Guidance on Privacy Impact Assessment in Health and Social Care: Version 2.0', Health Information and Quality Authority, Ireland, October, 2017, https://www.hiqa.ie/sites/default/files/2017-10/Guidance-on-Privacy-Impact-Assessment-in-health-and-social-care.pdf; 'Data Protection Impact Assessments', Data Protection Commission, Ireland, https://www.dataprotection.ie/en/organisations/know-your-obligations/data-protection-impact-assessments#describing-the-information-flows. See also, Alan Toy and David Hay, 'Privacy Auditing Standards', *Auditing: A Journal of Practice and Theory*, Vol. 34, No. 3, August 2015, https://www.researchgate.net/publication/283689170_Privacy_Auditing_Standards

4   Sakshi Singh and Sandeep Kumar, 'Tuberculosis in India: Road to Elimination', *International Journal of Preventive Medicine*, Vol. 10, No. 114, 2019, https://www.ncbi.nlm.nih.gov/pmc/articles/PMC6592106/; 'Revised National Tuberculosis Control Programme', Ministry of Health and Family Welfare, Government of India, 6 September 2019, https://dghs.gov.in/content/1358_3_RevisedNationalTuberculosisControlProgramme.aspx

5   'The National Strategic Plan for TB Elimination 2017-2025', Ministry of Health and Family Welfare, 2017, Government of India, https://bit.ly/3bVdt7C.

6   'National Strategic Plan for TB Elimination 2020-2025 draft v.7', Ministry of Health and Family Welfare, Government of India, 28 August 2020, https://bit.ly/3qkCFwX.

7   'Notification of TB Cases - No. Z-28015/2012-TB', Ministry of Health and Family Welfare, Government of India, 7 May 2012, https://tinyurl.com/h3364hn8; and 'Notification F No. Z-28015/2/2012-TB', Ministry of Health and Family Welfare, Government of India, 16 March 2018, https://bit.ly/3010ONQ

8   'Revised National Tuberculosis Control Programme', Directorate General of Health Services, Government of India, 6 September, 2019, https://bit.ly/3o8QEmQ

9   'Notification of TB Cases – No. Z-28015/2012-TB', Ministry of Health and Family Welfare, Government of India, 7 May 2012, https://tinyurl.com/h3364hn8

10 'Notification F No. Z-28015/2/2012-TB', Ministry of Health and Family Welfare, Government of India, 16 March 2018, https://bit.ly/3H4Oop3

11 'Intersectoral Convergence Between DWCD and DHFW – DOHW', Ministry of Health and Family Welfare, Government of India, https://bit.ly/30bdWQU
12 'Janani Suraksha Yojana: Features and FAQs', Ministry of Health and Family Welfare, Government of India, https://bit.ly/3jKrvy1
13 'Janani Suraksha Yojana: Features and FAQ, Annexure II', Ministry of Health and Family Welfare, Government of India, https://bit.ly/3jKrvy1.
14 A. Sreeranjini, Asha T. Chacko and Anil Kumar, 'An Overview of MCH Services in Idukki District Based on MCTS and Client's Satisfaction', in C. R. K. Nair and K. S. James (eds.), *Maternal and Child Health in India* Ministry of Health and Family Welfare, Government of India, 2016, https://bit.ly/3hEFYsG
15 See for instance, 'Pregnancy, Child Tracking and Health Services Management System', Government of Rajasthan, https://pctsrajmedical.raj.nic.in/private/login.aspx
16 'Reproductive and Child Health Portal', Health and Family Welfare Department, Government of India, 1 November 2021, https://rch.nhm.gov.in/RCH/about-rch.aspx
17 'Anmol AIS', Ministry of Health and Family Welfare, Government of India, https://tinyurl.com/4nuxvrp2
18 56.3% of respondents had low acceptance of mHealth facilities. Prakash Babu Kodali and Shankar Das, 'Acceptance of mHealth Technologies among Auxiliary Nurse Midwives in Andhra Pradesh, India: A Mixed Method Study', *Medical Science*, Vol. 25, No. 111, May 2021, https://bit.ly/36cnfiL
19 Chandrakant Lahariya, 'Ayushman Bharat Program and Universal Health Coverage in India', *Indian Pediatrics*, Vol. 55 June 2018, https://indianpediatrics.net/june2018/june-495-506.htm; Indrani Gupta, 'Out of Pocket Expenses and Poverty: Estimates from NSS 61st Round', eSocial Sciences Working Paper, id:5419 2013, https://bit.ly/3AptaiB; 'Tracking Universal Health Coverage: Global Monitoring Report', World Health Organization, 10 January 2017, https://bit.ly/3higG4H
20 National Health Authority, 'About Pradhan Mantri Jan Aarogya Yojana', https://pmjay.gov.in/about/pmjay; 'National Health Stack: Strategy and Approach (Consultation Document)', NITI Aayog, July 2018, https://bit.ly/36cizJQ
21 National Health Authority, 'Cyber Security and Privacy Strategy', Last modified 2020, https://bit.ly/3dLrx51
22 National Health Authority, 'Cyber Security and Privacy Strategy'.

23 National Health Authority, 'Data Privacy Policy 2.0', Last modified July 2020, https://bit.ly/3wk63Tk
24 'Acceptable Use Policy Version 1.0', National Health Authority, Last modified August 2019, https://bit.ly/3qPJtk5
25 National Health Authority, Beneficiary Identification Guidelines: Ayushman Bharat – Pradhan Mantri Jan arogya Yojana, https://www.pmjay.gov.in/sites/default/files/2018-07/GuidelinesonProcessofBeneficiaryIdentification_0.pdf
26 'Guidance Tool for Direct Benefit Transfer', Ministry of Health and Family Welfare, Government of India, D.O. No. Z-28015/24/2017-TB, 27 November 2017, https://tbcindia.gov.in/showfile.php?lid=3304
27 *K.S. Puttaswamy v. Union of India* (2019) 1 SCC 1
28 National Health Authority, 'Data Privacy Policy 2.0', Sections 8.3, 9.2, 9.4 and 9.5.
29 National Health Authority, 'Fundamentals on Security and Privacy', August 2018, pp. 2–3, https://bit.ly/3jQvkSA; National Health Authority, 'Data Privacy Policy 2.0', Sections 9.4 and 9.5
30 Rohan Jahagirdar and Praneeth Bodduluri, 'Digital Economy: India's Account Aggregator System Is Plagued by Privacy and Safety Issues', *EPW Engage*, Vol. 55, No. 22 30 May 2020, https://bit.ly/3CYvHAZ; Shweta Reddy, Pallavi Bedi, Anubha Sinha and Shweta Mohandas, 'Data Empowerment and Protection Architecture', Centre for Internet and Society, 30 November 2020, https://cis-india.org/depacomments1
31 Soumyarendra Barik, 'Anja Kovacs On The Problems With India's Report On Non-Personal Data Governance Framework', *Medianama*, 13 August 2020, https://bit.ly/3klnPCj
32 National Health Authority, 'Data Privacy Policy 2.0', Sections 6 and 8.5.
33 Ibid., Section 9.8.2.
34 Kalyani Pillai, 'Assessing the Implementation of India's New Health Reform Program, Ayushman Bharat, in Two Southern States: Kerala and Tamil Nadu', Undergraduate Honours Thesis, College of William and Mary, Paper 1523, 2020, https://bit.ly/3DaSaLa; PTI, 'Aadhaar Mandatory to get Treatment under Ayushman Bharat for Second Time', *Mint*, 7 October 2018, https://bit.ly/3kmfTkl
35 Prakhar Mishra and Alexander Fager, 'Privacy in Healthcare: The Role of the National Digital Health Blueprint', Data Governance Network, Working Paper 10, September 2020, https://datagovernance.org/files/research/1606372199.pdf

36 MoHFW, 'The National Strategic Plan for TB Elimination 2017-2025', pp. 92–93, 116–117; MoHFW, 'The National Strategic Plan for TB Elimination 2020-2025', Sections 7.2, 11.1.1, 12.4, 15.4.1.8.5, 18.1, 18.3 and 25.4.
37 Ibid., Sections 7.2 and 17.4.
38 National Health Authority, 'Data Privacy Policy 2.0', Sections 8.6, 9.2.2.
39 Ibid., Section 9.8.2.
40 Ibid., Section 9.6.
41 Ibid., Sections 9.6.5–6, 9.8.2.
42 MoHFW, 'The National Strategic Plan for TB Elimination 2020-2025', p. 82.
43 Nandita Saikia, Zakir Husain and Rimon Bora, 'Challenges of the HMIS in India: A case study of Udham Singh Nagar, Uttarakhand', Institute of Economic Growth, 1/2013, January 2018, https://bit.ly/3xfuF0G
44 MoHFW, 'The National Strategic Plan for TB Elimination 2017-2025', pp. 25–26; MoHFW, 'The National Strategic Plan for TB Elimination 2020–2025', p. 82.
45 'Nikshay Training Module: AarogyaSathi App', Ministry of Health and Family Welfare, Government of India, https://bit.ly/3EZB7fW
46 National Health Authority, 'Data Privacy Policy 2.0', Sections 8.7, 9.5.
47 Ibid., Section 9.11.
48 National Health Authority, 'Consultation Paper on Proposed Health Data Retention Policy', CP 04/2021, Ministry of Health and Family Welfare, Government of India, 23 November 2021, https://abdm.gov.in/assets/uploads/consultation_papersDocs/Consultation_Paper_on_Health_Data_Retention_Policy_21.pdf
49 National Health Authority, 'Data Privacy Policy 2.0', Sections 9.8, 9.11.6.
50 'The National Framework for a Gender Responsive Approach to TB in India', Ministry of Health and Family Welfare, Government of India, December 2019, https://tbcindia.gov.in/showfile.php?lid=3496
51 'Nikshay Version 2.0', Ministry of Health and Family Welfare, Government of India, https://bit.ly/3hAkoWd
52 National Health Authority, 'Data Privacy Policy 2.0', Sections 9.6–9.
53 National Health Authority, 'Fundamentals on Security and Privacy', August 2018, p. 3, https://bit.ly/3jQvkSA; National Health Authority, 'Data Privacy Policy 2.0', Section 9.7. Execution of a non-disclosure agreement and confidentiality undertakings is also mandated by Section 31.4 of the Contract Agreement for Implementation Support Agencies. 'Implementation Support Contract', National Health Authority, 2021, https://bit.ly/3kmgmTD

54 MoHFW, 'The National Strategic Plan for TB Elimination 2017-2025', pp. 36, 48, 52, 56, 75, 116.
55 MoHFW, 'The National Strategic Plan for TB Elimination 2020-2025', Section.12.2.i.
56 National Health Authority, Section 18.1.11.2; 'Nikshay: Treatment Initiation and Patient Management: Module 3', Government of India, https://bit.ly/3hhOIGi
57 The JSY Guidelines envisage an ombudsman at national, state and district level and nodal officers at the district level. These mechanisms are to take complaints pertaining to eligibility for the scheme, quantum and delays of cash disbursals, etc. The central and state governments are to also establish independent review and monitoring mechanisms. These focus on performance of the programme.' Janani Suraksha Yojana Guidelines for Implementation', paras 23 and 25, https://bit.ly/3hBaNyD
58 National Health Authority, 'Data Privacy Policy 2.0', Section 13.
59 National Health Authority, 'Data Privacy Policy 2.0', Section 10; National Health Authority, 'User Manual for Grievance Redress Portal', https://bit.ly/2Ysi9ic
60 National Health Authority, 'User Manual for Grievance Redress Portal', https://bit.ly/2Ysi9ic
61 National Health Authority, 'Data Privacy Policy 2.0', Sections 11, 12.
62 Another important reason for inaccessibility of the documentation is the poor state of websites and portals under NRHM. At the time of writing this, the various sites and portals under NHM/NRHM were missing valid security certificates. The security certificate for HMIS portal (https://nrhm-mis.nic.in/SitePages/Home.aspx) expired on 25/March/2021 and for the NHM website (https://nhm.gov.in/) expired on 27/May/2021.
63 National Health Authority, 'Data Privacy Policy 2.0', Section 8.2.
64 'National Health Stack (NHS) Open House on Open Health Services Network', iSPIRT, 1 August 2020, https://pn.ispirt.in/tag/health-stack/
65 National Health Authority, 'Data Privacy Policy 2.0', Section 10.
66 National Health Authority, 'Data Privacy Policy 2.0'.
67 Ibid., 'Data Privacy Policy 2.0', Section 9.6.3.
68 'ASHA Which Way Forward? Evaluation of ASHA Program', NHSRC and NRHM, Government of India, 2011, https://bit.ly/36iCyqw
69 Siddharth Tiwari, 'Privacy Concerns: ASHA Workers to Shun Track App', *The Times of India*, 13 June 2021, https://bit.ly/3dM8A2a; Tanvi

Roy, 'Privacy of the People - ASHA Workers and Employee Surveillance', Internet Freedom Foundation, 23 June 2021, https://internetfreedom. in/privacyofthepeople-asha-workers-and-employee-surveillance/; Rohtak Bureau, 'ASHA Workers Ne MDM Shield 360 App Download Karne Say Kiya Inkaar', *Amar Ujala* (Hindi), 8 June 2021, https://bit. ly/3yqiuyl

70 See generally, Daniel Solove, 'Privacy Self-management and the Consent Dilemma', *Harvard Law* Review, Issue No. 126, p. 1880, 2013, https://bit.ly/3EZCPxO; Rishab Bailey, Smriti Parsheera, Faiza Rahman and Renuka Sane, 'Disclosures in Privacy Policies: Does Notice and Consent Work?', *Loyola Consumer Law Review*, Vol. 33, No. 1, 2022.

71 Torsha Sarkar, Swagam Dasgupta and Swaraj Paul Barooah, 'Comments on National Health Stack: Strategy and Approach', Centre for Internet and Society, 31 July 2018, https://bit.ly/3bU5CaE

72 Reetika Khera and Jean Dreze, 'Six Types of Problems Aadhaar is Causing and Safeguards Needed Immediately', *Scroll.in*, 2 January 2022, https://scroll.in/article/1013700/six-types-of-problems-aadhaar-is-causing-and-safeguards-needed-immediately

73 Torsha Sarkar, Swagam Dasgupta and Swaraj Paul Barooah, 'Comments on National Health Stack'; Anja Kovacs and Nayantara Ranganathan, 'Data Sovereignty of Whom? Limits and Suitability of Sovereign Frameworks for Data in India', Data Governance Network, Working Paper 03 November 2019, https://bit.ly/3H4NLMd

74 Shashidhar K. J., Kriti Kapur, and Oommen C. Kurian, 'India's Draft Health Data Management Policy: ORF Recommendations', Observer Research Foundation, Special Report No. 122, November 2020, https://bit.ly/3hzE10J.

75 NITI Aayog, 'National Health Stack: Strategy and Approach', July 2018, https://bit.ly/3qP3cjY

76 Navdeep Yadav, 'Centre Earned Rs 100 Crores by Sharing Vehicle Registration Data with Companies Such as BMW, Axis Bank, Bajaj Allianz L&T and Others', *Business Insider*, 12 February 2021, https://bit.ly/3xpUNpW; Shreegireesh Jalihal, 'Quietly, Govt Sold Vehicular Bulk Data to Firm Without Price Discovery, Privacy Protection', *The Wire*, 8 April 2021, https://bit.ly/3jHtGCF; Sreemoyee Mukherjee, 'How Poor Data Protection Can Endanger Communities During Communal Riots', *The Wire*, 6 March 2020, https://thewire.in/rights/vahan-database-protection-riots; Aditya Chunduru, 'VAHAN Data used to Target Muslims', *Deccan Chronicle*, 29 February 2020, https://bit.ly/36c7EA1

77 Abantika Ghosh, 'Ayushman Bharat and All Other Govt Health Schemes to Integrate with Digital Health Mission', *The Print*, 6 August 2020, https://bit.ly/3mXmuDt

8: Trust: The Cornerstone of Health Interventions

1 Lucy Gilson, 'Trust and the Development of Healthcare as a Social Institution', *Social Science and Medicine*, Vol. 56, 2003, pp. 1453–68; Michael Calnan and Rosemary Rowe, *Trust Matters in Healthcare*, Open University Press, 2008.
2 World Health Organization, 'Human Rights and Health'. WHO Constitution 1946, https://www.who.int/news-room/fact-sheets/detail/human-rights-and-health
3 Dmitry Khodyakov. 'Trust as a Process: A Three-dimensional Approach', *Sociology*, Vol. 41, No. 1, 2007, pp. 115–32.
4 Olinda Timms, 'Doctor Patient Relationship', *Biomedical Ethics*, Elsevier, 2019, p. 58.
5 World Medical Association Declaration of Geneva, May 2006, https://www.wma.net/policies-post/wma-declaration-of-geneva/
6 S. D. Pearson and L. H. Raeke. 'Patients' Trust in Physicians: Many Theories, Few Measures, and Little Data', *Journal of General Internal Medicine*, Vol. 15, No. 7, 2000, pp. 509–13, doi:10.1046/j.1525-1497.2000.11002.x)
7 Sumit Kane, Michael Calnan and Anjali Radkar, 'Trust and Trust Relations from the Providers' Perspective: The Case of the Healthcare System in India', *Indian Journal of Medical Ethics*, Vol. 12, No. 3, 2016, pp. 157, https://ijme.in/articles/trust-and-trust-relations-from-the-providers-perspective-the-case-of-the-healthcare-system-in-india/
8 Adam Oliver, *Nurturing Reciprocity in Public Policy*, (Cambridge University Press, 2019, https://www.cambridge.org/core/books/abs/reciprocity-and-the-art-of-behavioural-public-policy/nurturing-reciprocity-in-public-policy/55C9E17E945776BD518097454E36C88A
9 Sumit Kane, Michael Calnan and Anjali Radkar, 'Trust and Trust Relations'.
10 Philosophy Encyclopedia Britannica. Simon Lee, 'Common Good', https://www.britannica.com/topic/common-good
11 Tamer Oraby, Michael G. Tyshenko, Jose Campo Maldonado, Kristina Vatcheva, Susie Elsaadany, Walid Q. Alali, Joseph C. Longenecker and Mustafa Al-Zoughool, 'Modeling the Effect of Lockdown Timing as a COVID-19 Control Measure in Countries with Differing Social

Contacts', *Sci Rep* 11, 3354 (2021), https://doi.org/10.1038/s41598-021-82873-2

12 'Govt Invokes Disaster Management Act to Enforce COVID19 Lockdown', *Hindustan Times*, 24 March 2020, https://www.hindustantimes.com/india-news/govt-invokes-disaster-management-act-to-enforce-covid-19-lockdown/story-AOGxaElEOHpHWDPyUYSiaP.html

13 'Coronavirus: India Doctors "spat at and attacked"', BBC News, 3 April 2020, https://www.bbc.com/news/world-asia-india-52151141

14 Sarojini Nadimpally, 'COVID-19 Has Exposed Deep Cracks in the Indian Healthcare System', *The BMJ Opinion*, 21 May 2021, https://blogs.bmj.com/bmj/2021/05/21/sarojini-nadimpally-covid-19-has-exposed-deep-cracks-in-the-indian-healthcare-system/

15 Kenneth Grace Mascarenhas Danabal, Shiva Shankar Magesh, Siddharth Saravanan and Vijayaprasad Gopichandran, 'Attitude Towards COVID-19 Vaccines and Vaccine Hesitancy in Urban and Rural Communities in Tamil Nadu, India – A Community Based Survey', *BMC Health Services Research*, Vol. 21, No. 994, 2021, https://doi.org/10.1186/s12913-021-07037-4

16 National Health Authority, 'Patient's Rights and Responsibilities Charter', Ayushman Bharat, March 2021, https://pmjay.gov.in/sites/default/files/2021-05/Patient-Rights-Responsibilities-Charter.pdf

17 Indian Council of Medical Research, 'Informed Consent: National Ethical Guidelines for Biomedical and Health Research Involving Human Participants', 2017, pp. 5, 49–55, https://main.icmr.nic.in/sites/default/files/guidelines/ICMR_Ethical_Guidelines_2017.pdf

18 Supriya Subramani, 'Patient Autonomy Within Real or Valid Consent: Samira Kohli's Case', *Indian Journal of Medical Ethics*, Vol. 2, No. 3, 2017, p. 184, https://ijme.in/articles/patient-autonomy-within-real-or-valid-consent-samira-kohlis-case/

19 World Medical Association, 'International Code of Medical Ethics', May 2006, https://www.wma.net/policies-post/wma-international-code-of-medical-ethics/

20 N. N. Mishra, Lisa S. Parker, V.L. Nimgaonkar and S.N. Deshpande, 'Privacy and the Right to Information Act, 2005', *Indian Journal of Medical Ethics*, Vol. 5, No. 4, 2008, pp. 158–61 doi:10.20529/IJME.2008.057; Article 21, Constitution of India.

21 Personal Data Protection Bill, 2019, http://164.100.47.4/BillsTexts/LSBillTexts/Asintroduced/373_2019_LS_Eng.pdf

22 'National Digital Health Mission, 2021', Ayushman Bharat Health Mission, https://abdm.gov.in/
23 'Aarogya Setu', National Informatics Centre, Ministry of Electronics and Information Technology, Government of India, 2020, https://www.aarogyasetu.gov.in/
24 Dinesh C. Sharma. 'Rights Violation Found in HPV Vaccine Trial in India', *The Lancet Oncology*, Vol. 14, No. 11 2013, https://www.thelancet.com/journals/lanonc/article/PIIS1470-2045(13)70420-0/fulltext
25 Indian Council of Medical Research, 'Informed Consent'.
26 Accountability Initiative Staff, 'COVID-19 Appropriate Behaviour, Community Backlash among Major Concerns for Frontline Workers during Pandemic', 22 April 2021, https://accountabilityindia.in/blog/covid-appropriate-behaviour-asha-anm-inside-districts/; V. Gopichandran and K. Sakthivel 'Doctor-patient communication and trust in doctors during COVID-19 times: A cross sectional study in Chennai, India', PLoS One, Vol. 16, No. 6, 23 June 2021
27 M. Akshatha, 'Expertise of over 50 NGOs to help Bengaluru manage rising coronavirus cases'. *Economic Times*. 11 August 2020, https://economictimes.indiatimes.com/news/politics-and-nation/expertise-of-over-50-ngos-to-help-bengaluru-manage-rising-coronavirus-cases/articleshow/77477862.cms
28 John W. Kieffer, 'Subsidiarity: Restoring a Sacred Harmony', *The Linacre Quarterly*, Vol. 84, No. 1, 2017, pp. 1–9, doi:10.1080/00243639.2016.1264249
29 Shweta Marathe, Benjamin M. Hunter, Indira Chakravarthi, Abhay Shukla and Susan F. Murray, 'The Impacts of Corporatisation of Healthcare on Medical Practice and Professionals in Maharashtra, India', *BMJ Global Health*, Vol. 5, No. 2, , 2020, doi:10.1136/bmjgh-2019-002026
30 Laishram Ladusingh and Anamika Pandey. 'Health Expenditure and Impoverishment in India', *Journal of Health Management*, Vol. 15, 2013, pp. 57–74, doi:10.1177/0972063413486031.
31 Arun K. Aggarwal, 'Strengthening Healthcare System in India: Is Privatization the Only Answer?' *Indian Journal of Community Medicine*, Vol 33, No. 2, 2008, pp. 69–70, doi:10.4103/0970-0218.40869
32 Sanjay Nagral, 'Doctors and Violence', *Indian Journal of Medical Ethics*, Vol. 9, No. 4, 2016, p. 107, https://ijme.in/articles/doctors-and-violence/
33 Michael Calnan and Rosemary Rowe, *Trust Matters in Healthcare*, Open University Press, 2008.

34 R. Narayan and T. Narayan, 'Universal Health Coverage for India', *BMJ Editorial*, 2012.
35 National Medical Commission, 'AETCOM Curriculum', 2019, https://www.nmc.org.in/wp-content/uploads/2020/01/AETCOM_book.pdf
36 Susan Goold, 'Trust and the Ethics of Healthcare Institutions', *The Hastings Center Report*, Vol. 31, No. 6, 2001, pp. 26–33. doi:10.2307/3527779
37 COPASAH – Community of Practitioners on Accountability and Social Action in Health, www.copasah.net
38 Nishant Sirohi, 'Declaring the Right to Health a Fundamental Right', Health Express, Observer Research Foundation, 14 July 2020, https://www.orfonline.org/expert-speak/declaring-the-right-to-health-a-fundamental-right/
39 UNESCO, Article 14, Universal Declaration on Bioethics and Human Rights. www.unesco.org/en/legal-affairs/universal-declaration-bioethics-and-human-rights
40 Sanjay Zodpey and Habib Hasan Farooqui, 'Universal Health Coverage in India: Progress Achieved & the Way Forward', *The Indian Journal of Medical Research*, Vol. 147, No. 4, 2018, pp. 327–29, doi:10.4103/ijmr.IJMR_616_18
41 National Health Mission, https://nhm.gov.in/
42 UNDP India, 'Sustainable Development Goals 2030', 2015, https://www.in.undp.org/content/india/en/home/sustainable-development-goals.html
43 UNDP, 'Human Development Reports HDI Ranking', 2020, http://hdr.undp.org/en/content/latest-human-development-index-ranking

9: Regulating the Womb: Reproductive Health, Bodily Integrity and Autonomy in Contemporary India

1 H.E. Dillaway, 'Are Hysterectomies Necessary? Racial-ethnic Differences in Women's Attitudes', *Journal of Women & Aging*, Vol. 28, No. 4, p. 309; Fouzieya Towghi, 'Cutting Inoperable Bodies: Particularizing Rural Sociality to Normalize Hysterectomies in Balochistan, Pakistan', *Medical Anthropology*, Vol. 31, No. 3, 2012, p. 229.
2 S. Ghosh and K.S. James, 'Levels and Trends in Caesarean Births: Cause for Concern?', *Economic and Political Weekly* 2010, p. 19.
3 K. Vora, 'Experimental Sociality and Gestational Surrogacy in the Indian ART Clinic', *Ethnos*, Vol. 79, No. 1, 2014, pp. 63–83.

4   P. Chatterjee, 'Hysterectomies in Beed District Raise Questions for India', *The Lancet*, Vol. 394, No. 10194, 2019, p 202.
5   Madhukar Pai, 'Unnecessary Medical Interventions: Caesarean Sections as a Case Study', *Economic and Political Weekly* 2000, p. 2755.
6   Anindita Majumdar, 'Conceptualizing Surrogacy as Work-labour: Domestic Labour in Commercial Gestational Surrogacy in India', *Journal of South Asian Development*, Vol. 13, No. 2, 2018, p. 210. Amrita Pande, 'Transnational commercial Surrogacy in India: Gifts for Global Sisters?', Reproductive Biomedicine Online, Vol. 23, No. 5, 2011, p. 618.
7   N. Chatterjee and N. E. Riley, 'Planning an Indian Modernity: The Gendered Politics of Fertility Control', *Signs: Journal of Women in Culture and Society*, Vol. 26, No. 3, 2001, p. 811.
8   Fouzieya Towghi and Kalindi Vora, 'Bodies, Markets, and the Experimental in South Asia', *Ethnos*, 2014, Vol. 79, No. 1, pp. 1–18.
9   Lawrence Cohen, 'Where it Hurts: Indian Material for an Ethics of Organ Transplantation', Vol. 128, No. 4, 1999, p. 135; K.S. Rajan, *Biocapital: The Constitution of Postgenomic Life* Durham, NC: Duke University Press, 2006.
10 Ibid.
11 Lawrence Cohen, 'Operability, Bioavailability, and Exception', in Aihwa Ong and Stephen J. Coller (Eds), *Global Assemblages: Technology, Politics, and Ethics as Anthropological Problems*, London: Blackwell Publishing, 2005, pp. 79–90; Cecilia Van Hollen, *Birth on the Threshold: Childbirth and Modernity in South India* Berkeley, CA: University of California Press, 2003.
12 Scott Carney, *Red Market*, UK: Hachette, 2011.
13 Cecilia Van Hollen, *Birth on the Threshold: Childbirth and Modernity in South India*, Berkeley, CA: Univ of California Press, 2003.
14 Towghi, 'Cutting Inoperable Bodies'; B.S. Subha Sri, 'Women's Bodies and the Medical Profession', *Economic and Political Weekly*, 2010, Vol. 45, No. 17, pp. 52–57.
15 Kim Gutschow, 'Going "Beyond the Numbers": Maternal Death Reviews in India', *Medical Anthropology*, Vol. 35, No. 4, 2016, p. 322; Victoria Loblay, 'Spatial Boundaries and Moralities of Gender: Considerations from Obstetric and Gynaecological Practice in Chennai, South India', *South Asian History and Culture*, Vol. 1, No. 2, 2010, p. 213.
16 R.S. Rajan, *The Scandal of the State: Women, Law, and Citizenship in Postcolonial India* Durham, NC: Duke University Press, 2003.

17 S. Desai, T. Sinha and A. Mahal, 'Prevalence of Hysterectomy Among Rural and Urban Women With and Without Health Insurance in Gujarat, India', *Reproductive Health Matters*, Vol. 19, No. 37, 2011, p. 42; Dillaway, 'Are Hysterectomies Necessary'; Towghi 'Cutting Inoperable Bodies'.
18 S. Desai, O.M. Campbell, T. Sinha, A. Mahal and S. Cousens, 'Incidence and determinants of hysterectomy in a low-income setting in Gujarat, India', *Health Policy and Planning*, Vol. 32, No. 1, 2017, p. 68.
19 Ibid., p. 72.
20 Towghi, 'Cutting Inoperable Bodies'.
21 Desai, Sinha and Mahal, 'Prevalence of Hysterectomy'.
22 Towghi, 'Cutting Inoperable Bodies'; Desai, Sinha and Mahal, 'Prevalence of hysterectomy', p. 239.
23 Towghi, 'Cutting Inoperable Bodies'.
24 Desai, Campbell, Sinha, Mahal and Cousons, 'Incidence and determinants', p. 69.
25 Rajan, *Scandal of the state*.
26 *Economic and Political Weekly*, 'Editorial: Under the Surgeon's Knife', Vol. 29, No. 8, 1994, p. 391.
27 N. Rao and S. Pungaliya, 'Human Concern or Convenience? Debate on Hysterectomies of Mentally Handicapped', *Economic and Political Weekly*, 1994, Vol. 29, No. 11, p. 604.
28 P. Chatterjee, 'Hysterectomies in Beed District Raise Questions for India', *The Lancet*, Vol. 394, No. 10194, 2019, p. 202; A. Gopinathan, 'Wombless in Maharashtra', *BMJ*, Vol. 333, No. 7568, 2006, p. 609.
29 Ibid.
30 Chatterjee, 'Hysterectomies in Beed'.
31 M. Lock and P. Kaufert, 'Menopause, Local Biologies, and Cultures of Aging', *American Journal of Human Biology*, Vol. 13, No. 4, 2001, p. 494.
32 Loblay, 'Spatial Boundaries and Moralities'.
33 Chatterjee and Riley, 'Planning and Indian Modernity'; Van Hollen, *Birth on the Threshold*.
34 Gutschow, 'Going "Beyond the Numbers"'.
35 S. Goli et al., 'Labour Room Violence in Uttar Pradesh, India: Evidence From Longitudinal Study of Pregnancy and Childbirth', *BMJ Open*, , Vol. 9, No. 7, 2019, p. 2.
36 Dana Ain Davis, 'Obstetric Racism: The Racial Politics of Pregnancy, Labor, and Birthing', *Medical Anthropology*, Vol. 28, No. 7, 2019, p. 560.
37 Gutschow, 'Going "Beyond the Numbers"'.

38 '"Alarming" Trend of Very High C-section Births, Says Survey', *Indian Express*, 15 December 2020, https://indianexpress.com/article/cities/pune/sharp-jump-in-c-section-deliveries-in-several-states-including-maharashtra-and-wb-shows-nfhs-data-of-2019-20-7104926/
39 Ghosh and James, 'Levels and Trends'.
40 N. Muzaffar and M. Akram, 'Alarming Rise of Caesarean Section Deliveries', *Economic & Political Weekly*, Vol. 54, No. 24, 2019, p. 55.
41 Ghosh and James, 'Levels and Trends'.
42 Muzaffar and Akram, 'Alarming Rise', p. 55.
43 Ibid.
44 Ibid.
45 Ghosh and James, 'Levels and Trends', p. 21.
46 Ibid.
47 Muzaffar and Akram, 'Alarming Rise'.
48 Sreeparna Chattopadhyay, Arima Mishra and Suraj Jacob, '"Safe", Yet Violent? Women's Experiences With Obstetric Violence During Hospital Births in Rural Northeast India', *Culture, Health & Sexuality*, Vol. 20, No. 7, 2018, p. 815; Johns Hopkins Medicine https://www.hopkinsmedicine.org/health/treatment-tests-and-therapies/episiotomy
    According to the John Hopkins Medical dictionary, 'an episiotomy is an incision through the area between your vaginal opening and your anus. This area is called the perineum. This procedure is done to make your vaginal opening larger for childbirth'.
49 Davis, 'Obstetric Racism'.
50 Ibid.
51 Chattopadhyay, Mishra and Jacob, '"Safe", Yet Violent?', p. 7.
52 Gutschow, 'Going "Beyond the Numbers"'; Davis, 'Obstetric Racism'; Chattopadhyay, Mishra and Jacob, '"Safe", Yet Violent?'.
53 Loblay, 'Spatial Boundaries and Moralities'; Subha Sri, 'Women's Bodies'.
54 Loblay, 'Spatial Boundaries and Moralities'.
55 N. B. Sarojini and A. Sharma, 'The Draft ART (Regulation) Bill: In Whose Interest', *Indian Journal of Medical Ethics*, Vol. 6, No. 1, 2009, p. 36.
56 Sama, *Birthing a Market: Commercial Surrogacy in India* New Delhi: Sama Resource Group for Women and Health, 2010; K. Vora, 'Experimental Sociality and Gestational Surrogacy in the Indian ART Clinic', *Ethnos*, Vol. 79, No. 1, 2014, p. 63.
57 S. Nadimpally and A. Majumdar, 'Recruiting to Give Birth: Agent-facilitators and the Commercial Surrogacy Arrangement in India, in

Babies for Sale, Miranda Davies (ed.), (London: Zed Books, 2017, pp. 48–68; A. Pande, *Wombs in Labor: Transnational Commercial Surrogacy in India*, New York: Columbia University Press, 2014; S. Rudrappa, *Discounted Life: The Price of Global Surrogacy in India* New York: NYU Press, 2015.

58 V.A. Zelizer, 'The Purchase of Intimacy', *Law & Social Inquiry*, Vol. 25, No. 3, 2000, pp. 817.
59 M. Rao, 'Why All Non-altruistic Surrogacy Should Be Banned', *Economic and Political Weekly*, 2012, Vol. 47, No. 21, pp. 15-17.
60 Department-Related Parliamentary Standing Committee, 'One Hundred Second Report: The Surrogacy (Regulation) Bill, 2016', August 2017, https://prsindia.org/files/bills_acts/bills_parliament/2016/SCR-%20Surrogacy%20Bill,%202018.pdf
61 Rajan, *Biocapital*.

10: Confidentiality and HIV/AIDS: The Need for Humaneness and Precision in the Law

1 Gregg Gonsalves and Peter Staley, 'Panic, Paranoia, and Public Health – The AIDS Epidemic's Lessons for Ebola', *New England Journal of Medicine*, Vol. 371, 2014, pp. 2348–49, https://www.nejm.org/doi/full/10.1056/NEJMp1413425
2 For a discussion on this see 'Risks, Rights & Health', the report of the Global Commission on HIV and the Law, https://hivlawcommission.org/wp-content/uploads/2017/06/FinalReport-RisksRightsHealth-EN.pdf
3 Stephanie Pappas, 'HIV Laws That Appear To Do More Harm Than Good', *Monitor on Psychology*, Vol. 49, No. 9, October 2018, https://www.apa.org/monitor/2018/10/ce-corner
4 Pappas, 'HIV Laws That Appear To Do More Harm Than Good', pp. 45–46.
5 Pappas, 'HIV Laws That Appear To Do More Harm Than Good'.
6 Smarajit Jana, Bharati Dey, Sushena Reza-Paul and Richard Steen, 'Combating Human Trafficking in the Sex Trade: Can Sex Workers Do It Better?', *Journal of Public Health*, Vol. 36, No. 4, 2014, pp. 622–28, https://doi.org/10.1093/pubmed/fdt095; See also, Toorjo Ghose et al., 'The Role of Brothels in Reducing HIV Risk in Sonagachi, India',

Qualitative Health Research, Vol. 21, No. 5, 2011, pp. 587–600, doi: 10.1177/1049732310395328

7   Goa Public Health (Amendment) Act, 1987, http://dhsgoa.gov.in/documents/goa-public-health-act.pdf
8   Amendment to Section 53, Goa Public Health (Amendment) Act, 1987.
9   See https://lawyerscollective.org/our-initiatives/hiv-and-law/. Also, see Lisa Monteiro, 'Dominic Made Me Promise That I Would Work for PLHIV As a Lawyer', *The Times of India*, 6 May 2017, https://timesofindia.indiatimes.com/city/goa/dominic-made-me-promise-that-i-would-work-for-plhiv-as-a-lawyer/articleshow/58541852.cms
10 Benedito R Ferrão, '40 Years After AIDS, Remembering Dominic D'Souza, the First Indian Diagnosed with HIV Infection', *Scroll.in*, 27 May 2021, https://scroll.in/article/995839/40-years-after-aids-remembering-dominic-dsouza-the-first-indian-diagnosed-with-hiv-infection
11 Stephen Marks, 'Jonathan Mann's Legacy to the 21st Century: The Human Rights Imperative for Public Health', *Journal of Law, Medicine & Ethics*, Vol. 29, 2001, pp. 131–38.
12 Elizabeth Fee and Manon Parry, 'Jonathan Mann, HIV/AIDS, and Human Rights', *Journal of Public Health Policy*, Vol. 29, 2008, pp. 54–71, https://doi.org/10.1057/palgrave.jphp.3200160
13 Wayne T. Steward, Gregory M. Herek, Jayashree Ramakrishna, Shalini Bharat, Sara Chandy, Judith Wrubel and Maria L. Ekstrand, 'HIV-Related Stigma: Adapting a Theoretical Framework for Use in India', *Social Science & Medicine*, Vol. 67, No. 8, October 2008, pp. 1225–35: 10.1016/j.socscimed.2008.05.032 offers an account of the different types of stigmas experienced by people living with HIV in India.
14 Michael Kirby, 'Human Rights and the HIV Paradox', *The Lancet*, Vol. 348, No. 9036 2 November 1996 1217–18, https://doi.org/10.1016/S0140-6736(96)05468-2
15 Vivek Divan, 'COVID-19 Is a Ripe Opportunity to Strengthen the Public Health and Social Security System', *The Indian Express*, 27 May 2020, https://indianexpress.com/article/opinion/columns/coronavirus-india-lockdown-vaccine-tests-migrants-hiv-lessons-for-covid-19-vivek-divan-6428697/
16 UNAIDS, 'Rights in the Time of COVID-19: Lessons From HIV For an Effective, Community-led Response', 2020, https://www.unaids.org/sites/default/files/media_asset/human-rights-and-covid-19_en.pdf

17 Commission on Social Determinants of Health, 'Closing the Gap in a Generation: Health Equity Through Action on the Social Determinants of Health', Final Report of the Commission on Social Determinants of Health, Geneva, World Health Organization, 2008, https://www.who.int/social_determinants/final_report/csdh_finalreport_2008.pdf
18 (2017) 10 SCC 1.
19 Section 129, Indian Evidence Act, 1872.
20 Lawyers Collective, *Legislating an Epidemic: HIV/AIDS in India*, New Delhi: Universal Law Publishing, 2003.
21 Ibid.
22 Ibid.
23 [1988] 2 AII ER 648.
24 Ibid.
25 Rachel Hajar, 'The Physician's Oath: Historical Perspectives', *Heart Views*, Vol. 18, No. 4, 2017, pp. 154-59, 10.4103/HEARTVIEWS.HEARTVIEWS_131_17
26 Clause 2.2, Indian Medical Council (Professional Conduct, Etiquette and Ethics) Regulations, 2002.
27 Lawyers Collective, *Legislating an Epidemic*.
28 Article 12, Universal Declaration of Human Rights; Article 17, International Covenant on Civil and Political Rights.
29 Paragraphs 65(g) and 69(a), UN General Assembly Political Declaration on HIV and AIDS: Ending Inequalities and Getting on Track to End AIDS by 2030, https://www.unaids.org/sites/default/files/media_asset/2021_political-declaration-on-hiv-and-aids_en.pdf
30 (1998) 8 SCC 296.
31 (2003) 1 SCC 500.
32 17 Cal.3d 425.
33 Ibid.
34 Ibid.
35 Ibid.
36 Chapter IV of the HIV/AIDS (Prevention and Control) Act, 2017.
37 Section 8, Ibid.
38 Section 9, Ibid.
39 Section 10, Ibid.
40 The HIV/AIDS (Prevention and Control) Act, 2017, was drafted by a team at Lawyers Collective HIV/AIDS Unit, the pioneering non-profit organization with vast experience in the realm of HIV and human

rights, including an extensive legal aid practice serving those affected by the epidemic. The authors were actively in this work at the Unit for several years, and often experienced lengthy delays in the traditional court system in representing HIV-affected clients. The Act itself was borne of this experience, and drafted at the behest of the government after an extensive process of civil society consultation across the country with a wide variety of stakeholders including people living with HIV, vulnerable communities such as sex workers and queer people, child rights groups, healthcare workers, unions and employers, women's organizations, and lawyers.

41 Section 21, HIV/AIDS (Prevention and Control) Act, 2017.
42 Rule 10, HIV/AIDS (Prevention and Control) Rules, 2018, available at http://www.naco.gov.in/sites/default/files/egazette%20HIV%20AIDS%20Act_0.pdf
43 Rule 9, HIV/AIDS (Prevention and Control) Rules, 2018.
44 Rule 13, Ibid.
45 Section 34, HIV/AIDS (Prevention and Control) Act, 2017.
46 Chapter X, Ibid.
47 Section 26, Ibid.
48 Tarun Bathini, 'Two Years Since HIV and AIDS Act Was Notified, Govts Have Done Little to Implement It', *The Wire*, 10 September 2020, https://thewire.in/government/hiv-aids-act-two-years-implementation
49 Section 28, HIV/AIDS (Prevention and Control) Act, 2017.
50 United Nations General Assembly, 'Political Declaration on HIV and AIDS: Ending Inequalities and Getting on Track to end AIDS by 2030', 2021, https://www.unaids.org/sites/default/files/media_asset/2021_political-declaration-on-hiv-and-aids_en.pdf
51 Jane M. Simoni, Bryan A. Kutner and Keith J. Horvath, 'Opportunities and Challenges of Digital Technology for HIV Treatment and Prevention', *Current HIV/AIDS Reports*, Vol. 14, No. 2015, pp. 437–40, https://doi.org/10.1007/s11904-015-0289-1
52 World Health Assembly Resolution, WHA 71.7 2018 on Digital Health, https://apps.who.int/gb/ebwha/pdf_files/WHA71/A71_R7-en.pdf; World Health Organization, 'Global Strategy for Digital Health', 2020, https://www.who.int/docs/default-source/documents/gs4dhdaa2a9f352b0445bafbc79ca799dce4d.pdf
53 (2017) 10 SCC 1
54 Section 11, HIV/AIDS (Prevention and Control) Act, 2017.

55 The Aadhaar identification system provides each resident in India with a 12-digit unique identification number, linked to demographic and biometric data.
56 Bernd Blobel, 'Authorisation and Access Control for Electronic Health Record Systems', *International Journal of Medical Informatics*, Vol. 73, add year, pp. 251–7, 10.1016/j.ijmedinf.2003.11.018
57 Section 8, HIV/AIDS (Prevention and Control) Act, 2017.
58 UNAIDS, 'Considerations and Guidance for Countries Adopting National Health Identifiers', 2014, https://www.unaids.org/sites/default/files/media_asset/JC2640_nationalhealthidentifiers_en.pdf
59 Privacy by Design extends to a Trilogy of encompassing applications: 1) The IT systems; 2) accountable business practices; and 3) physical design and networked infrastructure. See Ann Cavoukian, 'Privacy by Design: The 7 Foundational Principles, 2011, https://www.ipc.on.ca/wp-content/uploads/resources/7foundationalprinciples.pdf
60 Centre for Health Equity, Law and Policy & Internet Freedom Foundation, 'Working Paper: Analysing the NDHM Health Data Management Policy', June 2021, available at https://ea51c4f6-3257-4b64-b189-d18d2b68e428.filesusr.com/ugd/bfda9b_14f8cf90a45b48958b4209442e8db9f8.pdf
61 National AIDS Control Programme, 'Data Management Guidelines For Data Collection, Protection and Sharing', 2020, http://naco.gov.in/sites/default/files/Draft%20NACP%20Data%20Management%20Guidelines%202020.pdf
62 Shefali Malhotra, Rohin Garg, and Shivangi Rai, 'Analysing the NDHM Health Data Management Policy', June 11 June https://ssrn.com/abstract=3947598
63 Luc Rocher, Julien M. Hendrickx and Yves-Alexandre de Montjoye, 'Estimating the Success of Re-identifications in Incomplete Data sets Using Generative Models', *Nature Communications*, Vol. 10, No. 3069, 2019, https://doi.org/10.1038/s41467-019-10933-3
64 Sarthak Dogra, 'Took Covid Vaccine Using Aadhaar? Your National Health ID Has Been Created Without Your Permission', *India Today*, 24 May 2021, https://www.msn.com/en-in/news/other/took-covid-vaccine-using-aadhaar-your-national-health-id-has-been-created-without-your-permission/ar-AAKkntq
65 Aarti Dhar, 'HIV Treatment to be Linked to Aadhaar', *The Hindu*, 2 February 2015, https://www.thehindu.com/news/national/hiv-treatment-to-be-linked-to-aadhaar/article6845900.ece

66 Shruti Tomar, 'Linking Benefits for AIDS Patients to Aadhaar Triggers Privacy Concerns', *Hindustan Times*, 3 April 2017, https://www.hindustantimes.com/bhopal/linking-benefits-for-aids-patients-to-aadhaar-triggers-privacy-concerns/story-iR6HB8RmqPDaNwkX2Oj5EJ.html
67 Menaka Rao, 'Why Aadhaar Is Prompting HIV-Positive People to Drop Out of Treatment Programmes in India', Scroll.in, 17 November 2017, https://scroll.in/pulse/857656/across-india-hiv-positive-people-drop-out-of-treatment-programmes-as-centres-insist-on-aadhaar
68 Ibid.
69 Ibid.

11: Decisional Privacy and Decisional Autonomy: A Rights-Based Paradigm for Mental Healthcare in India

1 G. Gururaj, M. Varghese, V. Benegal, G.N. Rao, K. Pathak, L.K. Singh, R.Y. Mehta, D. Ram, T.M. Shibukumar, A. Kokane, R.K. Lenin Singh, B.S. Chavan, P. Sharma, C. Ramasubramanian, P.K. Dalal, P.K. Saha, S.P. Deuri, A.K. Giri, A.B. Kavishvar, V.K. Sinha, J. Thavody, R. Chatterji, B.S. Akoijam, S. Das, A. Kashyap, V.S. Ragavan, S.K. Singh, R. Misra and NMHS collaborators group. National Mental Health Survey of India, 2015-16: Mental Health Systems. Bengaluru, National Institute of Mental Health and Neuro Sciences, NIMHANS Publication No. 130, 2016. http://indianmhs.nimhans.ac.in/Docs/Report1.pdf
2 Ibid.
3 Richard M. Duffy and Brendan D. Kelly, *India's Mental Healthcare Act, 2017: Building Laws, Protecting Rights*, Singapore: Springer Nature, 2020, pp. 51–61.
4 Dinesh Bhugra, Dinesh Bhugra, Soumitra Pathare, Chetna Gosavi, Antonio Ventriglio, Julio Torales, João Castaldelli-Maia, Edgardo Juan L Tolentino Jr and Roger Ng, 'Mental Illness And The Right to Vote: A Review of Legislation Across the World', *International Review of Psychiatry* Vol No. 28, No.4, 2016, pp. 395–99. Dinesh Bhugra, Soumitra Pathare, Renuka Nardodkar, Chetna Gosavi, Roger Ng, Julio Torales and Antonio Ventriglio, 'Legislative Provisions Related to Marriage and Divorce of Persons with Mental Health Problems: A Global Review', *International Review of Psychiatry* Vol No. 28, No.4, 2016, 386–92, https://doi.org/10.1080/09540261.2016.1210577.

5   Bert-Jaap Koops, Bryce Clayton Newell, Tjerk Timan, Ivan Škorvánek, Tom Chokrevski and Maša Galič, 'A Typology of Privacy', *University of Pennsylvania Journal of International Law*, Vol. 38, 2017, 483–575.
6   Soumitra Pathare and Arjun Kapoor, 'Decisional Autonomy and India's Mental Healthcare Act: A Comment on Emerging Jurisprudence', in *Mental Health, Legal Capacity and Human Rights*, ed. Michael Ashley Stein et al, (Cambridge: Cambridge University Press, 2021), pp. 155–170.
7   Bert-Jaap Koops, 'A Typology of Privacy'.
8   Anita Allen, 'Privacy in Healthcare', in Stephen G. Post (Ed.) *Encyclopedia of Bioethics*, New York: MacMillan Reference Books, 1995, pp. 2064–73.
9   Daniel J. Solove, *Understanding Privacy* Harvard University Press, 2018.
10 Jonathan Pugh, *Autonomy, Rationality, and Contemporary Bioethics* Oxford University Press, 2020, pp. 8–15.
11 Daniel J. Solove, *Understanding Privacy* Harvard University Press, 2018.
12 Solove, *Understanding Privacy* Gerard Quinn, 'Personhood and Legal Capacity Perspectives on the Paradigm Shift of Article 12 CRPD', paper presented at the Harvard Project on Disability Conference, Harvard Law School, 20 February 2010.
13 Jennifer Hawkins and Louis C. Charland, 'Decision-Making Capacity', *Stanford Encyclopedia of Philosophy*, Fall 2020, https://plato.stanford.edu/archives/fall2020/entries/decision-capacity/
14 Committee on the Rights of Persons with Disabilities, 'General Comment 1: Article 12 Equal Recognition Before the Law', United Nations, CRPD/C/GC/1 (2014), http://daccess-dds-ny.un.org/doc/UNDOC/GEN/G14/031/20/PDF/G1403120.pdf?OpenElement Amita Dhanda, 'Legal Capacity in the Disability Rights CRPD: Stranglehold of the Past or Lodestar for the Future?', *Syracuse Journal of International Law and Commerce* Vol. 34, No. 2, 2007, p. 429.
15 Paul S. Appelbaum, 'Assessment of Patients' Competence to Consent to Treatment', *New England Journal of Medicine* Vol. 357 2007, pp. 1834–40, https://doi.org/10.1056/nejmcp074045
16 Europen Group of National Human Rights Institutions in the European Court of Human Rights, 'Amicus Brief, Written Comments by the European Group of National Human Rights Institutions in the European Court of Human Rights, D.D. v. Lithuania, Application No. 13469/06', http://www.interights.org/app/webroot/userimages/file/DD Amicus Human rights institutions.pdf
17 Michael Bach and Lana Kerzner, 'A New Paradigm for Protecting Autonomy and the Right to Legal Capacity', paper submitted to the

	Law Commission of Ontario for its Advancing Substantive Equality for Persons with Disabilities through Law, Policy and Practice project, October 2010, https://www.lco-cdo.org/wp-content/uploads/2010/11/disabilities-commissioned-paper-bach-kerzner.pdf.
18	Ibid.
19	Jennifer Hawkins and Louis C. Charland, 'Decision-Making Capacity.'
20	John Dawson, 'A Realistic Approach to Assessing Mental Health Laws' Compliance with the UNCRPD', *International Journal of Law and Psychiatry* Vol. 40 2015, pp. 70–9, https://doi.org/10.1016/j.ijlp.2015.04.003
21	Ibid; Matthé Scholten and Jakov Gather, 'Adverse Consequences of Article 12 of the UN Convention on the Rights of Persons with Disabilities for Persons with Mental Disabilities and an Alternative Way Forward', *Journal of Medical Ethics* vol. 44 No.4, 2018, pp. 226–33, https://doi.org/10.1136/medethics-2017-104414. George Szmukler, 'Involuntary Detention and Treatment: Are We Edging Toward a Paradigm Shift?', *Schizophrenia Bulletin* Vol. 46, No.2, 2020, pp. 231–35, https://doi.org/10.1093/schbul/sbz115.
22	(2017) 10 SCC 1.
23	AIR 2014 SC 1863.
24	(2018) 10 SCC 1.
25	AIR 2010 SC 235.
26	(2018) 5 SCC 1.
27	Isaiah Berlin, *Liberty: Four Essays on Liberty*, New York: Oxford University Press, 2002.
28	Suresh Bada Math, Vinay Basavaraju, Shashidhara Nagabhushana Harihara, Guru S Gowda , Narayana Manjunatha, Channaveerachari Naveen Kumar and Mahesh Gowda, 'Mental Healthcare Act 2017 – Aspiration to Action', *Indian Journal of Psychiatry* Vol. 61, Suppl 4, pp. 660–66, https://doi.org/10.4103/psychiatry.IndianJPsychiatry_91_19
29	Natalie F. Banner, 'Unreasonable Reasons: Normative Judgements in the Assessment of Mental Capacity', *Journal of Evaluation in Clinical Practice* Vol. 18, No. 5, 2012, pp. 1038–44 https://doi.org/10.1111/j.1365-2753.2012.01914.x
30	Dan Ariely, *Predictably Irrational, Revised: The Hidden Forces That Shape Our Decisions* (New York: Harper Perennial, 2010). A. Tversky, and D. Kahneman, 'Judgment Under Uncertainty: Heuristics and Biases', *Science*, Vol. 185, No. 4157, 1974, pp. 1124–31,, https://doi.org/10.1126/science.185.4157.1124.

31 Camillia Kong, *Mental Capacity in Relationship: Decision-making, Dialogue, and Autonomy*, Cambridge University Press, 2017, https://doi.org/10.1017/9781316683088.
32 Soumitra Pathare and Arjun Kapoor, 'Implementation Update on Mental Healthcare Act, 2017', in Richard M. Duffy and Brendan D. Kelly (Eds.), *India's Mental Healthcare Act, 2017*, Singapore: Springer Nature, 2020, pp. 251–265.
33 Maria Rodrigues, Helen Herrman, Silvana Galderisi and John Allan, 'Position Statement of the World Psychiatric Association: Implementing Alternatives to Coercion: A Key Component of Improving Mental Healthcare', October 2020, https://3ba346de-fde6-473f-b1da-536498661f9c.filesusr.com/ugd/e172f3_635a89af889c471683c29fcd981db0aa.pdf

12: State Legibility of Personal Health Data in India

1 Adam C. Powell, Hanu Tyagi and Jasmine K. Ludhar, 'Digitising Indian Healthcare Records', ISB Insight, 28 August 2018, https://isbinsight.isb.edu/digitising-indian-healthcare-records
2 National Health Authority, 'National Digital Health Mission: Strategy Overview', July, 2020 https://archive.org/details/ndhm-strategy-overview
3 Melissa M. Lee and Nan Zhang, 'Legibility and the Informational Foundations of State Capacity', *The Journal of Politics*, Vol. 79 No. 1, 2017.
4 Julie Myers, Thomas R. Frieden, Kamal M. Bherwani and Kelly J. Henning, 'Ethics in Public Health Research: Privacy and Public Health at Risk: Public Health Confidentiality in the Digital Age', *American Journal of Public Health*, Vol. 98 No. 5, 2008, pp. 793–80.
5 Vijay Kelkar and Ajay Shah, *In Service of the Republic: The Art and Science of Economic Policy* (Penguin Books, 2020); Arvind Kasthuri, 'Challenges to Healthcare in India – The Five As', *Indian Journal of Community Medicine*, Vol. 43 No. 3, 2018, pp. 141–143.
6 Merriam Webster's Dictionary, https://www.merriam-webster.com/dictionary/surveillance
7 David Lyon, *Surveillance Studies: An Overview*, Polity Press, 2007, p. 123.
8 Ashley Deeks, 'Framework for Surveillance', *Virginia Journal of International Law*, Vol. 55, 2015, pp. 293–367.

9   Shoshana Zuboff, *The Age of Surveillance Capitalism: The Fight for a Human Future at the New Frontier of Power*, Public Affairs Books, 2019.
10 Daniel Citron and David Grey, 'Addressing the Harm of Total Surveillance: A Reply to Professor Neil Richards', *Harvard Law Review Forum*, 2013, p. 262.
11 Bert Jaap-Koops, 'The Concept of Function Creep', *Law, Innovation and Technology*, Vol. 13, 2021.
12 Usha Ramanathan, 'The Function Creep that is Aadhaar', The Wire, 25 April 2017, https://thewire.in/government/aadhaar-function-creep-uid)
13 Daniel J. Solove, 'A Taxonomy of Privacy', *University of Pennsylvania Law Review*, Vol. 154 No. 3, 2006, pp. 477–558.
14 Freedom House, 'Report: Global Internet Freedom Declines in Shadow of Pandemic,' 2020, https://freedomhouse.org/article/report-global-internet-freedom-declines-shadow-pandemic
15 Adam Schwartz, 'COVID-19 and Surveillance Tech: Year in Review 2020', Electronic Frontier Foundation, 2021.
16 Introduction to Public Health Surveillance, Centers for Disease Control and Prevention, https://www.cdc.gov/training/publichealth101/surveillance.html
17 Harleen Kaur, 'Electronic Health Records in India: Legal Framework and Regulatory Issues,' RGNUL Student Research Review (RSSR), Vol. 6, No. 1, http://rsrr.in/wp-content/uploads/2020/08/ELECTRONIC-HEALTH-RECORDS-IN-INDIA.pdf
18 Powell et al., 'Digitising Indian Healthcare Records'.
19 Vineet Washington, 'Indian Wearable Market Grew 144.3 Percent YoY in 2020, With Earwear Taking 83.6 Percent Market Share: IDC', Gadget 360, 5 March 2021, https://gadgets.ndtv.com/wearables/news/indian-wearable-market-144-3-percent-growth-yoy-2020-earwear-83-6-percent-idc-2384464
20 Aditi Bisht, 'From Minding Water Intake To Mental Health, Here Are The Indian Healthtech Products That Track The Modern Lifestyle', *Inc42*, March 2021, https://inc42.com/features/from-minding-water-intake-to-mental-health-here-are-the-indian-healthtech-products-that-track-the-modern-lifestyle/
21 Powell et al., 'Digitising Indian Healthcare Records'.
22 NITI Aayog, National Health Stack: Strategy and Approach, July, 2018, https://www.niti.gov.in/writereaddata/files/document_publication/NHS-Strategy-and-Approach-Document-for-consultation.pdf

23 Express Web Desk, 'PM Modi Launches National Digital Health Mission, Says Every Indian to Get a Unique Health ID', *The Indian Express*, 15 August 2020, https://indianexpress.com/article/india/national-digital-health-mission-indians-health-identity-cards-6555529/
24 National Health Authority, 'National Digital Health Mission: Strategy Overview', July 2020, https://www.niti.gov.in/sites/default/files/2021-09/ndhm_strategy_overview.pdf
25 For example, private entities can develop solutions for other components such as electronic medical record (EMR). See National Health Authority, 'Hon'ble Prime Minister Announces National Digital Health Mission on India's 74th Independence Day - Press Release', https://ndhm.gov.in/media/pressReleasePdf
26 Seema Singh and Maitry Porecha, 'Behind the Rush and Hush of India's National Digital Health Mission', *The Ken*, 22 September 2020, https://the-ken.com/story/behind-the-rush-and-hush-of-indias-digital-health-mission/
27 Anand Mishra, 'Centre to Roll Out Unified Health Interface Under NDHM', *The Deccan Herald*, 27 May 2021, https://www.deccanherald.com/national/centre-to-roll-out-unified-health-interface-under-ndhm-990709.html
28 Section 25, 26 of the DNA Bill.
29 Vrinda Bhandari and Faiza Rahman, 'Constitutionalism During a Crisis: The Case of Aarogya Setu', in Coronavirus Pandemic: Lessons and Policy Responses (2020); Prabhakar Thakur, 'Aarogya Setu App Mandatory for Airline Passengers, No Entry Without "Green" Status', NDTV.com, 21 May 2020, https://gadgets.ndtv.com/apps/news/aarogya-setu-mandatory-domestic-airline-passengers-aai-sop-2232576
30 Anirudh Burman, 'Intrusive Pandemic-Era Monitoring Is the Same Old Surveillance State, Not a New One', Carnegie India, 7 May 2020, https://carnegieindia.org/2020/05/07/intrusive-pandemic-era-monitoring-is-same-old-surveillance-state-not-new-one-pub-8172
31 Gaurav Bhatnagar, 'Aarogya Setu Data Was Made Available to J&K Police in Kulgam, Reveals RTI', *The Wire*, 1 April 2021, https://thewire.in/government/aarogya-setu-data-was-made-available-to-jk-police-in-kulgam-reveals-rti
32 SFLC.in, 'Analysis of the Indian COVID-19 Apps', https://sflc.in/our-analysis-indian-covid19-apps
33 After receiving criticisms, the government has permitted access to vaccination without prior registration on CoWin. See Ananthakrishnan

G, 'Supreme Court Tells Government: Wake Up and Smell The Coffee, Let Vaccine Policy Be Flexible', *The Indian Express*, 1 June 2021, https://indianexpress.com/article/india/policy-must-change-as-per-ground-situation-sc-on-mandatory-cowin-registration-for-covid-19-vaccine-7337921/. However, people faced difficulties in accessing walk-in vaccination without COWIN registration. See Snehil Sinha, 'Another Day, Same Issue: No Walk-in Vax', *The Times of India*, 21 August 2021, https://timesofindia.indiatimes.com/city/noida/another-day-same-issue-no-walk-in-vax/articleshow/85501506.cms

34 Apar Gupta and Anushka Jain, 'India's Technocratic Approach to Vaccination Is Excluding the Digitally-Deprived', *The Indian Express*, 15 May 2021, https://indianexpress.com/article/opinion/columns/indias-technocratic-approach-to-vaccination-is-excluding-the-digitally-deprived-7315442/

35 Sarthak Dogra, 'Took Covid Vaccine Using Aadhaar? Your National Health ID Has Been Created Without Your Permission', *India Today*, 24 May 2021, https://www.indiatoday.in/technology/features/story/took-covid-vaccine-using-aadhaar-your-national-health-id-has-been-created-without-your-permission-1806470-2021-05-24

36 National Health Portal Indradhanush Immunization, https://www.nhp.gov.in/mobile-app-indradhanush

37 Government of Rajasthan, Department of Medical Health and Welfare, ttps://pctsrajmedical.raj.nic.in/private/login.aspx

38 Sections 3, 4, 5 and 6 of the Criminal Procedure Identification Act, 2022.

39 Harleen Kaur, 'Electronic Health Records in India: Legal Framework and Regulatory Issues'; Rina Chandran, 'Privacy Concerns as India Pushes Digital Health Plan, ID', Reuters, 22 September 2020, https://www.reuters.com/article/india-health-tech/analysis-privacy-concerns-as-india-pushes-digital-health-plan-id-idUKL8N2G536U

40 Neil Richards, 'The Dangers of Surveillance', *Harvard Law Review*, Vol. 126 2013, pp. 1934–1965.

41 For instance, the Indian government sold vehicle registration and driving license records to private companies. See Sidharth Mishra, 'Privacy Breach? Transport Ministry Selling Driving License, Vehicle Registration Data To Commercial Firms', *Outlook*, 15 July 2019, https://www.outlookindia.com/website/story/india-news-legal-or-not-why-has-the-roads-ministry-sold-our-data/334278

42 Richards, 'The Dangers of Surveillance'.

43 There are a number of harms that occur due to extensive collection and analysis of health data by private actors. These include financial and employment loss, discriminatory pricing of health services, loss of reputation and familial/community membership. These harms merit a separate and detailed examination.
44 John Sebastian and Aparajito Sen, 'Unravelling the Role of Autonomy and Consent in Privacy', *Indian Journal of Constitutional Law*, Vol. 9.
45 Solon Barocas and H. Nissenbaum, 'On Notice: The Trouble with Notice and Consent', Proceedings of the Engaging Data Forum: The First International Forum on the Application and Management of Personal Electronic Information, 2009.
46 Daniel J. Solove, 'Privacy Self Management and the Consent Dilemma', *Harvard Law Review*, 2013, p. 1880.
47 Solove, 'A Taxonomy of Privacy'.
48 Sneha Mahale, 'Are You Okay With Apps That Get Intimate?' *The New Indian Express*, 21 March 2020, https://www.newindianexpress.com/lifestyle/health/2020/mar/22/are-you-okay-with-apps-that-get-intimate-2118992.html
49 Drew Harwell, 'Is Your Pregnancy App Sharing Your Intimate Data With Your Boss?', *The Washington Post*, 11 April 2019, https://www.washingtonpost.com/technology/2019/04/10/tracking-your-pregnancy-an-app-may-be-more-public-than-you-think/
50 Jerry Beilson, 'Glow Pregnancy App Exposed Women to Privacy Threats, Consumer Report Finds', Consumer Report, September 2020, https://www.consumerreports.org/mobile-security-software/glow-pregnancy-app-exposed-women-to-privacy-threats/
51 Joy Buchanan, 'Court Rejects U.S. Bid to Subpoena Records of Planned Parenthood', *Los Angeles Times*, 6 March 2004, https://www.latimes.com/archives/la-xpm-2004-mar-06-me-files6-story.html
52 Sharifah Sekalala et al., 'Analyzing the Human Rights Impact of Increased Digital Public Health Surveillance during the COVID-19 Crisis', Health and Human Rights Journal, Vol. 22 No. 2, December 2020, pp. 7–20.
53 Notably, Article 15(2) of the Indian Constitution prohibits discrimination on the basis of these grounds by private individuals, companies as well as the state.
54 Alexandra Sternlicht, 'With New COVID-19 Outbreak Linked to Gay Man, Homophobia on Rise in South Korea', *Forbes*, 12 May 2020, https://www.forbes.com/sites/alexandrasternlicht/2020/05/12/with-new-covid-19-outbreak-linked-to-gay-man-homophobia-on-rise-in-south-korea/?sh=4cbb38ae4909

55 Scroll Staff, 'Covid-19: Mumbai Man Arrested For Refusing to Accept Groceries from Muslim Delivery Agent', *Scroll.in*, 23 April 2020, https://scroll.in/latest/960007/covid-19-mumbai-man-arrested-for-refusing-to-accept-groceries-from-muslim-delivery-agent

56 Hannah Ellis-Petersen and Sheikh Azizur Rahman, 'Coronavirus Conspiracy Theories Targeting Muslims Spread in India', *The Guardian*, 13 April 2020, https://www.theguardian.com/world/2020/apr/13/coronavirus-conspiracy-theories-targeting-muslims-spread-in-india

57 Mohammed Afeef, 'Does Law Allow Calls to Boycott Muslims During the COVID-19 Lockdown?' *The Wire*, 28 May 2020, https://thewire.in/communalism/covid-19-lockdown-muslims-boycott-law

58 Pratik Chakrabarti, 'Covid-19 and the Spectres of Colonialism', The India Forum, 9 July 2020, https://www.theindiaforum.in/article/covid-19-and-spectres-colonialism

59 Vrinda Bhandari and Karan Lahiri, 'The Surveillance State, Privacy and Criminal Investigation in India: Possible Futures in a Post-Puttaswamy World', *University of Oxford Human Rights Hub Journal*, Vol. 3 No. 2, 2020.

60 Michel Foucault, *Discipline and Punish: The Birth of the Prison*, translated by Alan Sheridan, New York: Vintage Books, 1979.

61 Solove, 'A Taxonomy of Privacy'.

62 Anand Venkat, 'The Aadhaar Judgment and Reality – III: On Surveillance', Indian Constitutional Law and Philosophy Blog, 2018, https://indconlawphil.wordpress.com/2018/10/02/the-aadhaar-judgment-and-reality-iii-on-surveillance-guest-post/

63 PEN America, 'Chilling Effects: NSA Surveillance Drives U.S. Writers to Self-Censor', 2013, https://pen.org/research-resources/chilling-effects/

64 Jeffrey H. Reiman, 'Driving to the Panopticon: A Philosophical Exploration of the Risks to Privacy Posed by the Highway Technology of the Future', *Santa Clara High Tech Law Journal*, Vol. 11 No. 27, 1995.

65 Maneka Rao, 'Why Aadhaar is Prompting HIV Positive People to drop out of Treatment Programmes Across India', *Scroll.in*, 17 November 2017, https://scroll.in/pulse/857656/across-india-hiv-positive-people-drop-out-of-treatment-programmes-as-centres-insist-on-aadhaar

66 Alex Marthews and Catherine Tucker, 'Government Surveillance and Internet Search Behavior', 2017, https://papers.ssrn.com/sol3/papers.cfm?abstract_id=2412564

67 See National Health Authority, National Digital Health Mission: Strategy Overview.

68 Rishab Bailey, Vrinda Bhandari, Smriti Parsheera and Faiza Rahman, 'Use of Personal Data by Intelligence and Law Enforcement Agencies', August 2018, https://macrofinance.nipfp.org.in/PDF/BBPR2018-Use-of-personal-data.pdf
69 A draft 'Health Data Management Policy' document was released by the government for public consultation. A draft 'Digital lnformation Security in Healthcare, Act (DISHA)' had also been released, https://www.nhp.gov.in/NHPfiles/R_4179_1521627488625_0.pdf. Thereafter, DISHA was submitted to Ministry of Electronics and Information Technology to be subsumed within the PDP Bill. Ministry of Health and Family Welfare, 'Data Transfer of Digital Health Records', Press Information Bureau, 16 July 2019, https://pib.gov.in/Pressreleaseshare.aspx?PRID=1578929
70 Rule 9, Pre-Conception and Pre-Natal Diagnostic Techniques (Prohibition of Sex Selection) Rules, 1996.
71 Section 29, PNDT Act. See also Section 22, Rights of Persons with Disabilities Act, 2016.
72 See Section 8(2) (f) of the HIV Act.
73 See ICMR, 'Specimen Referral Form for COVID-19', https://www.icmr.gov.in/pdf/covid/labs/archive/SRF_v11.pdf
74 Harleen Kaur, Ameya Paleja and Siddharth Srivastava, 'Legal and Regulatory Framework for Laboratory Testing in India: A Case Study for COVID-19', The Leap Blog, 2020, https://blog.theleapjournal.org/2020/07/legal-and-regulatory-framework-for.html
75 Bhandari and Rahman, 'Constitutionalism During a Crisis: The Case of Aarogya Setu'.
76 Sarthak Dogra, 'Took Covid Vaccine Using Aadhaar?'
77 Soumyarendra Barik, 'Govt Withdraws Data Protection Bill to Bring Revamped, Refreshed Regulation', *The Indian Express*, 4 August 2022, https://indianexpress.com/article/india/government-withdraws-data-protection-bill-8068257/.
78 Clause 2(21), PDP Bill.
79 Clause 35, PDP Bill.
80 Rishab Bailey, Vrinda Bhandari, Smriti Parsheera and Faiza Rahman, 'Comments on the Draft Personal Data Protection Bill, 2019', The Leap Blog, 2020, https://blog.theleapjournal.org/2020/04/comments-on-draft-personal-data.html.
81 *KS Puttaswamy v. Union of India*, 10 SCC 1 (2017); *KS Puttaswamy v. Union of India* (2019) 1 SCC 1.

82 Section 33(2), Aadhaar (Targeted Delivery of Financial and Other Subsidies, Benefits and Services) Act, 2016.
83 Coronavirus (COVID-19) Infection Survey: Methods and Further information, https://www.ons.gov.uk/peoplepopulationandcommunity/healthandsocialcare/conditionsanddiseases/methodologies/covid19infectionsurveypilotmethodsandfurtherinformation

13. Health Tracking Technologies: Privacy and Public Health

1 Shoshana Zuboff, *The Age of Surveillance Capitalism: The Fight for a Human Future at the New Frontier of Power*, Hachette UK, 2019.
2 Zuboff, *The Age of Surveillance Capitalism*.
3 Rachael Kent, 'Self-Tracking Health Over Time: From the Use of Instagram to Perform Optimal Health to the Protective Shield of the Digital Detox', *Social Media + Society*, Vol. 6 No. 3, 1 July 2020, https://doi.org/10.1177/2056305120940694
4 'Best Pulse Oximeters to Keep a Check on Your SpO2 Readings', *Business Insider*, https://www.businessinsider.in/insider-reviews/best-pulse-oximeters-to-keep-a-check-on-your-spo2-readings/articleshow/82192832.cms
5 'Oxitone 1000M', *Oxitone*, https://www.oxitone.com/oxitone-1000m/; Delaram Jarchi et al., 'Estimation of HRV and SpO2 from Wrist-Worn Commercial Sensors for Clinical Settings', in *2018 IEEE 15th International Conference on Wearable and Implantable Body Sensor Networks (BSN)*, 2018, pp. 144–47, https://doi.org/10.1109/BSN.2018.8329679
6 'MH2O App', MobileH2O, LLC, https://www.mobileh2o.com/mh2oapp
7 Chia-Fang Chung, Nanna Gorm, Irina A. Shklovski and Sean Munson, 'Finding the Right Fit: Understanding Health Tracking in Workplace Wellness Programs', in *Proceedings of the 2017 CHI Conference on Human Factors in Computing Systems*, CHI '17, New York, Association for Computing Machinery, 2017, pp. 4875–86, https://doi.org/10.1145/3025453.3025510; Elizabeth A. Brown, 'The Fitbit Fault Line: Two Proposals to Protect Health and Fitness Data at Work', *Yale Journal of Health Policy, Law and Ethics*, Vol. 16, 2016, p. 1; Laurie Giddens, Dorothy Leidner, and Ester Gonzalez, 'The Role of Fitbits in Corporate Wellness Programs: Does Step Count Matter?', 2017, https://doi.org/10.24251/HICSS.2017.438

8 For instance, see Ruth Ravichandran, Sang-Wha Sien, Shwetak N. Patel, Julie A. Kientz and Laura R. Pina, 'Making Sense of Sleep Sensors: How Sleep Sensing Technologies Support and Undermine Sleep Health,' in *Proceedings of the 2017 CHI Conference on Human Factors in Computing Systems*, CHI '17, New York, Association for Computing Machinery, 2017, pp. 6864–75, https://doi.org/10.1145/3025453.3025557
9 See Kent, 'Self-Tracking Health Over Time'.
10 Radhika Radhakrishnan, 'Health Data as Wealth: Understanding Patient Rights in India within a Digital Ecosystem through a Feminist Approach', Data Governance Network Working Paper No.19, October 2021.
11 Btihaj Ajana, *Metric Culture: Ontologies of Self-Tracking Practices*, Emerald Group Publishing, 2018, p. 2.
12 For more on the impact of datafication of bodies, see Anja Kovacs, 'When Our Bodies Become Data, Where Does That Leave Us?', Medium, 8 June 2020, https://deepdives.in/when-our-bodies-become-data-where-does-that-leave-us-906674f6a969
13 Chia-Fang Chung, Nanna Gorm, Irina A. Shklovski and Sean Munson, 'Finding the Right Fit'; Chantal Lidynia, Philipp Brauner, and Martina Ziefle, 'A Step in the Right Direction – Understanding Privacy Concerns and Perceived Sensitivity of Fitness Trackers', in Tareq Ahram and Christianne Falcão (eds.), *Advances in Human Factors in Wearable Technologies and Game Design*, Cham: Springer International Publishing, 2018, pp. 42–53, https://doi.org/10.1007/978-3-319-60639-2_5; Jessica Vitak, Yuting Liao, Priya Kumar, Michael Zimmer and Katherine Kritikos, 'Privacy Attitudes and Data Valuation Among Fitness Tracker Users', in *Transforming Digital Worlds*, Cham: Springer International Publishing, 2018, pp. 229–39, https://doi.org/10.1007/978-3-319-78105-1_27
14 Leah R. Fowler, Charlotte Gillard and Stephanie Morain, 'Teenage Use of Smartphone Applications for Menstrual Cycle Tracking', *Pediatrics*, Vol. 145 No. 5, 1 May 2020, https://doi.org/10.1542/peds.2019-2954
15 Recent amendments to the Medical Devices Rules, 2017 have expanded the scope of medical devices, suggesting that more devices will be regulated with a heavier hand going forward. However, as at the time of writing there are no additional regulatory requirements applicable to such devices in the context of collection and processing of user data.
16 'Govt Withdraws Data Protection Bill, 2021,' *The Economic Times*, 4 August 2022, https://economictimes.indiatimes.com/tech/technology/govt-withdraws-data-protection-bill-2021/articleshow/93334281.cms

17 Graham Greenleaf, 'Global Data Privacy Laws 2021: Despite COVID Delays, 145 Laws Show GDPR Dominance', Privacy Laws & Business International Report 169 No. 1 2021 pp. 3-5, http://classic.austlii.edu.au/au/journals/UNSWLRS/2021/60.html
18 Rule 2(i), Information Technology (Reasonable Security Practices and Procedures and Sensitive Personal Data or Information) Rules, 2011.
19 Rule 3, ibid.
20 Article 4(15) of the UK GDPR.
21 The UK's independent authority set up to uphold information rights in the public interest, promoting openness by public bodies and data privacy for individuals.
22 'What Is Special Category Data?', Information Commissioner's Office, 1 January 2021, https://ico.org.uk/for-organisations/guide-to-data-protection/guide-to-the-general-data-protection-regulation-gdpr/special-category-data/what-is-special-category-data/
23 Clause 3(36), Personal Data Protection Bill, 2019.
24 'The Quantified Self in Precarity: Work, Technology and What Counts', Routledge & CRC Press, n.d., https://www.routledge.com/The-Quantified-Self-in-Precarity-Work-Technology-and-What-Counts/Moore/p/book/9780367872908; Kate Crawford, Jessa Lingel and Tero Karppi, 'Our Metrics, Ourselves: A Hundred Years of Self-Tracking from the Weight Scale to the Wrist Wearable Device,' *European Journal of Cultural Studies*, Vol. 18, No. 4–5, 1 August 2015, pp. 479–96, https://doi.org/10.1177/1367549415584857
25 Crawford, Lingel and Karppi, 'Our Metrics, Ourselves'.
26 Lidynia, Brauner and Ziefle, 'A Step in the Right Direction – Understanding Privacy Concerns and Perceived Sensitivity of Fitness Trackers'; Vitak et al., 'Privacy Attitudes and Data Valuation Among Fitness Tracker Users.'
27 Described in this case as a concept attributed to user's lack of awareness of privacy issues associated with use of such platforms and lack of knowledge of ways to protect privacy. See Vitak et al., 'Privacy Attitudes and Data Valuation Among Fitness Tracker Users.'
28 Sandra Gabriele and Sonia Chiasson, 'Understanding Fitness Tracker Users' Security and Privacy Knowledge, Attitudes and Behaviours', in *Proceedings of the 2020 CHI Conference on Human Factors in Computing Systems*, New York, Association for Computing Machinery, 2020, pp. 1–12, https://doi.org/10.1145/3313831.3376651
29 Vitak et al., 'Privacy Attitudes and Data Valuation Among Fitness Tracker Users'.

30 Clause 15, Personal Data Protection Bill, 2019.
31 Crawford, Lingel and Karppi, 'Our Metrics, Ourselves'; WIRED Staff, 'Know Thyself: Tracking Every Facet of Life, from Sleep to Mood to Pain, 24/7/365', *Wired*, n.d., https://www.wired.com/2009/06/lbnp-knowthyself/
32 Crawford, Lingel and Karppi, 'Our Metrics, Ourselves'.
33 Section 27, Personal Data Protection Bill, 2019; 'Data Protection Impact Assessments', Information Commissioner's Office, 11 January 2021, https://ico.org.uk/for-organisations/guide-to-data-protection/guide-to-the-general-data-protection-regulation-gdpr/accountability-and-governance/data-protection-impact-assessments/
34 Ana C. Rivera-Rios, 'Gaps and Overlaps in US Data Health Privacy Oversight: Preventing Health Tech Consumer and Patient Health Data From Becoming the Product', *Journal of Healthcare Finance*, 19 June 2020, https://www.healthfinancejournal.com/index.php/johcf/article/view/225
35 For instance, a study that involved a survey of healthcare professionals in Austria suggested that medical doctors and professionals may have a less favourable impression of the positive benefits of ICT-based health services, see Daniela Haluza and David Jungwirth, 'ICT and the Future of Healthcare: Aspects of Pervasive Health Monitoring,' *Informatics for Health and Social Care* 43, Vol. No. 1, 2 January 2018, pp. 1–11, https://doi.org/10.1080/17538157.2016.1255215
36 Transcript, Federal Trade Commission, Spring Privacy Series, Consumer Generated and Controlled Health Data, 7 May 2014; Lee Tien, 'Big Data Profits If We Deregulate HIPAA', Electronic Frontier Foundation, 10 June 2021, https://www.eff.org/deeplinks/2021/06/big-data-profits-if-we-deregulate-hipaa
37 The Editorial Board, 'Smartwatches and Weak Privacy Rules', *The New York Times*, 16 September 2014, https://www.nytimes.com/2014/09/16/opinion/smartwatches-and-weak-privacy-rules.html
38 Brown, 'The Fitbit Fault Line'.
39 See Brown, 'The Fitbit Fault Line'; Giddens, Leidner, and Gonzalez, 'The Role of Fitbits in Corporate Wellness Programs'; Macy Bayern, 'Why Corporate Wellness Programs Are More Important than Ever', *TechRepublic*, 29 April 2020, https://www.techrepublic.com/article/why-corporate-wellness-programs-are-more-important-than-ever/
40 Giddens, Leidner and Gonzalez, 'The Role of Fitbits in Corporate Wellness Programs'.

41 Brown, 'The Fitbit Fault Line'.
42 Philippa M. Collins and Stefania Marassi, 'Is That Lawful?: Data Privacy and Fitness Trackers in the Workplace', *International Journal of Comparative Labour Law*, Vol. 37 No. 1, 1 February 2021, https://research-information.bris.ac.uk/en/publications/is-that-lawful-data-privacy-and-fitness-trackers-in-the-workplace
43 Clause 13, Personal Data Protection Bill, 2019.
44 Ibid.
45 'Data Protection In The Indian Insurance Sector – Regulatory Framework Part I - Insurance - India', *Mondaq*, https://www.mondaq.com/india/insurance-laws-and-products/809122/data-protection-in-the-indian-insurance-sector-regulatory-framework-part-i
46 Crawford, Lingel and Karppi, 'Our Metrics, Ourselves'; Collins and Marassi, 'Is That Lawful?'
47 B.N. Srikrishna et al., 'Report of the Committee of Experts on A Free and Fair Digital Economy: Protecting Privacy, Empowering Indians', 2018, https://meity.gov.in/writereaddata/files/Data_Protection_Committee_Report.pdf
48 Jack M. Balkin, 'Information Fiduciaries and the First Amendment', *U.C. Davis Law Review*, Vol. 49, 2016, pp. 1183–1234.
49 Smitha Krishna Prasad, 'It's A Matter of Trust: Exploring Data Fiduciaries in India', *Data Catalyst*, https://datacatalyst.org/reports/its-a-matter-of-trust-exploring-data-fiduciaries-in-india/
50 Ibid.
51 Crawford, Lingel and Karppi, 'Our Metrics, Ourselves'.
52 Renae Cheng, 'The National Steps Challenge™ Season 4 Lets You Win A Pair of SQ New York Business Class Tickets By Tracking Your Physical Activity', *TheSmartLocal*, 5 November 2018, https://thesmartlocal.com/read/national-steps-challenge-2018/
53 'LiveHealthy SG: What Is It and When Can Singaporeans Sign Up?,' https://sg.finance.yahoo.com/news/live-healthy-sg-hpb-fitbit-003335075.html
54 'FAQs,' Lu, https://www.lumihealth.sg/faq#getting-started-4
55 'Live Healthy SG'
56 'Health Insights Singapore (HISG) Sg100k,' n.d., https://www.hpb.gov.sg/hisg/sg100k
57 'Privacy Statement,' n.d., https://www.hpb.gov.sg/privacy-statement.
58 'Norwegian DPA: Ålesund Municipality Fined for Use of Strava, European Data Protection Board', n.d., https://edpb.europa.eu/news/

national-news/2021/norwegian-dpa-alesund-municipality-fined-use-strava_en

59 Press Release, 'Khelo India Supports India Steps Challenge to Encourage Healthy Lifestyle', InsideSport (blog), 14 March 2019, https://www.insidesport.co/khelo-india-supports-india-steps-challenge-to-encourage-healthy-lifestyle/; 'GOQii Charts 2020 Roadmap of New Products, Services and Partnerships', Express Healthcare (blog), 5 December 2019, https://www.expresshealthcare.in/news/goqii-charts-2020-roadmap-of-new-products-services-and-partnerships/415613/

60 'Big Data and Reproductive Health in India: A Case Study of the Mother and Child Tracking System', The Centre for Internet and Society, n.d., https://cis-india.org/raw/big-data-reproductive-health-india-mcts

61 H. Ceren Ates, Ali K. Yetisen, Firat Güder and Can Dincer, 'Wearable Devices for the Detection of COVID-19', *Nature Electronics*, Vol. 4, No. 1, January 2021, pp. 13–14, https://doi.org/10.1038/s41928-020-00533-1; Md Milon Islam et al., 'Wearable Technology to Assist the Patients Infected with Novel Coronavirus (COVID-19)', *SN Computer Science*, Vol. 1 No. 6, 1 October 2020, p. 320, https://doi.org/10.1007/s42979-020-00335-4; 'Empatica's Wearable Technology Receives CE Mark for COVID-19 Detection', n.d., https://www.medicaldevice-network.com/news/empatica-wearable-technology-covid-19/

62 Md Milon Islam, Saifuddin Mahmud, L.J. Muhammad, Md Rabiul Islam, Sheikh Nooruddin and Safial Islam Ayon, 'Wearable Technology to Assist the Patients Infected with Novel Coronavirus'.

63 'How Wearable Tech Is Combating COVID-19 in the Workplace', n.d., https://www.supplychainbrain.com/blogs/1-think-tank/post/32742-how-wearable-tech-is-combating-covid-19-in-the-workplace; 'Wearable Devices May Help Stop COVID-19 Workplace Spread,' Business Insurance, n.d., http://www.businessinsurance.com/article/20210401/NEWS08/912340646/Wearable-devices-may-help-stop-COVID-19-workplace-spread-coronavirus-pandemic-vi

64 Ida Tin, 'The Journey of a Single Data Point: What Happens to Your Period Tracking Data', n.d., https://helloclue.com/articles/about-clue/the-journey-of-a-single-data-point; Shivam Soni, 'Explorer | The Data Economy Lab', The Data Economy Lab (blog), 12 June 2020, https://thedataeconomylab.com/tracking-stewardship/

65 'Ginger Research', n.d., https://www.ginger.com/research

66 'Research Pledge, Fitbit Health Solutions', n.d., https://healthsolutions.fitbit.com/research-pledge/; 'Researchers FAQs',

Fitbit Health Solutions, n.d., https://healthsolutions.fitbit.com/researchers/faqs/
67 Article 89 of the GDPR.
68 Clause 38 of the PDP Bill.
69 Aditya Chunduru, '"Bonded Labour": ... Sanitation Workers in Chandigarh Protest against Being Forced to Wear GPS Tracking Devices', *MediaNama*, 28 October 2020, https://www.medianama.com/2020/10/223-chandigarh-smart-watches-sanitation-workers/
70 Crawford, Lingel and Karppi, 'Our Metrics, Ourselves'.

14: Data Stewardship: Solutions for Sharing of Health Data

1   World Health Organisation, 'Background Briefing for WHO Consultation on Data and Results Sharing During Public', 2015, https://www.who.int/medicines/ebola-treatment/background_briefing_on_data_results_sharing_during_phes.pdf
2   WHO, 'Background briefing on data sharing'.
3   Vasee Moorthy, Ana Maria Henao Restrepo, Marie-Pierre Preziosi and Soumya Swaminathan, 'Data Sharing for Novel Coronavirus', *Bull World Health Organ*, Vol. 98 No. 150, 2020, doi: http://dx.doi.org/10.2471/BLT.20.251561
4   Moorthy et al., 'Data Sharing for Novel Coronavirus'.
5   The Bermuda Principles set out rules for the rapid and public release of DNA sequence data. The Human Genome Project, a multinational effort to sequence the human genome, generated vast quantities of data about the genetic make-up of humans and other organisms.
6   Charlie Warzel, 'All Your Data Is Health Data', *The New York Times*, August 2021, https://www.nytimes.com/2019/08/13/opinion/health-data.html
7   Tamar Sharon, 'Blind-sided by Privacy? Digital Contact Tracing, the Apple/Google API and Big Tech's Newfound Role as Global Health Policy Makers'. *Ethics and Information Technology*, Vol. 23 No. 1, 2021, pp. 45–57.
8   Nina Schwalbe, Brian Wahl, Jingyi Song and Susanna Lehtimaki, 'Data Sharing and Global Public Health: Defining What We Mean by Data', *Frontiers in Digital Health*, 2:612339 (2021). doi: 10.3389/fdgth.2020.612339
9   Ernst and Young, 'Realising the Value of Healthcare Data: A Framework for the Future', 2019.

10 Wellcome, 'Data Sharing in Public Health Emergencies'. https://wellcome.org/what-we-do/our-work/data-sharing-public-health-emergencies.

11 Urs Gasser, Marcello Ienca, James Scheibner, Joanna Sleigh and Effy Vayena, 'Digital Tools Against COVID-19: Taxonomy, Ethical Challenges, and Navigation Aid', *The Lancent Digital Health*, Vol. 2 No. 8, 2020, pp. e425-e434.

12 Ajeet Mahale. 'BMC's 24×7 Decentralised "War rooms" Helping Stem COVID-19 Cases in Mumbai', *Down to Earth*, May 2021.

13 James Wilson, Daniel Herron, Parashkev Nachev and Nick McNally, 'The Value of Data: Applying a Public Value Model to the English National Health Service,' *Journal of Medical Internet Research*, 2020.

14 Ibid.

15 Ed Yong, 'How Science Beat the Virus', *The Atlantic*, February 2021, https://www.theatlantic.com/magazine/archive/2021/01/science-COVID-19-manhattan-project/617262/

16 Nuffield Council on Bioethics, 'The Collection, Linking and Use of Data in Biomedical Research and Healthcare', 2015, https://www.nuffieldbioethics.org/wp-content/uploads/Biological_and_health_data_web.pdf

17 Sarah Cheung, 'Disambiguating the Benefits and Risks from Public Health Data in the Digital Economy', *Big Data and Society*, Vol. 7 No. 1, 2020.

18 Sharon, 'Blind-sided by Privacy?'

19 Mhairi Aitken, Jenna de St Jorre, Claudia Pagliari, Ruth Jepson and Sarah Cunningham-Burley, 'Public Responses to the Sharing and Linkage of Health Data for Research Purposes: A Systematic Review and Thematic Synthesis of Qualitative Studies', *BMC Med Ethics*, Vol. 17 No. 1, 2016, p. 73, doi: 10.1186/s12910-016-0153-x

20 Understanding Patient Data, 'Public Attitudes to Patient Data Use', September 2018, https://understandingpatientdata.org.uk/sites/default/files/2020-10/Public%20attitudes%202010-2018.pdf

21 Daniel J. Solove, 'A Taxonomy of Privacy', *University of Pennsylvania Law Review*, Vol. 154 No. 3, 2006, pp. 477–558.

22 Internet Freedom Foundation, 2021, https://internetfreedom.in/page/4/

23 Soujanya Sridharana, Siddharth Manohar and Astha Kapoor, 'Health Data Stewardship: Learning from Use Cases', Aapti Institute, July 2021, https://thedataeconomylab.com/wp-content/uploads/2021/09/Aapti-Combined-Updated-w-Foreword.pdf

24 OECD, 'Health Data Governance: Privacy, Monitoring and Research', 2015.
25 Department of Health and Social Care, UK Government. 'New Data Strategy Launched to Improve Patient Care and Save Lives', 2021, https://www.gov.uk/government/news/new-data-strategy-launched-to-improve-patient-care-and-save-lives
26 Department of Health and Social Care, 'New Data Strategy'.
27 Saraa Malkamaki, 'Findata and Finnish Legislation on Secondary Use of Health Data', 2019, tinyurl.com/32r9ts53
28 Malkamaki, 'Findata and Finnish Legislation'.
29 The Act on the Secondary Use of Health and Social Data, 2019, can be accessed here: https://stm.fi/documents/1271139/1365571/The+Act+on+the+Secondary+Use+of+Health+and+Social+Data/a2bca08c-d067-3e54-45d1-18096de0ed76/The+Act+on+the+Secondary+Use+of+Health+and+Social+Data.pdf
30 Sridharana et al., 'Health Data Stewardship'.
31 Ibid.
32 Government of India. 'Personal Data Protection Bill', 2019.
33 Mohan Basu, 'What Modi Govt's 'DNA Bank' Will Look Like and the Concerns Over Its Misuse', *The Print*, October 2019, https://theprint.in/theprint-essential/modi-govts-dna-bank-and-concerns-over-its-misuse/309463/
34 Inika Charles, Aaron Kamath and Huzefa Tavawalla, 'Indian Judiciary's Take on Storage of COVID-19 Data Outside India', Nishith Desai Associates, June 2020, https://nishithdesai.com/information/news-storage/news-details/article/indian-judiciarys-take-on-storage-of-COVID-19-patient-data-outside-india.html
35 Kerala High Court, WP (C) Temp. No. 84 (2020), 24 April 2021.
36 Internet Freedom Foundation, Joint Statement: Ensure equitable access to COVID-19 vaccines and health care resources, 2021, https://internetfreedom.in/joint-statement-ensure-equitable-access-to-covid-vaccines/
37 National Digital Health Mission. 'Strategy Overview, NDHM', July 2020, https://ndhm.gov.in/documents/ndhm_strategy_overview.
38 Soujanya Sridharana, Siddharth Manohar and Astha Kapoor, 'Health Data Stewardship'.
39 Ibid.
40 Susan Bull et al., 'Best Practices for Ethical Sharing of Individual-Level Health Research Data From Low- and Middle-Income Settings'. *J Empir Res Hum Res Ethics*, 2015, pp. 302–313.

41 Bull et al., 'Best Practices for Ethical Sharing'.
42 Ibid.
43 Sridharana et al., 'Health Data Stewardship'.
44 Siddharth Manohar, Astha Kapoor and A. Ramesh, 'Data Stewardship – A Taxonomy', Aapti Institute, 2019.
45 T.C. Turin, I. Naeem, Akmn Nurul, M. Vaska, S. Goopy, R. Rashid, A. Kassan, F. Aghajafari, I. Ferrer, A. Kazi, I. Sadi, M. O'Beirne and C. Leduc, 'Community-based Health Data Cooperatives Towards Improving the Immigrant Community Health: A Scoping Review to Inform Policy and Practice', *International Journal Population Data Science*, Vol. 5 No. 1, June 2020, p. 1158, doi: 10.23889/ijpds.v5i1.1158
46 App Drivers and Courier Union, 'Uber Drivers Take Unprecedented International Legal Action to Demand Their Data', 2021, https://www.adcu.org.uk/news-posts/uber-drivers-take-unprecedented-international-legal-action-to-demand-their-data
47 Nesta, 'Midata.coop', https://www.nesta.org.uk/feature/me-my-data-and-i/midatacoop/
48 Turin et al., 'Community-based Health Data Cooperatives'.
49 Ibid.
50 Health Data Collaborative, https://www.healthdatacollaborative.org/.
51 S. Delacroix and N. Lawrence, 'Bottom-up Data Trusts: Disturbing the "One Size Fits All" Approach to Data Governance', *International Data Privacy Law*, 2019, pp. 236–252.
52 Variant Bio, https://www.variantbio.com/

15: Artificial Intelligence and Healthcare

1 John McCarthy and Patrick Hayes, 'Some Philosophical Problems from the Standpoint of Artificial Intelligence', in B. Melzer and Donald Michie (eds.), *Machine Intelligence*, Edinburgh University Press, 1969.
2 Ajay Agrawal, Joshua Gans and Avi Goldfarb, *Prediction Machines*, Harvard Business Review Press, 2018.
3 Patrick Gother, Mei Ngan and Kayee Hanaoka, 'Face Recognition Vendor Test Part 3: Demographic Effects', NIST Interagency/Internal Report- NSTIR 8280, 2019, https://doi.org/10.6028/NIST.IR.8280.
4 Chayakrit Krittanawong, HongJu Zhang, Zhen Wang, Mehmet Aydar and Takeshi Kitai, 'Artificial Intelligence in Precision Cardiovascular Medicine', *Journal of Amercan College of Cardiology 69*, Vol. No. 21, 30 May 2017, pp. 2657–2664.

5   Jennifer Yang Hui and Dymples Leong, 'The Era of Ubiquitous Listening: Living in a World of Speech-Activated Devices', Research Paper No. 17–21, Lee Kuan Yew School of Public Policy (2017), https://ssrn.com/abstract=3021623
6   Patil and Ajay Rasave, 'Artificial Intelligence Chat Bot for Counselling Therapy', *SSRN*, 7 May 2021, https://ssrn.com/abstract=3866861
7   Tom B. Brown, Benjamin Mann, Nick Ryder, Melanie Subbiah, Jared Kaplan, Prafulla Dhariwal, Arvind Neelakantan, Pranav Shyam, Girish Sastry, Amanda Askell, Sandhini Agarwal, Ariel Herbert-Voss, Gretchen Krueger, Tom Henighan, Rewon Child, Aditya Ramesh, Daniel M. Ziegler, Jeffrey Wu, Clemens Winter, Christopher Hesse, Mark Chen, Eric Sigler, Mateusz Litwin, Scott Gray, Benjamin Chess, Jack Clark, Christopher Berner, Sam McCandlish, Alec Radford, Ilya Sutskever and Dario Amodei, 'Language Models are few short learners', *arXiv*, 22 July, 2020, arXiv:2005.14165v4.
8   Brandon Walker, 'The Games That AI Won', *Towards data science*, 15 March 2020, https://towardsdatascience.com/the-games-that-ai-won-ff8fd4a71efc
9   Ajay Agarwal, *Prediction Machines*.
10 Ibid.
11 Rahul C. Deo, 'Machine Learning in Medicine', *Circulation*, Vol. 132 No. 20, 2015, https://dx.doi.org/10.1161%2FCIRCULATIONAHA.115.001593
12 Ibid.
13 Ibid.
14 Jussi Tohka and Mark van Gils, 'Evaluation of Machine Learning Algorithms for Health and Wellness Applications: A Tutorial', *Computers in Biology and Medicine*, Vol. 132 No. 104324, 2021, https://doi.org/10.1016/j.compbiomed.2021.104324
15 Venkatesh Rao, 'Superhistory and Not Superintelligence', Breakingsmart (blog), 12 May 2021, https://breakingsmart.substack.com/p/superhistory-not-superintelligence
16 The same information the subject of study collected over multiple points in time.
17 Will Douglas Heaven, 'Hundreds of AI Tools Built to Catch Covid. None of Them Helped', Technology Review (blog), 30 July 2021, https://www.technologyreview.com/2021/07/30/1030329/machine-learning-ai-failed-covid-hospital-diagnosis-pandemic/
18 Ayanna Howard, and Jason Borenstein, 'The Ugly Truth About Ourselves and Our Robot Creations: The Problem of Bias and Social

Inequity', *Science and Engineering Ethics*, Vol. 24 No. 1521, 2018, https://doi.org/https://doi.org/10.1007/s11948-017-9975-2

19 Barry R. Furrow, 'Searching for Adverse Events: Big Data and Beyond', *Annals of Health Law*, Vol. 27 No. 149, 2018, https://lawecommons.luc.edu/annals/vol27/iss2/5/

20 Claire Munoz Parry and Urvashi Aneja, 'Artificial Intelligence for Healthcare: Insights From India', Chatham House Research, 30 July 2020, https://www.chathamhouse.org/2020/07/artificial-intelligence-healthcare-insights-india-0/3-ai-healthcare-india-applications

21 Ibid.

22 Radhika Radhakrishnan, 'Interrogating the AI Hype: A Situated Politics of Machine Learning in Indian Healthcare,' *EPW*, 27 May 2021, https://www.epw.in/engage/article/interrogating-ai-hype-situated-politics-machine

23 In 2016 a Mumbai based diagnostic laboratory was hacked leading to a leakage of health records of 35,000 persons. Parry and Aneja, 'Artificial Intelligence for Healthcare'.

24 NSS, 'Key Indicators of Social Consumption in India', November 2019, http://mospi.nic.in/sites/default/files/publication_reports/KI_Health_75th_Final.pdf

25 Data from NSS from round 71st to 75th suggest a percentage decline in small practitioners/clinics, an increase in public health centres and roughly no percentage change in private hospitals. The percentage use of private hospitals is higher in urban areas in both reports.

26 Adam C. Powell et al., 'Digitizing Indian Health Records', *ISB Insight*, 28 August 2018, https://isbinsight.isb.edu/digitising-indian-healthcare-records/

27 Adam Bohr and Kaveh Memarzadeh, 'Current Healthcare, Big Data, and Machine Learning,' in Adam Bohr and Kaveh Memarzadeh (eds.), *Artificial Intelligence in Healthcare*, Academic Press, 2020, pp. 1–24, https://www.sciencedirect.com/science/article/pii/B9780128184387000010

28 Ministry of Health and Family Welfare, 'National Digital Health Blueprint', April 2019, https://www.nhp.gov.in/NHPfiles/National_Digital_Health_Blueprint_Report_comments_invited.pdf

29 Louis Enriquez-Sarano, 'Data-Rich and Knowledge-Poor: How Privacy Law Privatized Medical Data and What to do About it', *Columbia Law Review*, Vol. 120 No.8, 2020, pp. 2319–58, www.jstor.org/stable/26965837

30 Wei-Chun Lin, Jimmy S. Chen, Michael F. Chiang and Michelle R Hribar, 'Applications of Artificial Intelligence to Electronic Health Record Data

in Ophthalmology,' *Translational Vision Science & Technology*, Vol. 9 No. 13, February 2020, https://doi.org/10.1167/tvst.9.2.13

31 Abhinav Verma, Krisstina Rao, Vivek Eluri and Yukti Sharma, 'Regulating AI in Public Health: System Challenges and Perspectives', ORF Occasional Paper No. 261, July 2020, https://www.orfonline.org/research/regulating-ai-in-public-health-systems-challenges-and-perspectives/

32 Manohara M.M. Pai Raghavendra Ganiga, Radhika M. Pai and Rajesh Kumar Sinha, 'Standard Electronic Health Record (EHR) Framework for Indian Healthcare System' *Health Services and Outcomes Research Methodology*, Vol. 21, 2021, pp. 339–62, https://doi.org/10.1007/s10742-020-00238-0

33 Suptendra Nath Sarbadhikari, 'The Role of Standards for Digital Health and Information Management', *Journal of Basic and Clinical Research*, Vol. 6 No. 1, 2019–20, pp. 4–9, https://jbcr.net.in/JBCR-VOL-6-issue-1-2019-20/pdf/1.pdf

34 Kathryn Montgomery Jeff Chester and Katharina Kopp, 'Health Wearables: Ensuring Fairness, Preventing Discrimination, and Promoting Equity in an Emerging Internet-of-Things Environment', *Journal of Information Policy*, Vol. 8, 2018, p. 37, www.jstor.org/stable/10.5325/jinfopoli.8.2018.0034

35 'Continuous Glucose Monitoring', National Institute of Diabetes and Digestive and Kidney Diseases, US Department of Health and Human Services, https://www.niddk.nih.gov/health-information/diabetes/overview/managing-diabetes/continuous-glucose-monitoring

36 Kim Ann Zimmermann, 'Heart Rate Monitors: How They Work?', *Livescience*, 28 December 2013, https://www.livescience.com/42220-heart-rate-monitors.html

37 Husain Sumra, 'How FDA approval affects your wearables, and how its going to change', *Wareable*, 17 January 2018, https://www.wareable.com/wearable-tech/fda-wearables-state-of-play-239

38 'Kinsa Smart Thermometers,' Kinsa, https://kinsahealth.com/thermometers.

39 'Dr Trust Smart Weighing Scales,' Dr. Trust, https://drtrust.in/products/dr-trust-smart-connect-body-fat-scale-2-0

40 'Fitbit Sense', Fitbit, https://www.fitbit.com/global/us/technology/sleep

41 'Omron Heart Guide', OMRON, https://omronhealthcare.com/products/heartguide-wearable-blood-pressure-monitor-bp8000m/

42 Keshav Shree Mudgal and Neeranjan Das, 'The ethical adoption of artificial intelligence in radiology,' *The British Journal of Radiology*, Vol. 2 No. 1, 2019, https://www.birpublications.org/doi/full/10.1259/bjro.20190020

43 Larry Goldenberg, Guy Nir and Septimiu E. Salcudean, 'A New Era: Artificial Intelligence and Machine Learning in Prostate Cancer', *Nature Reviews Urology*, Vol. 16, 2019, p. 391, https://doi.org/10.1038/s41585-019-0193-3

44 Artificial intelligence performs better at radiology than human doctors. Ahmed Hosny Chintan Parmar, John Quackenbush, Lawrence H. Schwartz and Hugo J.W.L. Aerts, 'Artificial Intelligence in Radiology' *Nature Reviews Cancer*, Vol. 18 No. 8, 17 August 2018, pp. 500–10, https://doi.org/10.1038/s41568-018-0016-5

45 An algorithm developed by Google is now screening patients of diabetic retinopathy in Aravind Eye Hospital in Madurai. Christina Farr, 'Google Launches India Program to Screen Diabetics for Eye Conditions that Can Cause Blindness,' *CNBC*, 25 February 2019, https://www.cnbc.com/2019/02/25/google-verily-launch-diabetic-eye-condition-screening-tech-in-india.html

46 Syndromic surveillance refers to the process of detecting individual and population health indicators before actual diagnosis has been made.

47 Target was able to predict if women were in their second trimester of pregnancy, or in their first twenty weeks or if they are approaching delivery date by analyzing a number of shopping patterns. Tyler J. Smith, 'Haystack in a Hurricane: Mandated Disclosure and the Sectoral Approach to the Right to Privacy' *Yale Journal on Regulation*, Bulletin, 12 February 2020, https://www.yalejreg.com/bulletin/haystack-in-a-hurricane-mandated-disclosure-and-the-sectoral-approach-to-the-right-to-privacy/

48 Logan Kugler, 'What Happens When Big Data Blunders', *Communications of the ACM*, Vol. 5 No. 6, 2016, p. 15, https://dl.acm.org/doi/fullHtml/10.1145/2911975

49 Mollie Bloudoff-Indelicato, 'This Company Claims its Smart Thermometer Could Help Detect Coronavirus Hot Spots Faster Than the CDC', *CNBC*, 2 April 2020, https://www.cnbc.com/2020/04/02/this-smart-thermometer-could-help-detect-covid-19-hot-spots.html

50 Rahul Matthan, 'Skinny Solstice', *Livemint*, 9 January 2018, https://www.livemint.com/Opinion/2TV4ygFnhiENPzeUzJV92K/Skinny-Solstice.html

51 'Home, Health Heatmap of India', https://healthheatmapindia.org/

52 Diseases that spread to humans from animal hosts.

53 Bibhu Ranjan Mishra, 'Aarogya Setu Data Help in Accurately Predicting Covid-19 Hot spots', *Business Standard*, 10 May 2020, https://www.business-standard.com/article/current-affairs/aarogya-setu-data-helping-detect-covid-19-hot spots-accurately-report-120051000323_1.html

54 Rahul Matthan, 'Aarogya Setu and the Value of Syndromic Surveillance', *Livemint*, 13 May 2020, https://www.livemint.com/opinion/columns/aarogya-setu-and-the-value-of-syndromic-surveillance-11589304017285.html

55 Linus Bengtsson Jean Gaudart, Xin Lu, Sandra Moore, Erik Wetter, Kankoe Sallah, Stanislas Rebaudet and Renaud Piarroux, 'Using Mobile Phone Data to Predict the Spatial Spread of Cholera', *Scientific Reports*, Vol. 5, 2015, p. 8923, https://doi.org/10.1038/srep08923

56 Carolyn Y. Johnson, 'New England Researchers Help Shape the Fight on Ebola', *Boston Globe*, 14 November 2014, https://www.bostonglobe.com/metro/2014/11/02/ebola-disease-modelers-new-england-help-predict-future-spread-best-strategies/LZHSEGlInJs6SflLWW0yaP/story.html

57 Caroline O. Buckee and Kenth Engø-Monsen, 'Mobile Phone Data for Public Health: Towards Data Sharing Solutions That Protect Individual Privacy and National Security', R2/2016 (2014) 4, https://arxiv.org/ftp/arxiv/papers/1606/1606.00864.pdf

58 Facebook, 'Data for Good', https://dataforgood.fb.com/docs/covid19/

59 Google, 'Covid-19 Community Mobility Report', India, 12 June 2021, https://www.gstatic.com/covid19/mobility/2021-06-12_IN_Mobility_Report_en-GB.pdf

60 The Open Data Institute, 'The Use of Mobility Data for the Spread of Covid-19', 2021, http://theodi.org/wp-content/uploads/2021/03/Data4COVID19_0318.pdf

61 David Ferrucci, Anthony Levas, Sugato Bagchi, Gavid Gondek and Erik T. Mueller, 'Watson: Beyond Jeopardy!', *Artificial Intelligence*, (2013) 95, https://doi.org/10.1016/j.artint.2012.06.009

62 Titus J. Brinker, Achim Hekler, Alexander H Enk, Joachim Klode, Axel Hauschild, Carola Berking, Bastian Schilling, Sebastian Haferkamp, Dirk Schadendorf, Tim Holland-Letz, Jochen S. Utikal and Christof von Kalle, 'Deep Learning Outperformed 136 of 156 Dermatologists in Ahead-to-head Dermoscopic Melanoma Image Classification Task', *European Journal of Cancer* 113, Vol. May 2019, pp. 47–52, https://doi.org/10.1016/j.ejca.2019.04.001

63. M. Angulakshmi and G. Lakshmi Priya, 'Automated Brain Tumour Segmentation Techniques - A Review', *International Journal of Imaging Systems and Technology*, Vol. 27 No. 1, 21 March 2017, pp. 66–77, https://doi.org/10.1002/ima.22211
64. A. Michael Froomkin, and Ian R. Kerr Joelle Pineau, 'When AIs Outperform Doctors: Confronting the Challenges of a Tort-Induced Over-Reliance on Machine Learning', *Arizona Law Review*, Vol. 61, 20 February 2019, p. 49, https://dx.doi.org/10.2139/ssrn.3114347
65. Arieh Gomolin, Elena Netchiporouk, Robert Gniadecki and Ivan V. Litvinov, 'Artificial Intelligence Applications in Dermatology: Where Do We Stand?', *Frontiers in Medicine (Lausanne)*, Vol. 7, No. 100, 31 March 2020, https://dx.doi.org/10.3389%2Ffmed.2020.00100.
66. Heidi Ledford, 'Millions of Black People Affected by Racial Bias in Healthcare Algorithms', *Nature*, Vol. 26, October 2019, https://www.nature.com/articles/d41586-019-03228-6
67. David D. Luxton, 'Should Watson be Consulted?', *AMA Journal of Ethics*, Vol. 21 No. 2, 2019, https://journalofethics.ama-assn.org/article/should-watson-be-consulted-second-opinion/2019-02
68. Ahmed Hosny, Chintan Parmar, John Quackenbush, Lawrence H. Schwartz and Hugo J.W.L. Aerts, 'Artificial Intelligence in Radiology'.
69. Wei-Chun Lin, Jimmy S. Chen, Michael F. Chiang and Michelle R, Hribar, 'Applications of Artificial Intelligence to Electronic Health Record Data in Ophthalmology', *Translational Vision Science & Technology*, Vol. 9 No. 2, 2020, p.13, doi:10.1167/tvst.9.2.13
70. Lin et al., 'Applications of Artificial Intelligence to Electronic Health Record'.
71. Xin Yang, Yifei Wang, Ryan Byrne, Gisbert Schneider and Shengyong Yang, 'Concepts of Artificial Intelligence for Computer Assisted Drug Discovery,' *Chemical Review*, Vol. 119 No. 18, 2019, 9. 5, https://pubs.acs.org/doi/10.1021/acs.chemrev.8b00728#
72. Ibid.
73. Ibid., 7.1.
74. Ibid., 8.3.
75. Ibid., 8.1.
76. Joel J. P. C. Rodrigues, Dante Borges De Rezende Segundo, Heres Arantes Junqueira, Murilo Henrique Sabin, Rafael Maciel Prince, Jalal Al-Muhtadi and Victor Hugo C. De Albuquerque, 'Enabling Technologies for the Internet of Health Things', *IEEE Access*, Vol. 6, pp. 13129-41, 2018, doi: 10.1109/ACCESS.2017.2789329.
77. Rodrigues et al, 'Enabling Technologies'.

78 Sandeep Reddy, Sonia Allan, Simon Coghlan and Paul Cooper, 'A Governance Model for the Application of AI in Healthcare', *Journal of the American Medical Informatics Association*, Vol. 27 No. 3, March 2020, p. 491, doi: 10.1093/jamia/ocz192

79 Manuel Jesús-Azabal José Agustín Medina-Rodríguez, Javier Durán-García and Daniel García-Pérez, 'Remembranza Pills: Using Alexa to Remind the Daily Medicine Doses to Elderly', in Jose García-Alonso and Cesar Fonseca (eds.), *Gerontechnology*, Proceedings of the Second International Workshop, IWoG 2019, Cáceres, Spain, Springer International Publishing, 4–5 September 2019, https://link.springer.com/book/10.1007%2F978-3-030-41494-8

80 Shourjya Sanjyal, 'How Is AI Revolutionizing Elderly Care', *Forbes*, 31 October 2018, https://www.forbes.com/sites/shourjyasanyal/2018/10/31/how-is-ai-revolutionizing-elderly-care/?sh=7ab9bdf8e07d

81 Anita Ho, 'Are We Ready Artificial Intelligence Health Monitoring in Elder Care?', *BMC Geriatrics*, Vol. 20 No. 358, 2020, https://bmcgeriatr.biomedcentral.com/articles/10.1186/s12877-020-01764-9

82 Saharanaz Dilmaghani, Matthias R. Brust, Grégoire Danoy, Natalia Cassagnes, Johnatan Pecero and Pascal Bouvry, 'Privacy and Security of Big Data in AI Systems: A Research and Standards Perspective', (2019 IEEE International Conference on Big Data, 2019): 5737-5743, 10.1109/BigData47090.2019.9006283

83 Jian Chen and Yi Liu, 'The Secrets of Small Data: How Machine Learning Finally Reached the Enterprise', *Venturebeat*, 8 October 2020, https://venturebeat.com/2020/10/08/the-secrets-of-small-data-how-machine-learning-finally-reached-the-enterprise/

84 Amina Adadi, 'A Survey on Data-efficient Algorithms in Big Data Era', *Journal of Big Data*, Vol. 8, 2021, https://doi.org/10.1186/s40537-021-00419-9

85 Latanya Sweeney, 'Patient Identifiability in Pharmaceutical Data', Data Privacy Lab Working Paper 1015, 2011, https://dataprivacylab.org/projects/identifiability/pharma1.pdf

86 Ministry of Electronics and Information Technology, 'Constitution of a Committee of Experts to Deliberate on the Data Governance Framework', https://www.meity.gov.in/writereaddata/files/constitution_of_committee_of_experts_to_deliberate_on_data_governance_framework.pdf

87 Ministry of Information and Electronics Technology, 'Report by the Committee of Experts on Non-Personal Data Governance Framework

Version 2', 16 December 2020, https://static.mygov.in/rest/s3fs-public/mygov_160975438978977151.pdf
88 Ibid.
89 National Health Authority, 'National Digital Health Mission - Strategy Overview', July 2020, 2.2.6, https://ndhm.gov.in/documents/ndhm_strategy_overview
90 Sarah Zouinina, Younès Bennani, Nicoleta Rogovschi and A. Lyhyaoui, 'A Two-Levels Data Anonymization Approach', in I. Maglogiannis, L. Iliadis and E. Pimendis (eds.), *Artificial Applications and Innovations*, AIAI, IFIP Advances in Information and Communication Technology Book Series, No. 583, 2020, https://doi.org/10.1007/978-3-030-49161-1
91 Jackie Raskind, 'A Primer on Anonymization', *Medical Writing*, Vol. 28 No. 4, 2019, https://journal.emwa.org/artificial-intelligence-and-digital-health/a-primer-on-anonymisation/
92 Ibid.
93 George Kaissis, Marcus R. Makowski, Daniel Rückert and Rickmer F. Braren, 'Secure, Privacy-preserving and Federated Machine Learning in Medical Imaging', *Nature Machine Intelligence*, Vol. 2, 2020, pp. 305–11, https://doi.org/10.1038/s42256-020-0186-1
94 Ibid.
95 Brian M. Bot, Christine Suver, Elias Chaibub Neto, Michael Kellen, Arno Klein, Christopher Bare, Megan Doerr, Abhishek Pratap, John Wilbanks, E. Ray Dorsey, Stephen H. Friend and Andrew D. Trister, 'The mPower Study, Parkinson Disease Mobile Data Collected Using ResearchKit', *Scientific Data*, Vol. 3, No. 160011, 2016, https://doi.org/10.1038/sdata.2016.11
96 Elias Chaibub Neto, Abhishek Pratap, Thanneer M. Perumal, Meghasyam Tummalacherla, Phil Snyder, Brian M. Bot, Andrew D. Trister, Stephen H. Friend, Lara Mangravite, Larsson Omberg, 'Detecting the Impact of Subject Characteristics on Machine Learning-based Diagnostic Applications', *NPJ Digital Medicine*, Vol. 2, No. 99, 2019, https://doi.org/10.1038/s41746-019-0178-x
97 Rahul Matthan, 'Beyond Consent – A New Paradigm for Data Protection', Takshashila Discussion Document 2017-03, https://takshashila.org.in/wp-content/uploads/2017/07/TDD-Beyond-Consent-Data-Protection-RM-2017-03.pdf
98 Rahul Matthan, 'Privacy Checks Can Be Built Into Software Architecture', *Livemint*, 4 August 2021, https://www.livemint.com/opinion/columns/privacy-checks-can-be-built-into-software-architecture-11628016765657.html

Index

Aadhaar ID, 15, 40, 67, 89, 123, 124, 126–129, 137, 196–198, 229, 232, 233, 238–242, 273
Aarogya Setu app, 39, 61, 63, 65, 147, 230, 232, 240, 296
    contact tracing, 68–69, 77
    privacy policy, 75
Aarogya Setu Data Access and Knowledge Sharing Protocol, 2020, 69
ABDM. *See* Ayushman Bharat Digital Mission
Accredited Social Health Activist (ASHA) workers, 6, 73, 87, 103, 114, 115, 124, 136
    contact tracing, 69
    performance-based incentives, 104
    symptom tracking, 64
    training, 105, 117
Ackoff, R., 44
advance directive (AD), 215

AETCOM. *See* attitude, ethics and communication
Agrawal, P., 15
AHS. *See* Annual Health Survey
Ain-Davis, D., 170
air pollution, 5
Akram, M., 172
algorithmic fairness, 93–94
Alma Ata Declaration, 1978, 29, 101, 157
altruistic surrogacy, 177, 178
American Association of Community Health Workers, 116
Anganwadi workers (AWWs), 6, 87, 103–105, 115, 117
ANMs. *See* auxiliary nurse midwives
Annual Health Survey (AHS), 85, 295
anonymization, 57, 75, 92, 131, 135, 197, 272, 277, 278, 280, 304–305, 307

APIs. *See* application programming interfaces
Apollo Hospitals, 63
application programming interfaces (APIs), 50, 52
Arole, R., 103
artificial intelligence (AI)
   applications, 297–300
   and assisted living, 299–300
   creation, 289–290
   data-driven public health interventions, 294
   data for healthcare, 291–297
   description, 288–289
   diagnosis, monitoring and clinical decision support, 298
   digital health applications, 294
   EHRs, EMRs and PHRs, 291–292
   general, 288–289
   healthcare, 289–290
   hotspot detection, 295–296
   identifiable images, 307
   image recognition, 297–298
   locational privacy, 306–307
   mobility data, 296–297
   narrow, 288
   precision medicine and personalized health, 299
   and privacy, 300–306
   privacy harms, 290
   syndromic inferences, 294–295
   unintended privacy consequences, 307–308
   wearables and IoT, 292–293
ASHA. *See* Accredited Social Health Activist
assisted living, artificial intelligence, 299–300
Assisted Reproductive Technologies (Regulation) Bill, 173, 175, 176, 178
Assisted Reproductive Technology (Regulation) Act, 2021, 178
Astana Declaration, 101
attitude, ethics and communication (AETCOM) modules, 154
authorizations, 35, 67, 97–98
auxiliary nurse midwives (ANMs), 103, 115
   maternal and child health services, 102
   trainings, 104
Ayushman Bharat Digital Mission (ABDM), 14, 15, 17, 38, 39, 40, 146, 231

Bailey, R., 5
Banerjee, S., 15
Barefoot Doctors programme, 101
Berlin, I., 217
Bhandari, V., 8
big-data analytics systems, 89–90
biomedicalization, womb
   C-section births, 171
   episiotomy, 172–173
   LBV, 170
   LSCS, 171
   MDR, 170
   private hospitals, 172
   unnecessary c-sections, 172
biopolitics, 45
Blinkit, 64
bodily integrity, 10, 67, 76, 110, 164, 177, 180, 185, 211
Boudreaux, B., 62
breach of trust, 148

California Confidentiality of Medical Information Act, 251
call data records (CDRs), 296
calorie counters, 7

Index

cancer, 4, 278, 283, 293, 297
care protocols, 155
CDRs. *See* call data records
CDRS. *See* COVID data reporting score
Central Government Redressal Management System (CGRMS) portal, 133–134
Chatterjee, P., 169
Chattopadhyay, S., 172
Chaudhuri, B., 8, 9
Chaudhury, A.B.R., 32
cholera, 4, 79, 198, 296
CHWs. *See* community health workers
Clinical Establishments (Registration and Regulation) Act, 2010, 35
Clue app, 247, 262
CNNS. *See* Comprehensive National Nutrition Survey
Code of Criminal Procedure, Section 144, 32
code of ethics, CHWs, 116–117
comma-separated values (CSV), 50, 52
commercial surrogacy
 ban on, 174
 in-vitro fertilization, 175
 Surrogacy (Regulation) Bill, 174, 175
Committee of Experts on Data Protection, 37
Common Cause (A Registered Society) v. Union of India and another, 210–211
common good, 142, 146, 147
community advisory boards, 156
community health workers (CHWs), 7
 agents of privacy, 107–108

ASHAs, 6, 64, 69, 73, 87, 103–105, 114, 115, 117, 124, 136
AWWs, 6, 103–105, 115, 117
code of ethics, 116–117
digital, 115–116
empowering, 116–118
gender, 103
groups, 104
India, 102–106
privacy and confidentiality, operationalization, 110–115
role of, 101
training, ethics and professionalism, 117–118
trust, 108–109
Community of Practitioners on Accountability and Social Action in Health (COPASAH), 156
Comprehensive National Nutrition Survey (CNNS), 85
confidentiality
 EHRs, 196
 exception, 188–189
 fiduciary relationships, 186
 HDMP, 195–197
 health data, 194–198
 health system, 25–26
 Hippocratic Oath, 188
 HIV/AIDS, 186–188
 NDHM, 196
 and trust, 145–146
constitutional framework
 Article 21, the Constitution, 22–23
 Articles 23 and 24, the Constitution, 24
 intoxicating drinks and drugs, prohibition of, 24
 Justice K.S. Puttaswamy v. Union of India, 23

public health, 23, 24
contact tracing, 60, 77, 79, 85, 229, 236, 267, 270
   Aarogya Setu app, 61, 68–69, 86, 232
   apps, 66, 75, 230, 271
   CHWs, 114
   manual, 69
Convention on Rights of Persons with Disabilities, 29
Convention on the Elimination of All Forms of Discrimination against Women, the, 29
Convention on the Rights of the Child, 29
COPASAH. *See* Community of Practitioners on Accountability and Social Action in Health
Corona Watch app, 65
corporate wellness programmes, 248, 249, 255–258
COVA Punjab app, 69
COVID data reporting score (CDRS), 47
COVID-19 pandemic, 1, 17, 270. *See also* data infrastructure
   contact tracing, South Korea, 236
   data, collection and processing of, 31
   discriminatory behaviour, 236
   legal labelling as disaster, 32
   and trust, 142–143
   vaccines, 3
   wearable devices, 262
   work-life balance, 8
CoWin app, 70, 75, 232–233, 280
criminal laws, prohibitions and standards, 32–33

Criminal Procedure Identification Act, 2022, 233
CSV. *See* comma-separated values
Cukier, K., 42
Cyber Security and Privacy Strategy, 2020, 125

dangers, government access to health data
   dignity and autonomy, loss of, 234
   discrimination and identity-based violence / threats, 236–237
   society, democracy and public health, 237–239
   unfair leverage, 235–236
dashboards
   anonymization strategy, 57
   privacy policy, 56–57
   self-reporting feature, 58
   state, 47, 49, 56
data
   fiduciaries, 258, 264, 309
   management, 15, 39, 75, 195, 269, 279
   minimization, 72, 77, 132, 257, 263, 303–304, 308, 309
   protection laws, 14
   sharing, 74–76
Data Access and Knowledge Sharing Protocol, 39
databases, personal health information
   Aarogya Setu, 232
   ABDM, 231
   CoWin, 232–233
   Criminal Procedure Identification Act, 2022, 233

Index

DNA-based tracking, 231–232
emergence of, 230–233
data-driven pandemic, 45
datafication
   active contact tracing practice, 45
   and biopolitics, 45
   to dataism, 55–56
   DKIW hierarchy, 44
   ideology of, 45
   mismanagement and mistrust, data, 46
data governance
   Aarogya Setu app, 39
   ABDM, 38
   breach entries, 36
   DISHA, 38
   health data, 35–36
   non-legislative policy measures, 39
   non-personal data, 38–39
   PDP Bill, 37, 38
   personal data, protection of, 36, 37
data-information-knowledge-wisdom (DKIW) hierarchy, 44
data infrastructure, COVID-19
   clinical management data, 48
   dashboards, 49, 50
   data-driven narrative, 48–55
   datafication, 44–46
   datafication to dataism, 55–56
   data presentation, format of, 50
   dynamic data, 49
   enabling actions, 52–53
   fragmented nature, data, 52
   information infrastructure, 48–52
   methodology, 46–48
   policy guidelines and protocols, 49
   privacy, datafied pandemic, 56–58
   procedural data, 48
   representations and counter-representations, 53–55
   role-based logins, 51, 56
   state data platforms, 46–47
   status data, 48
   testing data, 48, 49
   vaccination related data, 49
data protection, public healthcare
   analysis, 135–138
   collection limitation, 128–129
   data quality and access/correction, 130–131
   enforcement and accountability, 133–134
   incident management, 134–135
   informed consent, 90–91
   integrity and confidentiality, 131–133
   JSY, 123–125, 127–135
   notice and consent, 90–91, 127–128
   NTEP, 122–123, 125, 127–131, 133, 135, 138, 139
   openness, 134
   PM-JAY, 125–135, 138, 139
   purpose limitation, 129–130
   standards, prescription of, 135
   storage limitation, 131
data sites (November 2020 and June 2021), 313–316
data stewardship
   health data governance, 282–285
   health data sharing, 281–282
   NDHM, 279–281

NPD report, 276–279
PDP Bill, 274–276
valuing health data, 269–274
Datta, A., 22
de-anonymization, 92
decisional autonomy
    Article 12 of the CRPD, 205
    assessments, 205
    definition, 203–204
    functional approach, 205
    Mental Healthcare Act, 2017, 213–217
    outcome approach, 204–205
    PwMI, supported decision-making, 206–209
    right to, 210, 212
    status approach, 204
decisional privacy, 202
    definition, 203
    India's Constitution, 209–213
    negative liberties, 219
    positive liberty, 217, 218
    public health challenges, 217–221
decision-making capacity (DMC)
    assessments, 219
    functional approach, 205
    outcome approach, 204–205
    status approach, 204
Department of Health and Human Services, United States, 36
Desai, S., 167, 168
diabetes, 4
differential privacy, 92–93
Digi-Doctor, 231, 279
digital community health work
    ANMs, 115
    data encryption, 115–116
    IDSP, 115
    MCTS, 115
Digital Information Security in Healthcare Act, 2017 (DISHA), 38, 274, 275
digitization
    Orwellian mass surveillance, 88
    secrecy aspect, privacy, 89
disaster, definition of, 32
Disaster Management Act, 2005, 31, 32, 71, 114, 142, 240
DISHA. *See* Digital Information Security in Healthcare Act
Divan, V., 10
DMSC. *See* Durbar Mahila Samanway Committee
DNA-based tracking, 231–232
DNA Technology (Use and Application) Regulation Bill, 2019 (DNA Bill), 231, 232
doctor-hospital relationship, 152
doctor-patient relationship, 141, 152
door-to-door symptom tracking, 64
drone surveillance, 65–66, 72
drug discovery, 299
Drugs and Cosmetics Act, 1940, 33
D'Souza, D., 184
Durbar Mahila Samanway Committee (DMSC), 183
Dwork, C., 93

Ebola epidemic, 266, 267
Ed Yong, 270
EHRs. *See* electronic health records
electronic health records (EHRs), 35, 195, 196, 279, 292
electronic medical record (EMR), 291–292
Environment Protection Act, 33
e-pass, 70

Epidemic Diseases Act, 1897, 9, 21, 30, 31, 32, 71, 142, 236, 240
episiotomy, 172–173
Eubanks, V., 90
European General Data Protection Regulation, 2016/679 (GDPR), 250, 252, 257
euthanasia, 210
ex-post accountability *vs. ex-ante* protection, 91

Facebook, 11
federated learning, 306
fiduciary relationship
　common good, 142
　confidentiality, 186
　doctor-patient, 141
　governments, 142
　reciprocity, 141–142
FinData, 272, 273
Fitbit, 247, 260, 262
5-SPICE model, 109
Food Safety Act, 33
Food Safety and Standards Act, 2006, 33
Foucault's idea of biopolitics, 45
function creep, 229

General Data Protection Regulation, Europe, 14
Ghar Ghar Nigrani app, 64, 73
Ghose, T., 32
Ghosh, S., 172
Global Burden of Disease study, 2019, 5
Google, 238, 267, 270, 297
Gopalakrishnan, K., 39
Gopichandran, V., 6, 7
Gopinathan, A., 169

Greater Chennai Corporation, 64, 68
Grofers, 64
Gujarat Prohibition Act, 1949, 25
Gutschow, K., 170, 171

harms, government access to health data
　dignity and autonomy, loss of, 234
　discrimination and identity-based violence/threats, 236–237
　society, democracy and public health, 237–239
　unfair leverage, 235–236
health
　definition, 7
　insurance, government-financed, 5
　-related programmes, India, 5
　and well-being, 7–8
healthcare insurance scheme, 231
health data
　cautious progress, 242–245
　dangers, government access, 233–239
　databases, emergence of, 230–233
　electronic, benefits of, 227–228
　function creep, 229
　governance, 282–285
　harms, individuals and society, 233–239
　public health surveillance, 229–230
　sharing, 281–282
　state legibility, 239–242
　surveillance, 228, 229

Index

health data architecture design
  authorization, 97–98
  implementation notes, 98–99
  operationalization and use cases, 86–88
  privacy and denial of rights, 88–94
  privacy architecture, elements of, 94–95
  public good, 84–86
  purpose limitation, 96
  use cases and ideal functionality, 95–96
  virtual identities, 97
Health Data Management Policy (HDMP), 11, 195, 269, 279
Health Facility Registry, 231
Health ID, 231
Health Insurance Portability and Accountability Act, 1996 (HIPAA), 251, 254
Health Management Information System (HMIS), 124
health-related data
  appropriation, 148
  clinical, 147
  public health programs and interventions, 147
  reciprocity, 147
  research, 147
health tracking technologies
  community fitness, digital governance and public health, 259–262
  corporate wellness, individual choice, and third-party responsibility, 254–259
  fitness and activity tracking wearables, 247, 250
  holistic approach, 264–265

monitoring technologies, 262–264
personal health information and law, 249–254
privacy paradox, 248
pulse oximeters, 247
high blood pressure, 5
high value data sets (HVDs), 277, 278, 305
Hindu, The, 42
Hindu Marriage Act, 1955, 201
Hippocratic Oath, 188
HIV/AIDS, 10
  antiretroviral treatment, 197
  confidentiality, 186–188
  directives, 182
  India HIV/AIDS Act, 190–193
  paradox, 183–186
  prevention initiative, 183
  SRBs, 183
  status, disclosure of, 188–190
  Tarasoff v Regents of University of California, 189–190
  transmission, 181, 182
  USA 'HIV exposure' laws, 182
HIV and AIDS (Prevention and Control) Act, 2017, 10, 26, 29, 240
  grievance redress, 192–193
  Section 8, 190–191
  Section 9, 191
  status, confidentiality of, 190, 191
HMIS. *See* Health Management Information System
HPB. *See* Singapore's Health Promotion Board
Human Development Index, 2020, 157

hysterectomies
   doctor-patient interactions, 167
   institutionalized medical procedures, 168
   menstruation, 168
   mental health institution, Mumbai, 168, 169
   normalization, 167
   and public insurance, 168
   redundant womb/uterus, 166
   reproductive rights, 168
   rural agrarian workers, 169
   rural and low-income women, 167

ICD. *See* International Classification of Disease
ICMR. *See* Indian Council of Medical Research
ICT-RTM. *See* Information Communication Technology enabled Real Time Monitoring
ideal functionality, 95–96
IDSP. *See* Integrated Disease Surveillance Programme
image recognition, 297–298
immunization passports, 69
Indian Council of Medical Research (ICMR), 63, 176, 240
Indian Medical Council (Professional Conduct, Etiquette and Ethics) Regulations, 2002, 188
Indian Software Product Industry RoundTable (ISPIRT), 134
Infant Milk Substitutes, Feeding Bottles and Infant Foods Act, 1992, 33
inferential privacy, 92–93

influenza pandemic, 4
Information and Communication Technology (ICT), 195
Information Communication Technology enabled Real Time Monitoring (ICT-RTM), 115
Information Technology Act, 2000, 36, 73, 146, 240, 251
informed consent, 90–91, 144–145, 214, 301–302
institutional trust, 149
Integrated Disease Surveillance Programme (IDSP), 115
International Classification of Disease (ICD), 45
International Health Regulations (IHR), 29, 30
Internet Democracy Project, 62

Jaap-Koops, B., 14
Jain, G., 5
James, K.S., 172
Jamkhed project, 103
Janani Suraksha Yojana (JSY)
   ANM/ASHA worker, 124
   cash incentives, pregnant women and healthcare workers, 123
   collection limitation, 128
   data quality and access/correction, 130, 131
   guidelines, 123
   HMIS, 124
   MCTS, 124
   purpose limitation, 129
   regulatory and policy framework, 123–124
   storage limitation, 131
JSY. *See* Janani Suraksha Yojana

Justice K.S. Puttaswamy v. Union of India, 23, 186, 194, 209

Kaf kaesque threats, privacy and liberty, 89, 90, 92
Kapoor, Arjun, 10, 11
Kapoor, Astha, 11
Khardekar, B.H., 24
Khelo India (Play India) program, 261
Kindig, D., 9
Kirby, M., 184
Krishnan, K.P., 5
Kurian, O.C., 36

labour room violence (LBV), 170–171
Landau, S., 77
lateral surveillance mechanisms, 68
LBV. *See* labour room violence
legal capacity, 202
legal framework, India
    allocation, legislative powers, 28–31
    balancing attempts, courts and policymakers, 25–27
    categorization, 31–35
    constitutional framework, 22–25
    criminal laws, prohibitions and standards, 32–33
    data governance, 35–39
    health services, provision of, 34–35
    protections, specific groups, 33–34
    public health emergencies, 31–32
Lipsky, M., 6
LiveHealthy SG, 260
locational privacy, 306–307
location tracking and syndromic surveillance, 65
Lock, M., 169
lower segment caesarean section (LSCS), 171
LSCS. *See* lower segment caesarean section
LumiHealth programmes, 260

Majumdar, A., 9, 10
malaria, 4
malnutrition, 5
Mann, J., 184
Maternal and Child Tracking Systems (MCTS), 115
maternal death register (MDR), 170
Matthan, R., 16
Mayer-Schoenberger, V., 42
McCarthy, J., 288
McDonald, S., 78
MCTS. *See* Mother and Child Tracking System
MDM 360 Shield app, 73
measles, 3
Medical Council of India's Code of Medical Ethics, 188
Medical Termination of Pregnancy Act, 1971, 210
Meghalaya High Court, 12
meningitis, 3
mental health, 201. *See also* persons with mental illness
    decisional privacy & decisional autonomy, 203–205
    and psychological well-being, 7–8
Mental Healthcare Act, 2017, 34, 213–217

Mental Health Review Boards
(MHRBs), 215, 218
Midata.coop, 283
Millennium Development Goals,
157
Ministry of Health and Family
Welfare (MoHFW), 35, 75, 122,
157, 279
Ministry of Housing and Urban
Affairs, 6
mobility and density mapping
drone surveillance, 65–66
location tracking and syndromic
surveillance, 65
Mother and Child Tracking System
(MCTS), 124
MPHWs. *See* multipurpose health
workers
multipurpose health workers
(MPHWs), 102, 103
Muthukrishnan, M., 8, 9
Muzaffar, N., 172

National AIDS Control Programme,
188
National AIDS Control Programme
Data Management Guidelines,
2020, 197
National Digital Health Blueprint
(NDHB), 89, 138
National Digital Health Mission
(NDHM), 14, 83, 85, 86, 91, 93,
195, 196, 225, 230, 269, 279–281
National Disaster Management Act,
2005, 21
National Family Health Survey
(NFHS), 85
National Health Authority (NHA),
125–126, 280

National Health Mission, 117
National Health Stack, 125
*National Legal Services Authority v.
Union of India and others,* 209
National Medical Commission Act, 34
National Medical Commission
(NMC), 34
National Nutrition Monitoring
Bureau (NNMB), 85
National Rural Health Mission, 103,
157
National Strategic Plan for TB
Elimination 2017-25 (NSP, 2017),
122, 132
National Tuberculosis Elimination
Programme (NTEP)
collection limitation, 128
data collection, 123
data quality and access/
correction, 130–131
enforcement and accountability,
133
governance framework, 122
Nikshay, 122–123, 132, 133
notice and consent, 127
NSP, 2017, 122, 134
purpose limitation, 129
storage limitation, 131
TB, elimination, 122
National Urban Health Mission, 157
*Navtej Singh Johar and Others v Union
of India,* 209
NDHB. *See* National Digital Health
Blueprint
NDHM. *See* National Digital Health
Mission
negative liberties, 219
NFHS. *See* National Family Health
Survey

NHA. *See* National Health Authority
NHA Acceptable Usage Policy, 126
NHA Data Privacy Policy, 133
NHA Data Privacy Policy 2.0, 125–126
Nikshay system, 115, 122–123, 132, 133, 134
NMC. *See* National Medical Commission
NNMB. *See* National Nutrition Monitoring Bureau
nominated representative (NR), 214–215
Non-Personal Data Committee Report (NPD report) 2020, 269
  anonymized data, sharing of, 276, 277
  community rights, 278
  HVDs, 277, 278
  Sprinklr, US-based company, 276, 277
NR. *See* nominated representative
NTEP. *See* National Tuberculosis Elimination Programme
Nuffield Council on Bioethics, 12
Nuffield Foundation, 270

obstetric violence, 169–173
occupational safety programs, 257
O'Neil, A., 89
open defecation, 2
Orwellian mass surveillance, 88
Ovia, pregnancy and period tracking app, 235

patient-government relationship, 153–154
patient-insurance relationship, 153
period trackers, 7

personal autonomy, 209
Personal Data Protection Bill, 2019 (PDP Bill), 11, 14, 15, 16, 22, 38, 146, 241, 250, 251, 252, 253, 263, 302
  data rights, 276
  DISHA, 274–275
  health data, definition, 274
  non-consensual processing, personal data, 74
  sensitive data, 37
  withdrawn bill, 275
personal health record (PHR), 292, 293, 301
persons with mental illness (PwMI)
  Article 12, CRPD, 205
  community-based facilities/services, 208
  decisional autonomy, 204–209
  decisional privacy, 203–204
  facilitated decision-making, 207
  families, treatment and care, 220
  independent decision-making, 206
  legal relationships, 201
  mental healthcare, 201
  MHCA, 203
  social determinants, 201
  structural discrimination, 200
  supported decision-making, 206, 207
physical activity, lack of, 4
Pipraiya, P., 16
plague, 4
PM-JAY. *See* Pradhan Mantri Jan Aarogya Yojana
polio, 3
population health, 9, 10
Poshan Abhiyan, 115

Index

positive liberty, 217–218
Pradhan Mantri Jan Aarogya Yojana (PM-JAY), 5, 231
  cashless insurance coverage, 125
  collection limitation, 128
  Cyber Security and Privacy Strategy, 2020, 125
  data collection and usage, 126
  data quality and access/correction, 131
  enforcement and accountability, 133
  incident management, 135
  integrity and confidentiality, 132
  interoperable IT platform, 125
  NHA Acceptable Usage Policy, 126
  NHA Data Privacy Policy 2.0, 125–126
  notice and consent, 127–128
  purpose limitation, 129–130
  regulatory/policy framework, 125
  SHAs, 125
  storage limitation, 131
Prasad, S.K., 7
precision medicine, 299
Pre-Conception and Pre-Natal Diagnostic Techniques (Prohibition of Sex Selection) Act, 1994 (PNDT Act), 239
Pre-conception and Techniques (Prohibition of Sex Selection) Act, 1994, 26
primary health care (PHC)
  approach, 101, 105, 117
principle of subsidiarity, 150
privacy, Indian communities, 106
privacy and public health

ABDM, 14, 15
  categories, 14
  COVID vaccination status, 12
  data protection laws, 14
  intervention ladder, 12, 13
  open defecation, 2
  Puttaswamy verdict, 11, 13
provision, health care services, 34–35
public good, 84–86
public health
  AI, healthcare, 16
  community health workers, 6–7
  COVID pandemic, 4, 6
  data sets, COVID-related, 8–9
  definition, 3
  emergencies, 31–32
  global deaths, 4
  health-related programmes, India, 5
  HIV/AIDS, 10
  internet, 11
  intervention ladder of, 12, 13
  interventions, 4
  mental health and psychological well-being, 7–8
  ordinance, 30
  PDP Bill, 11, 14, 15, 16
  persons with disability, 10–11
  physical and digital surveillance measures, 8
  population health, 9, 10
  privacy, data and beyond, 11–16
  private actors, role of, 7
  'public,' 9–11
  risk factors, death and disability, 5
  scientific successes, 3
  Smart Cities Mission, 6

Spanish flu/influenza pandemic, 4
street-level bureaucrats, 6
tracking technologies, 7
and well-being, 7–8
and women, 9–10
Public Health Act, 1987, 114, 184
Public Health (Prevention, Control and Management of Epidemics, Bio-terrorism and Disasters) Act, 2017, 30
Pungaliya, S., 168
Puttaswamy verdict, 11, 13, 14, 23, 25, 27, 28, 31, 40, 71, 241, 242
PwMI. *See* persons with mental illness

quarantine enforcement
  app-based surveillance, 66–67
  lateral surveillance, 68
  marking out, 67
  selfie requirement, 66, 67
Quarantine Watch app, 66
quasi-steward, 285

Rahman, F., 15
Rai, S., 10
Rajan, R.S., 168
Rao, M., 178
Rao, N., 168
Rapid Survey on Children (RSOC), 85
Reliance Jio, 63
Reproductive and Child Health (RCH) portal, 124
reproductive studies
  dispensable uterus, 166–169
  hysterectomies, normalization of, 166–169
  obstetric violence and biomedicalization, womb, 169–173
  surrogacy bill, 173–179
resident welfare associations (RWAs), 60, 68
respect, patients, 143–144
Rights of Persons with Disabilities Act, 2016, 29
right to confidentiality, 10, 143, 146, 215
right to explanation, 93
right to life and personal liberty, 209
right to privacy, 2, 3, 10, 22, 25, 61, 62, 71, 74, 118, 146, 186, 188, 190, 194, 195, 202, 209, 211, 212, 234, 241, 242, 276, 279
role-based logins, 51, 56
RSOC. *See* Rapid Survey on Children
RT-PCR tests, 70
RWAs. *See* resident welfare associations

safe motherhood, 5
Sagar, A., 15
Sama, 175
Samira Kohli judgment, 145
science and technology studies (STS), 43
SDF. *See* significant data fiduciaries
security breaches, 76–77
self-determination and autonomy, 211
self(ie)-governance, 22, 67
self-regulatory boards (SRBs), 183
sensitizing communities, 118
Shah, A., 15
Sharma, S., 15

SHAs. *See* State Health Agencies
Shelton, T., 46
Shrivastava Committee, 1974, 102
significant data fiduciaries (SDF), 275
Singapore's Health Promotion Board (HPB), 259–260
smallpox, 3, 4
Smart Cities Mission, 6
smart watches, 7
SMHAs. *See* State Mental Health Authorities
smoking, 4, 5
social distancing, 65–66
solid waste management, 6
Solove, J., 89, 91
Spanish flu, 4
special groups, protection for, 33–34
SRBs. *See* self-regulatory boards
Srikrishna, B.N., 13, 14, 37
state at home governance, 67
State Health Agencies (SHAs), 125
state legibility, personal health data
State Mental Health Authorities (SMHAs), 218
Stoddart, G., 9
Strava, fitness app, 247, 261
STS. *See* science and technology studies
Sucheta Srivastava v. Chandigarh Administration, 210
supervised learning, 289
surrogacy
   altruistic, 177, 178
   ARTs Bill, 175, 176, 178
   bodily integrity, 177
   commercial, 174, 175, 178
   infertility, positioning of, 176
   in-vitro fertilization, 173, 175
   public criticism and scrutiny, 174
   Surrogacy (Regulation) Bill, 2016, 174, 175, 177
   Surrogacy (Regulation) Act of 2021, 178
   Surrogacy (Regulation) Bill, 2016, 174, 175, 177
surveillance
   capitalism, 228
   definition, 228
   public health, 229–230
   syndromic, 294–295
surveillance measures, COVID-19 pandemic
   contact tracing, 68–69
   door-to-door tracking efforts, 64
   emergencies, 61
   lack of express/informed consent, 73–74
   legality and proportionality, 71–72
   mobility and density mapping, 64–66
   PDP Bill, 74
   privacy implications, 71
   privacy policies/protocols for data sharing, lack of, 74–76
   quarantine enforcement, 66–68
   self-assessment tools, 63–64
   suitability and efficacy, 77–78
   symptom tracking, 62–64
   temperature checks, workplace, 64–65
   travel passes and vaccination, 69–70
   unauthorized disclosure and security breaches, 76–77
Sustainable Development Goals, 157
Swachh Bharat Mission, 2

Swiggy, 64
symptom tracking
  door-to-door, 64
  geographical distribution, 62
  hospital-based reporting, 63
  self-assessment/self-reporting, 63–64
  temperature checks, workplace, 63, 64
syndromic mapping, 65
syndromic surveillance, 294–295

Tablighi Jamaat event, Delhi, 76
tamper-proof programs, 96
Tarasoff v Regents of University of California, 189–190
TEEs. *See* trusted execution environments
temperature checks, workplace, 63, 64
Thatcher, J., 90
TikTok, 11
Towghi, F., 167, 168
travel passes
  e-passes, 70
  immunization passports, 69
  RT-PCR tests, 70
  and vaccination, 70
trust
  building and preserving, 154–159
  care protocols, 155
  CHWs, 108–109
  community settings, 155–156
  and confidentiality, 145–146
  and COVID-19, 142–143
  doctor-patient relationship, 141, 152
  ethical and compassionate care, 149

fiduciary relationship, 141–142
health data, protection of, 147–148
informed consent, 144–145
institutional, 149
loss of, 148–149
news and social media, 151
patient-government relationship, 153–154
patient-insurance relationship, 153
public hospitals, health services and health schemes, 156–159
respecting persons, 143–144
training, 154–155
trustworthiness of systems, 150
trusted execution environments (TEEs), 98
tuberculosis elimination, 5

UHID. *See* unique health identity
unauthorized disclosure, personal information, 76–77
UNESCO Universal Declaration on Bioethics and Human Rights, 157
unique health identity (UHID), 196, 279
United Nations Convention on the Rights of Persons with Disabilities (CRPD), 202, 205, 213, 219
Universal Declaration of Human Rights, 11, 29
universal health coverage, 153
UN Resolutions and Political Declarations around Digital Health, 194
unsound mind, 201–202. *See also* persons with mental illness

unsupervised learning algorithms, 289
use cases
    operationalization, 86–88
    privacy analysis, 95–96
Uttar Pradesh Public Health and Epidemic Diseases Control Act, 2020, 31

vaccination
    mRNA vaccine, 267
    and travel, 70
valuing health data, 269–274

Vasudevan, V., 47
Village Health Guide scheme, 103
virtual identities, 97, 98
Vora, K., 175

wearable devices, 247, 250, 261, 262, 292–293, 297, 299–300, 303
Winslow, C-E. A., 3, 4
Woodburn, J., 21

Zelizer, V., 176
Zomato, 64
Zuboff, S., 90

Acknowledgements

THIS book project has come together thanks to the trust, hard work and kindness of many individuals. To begin with, I would like to thank Dinesh Thakur and Prashant Reddy at the Thakur Foundation for envisioning the need for this conversation on public health and privacy in India and offering me the support and independence to execute it. I am also grateful to the team at HarperCollins, particularly Suchismita Ukil, for their trust in this project and support through the book's journey. Vandana Rathore, Aman Arora, S.K. Ray Chaudhuri and Siddhesh Inamdar were among the others who helped along the way.

Needless to say, I am grateful to each one of the contributors whose knowledge and efforts have shaped this collection – this is as much their product as it is mine. Their patience and dedication through multiple rounds of deliberations and revisions, amidst the challenges thrown at us by the COVID situation, was a sign of having found a group that was truly passionate about unravelling the connections between public health and privacy. A special thanks to three of the contributors for help that went above and beyond their role as authors: Justice B.N.

Srikrishna, for reading through the first draft of the manuscript and agreeing to pen the foreword to this collection; K.P. Krishnan, for his guidance in planning the working paper workshop; and Rahul Matthan, for helping me navigate the publishing landscape.

Peer review and engagement were a key part of the book's development process and I remain indebted to all those who played a part in that process. Yamini Aiyar and her colleagues Sunil Kumar and Ragini Rao Munjuluri generously hosted us for the working paper workshop held at the Centre for Policy Research's office in New Delhi in October 2021. The initial drafts that were discussed at the workshop benefitted immensely from the insights and critiques offered by an extraordinary group of experts who joined us as discussants. My heartfelt gratitude to Indu Bhushan, Jai Vipra, Kiran Jonnalagadda, Maitreyi Misra, Maya Unnithan, Murali Neelakantan, Naveen Bagalkot, Naveen Thayyil, Prakhar Misra, Prashant Reddy, Shefali Malhotra, Siddharth Narrain, Tarunima Prabhakar, Vijayaprasad Gopichandran and Yamini Aiyar for their participation and feedback on the chapters.

Many others have helped along the way through useful conversations, encouragement, introductions and nudges. This is a long list that includes Justice A.P. Shah, Shaili Parsheera, Ila Patnaik, Amar Jesani, Apar Gupta, Madhumita Rajan, Ravinder Kaur, Harleen Kaur, Sujatha Rao, Usha Ramanathan and Shefali Malhotra.

Finally, nothing that I do would be possible without the love and support of my family. This covers the entire Parsheera clan but I must make a few special mentions. My father Bir Singh, who was both my hero and my biggest cheerleader, my mother Susheela who is the strongest person that I know and my brother Abhishek who always has my back.

About the Authors

Ajay Shah

Dr Ajay Shah is an economist. He does academic and policy-oriented research on India, at the intersection of economics, law and public administration. He has co-authored the book, *In Service of the Republic: The Art and Science of Economic Policy*.

Ambuj Sagar

Dr Ambuj Sagar is the founding head of the School of Public Policy at the Indian Institute of Technology Delhi. His interests broadly lie at the intersection of science, technology and development.

Anindita Majumdar

Dr Anindita Majumdar is an assistant professor of sociology in the Department of Liberal Arts at Indian Institute of Technology Hyderabad. Her research focuses on commercial surrogacy, kinship and infertility and the linkages between ageing and assisted reproductive technologies.

Arjun Kapoor

Arjun Kapoor is a lawyer and psychologist. He is a programme manager and research fellow at the Centre for Mental Health Law and Policy, Indian Law Society (ILS), Pune, and is co-leading various projects on law, policy and service reform for mental health and suicide prevention.

Astha Kapoor

Astha Kapoor is the co-founder of Aapti Institute, a research firm examining the interface between technology and society. She works on data governance, basic income, digitization of welfare, work and social architectures of technology.

B.N. Srikrishna

Justice B.N. Srikrishna is an eminent jurist and a former judge of the Supreme Court of India. He chaired the Committee of Experts constituted by the government to formulate a data protection framework for India. He has headed several other key commissions, including the Financial Sector Legislative Reforms Commission, the Sixth Central Pay Commission and the Commission on the Bombay Riots.

Bidisha Chaudhuri

Dr Bidisha Chaudhuri is an associate professor at the International Institute of Information Technology, Bengaluru. She works in the domain of IT and society. Her current research projects include information systems for sustainable development, politics of data and algorithms, political economy of digital identity and sociology of work and automation and AI ethics.

Faiza Rahman

Faiza Rahman is a doctoral candidate at the University of Melbourne. She was previously a technology policy researcher at the National Institute of Public Finance and Policy (NIPFP) and with the Judicial Reforms Initiative at the Vidhi Centre for Legal Policy.

Gaurav Jain

Gaurav Jain is a policy professional, currently working as a sector economist for the Disruptive Technology and Funds Sector for International Finance Corporation, World Bank Group. He was selected for the Young Leaders in Tech Fellow by the University of Chicago Trust India and Omidyar Network India. He has a master's degree in public Policy from the University of Oxford and a degree of Bachelor in Technology (Hons) from the Indian Institute of Technology Kharagpur.

K.P. Krishnan

Dr K.P. Krishnan served in the Indian Administrative Service for nearly thirty-seven years in various fields and secretariat positions, retiring as secretary, Ministry of Skill Development and Entrepreneurship in the Government of India. Following that he was the Investor Education and Protection Fund chair professor of economics at the National Council of Applied Economic Research, New Delhi.

Meera Muthukrishnan

Meera Muthukrishnan is a student at the International Institute of Information Technology, Bengaluru. Her research focuses on issues at the intersection of information technology and society.

Olinda Timms

Dr Olinda Timms is a medical doctor and adjunct associate professor in the Division of Health and Humanities at St Johns Research Institute, Bengaluru. She has been teaching and writing on medical ethics for several decades. Her book, *Biomedical Ethics,* was published by Elsevier India in 2016.

Prakhar Pipraiya

Prakhar Pipraiya is a fourth-year student in the BA, LLB (Hons) programme at the National Law School of India University (NLSIU), Bengaluru. He has been a part of the Law and Technology Society of NLSIU and was the first recipient of the Trilegal Research Fellowship in Law, Technology and Policy.

Prashant Agrawal

Prashant Agrawal is a PhD scholar in the Department of Computer Science and Engineering, Indian Institute of Technology Delhi. His research interests revolve around the areas of privacy, security and public policy. He has studied the problem of operationalizing privacy-by-design for public service applications and the problem of secure electronic voting.

Rahul Matthan

Rahul Matthan is a partner at Trilegal. He has been working on issues relating to technology law for over two decades and has been involved in a number of policy initiatives at the intersection of law, society and technology. He has a weekly column in *Mint* titled 'Ex Machina' and has authored the book, *Privacy 3.0: Unlocking Our Data-driven Future.*

Rishab Bailey

Rishab Bailey is a lawyer and technology policy researcher. He was previously a fellow at NIPFP, Delhi, and also worked with a global software company, and various human rights lawyers and NGOs on issues connected to internet governance, digital rights, civil liberties, technology law and intellectual property. He studied law at NLSIU, Bengaluru, and obtained an advanced master's degree in law and digital technology at Leiden University, Netherlands.

Shivangi Rai

Shivangi Rai is a deputy coordinator at the Centre for Health Equity, Law and Policy. She has over fifteen years of experience in advocacy and policy research in instilling a 'right to health' framework in legal and policy responses to HIV, tuberculosis and public health law, policies and programmes.

Smitha Krishna Prasad

Smitha Krishna Prasad is a Fritz Family Fellow at Georgetown University. She is also an assistant professor (on leave) at the NLSIU, Bengaluru, and a senior research fellow at the Digital Asia Hub. Prior to this, she was a director at the Centre for Communication Governance at National Law University, Delhi. Her primary research interests focus on issues around privacy, data protection and surveillance.

Smriti Parsheera

Smriti Parsheera is a fellow at the CyberBRICS Project at FGV Law School, Brazil, and a PhD scholar at IIT Delhi's School of Public Policy. From 2016 to 2013, she was involved in setting up and leading the technology policy group at NIPFP, Delhi. She has also worked with the Competition Commission of India, the United Nations Development Programme and the Financial Sector Legislative Reforms Commission. She studied law at NLSIU, Bengaluru and at the University of Pennsylvania School of Law.

Subhashis Banerjee

Dr Subhashis Banerjee is a professor in the Department of Computer Science and Engineering at IIT Delhi. His primary areas of research are computer vision and machine learning. He has also written extensively on policy issues related to digital identity, electronic voting, data and privacy protection, and fairness and reliability of machine-learning algorithms.

Subodh Sharma

Dr Subodh Sharma is an associate professor and the Pankaj Gupta chair professor in privacy and decentralization in the Computer Science Department at IIT Delhi. He is currently associate dean of academics at IIT Delhi. His research is primarily in the area of software engineering and formal methods. He has written about privacy issues in the context of Aadhaar and privacy-by-design in public service applications.

Vijayaprasad Gopichandran

Dr Vijayaprasad Gopichandran is a community physician currently serving as assistant professor of community medicine at the Employees State Insurance Companies Medical College and Postgraduate Institute of Medical Science and Research, Chennai. His areas of interest are medical and public health ethics and trust dynamics in doctor-patient relationships.

Vivek Divan

Vivek Divan heads the Centre for Health Equity, Law and Policy at ILS, Pune. His expertise for over two decades has been at the intersections of law, health and sexuality with particular focus on HIV, TB and LGBTQ concerns. He has worked both nationally and internationally on these issues, including drafting a bill that became the HIV and AIDS (Prevention and Control) Act in 2017 and co-authoring 'Legal Environment Assessment on TB in India' (2018).

Vrinda Bhandari

Vrinda Bhandari is a practising lawyer in Delhi, specializing in digital rights, privacy and technology issues. She has been involved in several key litigations, including the Aadhaar challenge, challenges against India's surveillance framework, and issues related to Aarogya Setu and the CoWin app. She graduated from NLSIU, Bengaluru, and completed her master's degree at the University of Oxford on a Rhodes Scholarship.

30 Years *of*

HarperCollins *Publishers* India

At HarperCollins, we believe in telling the best stories and finding the widest possible readership for our books in every format possible. We started publishing 30 years ago; a great deal has changed since then, but what has remained constant is the passion with which our authors write their books, the love with which readers receive them, and the sheer joy and excitement that we as publishers feel in being a part of the publishing process.

Over the years, we've had the pleasure of publishing some of the finest writing from the subcontinent and around the world, and some of the biggest bestsellers in India's publishing history. Our books and authors have won a phenomenal range of awards, and we ourselves have been named Publisher of the Year the greatest number of times. But nothing has meant more to us than the fact that millions of people have read the books we published, and somewhere, a book of ours might have made a difference.

As we step into our fourth decade, we go back to that one word – a word which has been a driving force for us all these years.

Read.